# UNSINKABL

# BRO...

## Cruise Confidential, Book 3

*by*
Brian David Bruns

A World Waters Publication

# Praise for Brian David Bruns

This man has seen it all.
—*Deborah Roberts, **ABC 20/20***

*Cruise Confidential* is a very funny, behind-the-scenes exploration of a cruise ship.
—***Booklist***

I found it absolutely hysterical.
—*Peter Greenberg, **NBC Today Show***

*Cruise Confidential* is a deliciously addictive read, a blistering kiss-and-tell.
—*Doug Lansky, **Travel Channel***

*Leviathan* marks a seamless transition into genre, fusing his passion for travel with horror.
—*Caitlyn Bahrenberg, **Downtown Magazine***

Bruns' prose not only invokes fear and suspense, but also proves his steady and deliberate writing voice.
—***Writer's Digest***

# Author's Note

Thank you for your interest in my continuing life at sea! This title finally reveals why I went there in the first place. Thus it opens with the past (Part 1) before continuing with the future (Part 2). Some events from *Cruise Confidential* are here in truncated form, and the events of *Ship for Brains* fit snugly between Parts I & II.

As usual, all names have been changed, excepting singer/songwriter Laureen Niamesny (her music is available). Oh, and Bruns really is Brown in Romanian.

The fourth book of the series, *High Seas Drifter*, continues with a travelogue feel. It reveals life on the largest sailing ship afloat and what—rather, who—scuttled my career at sea.

I highly recommend the audiobooks. Narrator Gary Furlong truly captures the feel of the sea with his dozens of global accents. Discover these and other titles on my website: BrianDavidBruns.com.


P.S.

Please remember to leave an honest review! Nothing helps an author more.

# Part 1:

# FROM ROMANIA WITH LOVE

Ah, women. They make the highs higher and the lows more frequent.

— Friedrich Nietzsche

# CHAPTER ONE

## *Transylvania Dreamin'*

### 1

BEING AN OPTIMIST SUCKS. Sometimes a wise man knows when to cut and run, but not me. Good, bad, or ugly, I simply must see a thing through. 'Life's a journey' and all that. Adhering to this philosophy has resulted in a few bizarre career moves. Good was being hired to explore content for a porn site, though perhaps I saw too much. Bad was creating software for a urology office, where I definitely saw too much. Ugly, of course, was working on cruise ships.

Yet my life was not truly rocked to its foundation until I applied this troublesome credo to that most complex thing called love. Like usual, it did not begin with love, but curiosity.

### 2

The engines woke from their trans-Atlantic drone with a backpedaling roar, signaling the jet's descent into Romania. I stared out the rain-streaked window, eager for my first glimpse of this country so steeped in legend. The weather kindly fulfilled my Hollywood-induced expectations as we slammed headlong into clouds of angry purple and black, heavy with moisture and pulsing with electricity. Strong winds—the kind designed to heap dead leaves onto an ancient tomb—battered the aircraft. Yes, this would do nicely!

The aircraft dominated the lonely airstrip in the middle of vast sodden fields. Sheets of rain raked triumphantly across surrounding rows of corn, but were shouldered aside by the imposing forest beyond. The plane came to a halt, and everyone began clapping.

Clapping? Was a safe landing here that rare? After a mind-numbing fifteen hours flying, this was the first hint that I was far from home.

But it didn't look any different. The mix of fields and forest was the same as where I grew up, if a bit more lush. How disappointing. Not that I expected the control tower to actually be Dracula's castle or anything, but I had hoped for something a little less, well, Iowan. A closer look offered me more when I noticed a row of combat aircraft sinking in the wet grass. They looked as old and worn as the concrete bunkers slumped across the misty distance. Memories of the Iron Curtain were not what I wanted, so I stared at the dark forest and imagined fearsome werewolves growling within.

Voices in Romanian and English informed me that this was not our final destination, but an unscheduled stop outside a city called Timişoara. We remained on the runway; a few people got off, a few got on.

A little old lady in tattered robes shuffled down the aisle and sat beside me. For lack of knowing a more appropriate label, I assumed she was a peasant. She wore patched and re-patched clothing more aged than me, and a shredded headscarf more hole than cloth. She wearily released a large bag that was a wonder to behold, an animal-looking thing surely made from some mammal slain decades ago and worked into a carry-on. I marveled that a woman so dressed had gotten her hands on a plane ticket.

Delays already. I had crossed North America, then the Atlantic, and finally Europe, to test my manliness against vampires and ghosts in Transylvania. Instead I got an old peasant woman. With the mild interest born of boredom, I regarded the fantastical lines of her face and the wisps of gray hair. Her thin bangs teased her eyes so that she squinted a lot.

My interest grew robustly when she opened her hirsute purse and pulled out a huge butcher knife.

I stared at her in open astonishment, but she was intent upon peeling an apple. It seemed ludicrous that her tiny, gnarled hands—spotted, scarred, and nearly broken from untold decades of toil—could so effectively wield such a weapon. Lightning flashed, reflecting sharply along the keen, ten-inch blade. A gust of wind shook the plane, and her slow reflexes brought the knife perilously close to my thigh.

What was the name of that artery in your thigh, the one that if cut would kill you? I had great difficulty focusing upon anatomy lessons at the moment and, needless to say, my Romanian language tapes had overlooked 'Please, ma'am, put away your weapon.'

Suddenly I understood why my Romanian host, Bianca, had been so insistent on the phone prior to my departure. "Let me know exactly when you arrive, and I'll be there to rescue you," she had said. "Romanian people are a little bit slippery until you know them better."

No kidding.

The plane surged once more into the storm-thrashed skies, and bucked like an angry bronco. With the very next pitch, the woman again uncontrollably thrust the knife at me—right at my crotch. I avoided crying out, instead mewling a pathetic whine. I quickly emptied the pocket in the seat-back before me to place as many layers as possible in my lap: magazines, safety instructions, even the barf bag.

Outside, lightning flashed in an obsessive display of raw power, eliciting oohs and aahs throughout the cabin. The noisy kids in the seats before me, who had been kicking and crying all damned flight, now fought and clawed and scrambled over each other for a better view. The old woman was apparently less impressed by the storm than by her apple, which she continued to peel in an ungainly, painfully slow manner. I, too, ignored the storm, my eyes never leaving that knife for the entire thirty minutes to Bucharest.

No, Romania was not at all like home!

## 3

Ah, but optimists are not fazed by reckless endangerment, nor really anything else, except maybe pimples. My friends all thought I was mad, particularly the one from Romania.

*Stupid*, said Mihaela—though as a professional at Microsoft, she frequently called me such.

*Crazy*, said Dave—who, as both a professional comedian and a member of Mensa, surely knew how to think outside the box.

*Inspiring*, said Ken—who, as a former Seventh Day Adventist now out of the closet, applauded following one's own path.

*Reckless*, said Bianca—the very woman who invited me to Romania after only knowing me three days!

While it was true I knew Bianca hardly at all, she was Mihaela's childhood friend, so how bad could she be? If I got into any trouble, Mihaela had strict orders to save me. She introduced us, after all. Actually, the only reason Bianca thought the trip was reckless was because I was flying out of New York City on September 11th, 2002. That was the only reason I could afford the tickets!

Alas, there had not been a retaliatory terrorist attack, but I was at risk of an unlikely, painful bleeding death at the hands of an elderly peasant woman. Perhaps my preparations had not been as thorough as I thought. I reread Bram Stoker's *Dracula*, of course, and got all the immunizations recommended by the CDC. The former was vastly more preferable than the latter. Dutifully I informed my long-suffering mother that I was covered for everything.

Well, almost.

Measles/mumps/rubella? Done. Diphtheria/pertussis/tetanus? I was all over it, not to mention that polio and hepatitis A and B were in the bag. Tuberculosis was a concern in parts of Romania, but encephalitis was happily on the decline. True, I didn't get my rabies shot, but Mihaela said Dracula was just a normal dude and the whole bat thing was just myth. So with the primary carrier of rabies out of the picture, what was there to worry about?

But I *was* beginning to worry. What if Bianca wasn't there to 'rescue' me when I stepped off the plane? If she wasn't there, I would be horrendously screwed. I didn't know a word of Romanian. I didn't even know how to make a phone call in Europe. There were country codes of some sort, and dialing a '1' at the beginning was not enough. Come to think of it, two months had passed since I met Bianca for those fateful—but short—three days. What if I didn't recognize her?

I need not have worried, for Bianca was waiting at the Bucharest airport as promised. She stands out in a crowd, not because of what she looks like or wears, but what she exudes. Her entire curvy figure radiates self-confidence. Below tussled black hair were black eyes twinkling with mischief, round cheeks, and pouty lips tinged with smug. She waited in a heavy green jacket over skin-tight jeans and a long, grey scarf wound loosely over her shoulders. A single white rose graced red-tipped fingers. We shared a hug, a laugh, and smalltalk as I gathered my luggage.

"Your flight was good?" she asked with her charming accent. Her English was quite capable, though her grammar was usually off. She was fluent in French, and had been taught the obligatory Russian in school, but only recently learned English—third-hand from movies and music.

"Oh, it was fine," I replied cheerily. "I was only mildly alarmed when the old lady next to me pulled out a butcher knife."

An understanding nod was not the response I had been hoping for, nor was it particularly reassuring. But if I had wanted something different, I certainly got it in the parking garage when Bianca pulled up the car. It was the tiniest car I had ever seen in my life—and even had four doors! The little European vehicle was literally half as long as my first car, an Oldsmobile, and probably a quarter as heavy. Though obviously used for a long, long time, the flat-white car hummed reliably.

"What the hell is that?" I blurted as she rose from the driver's side. Bianca smiled her smug smile and answered with a nonchalant toss of the scarf around her neck.

"This is Albişoara," she introduced, giving the car a loving pat (pronounced AL-bee-SHWAR-uh).

"How old is this thing?" I asked, too agog to realize I was being rude.

"I think she's almost as old as you, my dear," she said. "She was born in 1975. She's a Dacia, which were the only cars you could get in the communist days."

The small trunk in back was sufficient to fit my luggage, but fitting my legs in the front was quite a problem. Bianca wrestled the passenger seat as far back as it would go, and I squeezed in. My hair rubbed the roof just enough to crackle with static. Bianca found that delightfully funny. I did not.

The weather was a dreadful, punishing rain with thick grey mist, but Albişoara resolutely powered through it all. Bianca exited into heavy traffic and began grumbling at the unmoving mass of red taillights twinkling in the rain. Eager for every early glimpse of a new nation, I pressed my nose against the window. Had it not been raining, I would have stuck my head out and lolled my tongue like a dog.

Bianca was a woman blessed with tremendous enthusiasm and an infectious laugh; she would as soon dance as walk, and the day was not fit with enough hours to satisfy this need of hers. She always swung and pranced through the house, humming to the song in her head. She even wiggled while brushing her teeth. Also a loving person, she was quick to hug and quicker to kiss. These were all the graces of Bianca I would soon discover—and soon after require—to keep my own life sparkling. But none of it was apparent during that dreary, dismal drive from Bucharest.

"I hate Bucharest," she complained as she narrowly avoided yet another long line of stalled traffic—in so doing narrowly avoiding yet another aged fender. "The city is huge and grey and lifeless, yet the animals living here think they God's bloody gift to the world, as if there is no Romania beyond the capital's concrete."

She was far too surly, and I far too ignorant, to warrant a reply. Instead I began counting the Coca Cola signs along the road, for the weather was too gray to see much past them anyway. Certainly they fought hard enough for my attention—I was up to twenty-three before I saw a sign in Romanian. The sign featured a hilarious illustration of a donut with a frowning face, surrounded by steam and flames.

"That donut looks pissed as hell," I observed.

"*Gogoașa Înfuriatâ*," Bianca read. "It means 'angry donut'. *Înfuriatâ*—as in 'furious'."

"Exactly how can a donut get angry? Dunk it in coffee that's too hot?"

"She lives in Bucharest," Bianca explained bitterly.

"She? Donuts are girls in Romania?"

"Obviously," Bianca replied rather curtly.

I was tempted to ask if that was because they had a hole in the middle, but after seeing her fume like a donut, I decided to bite my tongue. We finally cleared the congestion of the city to turn onto the highway. Bianca pushed Albişoara for all she was worth, leaning forward over her steering wheel and all but slapping her fenders with a riding crop.

Albişoara's engine whined her high-pitched effort to appease Bianca's commands. The gloom suddenly spat out a dark mass directly before us. We swerved sharply to avoid a plodding, horse-drawn wagon. In the blink it took for us to pass I saw a farmer hunched over stolidly in the rain, both he and his horse long since used to noisy cars passing by. Even as we swerved into the left lane, we were suddenly passed ourselves on the left by a sleek new BMW. Gravel flashed across our windshield as his driver side tore up the far shoulder. Never even hanging up his cell phone, the driver expertly cut us off just in time as both he and Bianca surged right to avoid a head-on collision with a battered Mercedes truck.

The drive grew awkward. The fact that I had only known this woman three days before deciding to visit was weighing heavily upon me. I wondered when we would rekindle the intriguing vibe that had lured me here—or if. The rain's grey crept into the interior of poor, sweating and exhausted Albişoara and grew oppressive. Just then, a road sign caught my eye.

Ploieşti, it read. I leaned forward excitedly, promptly hitting my head on the windshield. Some hair remained where it had caught in a crevice.

"Ploy-ESHT!" I cried, also trying to rub my head without her noticing.

Bianca's tired eyes flew wide, and she stared at me in complete shock. No doubt I would have reacted the same if some foreigner had properly cried out, 'Arkansas!' She completely ignored the road, whereas I thought of nothing else.

A car zoomed by perilously close, reminding her with an angry horn of her inattention.

"How you know Ploieşti?" she asked. "And how you know our 'S' with a tail is your 'SH?'"

"That's where the oil refineries were that the Allies bombed in World War II."

Reminding someone about how your country bombed the hell out of their country is not usually a good icebreaker. In this case, however, it worked.

"You babaloo!" she snickered. "Mihaela always said you were history lover, and I forget you gave me the entire historical tour of that ghost town. You're right, of course."

Bianca sighed to release tension.

"Check me," she chided herself. "I'm sorry. I just hate Bucharest and this bloody rain! It always rains in my heart when I'm in Bucharest. I hoped your arrival would bring the sun."

"Stop, woman," I groaned. "After twenty hours in a plane, I can't handle poetry."

She smiled. "I get that from my father. If he were here, he would be driving and singing all those traditional Romanian songs. I've seen them bring him to tears, the babaloo."

"But who cares about Bucharest?" she continued, finally enervated. "I show you the real Romania! Transylvania is so much more pretty, and the bloody rain should be gone tomorrow. It's so beautiful and true, everything is natural and nothing made up to scratch your joy of life by artificiality or other human touch matters. And the trees will be foxy."

I listened to her intently, having forgotten how much I enjoyed listening to her speech. She always used words that I would never have thought of.

"Foxy?"

"*Da,*" she agreed. "All pretty and wild."

"And we will eat similar pigs!" she promised. "And drink cognac and wine like bigger pigs, and sing Romanian songs until midnight. And dance to dawn. You do like to dance, right?"

"You know what they say," I answered effusively. "White men can't dance."

"Who says that?" she asked, confused. "Everybody dances here. Well, you will dance, babaloo, because I am taking you to a Romanian wedding. Believe me, Romanian parties are the most cheerful and alive ones. Even on the cruise ships where I work, where is Tower of Babel, everybody admits that."

"What exactly does 'babaloo' mean?"

"Babaloo just means 'silly'," Bianca said, chuckling. "On ships you use lots of words from lots of places. Check I no call you something in Jamaican, like bamboclat or rasclat. That means you're in trouble."

I just smiled and nodded. Trying to change the subject away from dancing and weddings and insults, I fumbled with the glove compartment. I had to rearrange my knees just to get in.

"My first foreign babe's glove box," I commented. "Oh, wait, that sounded naughty. Sorry."

I expected to find the usual suspects: papers, pens, maybe a Kleenex or a parking ticket. Instead it was home to a foot-long, Rambo-style survival knife. This weapon made the old peasant lady look like she was just making pies.

"What the hell is this?" I gasped. "What is it with knives in this country?"

"Oh, that's Dad's," Bianca answered simply.

"He keeps this in the car?" I demanded. "What for?"

"He's a retired sergeant from the army," she explained. "He found it in the woods and decided to keep the extra knife in the car. He already has plenty at home."

"He found this in the woods," I repeated weakly. "Just lying there? Abandoned? In the Transylvanian woods? I guess the movies are true! Wait a minute—you said he's a retired sergeant from the army?"

"Da," she said.

"The Romanian army?"

"Where else?" she asked, unsure of my reaction.

"Under the Iron Curtain," I continued with growing alarm.

"Da," she said, growing impatient.

"So you're telling me that I have just arrived in a country— where even the donuts get violently angry—to visit the only daughter of a man who spent thirty years literally training to kill 'American capitalist pig dogs?'"

"He's a sweetie," she scoffed.

I was hardly convinced.


# 4


The drive continued for well over an hour, and as the lay of the land changed, so, too, did the name. The scenery was beautiful in the extreme. Lush forested mountains thrust up from the fertile plains. Rich forests—uncut since the Crusades —nuzzled sheer bluffs. The clouds broke against the bulk, leaving tatters and shreds to loaf about. This was now Transylvania.

Though thought by many to be entirely fictional, it is not so. Now a section of Romania, Transylvania had been a highly sought-after prize millennia before Bram Stoker ever dreamed up his famous tale, for the land provides a buffer between Europe and Asia. The Carpathian mountains shelter a plateau in a loving embrace, curving entirely around the south and east to form a natural defense that has proven most formidable. These bluffs broke wave after wave of invading Turks. Centuries before that, the rampaging Huns split their unstoppable charge around them. A millennium before that, the native Dacian people fought back the Romans until damn near the Dark Ages.

Ironically, the most accessible means to learn of this land is what so often maligns it. The vast bulk of vampire lore misses the truth entirely, whereas Bram Stoker's original novel *Dracula* was very accurate. While it is hotly debated whether or not the Irishman ever actually visited, none impugn his depiction of the local culture, their food, and their superstitions.

We finally neared our destination city of Braşov (pronounced Brah-SHOV). We neared a series of small mountains on three sides, the bowl in the middle filled with ancient, tiled roofs and centuries-old everything. The fourth side opened into a vast plain, and spilling from it like an oozing pool of filth was the urban sprawl of communist-era bloc apartments. These awful contraptions let the city cram 300,000 people into a space less than half the size of a comparable U.S. city, such as Cincinnati.

The rain renewed itself with vigor upon our entering the city, but Albişoara cut a neat line over the spluttering streets. I was surprised, though perhaps should not have been, at the amount of people outside. In the newer, bloc-heavy part of the city, the roads were wider and more heavily laden with Dacias. But as we neared the old city, narrowing streets made cars dwindle and pedestrians surge. I couldn't see any faces under the umbrellas, but definitely noted the bottoms—and was that ever something! Every pair of legs was magnificently tight. And, being Europe, every pair of pants was magnificently tight.

"What, is there a cheerleader convention in town?"

Bianca frowned in confusion. Eventually understanding blossomed.

"Ah, don't be fooled, gringo!" she said with a laugh. "In Romania we have a saying. It translates something like 'daughter in back, grandmother in front.'"

"What's that supposed to mean?"

"It means, rasclat, that you're drooling over women older than even me—and I'm over thirty. Romanian women have sexy legs from school right up until they become old hags. After that it doesn't matter anyway. We walk everywhere, check!—walking up ten bloody levels of stairs four bloody times a day makes great legs. Also, all our food is natural—no genetic mutation tomatoes here, papa! We eat all day long and don't gain weight."

I looked at her, not yet convinced. Soon enough I would be.

"Well, that's changing," she finally admitted. "McDonald's is here now."

She drove Albişoara down a gravel alleyway between a series of towering blocs, bottom floors of shops dark for the night. Unlike further out onto the plain, these blocs were older and spaced with sanity in mind, with plenty of huge trees covering the wide yards between them.

"How do you pronounce that?" I asked suddenly, having spied the tongue-twisting name of the alley.

"Strada Lâcramioarelor," Bianca answered smoothly, her tongue unperturbed in the slightest.

"Luckra...?"

"Lâcramioarelor," she repeated calmly. "Is a flower."

"Lucky-YODELADYHOO!" I finished with a yodel.

My look was smug. Her look was sour.

"You'll wish you tried harder before you know it," she prophesied rather ominously.

Bianca entered a gravel lot nestled in between the blocs. It was hardly formal, being little more than a section devoid of grass and lined with old Dacias at odd angles. They all were twins to Albişoara. I wondered how people could tell their cars apart. Bianca rushed us across the lot and nearly collided with a dumpster. At the very last second we scrunched to a halt. There was an awkward moment of silence after the near-impact, amplified by the thumping of rain.

"I once drove Mihaela's Volkswagen with modern brakes," Bianca offered with a shrug. "That's just a tickle to Albişoara. Sometimes you really have to stomp your foot to get her attention."

She gave me a very serious glance. "Don't tell my father about almost hitting that," she pleaded. "He is very, very protective of his ladies."

I smiled at her appreciatively, but my eyes lingered on the glove compartment.

# CHAPTER TWO

## *Meet the Parents*

### 1

WE RAN THROUGH the drizzle laden with luggage. Once under the sheltered doorway to the big bloc building, Bianca pressed a button next to the name Pop. A bent speaker crackled static, and she answered with words in Romanian. Curiously I browsed the names listed in scratchy text along the button box. Most were unfamiliar, of course. The first was Melci, (pronounced Melch), but there were actually two Pops. I discovered that 'escu' was a common suffix to Romanian names, for in this bloc alone was a Vasilescu, an Enescu, and even a Popescu. After a jarring clunk, the building's door was remotely unlocked.

A stairwell rose above us, yawning wide and darkening to blackness—like staring up a rearing dragon's throat. The concrete looked cold and damp and depressing, and each landing was adorned with rusted iron gripping a bouquet of dusty, plastic flowers. The silence was pregnant. It was creepy.

Up we went, lugging luggage. I couldn't get over how fast someone in America would slap down a lawsuit over those unlit stairs, while Bianca chatted excitedly about the upcoming introductions.

"I can't wait to hear my father greeting you in English," she bubbled. "He couldn't twist his tongue around certain words. I'm sure his English will be as bad as your Romanian."

"My Romanian?" I asked, panting behind her. Though in good shape, I was not used to stairs. By the third flight I was already winded, yet chain-smoking Bianca was fine. She wasn't kidding about Romanians climbing stairs all day long! I assuaged my embarrassment by blaming the long flight and heavy luggage.

"Da, bambo," she said. "You did learn some Romanian, didn't you? I ordered Mihaela to teach you basics."

"Well, she didn't," I replied tiredly. "Actually, Mihaela doesn't like to talk about Romania that much."

"That rasclat woman!" Bianca scoffed. "I should have known. Lots of Romanians don't advertise where they from. But you do know how to say 'is a pleasure to meet you?'"

"Uh, no," I admitted, trying to hide my panting.

Bianca paused and turned to me in the dark. "OK, repeat after me."

She then proceeded to speak some words. I stared at her blankly for a good long minute, then tried to repeat them. Her wince needed no translation.

"Forget it," she said. "At least tell me you have the gifts I asked you to bring."

"Da," I said. "See? I know Romanian. *Da* means yes, and *nu* means no, in case you didn't know."

"You genius, papa," she replied sarcastically.

On the fourth floor we stopped before a recessed doorway in absolute blackness. How she knew where the door was in order to knock defied explanation. My breath was raspy behind her, and I was happy for a moment to try and catch it. But immediately the door burst open with an explosion of bright light and noisy welcome.

"Aaaah!" exclaimed an enthusiastic voice. Bianca rushed into a big hug, as if she'd been on a contract with Carnival Cruise Lines, rather than gone for a day. I was still blinking from the brilliance when a hand reached forward to pull me inside. Foreign words enveloped me, along with unmistakable welcome.

Bianca's parents were tiny people. She herself was only 5'5", but was a head taller than both of them. The parents Pop were both white-haired and enjoyed the roundness happily attained through age, yet still sprightly. The many lines on their faces were predominantly around the eyes—unmistakably from laughter.

"Aaaah!" her father repeated as he thrust out his hand. Though a small man, his hand was not, and his grip was like steel. His nose was large and round, and his brow a mess of thick, white wires. An odd-shaped scar crinkled his lower lip, like an upside-down horseshoe.

"Velcome to Transylvania," he intoned with great sincerity, flashing huge, pearly white teeth. "It's nice to eat you."

He sounded exactly like Bela Lugosi. Had he not been a mere 130 pounds, I would have fainted. Even so, I worriedly looked around for large knives.

"*Mulțumesc foarte mult*," I replied in what I foolishly thought was surely flawless Romanian. (Pronounced MOOLTsoo-mesc f-WAHR-tay moolt) That meant 'thank you very much.' I think. He smiled even broader, delighted.

"Babaloo!" Bianca said, "You said you didn't know any Romanian."

"That's all I know," I replied, still shaking her father's hand. Finally he released me and gestured for his wife to step forward. Unlike her husband, her hair was not wispy-thin but wavy-thick. Her face boasted high cheekbones and a narrow, sharp nose. She gave me a big hug and a bigger smile. It was a warm welcome indeed.

"Everyone calls my father Piti," Bianca said. "His real name is pretty tough."

"Your dad sounds just like Dracula!" I commented enthusiastically.

"Yes, well, he is from Hungary, so he would," Bianca laughed. "My mother's name is Lâcramioara."

I stared at Bianca, drooping. "You've got to be kidding me. Lucra..."

"I warned you," Bianca said, smirking. "I don't want you getting a sore tongue already, so you can call her Lucky."

Piti removed his blue sweater vest and began tugging it over my arms—or attempting to. To say it was a tight fit was an understatement in any language, for my shoulders were nearly twice as wide as his. But he would not be deterred, and grunted under the strain of buttoning it closed around my chest.

His offerings were far from over. Piti kicked off his slippers and gestured for me to put those on, too. I tried to indicate it was unnecessary, using a smile. I couldn't use words anyway—not because of the language barrier, but because I was unable to draw breath in his tiny sweater vest.

Piti pointed to the slippers in a manner that indicated he expected to be obeyed. Though small, he was the very model of a modern major general.

"Papooch!" he ordered.

"You better put on the *papuci*," Bianca observed, elaborating the correct pronunciation.

I tried to protest how preposterous I would look in his tiny slippers, but only managed a sick wheeze. Stars were dancing in the corners of my vision. While Piti was distracted with the slippers, I unobtrusively unbuttoned the vest. Fresh, glorious air surged into my lungs.

Feeling renewed, I cheekily handed my hiking boot to Bianca. Lucky's eyes bulged, whereas Bianca began laughing. She egged her father on, and the papuci drama began.

Barely half my foot fit into his slipper, but Piti was unfazed. He rushed to a corner piled high with fuzzy footwear of all colors, and began digging. Slippers were flung aside with abandon as he dug to the bottom of the mound. Finally he found what he sought and returned with the chosen pair. Triumphantly he presented the pair of navy blue papuci.

They, too, were hopelessly small. Piti looked back and forth between the slippers and my Size 12 Wide feet. His bristly brows knit together, and with renewed vigor he tackled the heap of slippers. While he mumbled in annoyance, the ladies stifled giggles.

"Really," I said. "It's OK. I don't need any."

"Oh, no," Bianca said vehemently, dodging a slipper as it flew wide. She looked at me like I was a moron, and added, "You'll catch a cold with bare feet on the tile."

"It feels good to be barefoot after the long trip," I tried, but she would have none of it. Her eyes flew as wide as her mother's when she actually looked at my feet.

"Whoa, papa! Check your fingers!"

"What?" I asked, searching for something unsightly under my fingernails.

"No, bambo, on your feet."

"You mean my toes?" I said.

"Whatever. Both have same name in Romanian."

"Really?" I said, surprised. "You don't get confused?"

"How you confuse your feet with your hands? Mihaela said you were stupid, now I see why. Check your feet: get papuci on them. No colds on my watch."

"Come on, Bianca," I chided. "You can recite Mendeleev's Periodic Chart of the Elements—in order, no less—yet don't know that colds only come from a virus?"

Protestations were in vain, however. Piti shoved another pair of slippers at me. Too small. So was the fourth pair. Fighting anger now, Piti stomped out of the entryway and deeper into the apartment. We heard slamming cupboards and closets. Quietly, Lucky went after him.

"Wow," I said, now alone with Bianca. "This really isn't a big deal."

"He wants to be the perfect host," she explained with a smile. "Indulge him. American guest is very rare."

Lucky returned first, bringing the most surprising slippers I could have imagined: monstrously huge, fuzzy American flags.

"I forgot about those!" Bianca cried, laughing. "Don't ask where they came from. Long story."

Suddenly Piti burst from the other room, panting and disheveled—and empty handed. He froze and stared with disappointment at the ludicrously large American flag slippers. Rather than be out-done by his wife, he reached over and grabbed a bottle of liquor. Piti triumphantly held out this new offering and said two familiar words in an unfamiliar manner.

"Bree-ahn," he cried. "Alcool!"

"Now he's talking my language!" I agreed happily.

"Be careful with that," Bianca warned, rolling her eyes. She grabbed my arm and led me into the kitchen. "You don't have anything like it in America."

A moment later we four were crammed into a tiny kitchen around an even tinier table. Everything was communist-drab. It was bad enough that everything outside was nonstop grey concrete, but inside all was nonstop off-white tile. The floor, ceiling, and even walls were sheathed in aged tiles. The tabletop was off-white laminate. What is it about communists that they deny any color other than red? Everything was scrubbed perfectly clean with pride, however.

I feared that fitting four of us in the kitchen simultaneously would be problematic. This was a failure of my imagination. The table was pulled away from the wall and we squeezed around it. My shoulder rubbed against the refrigerator, which resembled a Sixties-era Frigidaire, while beside me sat Bianca with her back pressed against a decrepit stove. Piti was wedged against the wall, while Lucky's chair sat inside the walk-in cupboard. Any time someone needed to leave the kitchen, I had to pivot halfway around for them to pass.

With great ceremony, Piti readied tiny cups for each of us. They were perhaps half the size of a shot glass, shaped like a beer stein—for a doll. I felt like I was playing tea with my niece, until the unmistakable scent of raw liquor wafted up as we toasted. After one sip, I nearly choked.

"What the hell is this?" I spluttered, bringing a round of laughter. I looked into my empty thimble, looking for taste. It was nowhere to be found.

"This is țuica," Bianca explained.

"Zweeka?"

"There's a 'T' in front," she corrected gently. "When a 'T' has a little tail on it, it sounds like the 'TZ' in 'pizza'. Anyway, țuica is a traditional Romanian drink. You can buy it at the store, but the best is homemade. It's plum brandy. We drink it at special moments. And before every meal, of course, to stimulate appetite. Like vodka to Russians."

"I shudder to imagine America if we stimulated our appetites before every meal," I commented wryly. "Though I think it would be cool to have a drink we were internationally known for."

"Sure you do," Bianca replied. "Whiskey. How else was the West won?"

"Atta girl!" I laughed. "But try as I might, I cannot picture my mother doing shots of Jack before each meal. Anyway, what you have here is not exactly unknown in America. We call it moonshine, and it explains why your parents are so short. I have an inch or two to spare, so I'll have another."

"Aaaah!" said Piti excitedly, pouring another for me and himself. The ladies quietly demurred a repeat.

We settled in, and immediately began connecting. Though neither Piti nor Lucky were educated, both spoke three languages: Romanian, Hungarian, and Russian. I, being American, of course only spoke one. Bianca took her role as translator smoothly and with relish. In just my first five minutes squeegeed into that tiny kitchen, I learned a powerful lesson about humanity. Communication is different—and more important—than language. Goodwill needs no words. There was more laughter than talk, anyway.

And smoking. Oh, was there smoking.

I had been around smoking, of course. As a child, both my parents smoked until it was discovered to be unhealthy. Mom quit cold turkey, which in hindsight perhaps explains why my father began smoking more than ever. There is no lobbyist more passionate than one reformed. Eventually I found my way into smoke-filled bars when I became of age—or thereabouts, as far as my mother is concerned. But I had never encountered anything like this.

Bianca and Piti both puffed aggressively through a pack of green-tipped menthol cigarettes. While Lucky did not join them, she appeared completely unaffected by the thick haze that muscled out all the oxygen from the small room. Father and daughter shared a shallow ashtray no larger than a petri dish, which quickly overflowed with smashed and smoldering butts. Bianca must have contorted out of her chair to empty it half a dozen times in the first hour, yet when I suggested she get a larger ashtray she just called me American. I was beginning to truly marvel at how everything in this country was ridiculously small. It had not yet occurred to me that in America everything was ridiculously large.

Barely able to breathe, but not wanting to admit as much to my hosts, I excused myself. I claimed to need the restroom, but it was my lungs that needed a rest.

"I should warn you there's no hot water," Bianca said as I rose.

"Oh, OK," I said, trying not to look as surprised as I was.

"We're moving to the new house in a few weeks," she explained. "So we cancelled the contract with the private company rather than pre-pay for another year. We on city supply now, and they only get us hot water for about an hour in the afternoon. They deny that, of course, but you know: Romanian-style."

I did not know what Bianca meant by Romanian-style, but was beginning to learn. It was not a comfortable process.

The bathroom somehow managed to be smaller than even the kitchen. Beneath the window was a short bathtub, with a shorter hose and sprayer on a hook. So it was a quasi-shower. Or was it? There was no shower curtain. I guess if I wanted to skip a full bath I would have to squat in the tub and spray myself.

One thing was universal, however: a stack of magazines by the toilet. I flipped through them curiously, delighted to see the photographs featured only topless women. But this was not pornography, as it was obviously some sort of glorified *TV Guide*, printed on the worst kind of pulp paper, channel listings predominating. I doubted Romania featured a dozen-plus porn channels, but what did I know? Maybe Romania was cooler than I thought.

Then I encountered the toilet paper.

Now, I am no wuss. I am a man's man, not only content to squat in the woods and use leaves for sanitation, but prefer to do so, dammit. I had no time for quadruple-ply ultra-soft bathroom tissue featuring pictures of babies and angels at five bucks a roll. But this tissue was transparent-thin and rougher than a Brillo pad. It was so thin that I would have used half a roll, had it not been so painful.

When I returned, Bianca observed my haunted expression. "Everything OK?"

"I'll have to answer that later, I think," I replied, shaken. "The... uh... paper, is somethin' else. I knew communists disregarded human comfort and dignity on every level, but I didn't realize just how dehumanizing it is to wipe your butt with sandpaper."

She scrunched her face and said, "Oh, we all hate that soft, buttery toilet paper introduced from the West after the revolution. How do you know it's even working?"

I thought it best to drop the subject.

Happily, the windows had been opened in my absence. The air was far from clear, but was less foul. It was also colder. Lucky herself replaced Bianca's chair by the stove, having lit two burners with a wooden match. Upon one burner sat a battered percolator, while the other blazed away in blue flame —apparently intended to warm the kitchen. It didn't work. Neither did Piti's clinging sweater vest. I shivered in the cold, even as the fuzzy flag slippers made my feet sweat. Alas, coffee induced more smoking than even the alcohol, so soon steam and smoke tangoed above us.

I presented the gifts which Bianca had suggested I bring: a bottle of good cognac for her mother and a cowboy hat for her father. Oh, did Piti love his hat! He wore it all night, unsuccessfully fighting the urge to draw pretend pistols at every opportunity. Considering his background and mine, he made me flinch a bit too often. When Bianca explained to him that I bought it at a real Old West ghost town, where she and I had met, he was even more excited.

Eventually the older folks retired to the living room, where the couch unfolded into a bed. Bianca and I stayed up longer in the bedroom, sitting upon another couch that would eventually unfold for me. We listened to some quiet music and browsed through photographs of her fascinating time working on cruise ships. She ate copious amounts of M&Ms. We began quietly, speaking in hushed voices barely above the clicking of fingernails on candy, but as our enthusiasm over each other swelled, so did our volume. Soon we rekindled the playfulness and joy we had so surprisingly found in each other at our first meeting.

"It's 3 a.m.," Bianca finally said, pushing herself up from the couch. "Time for bed."

"Oh, wow," I said. "We've been in here for five hours! I'm sorry to keep you up so late. I guess I'm still on Nevada time."

"Don't worry, me night bird."

The bed was unfolded, Bianca taking great care to set it up nicely for me, and then she slipped off to somehow fit into bed with her parents. Sleep began elusively, though less because of my internal clock than from the street lamps that were level with the windows—which filled out one entire wall from waist-high to the ceiling. The room was bright enough to read in. In the distance I saw the bloc in which my friend Mihaela had grown up. She had been on the ninth floor, Bianca informed me, and they had communicated via flashlights when they were supposed to be in bed. Kids are kids everywhere.

Just a few short hours ago I had no idea whatsoever of what to expect from this visit-on-a-whim. I had been excited, of course, but it was so far out of the ordinary that it didn't seem real. Even as late as driving to the airport, it didn't really feel like I was about to fly to Romania—where I would be completely helpless and utterly reliant upon a stranger. But now I was here, and it was all right. I slept soundly.

## 2

I was awakened by a bizarre sound. The noise of traffic was dominant—a little vehicular and a lot pedestrian—obscuring the odd call that had awakened me. The noise was singularly strange, like that of a broken awhooga-style car horn from long before even Albişoara's time. But it wasn't a car horn, because it came from the living room.

I rubbed my eyes and rose, when suddenly the door burst open and Bianca stuck her head into the room. Her black hair was a mass of jutting angles, and her eyes were pronounced by dark circles. "Why you not answer chicken?"

"What?" I asked blearily.

"The chicken!" she repeated. "You didn't hear Piti calling *cucurigu?*"

"Chickens go cucurigu?"

"The male ones do. Don't you know anything?"

"So that was Piti imitating a rooster? I thought it was Albişoara's last gasp for breath in a cruel world. Or perhaps an asthmatic duck."

Bianca entered and began removing the blankets from the folding bed. "Don't be silly. Ducks say *mac.*"

"That's the dumbest thing I've ever heard in my life," I replied indignantly. "Ducks do not say mac."

"And why not?"

"Because ducks don't have lips. How's a duck going to make an 'm' sound? No ducks macking on chicks, thank you. What's wrong with you people?"

"Oh, by all means, dazzle me with your onomatopoeia."

"Roosters go cock-a-doodle-do," I declared with great solemnity. "I'll grant you that cucurigu sounds more accurate. But ducks quack. Chicks peep. Chickens cluck. Satisfied?"

"Chickens cluck?" she asked, frowning. "Chickens *cotcodac.*"

"See?" I mocked. "This is why America is superior. Our onomatopoeia is the best."

"It's not even your language, bamboclat," Bianca retorted. "And gooses?"

"Geese honk."

"Honk? Albişoara honks. You confuse foots with hands and gooses with cars. America sounds very strange."

Fortunately, breakfast stopped any debate, for we agreed to call it breakfast even if it was after twelve noon. We entered the kitchen and Piti rose from his steaming—and small—cup of coffee, doffed his new cowboy hat, and gave Bianca a big kiss on the forehead. Lucky leaned back from the stove to do the same. The sheer love and joy they exchanged was palpable, as if every single morning was cause for tremendous celebration. They all trilled like happy birds in spring. I have always been a morning person and a cheery soul, but they made me look like a surly Monday morning.

I, too, received a kiss from Lucky, while Piti aggressively shook my hand and bid me good morning in enthusiastic, if halting, English. To Bianca he then gave an exaggerated look of acute misery. His pronounced, white brows drooped like those of a sorrowful hound, while he rubbed his belly to indicate it was past time for repast.

The table was pulled from the wall and ready for action. Oh, was it ready! The table was so loaded with food that the plates were forced to compete for space. True to all-things-little form, every food item was on a small plate—like tapas—each devoted to its own offering. All were served cold: a dish of thinly-sliced sausages, another of smoked, fatty ribs, three bowls devoted to different cheeses, one of pickles, a jar of pickled hot peppers, a dish of fresh red peppers and one of them roasted in olive oil. The only large plate was loaded with gargantuan tomatoes. A round loaf of rustic bread waited—fresh from the farmer's market that morning, as was everything perishable.

I sat and was immediately presented with a steaming cup of both coffee and tea. Lucky pulled from the stove a pan loaded with slender sausages, cropped to about three inches, which had been cooking in oil. They glistened with welcome heat, the edges nicely browned and puffed into little Xs where she had cut them. She gave me four, then portioned two each for everyone else. Piti turned his puppy-dog eyes on her until she sacrificed one of her own sausages to his plate. Any attempt from me to more evenly apportion the food was scoffed at.

Piti was ready for the meal to begin, which meant he had the țuica handy. Unlike the bottle he had last night, this morning the supply came from a funny little brown-glazed container in the shape of a barrel with a gnome-like, drunken man draped over the top. It was mounted on a wooden rocking chair with a series of hooks for the thimble-sized țuica glasses. Lucky and Bianca preferred the cognac I had brought, but I was a good sport and joined Piti for țuica. I even more sportingly took a refill to ease the pain of the first. We toasted each other with each shot, grimacing all the while. On the third shot Piti turned towards the wall and instead toasted to something painted on the tiles.

"Well, I'll be damned!" I cried. "That really is a capitalist pig-dog!"

"What?" Bianca asked, frowning.

"Right there, painted on the wall!"

I indicated the odd illustration of a brown dog playing a cello that someone had painted directly onto the wall. It had the long, floppy ears of a dog, but the tail was decidedly cork-screwed like a pig's. Bianca laughed, having forgotten all about the decoration over years of familiarity. She didn't bother to translate, as Piti was already helping himself to the food with a satisfied, 'aaaah.'

Perhaps it was my Germanic ancestry—though more likely my much-closer Midwest American—but I immediately went for the sausages and cheese. The cheese was unlike anything I had ever encountered, and simply wonderful. My favorite tasted like parmesan, but instead of being hard it was semi-soft and a bit chalky. I was told this was sheep cheese. I decided not to admit that I didn't even know sheep made milk.

I began to feel guilty. The Pops were making a profound effort to be the best hosts possible, and had created a massive feast. The least I could do was accept with honest gratitude, for this was a moment where I was expected to indulge. Further, compared to them I was simply huge—a good seventy pounds heavier than Piti and obviously double Lucky. My issue was not with how much I ate, but what I selected. I was picking only the apparent luxuries.

Thus, I grudgingly took a tomato. I hated tomatoes. They were usually flavorless and always watery, insides like they were stuck in the larval stage. But these tomatoes were something of a completely different order. Even the very best homegrown garden tomatoes in the fertile soil of Iowa paled in comparison to the texture and robust flavor of these Romanian gems. Just one of these first-sized monsters weighed over a pound and was a meal in itself. It was a solid, meaty beast all the way through. I was so astounded I actually ate more of them than anything else!

Though Piti was first to begin filling his plate, he was last to eat anything. He arranged his food with military precision. He sliced his red peppers into short slivers and arranged them to formation around the entire rim of his plate. Bianca answered my querying look.

"Those are daddy's little soldiers," she explained. "Thirty years as a sergeant dies hard. Nothing begins until everyone is presented properly at attention."

Eventually Piti dipped the slices in a small dish of salt from a cruet set. A handle neatly held two bowls, clearly marked S and P, but both were brimming with salt. In fact, before anything was consumed by any of my three hosts, it was first dipped in salt.

"Salt!" I cried, flabbergast. "The forbidden seasoning! Mom would not allow it in our house."

"Why not?" Bianca asked, surprised.

"Oh, you know. Too much salt in our diets and high blood pressure and all that."

"How is this possible?" she asked. Then her eyes got wide in understanding. "Oh, check me! I forgot: you guys eat all that nonstop food with chemicals and artificiality. Ugh. Getting food out of a box is the same as getting wine out of a box. I did that once, and don't tell me that had anything to do with the wine experience!"

I nodded deeply, thinking her comparison particularly apt.

"Not here, papa," Bianca continued happily. "We have real food, and if we no salt it, we get no salt at all."

While no doubt the subtleties of our dialogue were not understood by Piti, he was well aware of the crux of it. His fourth shot of țuica was 'toasted' by clinking it against the salt bowl.

"*Mai vrei cafea?*" Bianca asked, holding up the coffee pot. It took me a moment to realize she was talking to me. Sometimes while translating she would accidentally say something English to her parents, or Romanian to me. But she was looking right at me, waiting for a reply.

"Oh, I'm sorry," I said. "You were speaking Romanian."

"I know, babaloo, we're in Romania. I noticed you tune out everything unless it is English. If you begin to listen, you begin to learn."

I looked up at her sheepishly. She was absolutely right.

She continued, "So in Romanian coffee is a feminine word: 'cafea'."

I gratefully held out my espresso-sized cup. "Thank you so much! I'm used to big mugs about half the size of that pot."

We continued our meal, but after a moment I spoke up again.

"You know," I commented. "It makes sense that coffee is a woman. It's hot and stimulating and you can't live without it, but is actually bad for you."

Bianca gave me a smug grin and retorted, "Not when you only have one."

3

After breakfast, Lucky and Bianca cleared the table while Piti and I did nothing. I was uncomfortable with the stereotypical male/female roles, but any efforts to assist in cleaning were roundly rejected. This, I was informed, was when the men enjoyed cigarettes and conversation. So I enjoyed more of Lucky's fantastic tea. To my astonishment, she made it herself from flowers and plants she picked while out walking in the forested hills surrounding their new house in Sighişoara.

Walking was in order for Bianca and I, too. She finally enjoyed her own cigarette, but then we readied ourselves for a tour of Braşov. Her parents joined us for the first block of our rainy walk, intent upon the nearby market to gather food for dinner. Even though they had already been to the market once already that day, it was only a block away so there was no need to buy in bulk. Besides, they had no room to store anything anyway!

"At first I thought the shops on the ground floor of the blocs would be annoying," I commented. "In America we value privacy and personal space over all; I guess that's where the suburbs came from. But living there is so far from everything: if I run out of milk for my coffee, it's eight miles round trip to get it. But here you get fresh everything every day."

"Oh, yes," Bianca agreed heartily. "Mihaela told me your bread is designed to stay alive for weeks. How can weeks-old bread compare to fresh-baked? And why you eat dead cheese?"

"I do *not* eat dead cheese," I retorted.

"Yes you do. You pasteurize away all the living cultures. That's where the health is, and the flavor, too. No dead cheese for me, papa!"

"Aren't things supposed to be dead before you eat them?" I joked. "But seriously, we pasteurize it so people don't get sick."

"Eating old food is supposed to make you sick," Bianca chided gently.

Good point.

For perhaps the first time, I reflected upon my eating habits. When I had worked in an office environment, my lunch was either microwaved food or fast food, and breakfast in the car was common. I had always been more excited about the act of eating than the substance of it. I had also been thirty pounds overweight. Was I really such a zombie that I was incapable of asking myself whether or not my habits brought me joy? Was this, like, the beginning of wisdom and stuff?

Huddled beneath our respective umbrellas in the dreary afternoon, the Pops made plans in Romanian. I opted out of trying to decipher their blur of words, but thought Bianca's point about opening up to learning was valid. I instead noted a nearby sign. It was white with red letters and a picture of a snarling dog. It read '*Câine rau.*'

"OK," I said, "At least I need no translation for that one. Câine rau means 'beware of dog.'"

"It's pronounced cu-eenay and *rau* rhymes with *how*," Bianca corrected. "It literally translates as 'bad dog.'"

"*Ham ham,*" Piti agreed, nodding.

Confusion, always hovering nearby, again pounced.

"Ham?" I said. "So I'm supposed to feed bad dogs ham to keep them happy, or what?"

"No, bamboclat," Bianca chided. "Ham ham is what dogs say."

# CHAPTER THREE
## *Bad Dog*

### 1

THOUGH THE WEATHER was rainy and cold, our tour of Brașov was still cozy. I had dressed appropriately—meaning something other than Piti's sweater vest—but was mostly warmed by sharing an umbrella with Bianca. When she slipped her arm through mine, I realized I had never actually strode arm in arm before. Bianca was a physical person, I was learning, and even held hands with her parents. My family was also loving, but three boys made affection a contact sport. As far as women went, my super hot ex-girlfriend had rarely been seen in public with me—no doubt to retain plausible deniability for all the other men she insisted she didn't see. My ex-wife, of course, was warm as North Atlantic cod.

Puddles were everywhere underfoot, as were cracks and other hazards: apparently plenty of people walked their dogs without bothering to clean up afterwards. People were everywhere: all walking, all wearing dark colors—black predominating—and all dressed nicely. This is not to imply expensively or formally, but merely that everyone gave some thought to how they looked before leaving home. No doubt this was why Walmart never bothered with Romania.

To my surprise, all the street signs were in both Romanian and German. Indeed, everyone looked German rather than Russian, though their suspicious glances implied the latter. I wondered if they knew that the Iron Curtain had, in fact, been lifted.

"Do my clothes really stick out so much?" I asked Bianca, concerned. "Really, I tried to dress appropriately. No tennis shoes and T-shirts and all that. But everyone is staring at me."

"We are speaking English," Bianca explained. "And I look Romanian. You not noticed that everyone here has black hair? Your hair is your name."

"My hair is my name?" I asked, confused. This was fast becoming my new normal.

"*Brun* is Romanian for brown," she answered.

"Really?" I said, surprised. "But my ancestry is German."

"Transylvania was populated by Germans for centuries, Mr. Brown," Bianca pointed out.

"I thought you were all Russian."

"Most Americans do," she agreed.

Etymology aside, Bianca was quite right. I had indeed noticed that everyone was homogenous in color. So were the buildings. Whatever the communists could not build with concrete was instead drowned in a pool of it. The weather amplified everything: structures, streets, walks, parks, expressions—all were dismal and depressed.

We approached a long, pedestrian-only street. Two buildings flanking the entrance were both modern—one even contained a McDonald's—but otherwise the entire street was filled with fascinating, centuries-old architecture shouldering the sky. A procession of name-brand clothiers receded into the distance. Now this was anything but communist!

"This is Strada Republicii," Bianca observed. "It leads to cool stuff."

"Strada Repooblichee," I repeated.

"Check the bullet holes," she suggested, pointing to the tops of the two modern buildings. "Those ones are from machine guns during the revolution."

Little holes peppered the upper floors of the concrete buildings, reminding me of a middle-aged man with acne. I paused to marvel, then finally asked what had been on my mind for a while. My friend Mihaela had always refused to talk about it, but now the subject had been broached.

"What was it like during the revolution?"

"Not good," she said dismissively, tugging on my arm to continue.

"But your dad wasn't retired then," I pressed. "He was in the army. What was his role in all that mess?"

"Check your McDonald's," she said instead. "Beside Dolce & Gabbana, as if both are equal premium. Ha!"

Bianca obviously didn't want to talk about the revolution any more than Mihaela, so I dropped the subject.

Strada Republicii was indeed cool stuff, and I gawked at the buildings like a peasant entering his first city. I had always imagined that super old buildings would look, well, super old. Yet these were beautifully maintained structures with scrubbed marble and painted pillars.

We browsed a bit in the shops, but the high prices would have sent a Manhattanite into cardiac arrest. Though I knew there were many thousands of Romanian lei to the US dollar, seeing eight digits on the tag for a suit freaked me out. All the employees, with slender bodies and slicked-back hair, were intensely attractive—and intensely indifferent. If Dracula himself flew in on bat wings and attacked me right there in the showroom, no one would have noticed.

The strada opened into a huge, irregularly-shaped square. It was more of a lopsided triangle, really, defined by red-tiled merchant houses from ages ago. A wide, low fountain burbled noisily in competition with the drizzle, but the real focus of the piața was a yellow building topped with a tower.

"That's Trumpet Tower," Bianca explained.

"Good God," I joked. "The Donald has prime real estate everywhere, doesn't he?"

Bianca leaned back in order to look at my face. "What's a Donald? Anyway, Trumpet Tower was originally a watchtower looking for barbarians. I think you'll like Biserica Neagră better. Check her in the corner there."

She waved a hand with grand flourish. I gasped.

"The Black Church," she proudly introduced.

The horror geek in me took over. I couldn't help it. Here I was in Transylvania, home of Dracula, standing before the largest Gothic cathedral I had ever seen, called the Black Church. This place must have more than merely bats in the belfry!

"It's spectacular," I breathed, staring at the stained glass windows rising ramrod straight, from pavement to tiles, marching down the long flanks of the building. Heavy stone supports offset the glass, each accented with slender columns that spiked above the slanting roof. A single, squat tower rose from the huge structure.

"She was a small church long ago," Bianca narrated. "But was destroyed by the Mongols in the 1200s."

"The Mongols?" I asked, surprised. "The Mongols were in the steppes and stuff."

"They were from Asia, yes," Bianca said. "Remember they invaded Europe, too."

I just nodded, embarrassed to find my historical knowledge was shallower than I had thought.

"We rebuilt her, but the Turks destroyed her again in the 1400s. So we rebuilt her again. She got the name Black Church in the 1600s when the Hapsburgs invaded and burned her down. The smoke turned the foundation black, and it took one hundred years to fix her up again."

As the tour continued, we eased up increasingly steep cobblestone streets, narrow enough to prevent cars, and meandered outward from the old city's center. The base of a mountain loomed above: tall, but predominantly a long, lumpy ridge smothered in thick forest. A neat cut of trees bisected the mountain's flank in deference to a cable car. The top of the funicular accessed a restaurant and radio tower, while the bottom platform rested near an ancient defensive wall and an accompanying tower of old, beaten stone.

"How old is this?" I asked, intrigued.

"Pretty old," Bianca said, shrugging. "I don't know when it was first built, but this one was rebuilt by Vlad Țepes. Actually he made the guilds do it. That's how it was done in those days."

"Vlad Tepes, the Impaler?" I asked, excitedly. "You mean Dracula?"

"Yes," she said simply. "It's pronounced Tse-PESH. The T and S have tails, making them different."

I stared in awe at the ruins. The city-side of the wall was about forty feet high, but being pressed up against the slope of the mountain would nullify such height from the outside—or so I thought. In fact, the entire hillside had been dug away from the base of the wall. There was no way to approach the defense without first walking into a flat kill zone.

"Aaaah," Bianca said, channeling her father's enthusiasm as she pointed to some words cut into the stone. "This part was built by the shoemaker's guild. See?"

"This is so awesome!" I said. "Dug by hand six hundred years ago, at the order of Dracula himself! Maybe he even walked by to supervise. My friends are gonna die when they hear this."

"Oh, no," Bianca groaned. "What are you, a peasant with superstitions and animal beliefs? Check, you like dead cheese and dead people! You even say your friends are going to die. Why you horror lovers all so creepy?"

"Not all horror fans are creepy," I grumbled, annoyed at her for dousing my enthusiasm. "Have you ever read the original book *Dracula*? It's very good. Why do you think it spawned a century's worth of fans?"

"Bah! Tolstoy is very good. I no even think about death. Why bother, when life is so full of love and warmth? Still, if you like vampires so much, you'll go coconuts when we go to my house in Sighişoara."

"Why, what's there?"

"You will see," she replied cryptically.

The low road stretched beneath the forest and along the defensive wall—built before Columbus was even born!—until we finally worked higher up the mountain. The lane was dripping with foliage dripping with water. We skirted the many pools on the path, pushing into each other with our hips and being generally playful. I felt fifteen years old, not thirty.

"Tell me this isn't where the teens go to make out," I observed, eyeing the shadowed benches along the walk. I nudged her and teased, "Any stories you want to tell me? First kiss here?"

Bianca harrumphed, then motioned to the mountain in general. "This is Tâmpa. She rises, oh, about 400 meters above the city. I don't know how many of your foots that is. 1200 or something."

"So mountains are girls, then?" I asked.

"No, mountains are boys," she corrected.

"But you called Timpa a girl."

"That's because Tâmpa is a girl," she said, looking at me like I was an idiot. "Ends with an 'A'. And it's Tâmpa, not Timpa. It's an 'A' in the middle, one wearing a cap."

Not hearing any difference, I just nodded. I thought it funny how she engendered inanimate objects all the time.

"Lots of walks wriggle around her," Bianca continued. "Because she's mostly a nature reserve now, with lots of rare animal species. Mucho bears."

"Bears?" I asked, surprised. It was a long ridge, sure, but looked awfully small to have 'lots' of bears. Why, the old city nuzzled right up to its base!

"Mucho," Bianca repeated cheerily. "Last week a bear killed a man here in Brașov, and mailed eight more."

"Mauled," I corrected.

"That one," she agreed. "Don't tell your mother, or she'll throw her feet."

I was too busy looking for bears, or bear spoor—as if I knew what that looked like—to immediately realize what she said.

"Throw her feet?"

"You throw feet," Bianca clarified. "And stomp them."

"You mean throw a fit," I said, laughing nervously. I was very distracted and mumbled, "Your accent is showing, my dear."

The forest was already very dark around us. I swear I heard a growl. Do bears growl?

"Here we go," she said, nodding to a unique restaurant with a long stone deck sprouting heavy woodwork. It was the perfect blend of forest, traditional design, and clean modernity. "Casa Pădurarului."

"Whoa," I said. "That's almost as hard to say as your street name."

"Maybe we eat here sometime. They have bear on the menu. But first, up we go! Funicular is here, with café at top. The view should be good, too, because the rain stopped."

"Coffee sounds perfect," I agreed, as we stepped onto the gently swaying cable car. Not surprisingly, it was painted to overtly advertise Coca Cola.

The view on our ascent was, in a word, magnificent. Though the clouds obscured the sun, the hour was obviously late enough for darkness to creep into the valley. Below spread the entire old city with networked, narrow lanes aglow in lamplight, like a spider web glistening after a twilight rain. As we rose higher, distance blurred the scars of age to turn the red tiled roofs—each independently faded—into a speckled band of multicolored pebbles. The Black Church reared above like a boulder on a beach. By the time we topped Tâmpa, the forested mountains that sheltered Braşov became mere lumps of green.

We arrived just in time for the café's closing. We had been walking a long, long time and were desperate to get off our feet and drink something warm or alcoholic. Ideally both. It was not to be.

"I think there are big rocks at the top with a view of the city," Bianca said as she searched her memory. She pointed to a sodden path leaving our concrete platform to disappear into the dark, dripping forest. "Check there. What you think?"

"I think it looks perfectly bear-sized."

"Bah! No bears here, papa."

"Lots of bears," I mocked with an obnoxiously high voice, quoting her from earlier. "Mucho bears. Bears mailed eight people."

"My feet need rest, bears or no."

"Yeah, I'd hate to cram my fingers in those, too," I said, eyeing her footwear. Below her swishing, full-length skirt were knee-high leather boots with high heels. "You sure? It looks pretty muddy."

"Is fine," she scoffed. "Last tram leaves in thirty minutes. Mucho time."

Thus we entered the black woods of Transylvania. I was getting my horror geek on. Guided by occasional peeks of the city below us, we followed several different paths that radiated around the cluster of mid-ridge modernity. It was impossible to get truly lost, because the drop-off to the city was quite steep and there was no going down that. The woods were dense and gnarled, but stony outcroppings created enough gaps for the decreasing twilight to filter through. The city below snapped alive with orange lights, promising fantastic views once we found our seats. But, alas, we did not. After twenty minutes of muddy stomping, we still had not found the rocks Bianca was looking for. Or bears.

After clambering up a wet, muddy slope, we suddenly found ourselves at the highest point of the whole mountain. The rocky outcropping was like an island over a sea of rippling forest—which dropped into the abyss like the ancient mariners feared lay at the end of the world. The city below was magnificent in night, with its orange lights burning the underside of the clouds.

We had no hope of returning the way we came, but fortunately our exit was clear: a bridge descended from the exposed knoll, passed over a chasm, and ended at the café. We appreciated the view only briefly, because the funicular's last car was swaying at the gate, impatient to be done with its duty for the day. This should have been the end to a mini adventure.

Should have.

"He's calling us," Bianca noted, waving back to a skinny man—wearing black, of course—who stood in the tram's gently swinging doorway.

We crossed the bridge over the deep gap, when something horrible happened. It began innocently, when the back door to the café was kicked open and a cook tossed out a platter of scrap food. I smiled as a mother dog loped from the woods, leading three shuffling, tumbling little balls of fur.

Suddenly I realized the food blocked our path to the tram. The bitch was a lean, street-tough sixty pounds or so, with swollen teats revealing the extreme youth of her pups. While they yipped and yapped and rolled happily in their food, their mother stood guard. The look she gave us needed no translation: she would block our exit as thoroughly as any border guard under the Iron Curtain.

"How we cross?" Bianca asked, blinking in surprise at just how quickly the difficulty had materialized.

"It could be worse," I joked, "At least she's not rabid."

The joke was on me when another dog approached, lured by the smell of a free meal. This was a larger, unkempt animal with extremely long legs. His fur was so shaggy that his weight was hard to gauge, but there was no mistaking whatsoever the flecks of white foaming at his mouth.

"Damn!" I blurted, astounded at the coincidence. The timing was so perfect I would have laughed, had we not been trapped on a rainy mountaintop at night.

The bitch growled a warning, but the feral newcomer ignored her—at his own peril. She leapt upon him, ferociously rending and tearing flesh and fur. The two savage combatants became a blur of spinning bodies, snapping fangs, and flying spittle. The bitch was particularly effective at darting in and slashing at her opponent, whose strategy appeared to be to stand firm and accept the attacks bodily while trying to clamp his foaming jaws upon her. This was a fight in earnest, a noisy, high-pitched ordeal of feral dominance and survival.

It was awful to behold.

The bitch fought to save her pups with a terrifying brutality, and the battle was soon over. The scruffy newcomer tucked tail and ran back into the night. The victor padded casually back to her pups, blood-shot eyes glaring at us, chest heaving—and flanks bleeding.

"Damn!" Bianca repeated, stunned.

I started laughing.

Bianca stared at me with wide eyes. Her expression made me laugh even more. I couldn't help it.

"What's with you, man?" she asked, eyeing me with perhaps more concern than even the bitch.

"Before I came to Romania," I explained, "I got all my shots except one: rabies. What are the odds? In my thirty years of life, I've never even seen a rabid dog. Yet on day one, here I am, cornered on a stormy mountaintop by an angry, rabid bitch. I mean really, what are the odds of this?"

"You think this is funny? You sick, papa!"

I just kept laughing, and pointed to the funicular—or, rather, where it had previously been. The last tram had descended for the night.

"The rasclat left us!" Bianca cried angrily. She stomped her feet in outrage for a while before finally shrugging her shoulders in defeat. She explained lamely, "Romanian-style."

I laughed even harder, barely able to speak between gasps for air. "Thanks for this wonderful tour! And to think I blew off my mother's fears that a trip to Romania would leave me stranded and exhausted... in the cold, wet wilderness... surrounded by dangerous animals... in the dark."

Bianca did not think it was funny at all.

"It could be worse," I added. "At least it stopped raining."

Of course, the downpour commenced almost instantly.

"Hey, American rau," Bianca said bitterly. "Shut up! You want suggest aliens come down and take us next?"

"Ham ham," I laughed quietly, earning an elbow in the ribs.

But then Bianca, too, began laughing—almost hysterically, in fact.

"What?" I asked, bewildered by her sudden lightening of mood.

"Check, babaloo," she said, pointing to the scraps the cook had thrown to the dogs. "It's ham!"

## 2

We eventually passed the angry—and now potentially rabid —bitch after the rain had cooled her temper. When we felt the moment was right, we eased slowly but confidently past her, making our path obvious and as far away from her pups as possible.

While squinting to follow the long, dark mountain trail, the entombing forest blocked the rain. Alas, the water made it through by collecting on leaves and forming heavy drops that smacked our umbrella with tremendous force. With miles to go, and already exhausted, we got a little crazy. We couldn't stop saying 'ham ham' and laughing. Had anyone been around to see us, they would have thought we were nuts—or, since this was Transylvania, possibly mad scientists.

"Tell me a story," Bianca said. "Something adventurous. Or about your marriage."

"The greatest adventure of them all," I commented dryly. "Don't get me started."

"We have a long walk," she pointed out.

"Well," I began, readying for the tale. "The story of how my ex-wife and I left Iowa is trippy. When we were twenty-five, my girlfriend and I both wanted to leave—we weren't married then—so Jen got a job as a chef at a Colorado ski resort. I had just graduated from college, but figured I would be a waiter until we figured things out. We loaded up her car, grabbed the cat, and drove out west. But when we got there, we absolutely hated the place. There was only the one restaurant for an hour's drive in every direction, and four ranches. There was no chance of us making it there, and no way in hell we were moving back to Iowa."

"What did you do?"

"We kept driving west," I answered. "We decided to just go until we found something we liked, or our money ran out. Living off my credit cards, we went all the way to the west coast and up and down California, looking for a fit. Unfortunately, everything in Cal was too expensive for us, so we ended up in Reno, Nevada. We were nearly broke and my credit cards were maxed. It was over 110 degrees and our only home was a metal car in the sun. I thought the poor cat was going to die, man.

"I drove us around town until I found a suitable neighborhood: not too good and not too bad. I approached the manager and told him, 'We have no money here, but plenty back home. I want to leave my girlfriend and our cat here— starting right now—for one week free. I will return to Iowa to get the rest of my money. If I don't return in seven days with all of next month's rent on top of this week's, you can throw my girlfriend and cat out onto the street.'"

Bianca laughed, and asked, "He no buy that Gypsy crap, did he?"

"He did. He said I looked just smart enough—and stupid enough—to be believable. We were obviously middle class and, to be honest, were his only white tenants, which I think influenced his decision. So I left Jen with the car to look for a job, and gave her the last of our cash. I kept twenty dollars only and took the train—yes, the train—across the country to Iowa. It took two and a half days, but I made it. I spent another day and a half in Iowa fattening up and gathering my stuff, then hopped in my car to go 'rescue' Jen. That led to one of the worst experiences of my life.

"You see, it takes thirty-two hours to drive from Cedar Rapids to Reno. Unfortunately, I took a wrong turn in there somewhere and added to the distance. I was really, really worried about Jen being left alone in that strange and none-too-safe neighborhood, and I had to get my ass back there and pay. She had almost no money for food and just barely enough for gas to drive around looking for a job. She had no phone to communicate with, which is why I didn't wire the money. She had no one to turn to at all. I hauled ass and drove straight through, hyped up on coffee. But my timing was off—dangerously off.

"Because of my wrong turn, I ended up entering Nevada on Highway 50. This, I discovered, was called the Loneliest Road in America. They weren't kidding! I was crossing mountains, which are hell on gas mileage..."

"Wait," Bianca interrupted. "Hell on what?"

"Gas mileage. You know, miles...?"

"Oh, da, da, of course. Please continue."

"After crossing the deserts of western Colorado and crossing all of Utah, I was running low on gas. I had never seen such vast distances without a gas station: it was crazy. I finally crossed into Nevada and reached a little mountain town at 9:05 p.m. I pulled into the only gas station just as they were closing up—or, rather, as he was closing up. There was only one guy, and only two pumps."

"Of course there was only he," Bianca interrupted again. "How many Americans it take to pump gas?"

"You haven't spent much time in America, have you?" I replied. "Most gas stations are big: dozens of pumps, big store, and all that."

"Anyway," I continued. "These were the old-fashioned kind of gas pumps, where you have to go inside to pay for gas. No credit cards or anything. He wouldn't let me have any gas because he had just closed up the cash register for the night. Can you believe that?

"So I had to keep driving. And driving. And driving. I was driving on fumes, man, and hadn't seen any cities at all. I passed one little town with a population of like twenty or something, but that was all dark and closed. I went up and down I don't know how many mountain ranges. Turns out Nevada is the most mountainous state in America, other than Alaska. I was less than five minutes from being stranded alone in the middle of the desert at midnight. If that happened I would survive, but I would have no chance of saving Jen from being kicked out on the street.

"Until!" I boomed, getting all melodramatic. "Until I saw a light ahead. A dirt road crossed this so-called 'highway,' marked by a single street lamp. Lo and behold, there was a single, dusty gas pump—in the dirt parking lot of a bar, of all things. I pulled up to the pump and parked. Even though it was dark, I intended to remain right there all damn night if need be.

"That bar was something else," I continued. "It was small, of course, and very rustic. The two bathrooms were differentiated by stolen highway signs—filled with bullet holes —indicating 'cow crossing' for the ladies and 'open range' for the men. At the bar were three men with the longest beards I had ever seen in my life. I still don't recall which was dirtier: them or their clothes. They looked just like Old West mining prospectors. The way they shot whiskey implied they were getting home by burro rather than car.

"'I need gas,' I said to the bartender. He looked just like the miners, by the way. He replied, 'Sure, after you buy a couple of beers or three.' I had been driving under extreme stress over Jen for about twenty-two hours straight at this point, and said as much. But he wouldn't turn on the gas pump until I bought a beer. So I did. The conversation was... interesting. These were men who had avoided civilization their entire lives. They referred to a town of 300 people as 'the big city.' It was bizarre."

"So you had a beer?" Bianca said. "When your woman was waiting for you, you sat and had a beer?"

"What else could I do?" I defended lightly, "I didn't drink it, because I would have passed out from exhaustion. On TV was the news, something about a woman running for governor or something like that. The bartender made his disgust at that turn of events very clear. I won't repeat what he said, but it nearly made me blush—no small feat. Then the patrons answered in kind, right down the line, until the guy beside me agreed by angrily spitting his chewing tobacco on the floor. Then all four stopped and stared at me, waiting.

"Now, I needed to get back to Reno," I clarified. "Which meant I needed to get gas. I played the part expected of me. I slammed my beer on the bar and said with great emphasis, 'God damn it! I was planning on moving to Nevada, but I won't until that bitch gets her fat ass back in the kitchen, barefoot and pregnant!'"

"'By God, son!' cried the bartender. 'Let's get that pump turned on straight away. We need more men like you here.'"

"So gas I got, and I pulled into Reno about 3:30 a.m. The next morning I was due to pay up, so it was just in time. All that, and yet we were doomed from the beginning," I finished. "I think the moral of the story is that I don't know when to quit."

"But you did quit," Bianca pointed out. "You divorced."

"Jeez," I grunted. "You don't have to get all serious and stuff. We got married in a drive-through ceremony, for cryin' out loud. I just found reverse a little late, that's all."

We continued in silence for a moment, and I wondered if Bianca would feel the need to share a similar story. With none forthcoming, I tested the waters.

"You said you had a big ex, too," I prompted. "There's got to be an interesting story in there somewhere."

Bianca stumbled, her foot disappearing into a puddle of surprising depth. Cold water splashed up, soaking her skirt and dousing my pants. She cursed with all the creativity of a sailor, which she was. Saved by the puddle, conversation ceased as we finally reached Casa Pădurarului—closed, of course—and wormed through the defenses of Brașov. The streets of the old city were deserted at this late hour in the rain, but I saw no less than three packs of stray dogs. Menacing, unkempt shapes darted over glistening brick, some melting into groups, others into shadow.

"How many goddamn dogs you got in this country?" I asked with that strange mixture of humor and irritability that comes with fatigue.

"Tens of thousands," Bianca answered tiredly, hanging on my arm heavily. Her feet must have hurt something fierce in those high-heeled boots, but she endured without complaint.

The night had become very cold, and we huddled together in clouds of our own puffing breath.

"Is real problem," she continued. "When Ceauşescu was in control, he forced thousands of people to leave their farms and move into the city. Every peasant had a dog, but had to leave him in the country. Dogs are smart, though, and came to the city themselves. Also, Ceauşescu destroyed mucho houses with gardens for blocs, so even city dogs became Gypsies."

"Well, at least that explains all the crap on the streets," I said with completely artificial cheeriness.

The rain pressed harder and the skies grumbled louder. There is something inherently romantic about sharing a good umbrella, arm in arm with a beautiful companion, wandering deserted brick streets and centuries-old architecture. We crossed a series of old, pillared structures wrapped around a dark alcove. Lightning flashed, and suddenly a huge statue leapt out of the blackness at us.

I actually jumped back, forcing Bianca to stumble after me. Her deer-in-the-headlights stare revealed that she, too, had been surprised.

Lit by a strobe light of smoldering lightning, a gargantuan, angry man glared down with bronze eyes from atop a stone pedestal. His posture was immensely intimidating, with arms rearing back but ready to thrust forward, hammy fists clenched and ready to grapple—or grab a battle axe. Even his facial hair was combative, with flowing whiskers flaring to sharp points.

"What kind of a goddamn statue is that?" I challenged, panting.

"That rasclat is Andre Mureşanu," Bianca said, shooting an accusing glare at the bronze. She straightened her skirt indignantly. "He was a poet."

"A poet?" I cried. "He looks like the slaughterer of armies and children, for Christ's sake."

As thunder growled, I left Bianca the umbrella and uncertainly stepped into the small courtyard for a closer look. It was lush with overgrowing plants and unkempt hedges. The grass beneath my feet was swamped, and pulsed with the erratic winds.

"He was a warrior poet," Bianca clarified, calling from the street. "Check the book in his hand."

"Book my ass," I snapped, gazing up at his aggressive stance. "He doesn't want to read it—he wants to bludgeon me with it."

"He was a revolutionary that was able to speak and write to the masses. So we say poet. This was two hundred years ago."

"Conan the Librarian, indeed," I muttered, rejoining her. Bookended by a violent dog fight and a violent revolutionary, any rapture we may have enjoyed was effectively crushed. But our fatigue was washed away by adrenaline, so we scampered hurriedly along to Strada Lâcramioarelor.

# 3

Slogging up the dark steps to the fourth floor after marching through hell and back—even meeting a demon poet —was just mean. Piti greeted us at the door with a weak 'Aaaah' before dropping melodramatically to the floor. There he moaned and rubbed his empty belly. We were quickly wrapped in sweater-vests and papuci of dubious fit, then led into the cozy kitchen for a steaming cup of Lucky's tea.

Lucky had made a traditional Eastern European dish called *sarmale*. These were pickled cabbage rolls stuffed with minced pork, slices of smoked bacon, and chunks of peeled tomatoes. It was served with steaming mounds of polenta and actual soured cream. The sourness of the cream was explosive and delicious—actual soured cream!—and was completely unlike any of our processed 'sour' cream in the States. This simple dish vastly exceeded the sum of its own parts.

After dinner we played a card game called whist. As the man of the house, Piti insisted on teaching me the rules, preferring minimal linguistic assistance from his daughter. Fortunately it was not an overly complex game. Piti, Bianca, and I played, while Lucky watched and fussed over snacks and drinks. I came in last each of the first three games, but at least learned numbers in Romanian. Bianca jokingly mentioned that if I managed to hit exactly zero when someone else topped 500, the zero won. Using this strategy I won the next three games, at which point Piti threw down his cards and blurted something at Bianca in exasperation.

"He hates losing," she snickered. "Careful, he'll start cheating now."

"What did he say?"

"He called you a typical American, because Americans always find a way to win."

Struggling in the cramped kitchen, I stuck my big feet in the air. Pointing to the tiny slippers desperately clinging to them—the American flag slippers were too hot for me to wear—I said, "Lucky papuci."

Piti was so delighted that he poured us a special round of țuica. A dubious reward if ever there was one.

But then disaster struck: we ran out of wine. We had been drinking Piti's homemade wine by the bottle—refilled Coca Cola two-liter bottles, that is. This was the strangest wine I had ever encountered, being somewhat sweet with a hint of natural effervescence. I could only describe it as happy, fruitless sangria.

"We can skip the wine," I said helpfully. "We have alternatives."

Piti grinned when he followed my gaze to the țuica bottle. But he sadly shook his head.

"Nu," he said, tapping his temple. "*Durere de cap.*"

He then rose and gathered his jacket, leaving Bianca to translate.

"Durere de cap," Bianca explained, "Means headache. *Durere* is pain, and *cap* means head. You know, you wear a cap on your head."

"I see," I said. "But we're gonna have a hangover after all this wine anyway."

"That's the beauty of it!" she exclaimed. "This homemade wine is so honest and natural, with no tannins or artificiality, that you can drink yourself unconscious and not have durere de cap in the morning."

I was a bit dubious over that claim, but let it be. Piti was about to leave for more wine, but instead gestured for us to join him. Bianca looked quite surprised, yet also a touch pleased, for some reason. Soon we three were descending the unlit steps. At the bottom of the stairwell we stood in the dark. Piti was busy doing something, but I couldn't imagine what it was.

"I swear I just heard him open a manhole cover," I commented, leaning into Bianca's warmth.

"Please no tell me about any of your holes," Bianca begged.

More sounds of movement resounded from the recess beneath the stairs, eventually capped by a click. A faint light shone up from a trapdoor in the concrete floor, which Bianca nudged me to enter. I hesitated. This had all the markings of a nasty twist in a horror movie.

"Down you go, amigo," Bianca said innocently enough. "Watch your head."

Not knowing how to get out of it, I mustered myself to enter their underground crypt, where no doubt they had some sort of torture device, or perhaps cave tunnels that led to the caverns below Dracula's castle.

Squeezing down through the manhole was tortuous. I dropped into a nasty little tunnel, illuminated only by a weak light glowing somewhere afar. Creepy was the only word to describe it. I felt the weight of the building above me, which shuddered at random intervals—presumably from the wind, but possibly from the machinery driving the pendulum over the pit. I was forced to hunch and half-shuffle, half-crawl beside steaming pipes. After a turn, I saw an opening broken in the stone wall, through which the weak light emanated. Piti's figure occasionally passed before the light, dropping me into blackness.

Once through the hole, I was able to stand erect in a little room—or so I thought. The ceiling was uneven, and I hit my head. Reflexively I swore, which brought gales of laughter from Piti. Bianca came in after me, and Piti immediately spoke to her at great length, sniggering the whole time. Soon she was laughing, too.

"Some friends you are," I muttered, rubbing my head. "Is this where I say 'durere de cap?'"

Piti began laughing even louder, but Bianca managed to stifle her tears long enough to explain.

"He didn't realize you swore," she explained. "You said 'Jesus Christ', but because it's different in Romanian, he heard '*Jesus Gras.*'"

"Which means?"

She rubbed her round cheeks to suppress another giggle. "It means 'fat Jesus.' That's such an odd thing to say."

"No kidding," I commented dryly, "And probably even more offensive than saying the Lord's name in vain."

We were in a tiny chamber lined with shelves loaded with wine bottles and miscellaneous wine-making accoutrements. Several huge glass jugs, holding perhaps forty gallons or so, competed with us for the limited floor space.

"This is Piti's room," Bianca explained, dusting off her skirt. "Nobody else wants it, of course. Whenever he needs to disappear, he comes here and squeezes his grapes or shakes his apples."

"I'd like to watch you shake your apples, baby."

"What?"

"Nothing. It's a wonder he ever found it. How exactly does Piti shake his apples?"

Bianca gestured to the large containers and said, "He throws one apple in each, and when it floats the wine is ready. Along the way he gives them a shake to wake them up."

Piti was humming as he searched the shelves for just the right two-liter Coke bottle. He found what he was looking for, then motioned for me to sit. I squatted atop one of the glass containers, unsure if it was able to support my weight. Bianca came up behind me and rested her arms on my shoulders.

"This is special treatment, you know," she whispered into my ear. "Radu and Adi, who you'll meet in Sighişoara, wanted to marry my two cousins but were not allowed into the family until they first came down here and got drunk with Piti. Check, Adi is taller than you, papa! Can you imagine them both drunk as apples trying to get out that tunnel?"

Rather than comment on her phrase 'drunk as apples,' my imagination flared. For a second, I pictured myself someday getting drunk down here with Piti. Emotion flashed through me, just for a second. Why, I was actually a bit jealous! Bianca was bewitching, to be sure, but we were just friends. Right?

Piti opened the bottle and took a swig. He concentrated a moment, contracting his bushy white brows and wrinkling his round nose. Finally he smiled and loosed a satisfied, "Aaaah."

The bulky bottle passed between the three of us, when we were joined by Lucky. It was a surprise to both my companions, and a welcome one at that. Now we were four in a place even smaller than the kitchen! Lucky, who usually avoided drinking wine, took up the bottle as eagerly as the rest of us. It was fun to see her high, rosy cheeks turn bright red with joy.

"Mihaela used to come here, too," Bianca began, but suddenly burst out laughing. She rattled a long story to her parents in Romanian, and soon the three of them were howling.

"You know," Bianca explained. "She was always so serious. But one day Piti cut his hand when waking up an apple. Those bottles are huge, and he accidentally hit the wall and shattered it. Mihaela actually fainted when she saw all the blood. She's the shortest one to ever hit their head in here, papa. And check: she was studying to be a doctor!"

"Mihaela studied to be a doctor?" I asked, surprised. "She works for Microsoft!"

"For two years," Bianca answered, smirking. "Because her boyfriend was a doctor, of course. 'You should have a smart boyfriend like me,' she would say. Rasclat! Well, she quit after that. I guess love doesn't conquer all."

"Not usually," I observed, taking a swig of wine. Then I flashed her a smile and added, "But that doesn't mean it can't."

# CHAPTER FOUR

## *My Big Fat Romanian Wedding*

### 1

IT WAS STILL DARK when I awoke the next morning. I was up before everyone else, no doubt suffering the dregs of jet lag. I tiptoed first around the three Pops snuggled in their little fold-out bed, then tiptoed second around the kitchen in Piti's tiny papuci. The slippers were so small that staying on my toes was the only way to stay clear of the cold floor. It promised to be a cold, drizzly day. I lit the burner with a match and heated a small pot of Lucky's tea that she always kept ready. Eventually Lucky joined me, wearing her robe, and immediately lit the remaining burners for warmth.

"Durere de cap?" she asked, running her hands through my hair in motherly fashion.

"Nu!" I cheerfully replied, now fully convinced of the superiority of Piti's wine. She smiled, then hopped about the kitchen preparing a meal, humming happily. She was shockingly talented, with a voice like a professional contralto. I could almost hear the accompaniment by the cello-playing pig-dog.

I sat at my usual spot, which meant my legs blocked access to the kitchen. Eventually Bianca arrived, and, motioning with a rotating finger, curtly ordered me to '*Roteste*'. I rotated. Then Piti arrived yawning—already wearing his cowboy hat while still in his pajamas—and the three of us sounded in unison, "Roteste!"

Piti's first order of business was always a kiss for his wife and his daughter, and a brisk shaking of my hand. Every morning together was a glorious one in the Pop household. Of course, afterwards Piti immediately planted himself in his chair, rubbed his belly, and began whining for food. Lucky didn't disappoint, and soon Piti had his little soldiers arrayed on the breakfast plate. For me the most satisfying part of the meal, amusingly enough, was my constant rotating. I was discovering the inherent joy of close physical proximity. In America we have a relatively large culturally-dictated sense of personal space, but I was realizing that it kept people at arm's length in more ways than one.

After breakfast and its subsequent smoky conversation, Bianca went into the living room to open a large box that had arrived for her the previous day.

"This is another box from Tommy," she declared.

"A fawning admirer?" I asked.

Her round cheeks turned a bit redder than usual, and her perky lips pursed to say, "The latest suitor."

I raised my eyebrows, then sat back on the couch to observe. Piti, beside me, leaned forward to stick his rather large nose into everything.

"Tommy is much older," Bianca explained as she tore open the box. She began pulling out load after load of teddy bears. There were blue bears, red bears, fuzzy bears, cute bears, even a sailor bear.

"Indeed," I teased. "Just how old does he think you are?"

She gave me a sour face, then removed the final stuffed animal. It was a horrendous looking, shaggy brown thing. Bianca and Piti burst out laughing, then looked to me.

"What?" I said. "It's not like I sent it."

"What is it?"

"That's the original teddy bear," I explained. "Named after President Teddy Roosevelt. Not exactly as cute as its descendants, is it?"

Surprisingly, Bianca didn't need to translate that for Piti, for upon hearing me say 'President Teddy Roosevelt,' he nodded. For some odd reason, it turned out that the origin of the teddy bear was common knowledge in Romania. They just hadn't seen one before.

The box contained a total of fifteen teddy bears, two boxes of chocolates, and an oversized Tommy Hilfiger beach towel decorated as a giant American flag.

"Aha!" I cried. "This is where you got the big-ass American flag papuci."

"Guilty," Bianca agreed. "This contract, an older man—a guest—fell in love with me, but madly. He promised me the moon and the sun and told me that he will wait for me until the end of time, if I would accept to be his wife. He offered to buy for me any house I want, anywhere in States, and he treated me like a princess. I believe him because I spent some time in his company. He is so respectful and kind, and he didn't touch me anyhow because I had a reserved attitude, and was honest with him. I can't feel for him the way he feels for me."

"That must have been one hell of a cruise!"

"Well," she admitted sheepishly. "After we met, he stayed on for two more weeks. He is very persistent."

She stumbled to add quickly, "So you see, I do in life what my mind and heart desires, and won't do any compromise— even for money or a Green Card."

"Or two dozen teddy bears," I added wryly.

"Oh, no," she corrected. "These are from Tommy. I'm talking about another one. If Tommy knew he had competition, he would offer me the planets!"

I raised an eyebrow and looked to Piti, who had been staring silently at the pile of stuffed animals. After a quiet moment of musing, he finally shrugged and said, "Jesus Gras."

## 2

In the afternoon I joined the Pops in dressing for a wedding. Bianca had warned me in advance, so I brought a good suit for the occasion. I shuffled into the kitchen wearing a dark double-breasted suit over a white shirt with a sharp collar, a pale silk tie, and garish American flag slippers. Lucky gave me a huge smile and clapped her hands to her chest. She was wearing a frilly, multi-colored dress with long skirts.

Bianca, in a body-hugging, vivid purple dress with an open back and even longer skirts, loosed a surprised squeak.

"*Oui!*" she said, stepping up and sliding an appreciative hand down my tie. "You clean up good. In Romanian we say '*foarte frumos.*'"

"Foarte frumos," I repeated. "That's an easy one: rolls off your tongue. Anyway, thank you. I want to make an impression."

"Oh, you will," she teased. "As the only one not talking to anybody. You nervous?"

"Should I be?"

"At your first Romanian wedding?" she said cryptically. "I would be. Love is in the air, papa. Check you don't get caught in some black widow web."

Piti joined us presently, wearing an old fabric suit of olive green. It was freshly brushed, and the way he presented himself for inspection was decidedly military. Lucky clapped her hands enthusiastically, then immediately rushed up to comb his hair again. He spluttered under her ministrations for a moment, then wisely acquiesced.

As I was tying the laces on my dress shoes, I suddenly broke a lace.

"Damn it!" I snapped.

"Jesus Gras!" Piti added happily.

"Why you Americans so violent?" Bianca asked, half-teasing, half-serious as she slid into purple high heels. "Not everything is a terrorist!"

"Oh, like women don't have their own cobbling issues?" I mocked.

We were all ready, but Lucky felt the need to comb Piti's hair one more time, murmuring to him as she would a pet, "Foarte frumos—similar Bree-ahn."

Piti glanced up at me, in my crisp new suit and a full foot taller, then began flapping his hands to stop Lucky's pampering. Exasperatedly he cried, "Jesus Gras, *femeia!*"

Bianca's perky lips formed her trademark smirk. "He's found a favorite phrase, I think."


# 3


Stalwart Albişoara took us to the cathedral, but not before Piti lovingly washed and squeegeed her windows—despite the spotty rain. We pulled up to a cathedral, ancient, towering, and almost leaning over the curb. The front area was lined with neat rows of plants and wet walkways holding pools of rainwater. Trampling through these puddles were the delicately-clad feet of dozens upon dozens of men and women, all pushing and fighting their way up to the steps of the cathedral. Only upon exiting the car did it strike me that I was about to be overwhelmed.

Bianca dove headfirst into the waves of humanity, dragging me along by the hand. It took everything I had to maintain that grip in the ebb and flow of the crowd. The bodies pressing against me were uniformly well-dressed in their wedding best, varying in age from ten to ninety. A great many surprised and pleased greetings were thrown Bianca's way. It became immediately apparent that she was something of a celebrity. She was a sort of ex-patriot now, after all. The Pops were universally loved for their charisma, and Bianca was no exception. Deeper we dove.

Words were flung at me, but it was easy to drown them out because I understood nothing. So I smiled a lot, which came naturally enough. Everyone could tell at a glance that I was not Romanian—brown hair aside—and all understood. Bianca took care to introduce me to a number of people upon the steps of the cathedral, apparently her peers. A few greeted me in halting English, but easily a dozen names passed through me without really being caught in my memory's hole-filled net.

From behind a pillar came two little girls in brightly colored dresses, aged ten or so, arms locked together. They attacked Bianca with enthusiasm, gazing up at her with big, adoring eyes. One was a rare blonde in a white dress, the other a brunette pretty in pink. Bianca gave the brunette a hug, then happily introduced her as Corina, the daughter of Sorin the Mustard King. I thought she was a very pretty girl, though she had yet to grow into her prominent nose and big teeth. The blonde was a friend of hers.

"Corina is learning English," Bianca boasted. Corina blushed.

"Oh?" I said, giving the girl a grin. "How do you say 'Mustard Princess'?"

"*Prinţesa Muştar,*" she answered with a giggle. Corina blushed even deeper when she met Bianca's smiling gaze. To her friend, however, she gave a look of great satisfaction. The blonde responded by sticking her tongue out at her.

We moved off into the crowd, and I shouted questions to Bianca.

"Who is getting married, again?"

"Flaviu Miere," she shouted back. "He's the older brother of Sorin the Mustard King. Their father is my Godfather. You'll meet Sorin inside, but I don't expect you'll talk much to Flaviu. Not because he's getting married, but because he's cold with everyone, including his family. As a lawyer, this works well for him. The bride Oana is a judge, and the coldest witch ever. They were made for each other."

Finally we made it into the cathedral. I gazed about in awe at the design, which was very different than anything I had visited before. I was raised Roman Catholic, which placed a premium on expensive decor, but what this lacked in gold it countered with art. Every square inch of wall was lavishly covered by the strokes of reverent artists, from marble floor to gilded ceiling so very, very high up. Smoke from numerous braziers lazily wafted upwards, content to take its time on the long journey to the top. For the most part, only candles lit the huge chamber, such that all was primarily dark.

"Since you don't know Romanian Orthodox," Bianca commented, "I will explain things for you. If it helps, think of it as Greek Orthodox, our brother."

"Not Russian?"

"We have Roman roots, babaloo, not Russian. The country is Roman-ia, not Russian-ia."

Though tall, the cathedral was not very long. Every available spot was filled with a body, and we struggled into a place a bit to the right of the entryway. The front section was corded off, and a ceremony involving four people and one priest was already occurring. While Bianca made conversation with various people, I spied Corina and her friend peeking at me from behind a pillar. Once observed, they threw a shy smile my way before vanishing. They were adorable.

Suddenly a large chunk of people began leaving. We pushed our way closer to the front via the right flank. Those that were here before were not part of our party at all, and the entire pool of humanity rotated in a counter-clockwise manner so our party could make its way to the front.

"Roteste!" I cried as we finally wound our way to the stand directly behind the cordoned front. Already a third group was pushing at our rear.

The bride and groom stood front and center, flanked by another young couple.

"The other couple are the Godparents," Bianca explained. "When we were growing up, Sorin used to comment that I would be Godparent at his wedding, but it couldn't happen."

"Why not? Were you at sea?"

"No, bambo, because I'm not married! Godparents have to be married. Duh."

"So you don't individually choose loved ones for however many bridesmaids and groomsmen you want, but have to agree on one married couple to become the Godparents?"

"Of course," she replied. "What do you mean, however many you want? How many Godparents you need?"

The ceremony progressed with the usual speaking and responding of vows. I heard additional responses to the priest from a chorus, but never saw where it was stationed. And then we were rotating out. Before I knew it, we were outside and yet another group was clambering to get in. Rotate!

"That ceremony was even faster than my drive-thru wedding in Reno," I marveled. "A short few minutes and 'move along, folks, nothing to see here,' even as dozens of others mill around, waiting for you to finish. Roman Catholic weddings can be tortuous, lasting hours."

"Hours?" Bianca repeated, shocked. "What you do for hours?"

"Wait for death," I replied with a grimace. "It's all rise, kneel, rise, kneel, toe the line, at attention!"

"No thank you," she said. "Who cares about the ceremony? It's the party that matters!"

"And that's why I love you," I replied cheekily. She paused a moment, then led me outside.

We crossed the street and spread out in a wide, grassy park. The dark clouds above were beginning to spit rain as the requisite group photos were taken. Though there was much joy in the air, I noticed that almost nobody smiled. What was it about Europeans that they thought bland stoicism was the only dignified way to celebrate momentous occasions? The bride Oana, in particular, was indeed the ice queen Bianca indicated. She was exquisitely beautiful, with porcelain features, flowing black hair, and a divinely trim figure. Her sculpted lips never once wiggled into a smile, though her finely-penciled eyebrow perversely shot up plenty. The photo shoot came to an end when Corina and her friend both stormed off in a huff, bored and tired of posing. Some things are universal!

It began to rain, so all commenced across the street to the dinner hall. I was informed that this was the nicest place in town for such gatherings. After all, Oana was tough enough to be a female judge in a heavily misogynist society, and subsequently highly prized. Beauty or no, she was the last judge I would ever want presiding over me.

The hall's entryway immediately surprised me with shallow, wide steps. Such steps were rare in America, where accessibility takes precedence over design, and—even more taboo—a candle burned on every step. It was a very simple, classy presentation, but one begging for a lawsuit in America, whether family or friend or not!

The hall was divided into two sections: a series of terraced tables filled the dark back, while a single row of six-foot tables hugged the wide dance floor. Piti and Lucky remained in the upper reaches with their good friends, the elder Mieres—surprising since they were the parents of the groom and so far in the back. Bianca also chose seats with Mieres—in this case Sorin and his wife. Horribly, however, they were also right next to the dance floor.

"Ah!" I cried, offering my hand. "The Mustard King himself!"

"Yes," said the short man in a dark suit and tie, as he shook my hand. "Is pleasure to meet you."

The Mustard King was in his mid-thirties, balding, somewhat portly and very smiley. I immediately recognized Corina's prominent nose on him, though he had grown into his, of course. In English, he introduced his wife, Moni, an equally smiley lady with long brown hair.

"I'm glad we can give Bianca a break," I said to Sorin. "She must be tired of translating."

"I study English," he agreed with a charming humility. His voice was very endearing, sounding like he was ready to giggle at any moment. "I do not speak well... but I understand all."

"So why are you called the Mustard King?"

Sorin laughed heartily at the question, but had to pull Bianca in to translate the answer.

"He has a mustard factory," Bianca explained. "It's very successful, supplying mustard to most restaurants in Braşov and selling in stores in half of all Romania. He's going to college now to learn more about business, which is why he's learning English. He's branching off into cola, too."

"Oh, wow," I replied, impressed. "Good luck competing with Coca Cola. They seem to have a monopoly here."

"Correct," Sorin said. "I want to... offer local product. I hope... to show you my factory."

Speaking of local produce, țuica was immediately served, as was a Romanian beer called Ursus. Sorin introduced me to Romania's fine wines, which I discovered were quite good—and not in a 'Piti's basement' manner. The first course of dinner was brought out, a series of smaller items in tapas-style. The assortment was reminiscent of Lucky's breakfasts, though also included sarmale. Soon afterwards dinner was served, an expensive river fish sautéed in a sweet white wine. Conversations waxed and waned. The very second we were through eating, Bianca was urging us to the dance floor.

"Uh, I think I need to digest this a bit first," I said.

I hated dancing, but knew that sooner or later I would have to do it. Later sounded preferable. After copious amounts of țuica sounded even more preferable.

"Dancing is how you digest," Bianca countered.

"But I ate similar pig!" I protested weakly.

"This is only the first course, you know," Bianca warned. "That's Romanian-style celebration: food, dance, food, dance, drinks through all."

Bianca rose and headed out to the dance floor. When she saw I wasn't following, she barked, "Sorin!"

Sorin gave his wife a painfully insincere look of apology, actually looking more like he was about to giggle, and Moni waved for him to go. He was gone in a blink. They began moving in an apparently Transylvanian version of ballroom dance. Bianca looked radiant in her sleek purple dress, shimmering under the mirror ball, her hair a mess falling over her eyes so that all you saw were round cheeks and perky lips. Sorin looked like a potato in a suit next to her—a very happy potato, to be sure. Moni gave a good-natured grimace and poured me another drink. We toasted each other, then watched our partners slink across the floor.

Alas, after the next round of food was served and devoured, I could hardly stall any longer—or hardly stand any longer, for that matter. Țuica was powerful stuff! So Bianca lured me onto the dance floor when the music changed to a funky 80s pop with non-English vocals. Though I had never heard any of the songs before, I was of course familiar with the disco genre. Classic hits like ABBA's 'Dancing Queen' melded naturally into Romanian and Italian pop.

To my absolute shock, I found dancing with Bianca exhilarating. A part of me had always wanted to dance, for I can feel the rhythm of music flowing through me, but don't know how to let it free. I knew the adage 'dance like no one else is in the room,' but was always too scared to try. Yet I was beginning to realize that, for Bianca, I would try anything.

Courtesy of lots of țuica, vin, and bere, I was ready to go out on a limb. This was fortunate, for the music soon changed to traditional Romanian, bringing the entire crowd down to dance. I didn't want to be rude, so I felt compelled to try the traditional dances. Transylvanian dances, I was informed, were particularly slow and laid-back. This allowed me to keep up with the simple, almost leisurely moves. But it was not to last, for the bride's family was from another area of Romania, called Moldova. The Moldavian dances were mind-numbingly fast and immediately caused durere de cap. We fled back to the table, content to down more booze and watch the completely uninhibited Piti and Lucky tear up the dance floor. They moved like they were still teens, as they were when they first fell in love. It was charming.

As Bianca had noted, the night stretched into a long series of food, dance, food, dance, with drinks throughout. During one break, while sitting at the table, Bianca received a delicate tap on her shoulder. We turned and saw little Corina, adorable in her pink dress. With a very shy smile, she asked Bianca something in Romanian.

Bianca replied slowly in English, "Would you like to dance with me?" She repeated it again, while Corina stumbled over the unfamiliar words. The girl then blushed and looked down. Bianca, smiling, encouraged her to try again. A moment later her bravery swelled, and Corina turned to me and asked in broken meter, "Would you like to dance with me?"

"Yes," I said, and thusly was soon dancing with a young Romanian girl. I, of course, was completely unfit to lead a dance, but being that I towered over her, we just held hands at arm's length and spun to the music. As we spun, I noticed Lucky dancing nearby, and she gave me a generous grin. The song died, and even as I thanked the girl for the dance, I was bodily snatched up by Lucky for the next one. I was suitably awkward, but she was patient. When through, she gave me a quick peck on the cheek. Then, spontaneously, she stuck a finger in my dimples, before fleeing as nervously as Corina.

Time passed, as did yet more courses and dances. I was really enjoying myself. At one point Bianca and Lucky left for the restroom, so I took the opportunity to sit next to Piti. We immediately downed shots of țuica and laughed together. Just then a particularly lovely example of Romanian beauty sashayed past, and we both stared like, well, drunk men.

"Frumos," I commented. He nodded deeply.

"*Frumoasa*," he corrected kindly. He pointed at me and said, "Frumos," then moved his hands into an hourglass shape and said, "Femeie: frumoasa."

We scanned the crowd and started pointing at various exemplary samples of the female persuasion. There were numerous such, and we identified a dozen in rapid succession. The ladies returned and we quickly dropped to silence.

"What are you doing?" Bianca asked, surprised at catching some talk.

"Oh, your father and I were just having a conversation."

She laughed. "Oh, really?"

"Yes," I replied solemnly, demonstrating by pointing to nearby babes. "Frumoasa, frumoasa..."

"Check!" Piti suddenly blurted. He pointed to Oana as she approached, and quickly received a smack atop the head from Lucky. But there was more to Piti's observation than just the most frumoasa lady in the room.

She was kidnapped before our very eyes.

Oana strode past us, eyes straight ahead and not deigning to glance down at her fawning admirers, when suddenly a group of men rushed her. They snatched her up as she kicked and screamed, then bodily carried her towards the front door. One of the abductors was kicked in the head and tumbled into the door as they passed through en masse.

"What the hell was that?" I blurted, standing up. But the Pops were all laughing and conversing jovially in Romanian.

"Hey, bamboclat woman!" I said to Bianca. "Should I be rushing to her defense, or not? What's going on?"

"They are stealing the bride," she answered simply.

"You think?" I replied sarcastically.

"No, no, you don't understand. It's a Romanian tradition to steal the bride from the party. Most women look forward to it, but I'm not surprised that Oana would protest. *Oui*, papa, I would be scared to abduct that one!"

"Where are they taking her?"

"Probably out to the car."

A cry rose from near the entrance, and soon swept through the entire hall. A spokesman for the abductors, hair still mussed and panting from the resisted arrest, limped in. He held above his head a trophy: one of Oana's white shoes. Hoots and hollers followed his progress down to the dance floor. The music stopped, and the groom was called up to verify if this was, indeed, proof of life from his missing bride.

"They usually ransom the bride for drinks," Bianca explained. "But sometimes money. If it happens before midnight, the Godparents have to pay up, but after midnight it's for the groom. I think they waited this late to get some of Flaviu's lawyer cash."

There was a lot of good-natured ribbing that Flaviu was so careless with his new wife. When he finally pulled out his money clip, there were many jeers. The abductor reviewed the dollar amount with skepticism, then held up the shoe to the hall, seeking consensus of whether or not it was enough money to fulfill the ransom. Boos answered. Reluctantly, Flaviu dug deeper into his pockets until he emptied them entirely. The spokesman triumphantly took the money and limped back outside.

"Sometimes they force the groom to do some embarrassing act to prove his love," Bianca continued. "But Flaviu has no sense of humor and wouldn't do it. Oh, I wish I could have seen Oana fighting those thieves outside! A fight for the ages, like Achilles and Hector."

Moments later the bride was ushered in on the shoulders of half a dozen men, none of whom appeared untrammeled, one even bleeding. Oana was returned to Flaviu, and the music flared up for a slow dance to rejoice their reunion.

As the night continued, I found myself slow dancing with Bianca—a lot. I felt very comfortable getting close with her, and though I moved horribly to her lead, we both seemed to fit very well. I hugged her close as we meandered about the dance floor. Song after song was now slow and romantic, and love was indeed in the air. I caught a glimpse of Piti stealing a kiss from Lucky nearby. I leaned forward and told Bianca how much fun I was having, even with the dreaded dancing for the first time in my life. She just laughed and held me close. We spun about, and I found myself whispering into her ear what few Romanian words I had learned already—any excuse to get closer.

"Frumoasa... sarmale... durere de cap...Strada Lucky-yodeladyhoo..."

She closed her eyes and smiled, and before I knew it, we were not lost in the dance, but in each other.

The night finally began to settle down. To my shock, it was already past 3 a.m. Piti and Lucky wanted to leave, but Bianca fought resolutely to remain. Her parents left in Albişoara, leaving Bianca and I to walk home. Bianca disappeared to change into jeans, and I found myself looking for little Corina. There was something I wanted to say to her. I spied her once on an upper balcony, playing with her blonde friend in white, but by the time I got there they had vanished. Bianca returned, and the dancing resumed.

Suddenly I found myself among a small circle of men who were surrounding the bride and a basket on the floor filled with money. Bianca handed me a Romanian bill with a long string of zeroes on it, and informed me that it was a dollar dance.

"That's one hell of a dollar!" I commented. "But then, Oana is pretty damn hot."

"30,000 Romanian lei to the US Dollar, remember," Bianca chided wryly.

I was nervous to dance with the ice queen, but soon found myself doing so. Oana joined me with extreme composure, holding her head high, revealing a flawless, milk-white neck. In faltering Romanian I asked if she spoke English, "*Vorbiţi Englezeşte?*"

She replied with a flat, "Nu."

"No problem," I said, and we danced in silence. Really, who needs words when dancing with such a staggering beauty? I was not bruised by the end of the song, as her abductors were, but I think my hands were frost-bitten.

Unfortunately it was only another half an hour of slow dancing with Bianca before everything came to an end. When we returned to our table, the Mieres were preparing to leave. Little Corina looked very tired. I made my way over to her, dropped low to be at eye level, and whispered in her ear what I had been wanting to say to her. I'm not sure why. I don't particularly like kids. I guess Oana wasn't the only cold one. But something about little Corina thawed me a bit.

"Foarte frumoasa," I said.

She smiled weakly and perked up a bit, but soon Sorin was hefting her up and carrying his sleeping daughter to the exit.

# 4

Bianca and I both expressed a desire to walk home together, not wanting our closeness to end. Unfortunately it was raining when we left. That may have felt refreshing, had it not been cold enough to clearly see our breath. Thus we opted for a taxi, which was a mistake. After the amazing night of beauty, a nasty Romanian cab killed the vibe. We were so distraught over the filthy vehicle that we asked the driver to drop us off a few blocks before we reached our bloc.

Arm in arm we rushed home, exhilarated to the point of giddiness by fatigue and the cold shower. We settled in the kitchen, Bianca upon a stool beneath the pig-dog mural and I beside her. The quiet of the little chamber thundered in our ears. Though still cold, we shared a cup of cold tea because we were too tired to heat it. She appeared pleasantly tired, but was far too excited to sleep. I felt the same. We conversed about the night, our words luring us into a heady, relaxed state. She leaned a bit forward and was narrating something. I, too, leaned forward, but wasn't listening at all.

As she spoke, I moved in closer and kissed her lightly on a rosy cheek. It was still cold. She paused in her speech. I stayed close, and teased her cheek with another few delicate kisses. Then I leaned even closer and kissed by her ear, our cheeks pressing together, finally warming.

Now she was completely silent, and I nudged her chin up so I could gently kiss her neck. My lips slid down slowly, exploring for a few more desirable spots to taste. I held the last, light kiss upon her delicate throat for a long moment, eyes closed and face pressed into the sheltering curve of her chin. Satisfied, I finally leaned back.

We locked eyes for a very, very rewarding moment.

"W-why you do that?" she asked brokenly. Her voice was quiet but playful.

"Do what?" I asked, returning close but pausing an inch away from her mouth. I cocked my head to the side and stared at those ruby lips.

"Make me forget my words…" she replied. I cut her off with a kiss, a real kiss, our first. It was light, soft, and very warm… and it lasted.

When I eventually pulled back, I asked her innocently, "What were you saying?"

She gave me a playful frown, but her smirk was wriggling into place.

"You always make me lose my thoughts!" she accused, her Romanian accent husky and thick.

"Oh," I said, giving her a smile. "I'm sorry."

"Don't be," she whispered back.

We enjoyed another few warm and gentle kisses, then acknowledged that we needed to go to bed. Alas, we both knew that we couldn't continue with what we wanted to, not with her parents nary five feet away. That, unfortunately, meant I would sleep alone and she would be with her parents. But when I drifted into dreams, I was far from unhappy.

# CHAPTER FIVE
## *The Worst Birthday*

### 1

AAAH... SIGHIŞOARA. The Old World hamlet will always be a special place for Bianca and I; a place resonating with a deep sense of peace and belonging; where we fell hopelessly in love; where we loosed unbridled passion with a ferocity most can scarcely conceive; where we beat our first Gypsy girl.

Not necessarily in that order.

Though geographically not too distant, getting from Braşov to Sighişoara required some time because the highway twisted through the rugged Carpathians. These mountains stayed the Romans for centuries, forced the Mongols elsewhere, and even kept the Turks at bay—but none of them had stalwart Albişoara. As always, Piti first had to shoo away the children laughing at his doting on the car with a thirty-point inspection. I tried, but concluded there was no chance to secretly ditch the Rambo knife from the glove compartment. It still made me nervous.

Far more unnerving was when Piti signaled that I was to remove my seatbelt. I kept it on, of course, but he actually reached over and unbuckled it! He answered my shocked look by indicating I just need it in my lap to placate passing police, no more. It was unmanly to have it secured, Bianca added helpfully.

The drive was pleasant, past robust forests, tumbling streams and menacing ridges. We passed occasional clusters of farmhouses on steep hillsides with old tiled roofs. I loved them, but Bianca hated them. To me they screamed Europe and romance, but to Bianca they were merely broken down remnants from another era. As we neared Sighişoara, Lucky reached forward and began quietly patting my shoulders. For nearly fifteen minutes she affectionately caressed them, very tender and very sweet. I couldn't help but smile, and wondered what Bianca had told her that morning while Piti and I were busy downing ţuica. Actually, Piti dutifully abstained because he was driving, but I had an appetite to stimulate.

Similar to our entry into Braşov, we first drove through the newer, ugly section of town. We crossed a wide, low river called Târnava Mare, upon whose bank rose a fantastic Byzantine cathedral. A few turns later, past the old stone Orthodox Church of Corneşti and up a hill, we finally rumbled along the cobblestone Strada Crişan, which held Bianca's house. Hers was at the end of the street, beyond which rose a tall, rounded hill loaded with massive oaks old as the city itself.

We idled Albişoara outside a metal wall that blocked our view of her house. Indeed, all of the neighbors had walls and gated yards. While this made the street itself less visually appealing, each home did enjoy a sense of privacy. Bianca pointed to the hill and the thick forest, explaining, "Carpathian bears live there and wander the streets at night. Check those oaks: they are favorite of Prince Charles. When he visited, he begged the people not to kill them. See? We can be civilized sometimes. No city sprawl here, papa!"

Piti became impatient and ordered Bianca to get out and unlock the gates with an exasperated, "Jesus Gras!"

"Câine rau?" I asked, pointing to the mildly weathered sign bolted to the extremely weathered metal wall.

Bianca smiled as she opened access for Albişoara. "Ask Piti."

The house was absolutely charming. It had lush gardens, courtesy of Lucky's green thumb, and a great view. I stared over an old brick wall across the top of the forest that snuggled the old town, canopy punctured by numerous spires from cathedrals and citadels. I could easily imagine a morning coffee watching the sun rise over all that awesomeness. The house was a freshly painted, comfortable, single story dwelling that included a three-season porch. Piti followed the two stone tracks set in the grass that led to a shiny new garage. When he came out, I asked him about the 'bad dog' sign out front.

"Check," he said, pointing to the steps leading up to the front door. Wet and bedraggled from remaining outside to stand guard, was a small toy chihuahua. "Ham ham!"

More than just building a garage and refurbishing the exterior, Bianca was also in the process of revamping the interior to modern standards. The floors were all torn up, so the tour was a short one. A small bedroom attached to the kitchen was for her parents, then a short hall led to the living room, a modern bathroom, and a sizable, sunny bedroom for Bianca. When complete, it would be a wonderful place that would allow the family both togetherness and privacy, as needed.

"I feel sorry for the workers," Bianca commented. "Piti orders them like they are his soldiers. The best part, though, is the cellar. Is huge, and Piti can make mucho more wine."

Simply put, I would have lived there in a heartbeat. Her parents were so excited it was palpable. The amount of satisfaction Bianca must have felt for being able to provide this for them—after a lifetime in a communist hell-bloc—was unimaginable. She was truly a classy woman.

Piti and Lucky eventually took the car to visit family in the new part of town. Bianca grabbed my arm and said, "Sighişoara is one of the best preserved medieval towns in all of Europe. Is UNESCO World Heritage site, with all its 16th century buildings still living. They say it equals even Prague and Vienna. Shall we wander?"

And wander we did. It was wonderful. All the streets of old Sighişoara were cobbled, the buildings classic, and the vibe one of contentment with the countless centuries. The citadel and subsequent town, which they called Schassburg, were founded by Romanian Saxons in the 1100s. Most of the structures clustering around the citadel were expanded in the 1400s. Striding up to it was a steep ramp, one side dropping into a thicket of ancient oaks, and the other a massive defensive wall of hand-hewn stone, dozens of feet high. Under the dappled sunlight, just before the curve that led to the citadel, I felt overwhelmed by the romance of it all. There, in the middle of the road, I stopped Bianca and kissed her.

"I like this spot!" I said.

"I do now," Bianca agreed with a chuckle.

"I declare that this spot shall forevermore be designated for mandatory kissing." It was painfully unmanly to think such thoughts, let alone speak them, but I was overcome by the romance of the place.

We strolled beneath an extremely impressive tower, rebuilt after an explosion of the gunpowder stores in the 17$^{th}$ century and later outfitted with a fantastic clock, complete with wooden figurines that changed in tandem with the clockworks. Nearby the tower was an old, three-story house painted ochre. Above the door was a wrought-iron dragon.

"You will like this one," Bianca observed. "This is Vlad Dracul's house. His son Dracula was born here in 1431."

"Dracul," I repeated in awe. "That means 'the dragon,' does it not?"

"It can," Bianca agreed. "It also means 'the devil.' So Dracula actually means 'son of the devil.' All you death-loving creeps forget the real Dracula is a hero to my people. He was a sick puppy, da, but we love him because he tried to kill all the Gypsies."

I opted out of responding to the strange statement.

"Anyway, the top is Museum of Weapons. The ground floor is restaurant."

My gaping earned a smirk. I desperately wanted to get a photo of the utter sweetness I was beholding, but the scene was ruined by a piece-of-crap Volkswagen Beetle parked in the way.

We searched for a café, choosing from among numerous scattered balconies and patios with tables and chairs tucked under canopies or perched atop roofs. Every direction and all descended with steep cobblestone streets, or steeper custom steps—all layered and folded atop centuries of additions. We opted for a narrow balcony, only three tables long, clinging to the stonework of an old tower. Here we could watch the streets spill into the valley below. It was no more beautiful than any of the others: they were all lovely.

A slim, middle-aged waitress with rollicking black hair but tired eyes took our order. We each ordered a Romanian coffee —in reality a Turkish coffee, though they refused to admit it— and a local cognac from Jidvei. Bianca lit a cigarette. I lit a cigar. We both gazed about and filled the sunshade with smoke.

The afternoon stretched out, and we wallowed in the peace. That is, until we were approached by a smelly girl of about Corina's age. She shuffled right up to us, eyes drooping and posture broken. She began to mumble in a most pitiful manner.

Bianca growled some menacing words at the girl. All sense of peace gone, what sat beside me was nothing less than the bitch on the mountaintop protecting her pups. Amazingly, the girl gave no reaction. She just continued her pathetic muttering at the ground.

"It's just a homeless girl," I said. "Should I give her something to make her go away?"

"You will not!" Bianca snapped. "She no homeless."

Bianca raised her arm as if to strike, and barked threateningly. Yet the girl remained, unintelligible words dribbling from her dirty mouth like sewage fouling a river. Time ticked by awkwardly, our pleasant vibe long since destroyed. I cannot truly convey how wretched this creature was, nor how provokingly annoying. Equally perplexing was how Bianca could claim the girl was not homeless. I had seen destitution before, and it looked a lot like this—though not even a fraction this bad. This seemed almost... intentional.

Tired of waiting, Bianca finally reared her arm back and— with great emphasis—walloped the girl right upside the head.

"Jesus Gras!" I cried in shock, rising halfway from my chair.

The girl did not react to the blow, other than to slowly turn about and wander off.

Bianca leaned back casually, brought her coffee to her lips, closed her eyes, and enjoyed a sip. She could not see my utter horror, so I made damn sure she heard it.

"What the hell was that?"

"That," Bianca answered, clinking cup on saucer, "was a Gypsy."

"Why did you hit her? She would have left if you just ignored her."

"I do her favor," Bianca explained. She frowned a moment, then understanding lit her face. "You thought she was a homeless person, and in the States homeless people are polite. You a long way from home, Brian."

She leaned forward and pointed across the distance to the street.

"Check him," she said, indicating a man standing in the afternoon shadows. He was dressed in ragged clothing, lounging against a wall with arms folded across his chest. He had the darkest skin I had yet seen in Romania, like a dark tan from being in the sun all day.

"Keep your eyes open, amigo. He targeted us—probably heard our English—and sent her in. If she went back without money, believe me, he would beat her half to death. No hospital, no treatment, just bruises and flies until she heals on her own. They are disgusting creatures, and this is business to them."

"How can beating your own child be business?"

"These are not a misunderstood minority," Bianca warned. "Waiting for the majority to embrace them and their different ways. They choose to live outside of cities, of civilization, to feed off the scraps. They speak only their own language and recognize only their own culture. They teach children to steal. They sell little girls into marriage. They refuse to civilize, to change, to evolve."

"Surely not all—"

"This not Hollywood," Bianca interrupted. "This is no—how you say?—stereotype. They are not exciting outcast dancers or any such things. This no American happy ending. I know you and your American sensibilities. You are idealists, but this is no ideal world. Gypsies have had centuries to go straight: they don't want to. They are dangerous."

I was silent, taken aback by her vehemence. Bianca's earlier comment about Vlad Dracula being a local hero now made more sense. I was, indeed, a long way from home.


# 2


Ironically, the most unique and fateful night of my entire life began with Bianca abandoning me. For nearly two weeks I had been pushing Bianca to give herself a break from the constant, tiring translations. The good thing was that she finally listened and left me. The bad thing was where she left me.

Fending for myself at her aunt and uncle's place may not sound so bad. They are family, after all. Because Lucky and he were spending the night there, Piti began drinking early. By the time Bianca disappeared into the bedroom, Piti and Uncle Loți had already plowed through all the wine and were arguing over politics—in Hungarian, no less. Apparently this was standard operating procedure with these two, though why they were speaking in Magyar was anybody's guess. Piti may have only been about 130 pounds, but watching him scream about elections would intimidate Mike Tyson.

I retreated to the kitchen and watched Lucky and Aunt Stefania prepare the night's meal. I enjoyed learning how to say the foods in Romanian, taking special care to remember Bianca's favorite thing: apples. Those were *mere*. My favorites were *usturoi şi ceapa*; that is, garlic and onions. Eventually the men stumbled in, drunk as mere. They managed to communicate their surprise that I would deign to such womanly activities. I managed to communicate that I prefer Romanian food over Romanian politics.

When Bianca finally bounced into the kitchen, dressed for the evening's activities, I knew I was in for a long night.

"How do I look?" she asked, whirling about. Lucky and Aunt Stefania clapped their hands enthusiastically. Bianca wore a fluttery silken top patterned after some sort of savannah, with tall grasses tickling the curves of her body. I found myself jealous of a shirt! Lucky adored the accompanying green scarf, whereas I preferred the tight leather pants. She looked fantastic. I had a flash of foresight that Bianca would be one of those women who, at age forty, would dress like she's twenty. Suited me fine.

It was a short walk in a chill evening to our destination.

"I have two cousins," Bianca explained as she clung to my arm. "Cristina and Laura. They always lived in Sighişoara, and I would stay with them during the summers. Cristina married Adi, and Laura married Radu. Those two bamboclat husbands have a rivalry going over everything, papa. Big drama choosing which apartment to have the party. Cristina and Adi won that one, because their daughters are easier to handle than Laura and Radu's baby. And, of course, is Cristina's birthday tomorrow."

"You're dressing awfully sexy for a dinner party with children," I teased.

"Oh, I have reputation to uphold," she answered. "And a job. I make life easier on my cousins. Adi and Radu both love to dance, but the girls are too tired. So I give them a break, taking care of their husbands for a night."

"How noble," I said drily. "You swoop in, get their husbands all hot and bothered, then leave the country."

"Hey, bambo," Bianca challenged. "What you think you gonna do to my cousins?"

When we arrived, both cousins smothered Bianca in hugs, leaving me for long minutes in the hallway holding the bags. Over their heads I met the gaze of a tall and ugly man, who rolled his eyes. Soon enough I was being shown off to the sisters, who spun me around, looked me up and down, and even rapped a knuckle on my chest like I was a melon at the market.

"My cousins," Bianca introduced. Both sisters shared nearly identical features, with dark eyes and narrow noses, like a soft hawk's beak. Strong laugh lines couched sumptuous lips, painted in the deep shades preferred by Romanian women. Only then did I realize how rare Bianca's usual bright red lipstick was. Cristina looked precisely like a middle-aged woman with two children: dressed for comfort in jeans, with curly hair left to fend for itself. Laura was a bit younger, still 'bothering' to apply makeup and dress with extra care.

"Be careful," Bianca warned me. "Laura knows some English. She doesn't speak it, but watch your tongue because we girls always find stuff out."

Laura smiled to reveal a charming little gap between her front teeth, blushed, and shook her head in denial. This, of course, only proved that she did understand.

"Are you two Bianca's only cousins, then?" I asked Laura.

Laura shot an unsure look at Cristina, and both overtly avoided Bianca's gaze. A long pause lengthened awkwardly, until Radu answered curtly in English.

"There is one other, in Timişoara. Forget about it, because Bianca hates Timişoara."

The moment was weird, and the discomfort obvious, even if the reason was not. I didn't press it. Immediately thereafter I was apprehended by Radu. Though six feet tall, he was not a big man. Rather, he reminded me of someone of average build accidentally run up to an awkward height. Without any meat on his bones, pale skin and deep-set, dark eyes, Radu's smile looked like a skull with a missing canine. He grabbed my arm and rather forcefully pulled me away from the women.

We sat at the kitchen table and he poured me a tall glass of red wine and Coca Cola. Yes: equal parts red wine and Coke. It looked as gross as it sounded, but a quick glance at Radu's posture made it clear that bravado was in order. I downed the whole thing as fast as he did—and the second—and by the third it was starting to taste pretty good. It was tough enough to choke down without Radu blasting through half a pack of smokes in mere minutes. When lighting up his dozenth or so cigarette, Radu suddenly spoke to me in my language.

"Romania is awful place," he said. "But it's home."

"You learned English in school?" I asked. Strange how we had been drinking for half an hour already and not communicating at all—not that Radu could have said much between those aggressive puffs.

"Yes," he replied. "I work winters in Germany. Germans, of course, speak English like civilized people. There I work to bring back huge money, earned with my own hands."

He held up his hands dramatically, splaying long, bony fingers.

"I was rusty, so didn't talk," he admitted. "But after drinking, everyone speaks all languages!"

Melodrama aside, Radu was right. After two weeks in Romania, I was already learning that what keeps most of us from using a second language is lack of courage to just say something. When in a foreign land, no one cares about syntax when you are obviously trying and actually communicating.

Radu proved to be every bit the Romanian man: arrogant, bigoted, and proudly assuming that being a good provider was enough to compensate for all of it. Who was I to argue? Then again, I need not when Bianca was around.

"Woman!" Radu suddenly bellowed. "Come feed me!"

Bianca entered the kitchen, bringing an even wider grin than usual to Radu's skeletal face. He looked her up and down a bit wolfishly, then asked, "Where is Laura?"

"You yelled in English," Bianca chided. "Who you think would answer?"

"Come to papa!" he cried gleefully, holding out his skinny arms.

Bianca stomped right past him, and past the stove, loaded with steam-spouting lids and bubbling sauces, to throw open a cupboard. She grabbed a bag of pretzel sticks, tore open the top, and smacked them on the table.

"Here you are, my sweet," she said, smiling smugly.

"What is this?" Radu asked, holding up a broken pretzel stick with profound disappointment.

"Freudian symbolism," Bianca muttered. Then more loudly added, "That's all you get until Adi comes home."

"Who cares about Adi?" Radu retorted loudly. "I am here!"

With a sniff, Bianca spun on her heel and departed, leaving Radu to his crumpled bag of broken pretzels. Things went downhill from there.

"Adi," Radu grumbled. "Ha! He is a good man, but not the provider I am. I work in Germany to provide a better life for my family, with my own two hands. I bought new computer, for example. I bought new stereo."

"All Laura wants is a real bed!" Bianca's voice called from the hallway.

"You'll like the stereo when you come dance at my home!" he yelled back. Then he gave a dismissive wave and said, "Women! I bought all new fixtures for the bathroom, so Laura could keep herself pretty. Now she wants a bed! What for? Our baby keeps us busy all night, so no time for sex anyway."

Time slowed to a crawl as Radu shared with me his profound insight into Romanian politics. As a product of the revolution, he wanted nothing to do with the current president, a long-time member of communist dictator Ceaşescu's regime. Radu thought he was a jerk. Radu thought he was corrupt. Radu told me every single reason why. I secretly prayed for Piti to show up, but only after first checking Albişoara's glove box. When Adi arrived with one of their daughters, it was the most ecstatic moment of my entire visit to Romania.

As I shook Adi's hand, I gazed upwards to assess his height at easily 6'5" tall. Aside from prodigious height, Adi was otherwise mercifully opposite of Radu, being robust and healthy in appearance, with tanned skin, thinning hair, and an extremely generous smile. Within seconds he was pouring himself wine and proving himself a real ham. Raluca, an enthusiastic six years old, was every bit her father's daughter.

Radu wanted food. Adi wanted wine. The ensuing argument was in Romanian, of course, but the body language was universal. The conversation moved away from the subject at hand and reverted to who had the most toys. Radu and his two hands won that battle; his new bathroom and computer trumping Adi's new kitchen cupboards. It is amazing how much can be understood when we just shut up and observe— and observe I did, for Bianca had no hope or intention of translating for seven people. Radu, of course, was quick to translate everything of importance that he, himself, said.

Over a forkful of scrumptious pork schnitzel, I asked Cristina, "What do you want for your birthday?"

Via Bianca, she answered, "All I want is a good night's sleep, a relaxed morning with Adi taking care of Raluca and Antonia—she's too young so friends are caring for her—and making breakfast, and the whole day to just relax."

Adi reached a lengthy arm around her and gave her a reassuring hug. They were a very smiley couple, unlike Laura and Radu.

"But first," Cristina added, "I want to dance with my husband."

The evening was much like the wedding, only of smaller scale. We ate, then danced, then ate, then danced. We drank throughout. A small music box was fired up, and Cristina had her dance with Adi. After only one, however, she trudged into the kitchen to clean. She refused any offers to assist, relenting only after Adi promised to do everything in honor of her birthday—after another wine and another dance, of course. Facing the inevitable, Cristina gestured to Bianca.

Silk fluttering and leather stretching, Bianca swirled through the living room like a dream: Adi and Radu's dream, apparently, based on the way they argued over each dance with her. The sisters directed narrowed eyes to them all, and I feared the annoyance was for Bianca. After all, she was the exotic one radiant with a joy of life that us 'normal' people did not possess, and frequently viewed with skepticism that hid jealousy. Bianca had no children and a figure that showed it. She was well dressed, well traveled, and had money. It just didn't seem fair.

Eventually I realized they were dismissive of Bianca rather than challenged by her, and mostly just disappointed with their husbands. Perhaps they longed for a time when their men fought for their own hand in a dance.

Much to my surprise, I spent most of the night talking to Raluca. It started when Radu plunked down at the table, having lost the next dance with Bianca. He lit a cigarette, and then spoke to Raluca. I heard my name in there somewhere. She began giggling.

"Mister Brown!" she said, pointing at me.

Radu blew a line of white into the air, and grinned. When directed at me, his smile looked hideous, but when directed at Raluca it just looked goofy. Though a misogynist, he was not a monster—though I usually thought them synonymous. But he was good with kids. Radu finally explained, "I asked her if she knew how to say your name in English."

"Funny how everyone thinks my name is Romanian," I commented wryly. I turned to Raluca and asked, "You are learning English?"

Her dimpled cheeks answered by turning red.

"Wow. How old are you?"

"Six!" she answered cheerfully, holding up the appropriate number of fingers.

"Cristina said she's learning body parts," Radu said. "Ask her if she knows what is 'elbow.'"

Instead, Raluca's face took on a mischievous look. She held up her hands with overt drama and intoned, with as much gravity as a six-year-old could muster, "Two hands!"

Radu retreated with a grimace, unable to cope with being unmanned by a little girl. My time would come soon. I pointed to various body parts and asked, 'How do you say this?' Raluca, the adorable little voracious monster, never tired of the game and after an hour I ran out of body parts. I began floundering for things like epiglottis.

Adi was a real ham, and the highlight of the night. He was a very, very insanely happy drunk—and drunk he got! The wine and Coke emptied faster than a gas tank in a Hummer. Indeed, every time Adi refreshed his drink, he toasted Detroit. I thought this rather odd, until Bianca explained that his friend had won the U.S. Green Card lottery and settled there.

Alas, the time came when Radu wanted to leave. Laura obediently gathered their things and pretended that Radu led the way home. Whenever he staggered down the wrong path, she waited dutifully until he corrected his mistake. This appeared to be a practiced routine.

Eventually Adi's bombastic tales of conquering Detroit slowed, too. He repeatedly muttered thanks to me for my 'services' to Raluca, griping in quieter and quieter terms that for the next three weeks he'll be up to his ears in 'elbows and noses.' Cristina quietly stroked Raluca's hair as she slept on the bench in the breakfast nook. Snuggling in my arms, Bianca softly translated Adi's dimming murmurs. What followed was a very touching and heartfelt moment. Adi was not just a clown, but a genuine, caring man who wanted to provide the best life possible for his family. He wanted to move to Detroit, knowing there was a large community of Romanians there to help Cristina adjust to their new home. There he would work for the railroad—the only thing he knew—and pay for Raluca to have the best education, where she would grow up and be a doctor. He finally drifted off to sleep on the kitchen floor, head resting on the base of the stove, with dreams for his family.

3

Bianca and I retired to what was akin to a torture chamber. The bed was a fold-out couch with a mattress that delighted in shifting its limited padding to maximize the discomfort from an iron bar under our backs. I could not fathom how Adi and Cristina slept on that rack nightly—only thumbscrews could have made it worse—and was downright baffled how they could maintain a cheery attitude.

This was the first time Bianca and I were able to share a bed. Since our first kiss after the wedding, we had been trying like crazy to find alone time, to no avail. Even had her father allowed us to sleep together in their apartment—and he most certainly had not—we would have been paralyzed in fear over the noisy fold-out bed. Every time I rolled over, I worried the whole bloc woke up. It was that bad. Thus, we had been left to steal snippets of passion in afternoon corners, work ourselves into a frenzy, then have to smile when called into the next room for dinner. Our growing love made us feel as vibrant as teenagers again, and being treated as such only enhanced the feeling.

Thus I was more than merely excited when it was time for bed, whether or not it was on a torture rack. Stealing kisses like children was fun, but we were adults and inclined to go further. Yet when I saw Bianca, I started laughing.

"You no like my Thousand Lips pajamas?" Bianca asked, spinning to show off the white silk shirt and pants, covered all over with red lips.

"Let's see how many of those lips I can kiss before—"

"—before?" she interrupted, teasingly. "Hey, babaloo, thin walls. Raluca is right behind that wall. Behave."

Adi's horrendous snoring came through the wall loud and clear. Despite being in another room, it seemed like we were all in the same bed as one big, happy family.

Fortunately sleep was furthest from my mind—there were a thousand lips to attend to. Our passion had been smoldering for a week since the wedding, and now it threatened to burst into a full conflagration. Our lips were wet and wanting and our enthusiasm flared with every kiss. Yet we had to slow down. Slowing down was hell.

But I was blinded with passion for Bianca. My mind was completely and utterly on her, and I couldn't stop. I had never felt such incredible, insatiable desire before—never before been enslaved by emotion. I saw nothing but red in the blackness. Her sighs and moans, her gasping breath, all filled me with a strength and power I did not know I possessed.

Finally, in a glorious moment where I lost awareness of all but those lips, we cast aside inhibition. She shuddered and her whole body rocked. I felt it throughout my entire body—my hips, my gut, my chest, my whole being—all shaking with sensations too intense to handle.

We made so much noise, I had no idea. The squeaking was horrendous, but I couldn't hear anything past the blood pounding in my ears and the panting. The whole world was gone. Never before had I ever been so focused on anything, so unaware of my surroundings.

Afterwards, when I buried my face in her neck, slippery from sweat, reality crashed over me like an ice-cold wave. The ragged heaves of Adi puking his guts out tore through the night, flimsy walls doing nothing to lessen the ugliness of the sound. Raluca's whining for him to stop so she could sleep were somehow both adorable and heartbreaking.

Pain stabbed through my back and it seized up. Bianca tried to squirm off the iron bar under the mattress but she, too, groaned as her muscles blazed in retaliation at such abuse. Too pained to do anything further, we lay and listened to Adi's vomiting. We tried to laugh, but were too bruised from our sport on the gridiron. Yet despite all this, if I ever had a chance to relive that moment, even once in my life, I would be the luckiest man ever.

The next morning the only thing that hurt worse than my back was my empathy for poor, poor Cristina. For her birthday, all she wanted in the world was a good night's sleep, to rise late, and have her family take care of everything for a whole, glorious day.

What did she get? A sleepless night sharing her daughter's tiny bed, on one side listening to her husband vomit continuously for several hours, and on the other her cousin and new boyfriend noisily knocking boots till dawn—in her bed. Obviously unable to sleep, she had risen and spent the long, cold night blearily cleaning the dishes from the big party and making breakfast not only for her family, but her guests as well.

# CHAPTER SIX

## *I'm Turning Japanese*

### 1

ONE THING WAS for sure: Bianca and I needed a vacation in our vacation. Her family and homeland were wonderful, but we wanted hot days on some beach and hotter nights under some sheets. When Bianca suggested Egypt, my heart leapt with joy. Ever since I was a child, I had fantasized of the Great Pyramid. Bianca was proving to me time and again that dreams can come true.

"I always fantasized about a night in the best hotel," Bianca said dreamily. "Where royalty and celebrities stay. Just one night."

"I don't know," I commented. "I'm living a fantasy in some pretty crappy Romanian blocs."

"Babaloo," she chided. "Anyway, we no play royalty today. We'll book through a Hungarian agency, because they have better quality. But promise me some day you get me a room where royalty and celebrities stay!"

"Deal," I said.

Because we chose a Hungarian agency, the departures were from Budapest. Surprisingly, the fastest way to reach Budapest from Braşov was to drive halfway across Hungary. Thus we took a train to Cluj in western Romania and from there hopped onto a bus for a drive through the night. Actually, it was not a bus, nor even a smaller autobus, but an autocar. The ungainly offspring from the unholy union of bus and van, the Romanian autocar was born with eight seats in the space meant for four. The driver, I presume, did not understand the Hungarian language Magyar, based upon his suicidal disregard for traffic signs. Taking this methodology a step further, he didn't read Romanian, either. It was a terrifying midnight drive on horrible, broken highways snaking through narrow mountain passes.

Crossing the border from Romania to Hungary was the stuff of Hollywood—or cardiac arrest. A vast field of concrete separated us from Hungary, the few structures present more bunker than building. In a bleak, black night of slashing rain and frigid cold, the bus was waved to a stop by armed guards in wool overcoats and warm hats. At a glance, there was little difference between a Russian soldier and a Romanian one, and I felt like I was living in a Tom Clancy movie. These facilities were built during the communist era to keep citizens locked inside their own borders, making our phrase 'America: Love it or Leave it,' sound insulting.

The autocar's door opened and a grumpy guard barked for everyone's papers. Passports were handed forward and received with disdain. The sentinel bantered with the driver for several minutes, and the conversation grew heated. More than a few of the passengers showed signs of real concern. These people remembered all too well decades of denial and oppression by their own government. The driver reluctantly pulled the autocar up to a drab, partially lit bunker and turned off the engine. We plunged into a silence broken only by rain hammering the roof.

Time crawled by tensely, but fifteen minutes later the forlorn sentry returned, approaching alone in the rain across the concrete plain. The driver obediently rolled down his window, and they again argued in Romanian until the sentry became irate. Suddenly everyone in the autocar stared at me. Accusing murmurs slid through the dark vehicle. I had rarely in my life felt so helpless and uncomfortable. Suddenly, breaking my back on Cristina's bed didn't sound so bad.

Bianca leaned forward to explain, "They looking for a Japanese man."

"Where?"

"Here, bambo."

"What, in our bus? There's only a bunch of old Romanian women, you and me."

"I know," she whispered back. "Something is wrong."

The sentinel demanded forcefully for the side door of the autocar to be opened again. We all perked up at the chilly wind —or the automatic rifle slung across his back. The sentinel suddenly jabbed a finger at me and began a tirade of angry-sounding accusations.

Bianca answered the man's queries, but he did not seem satisfied. He pored over my passport with his flashlight at length, then disappeared again into the night. Someone hastily closed the door against the bitter wind.

"He thinks you Japanese," Bianca said with a mixture of amusement and annoyance.

"Me? Do I look Japanese to you?"

"Obviously not," she snapped. "But the idiot couldn't tell you are over six feet tall and one hundred kilos."

"I also happen to be white," I added. "Most people would say frightfully so."

"Apparently the rasclat driver told the first sentry that we had all Romanians and one foreigner, but somehow they got Japanese out of American. Where do they find these guys?"

I resisted the urge to say 'Department of Homeland Security.'

Another five minutes passed even more tensely, and I grew annoyed and nervous that my passport was being tossed around by people so inept as to think I was Japanese. True, between World War II and the revolution, it was rare indeed for a Romanian to have actually seen anyone not white, but this was ridiculous. I was about to offer to talk with them, but more visions of Cold War-era movies made me just shut up and wait. Finally, sometime well after midnight, the sentry returned our passports and motioned for us to roll on through to Hungary.

Intent on recovering lost time, the driver drove even more erratically, if that were possible. In an effort to settle our nerves after the border checkpoint and ignore the crazy driving, Bianca and I began to whisper back and forth sweet nothings. These turned into rather explicit reminisces about what we had managed to accomplish thus far, which then turned into a full-on list of proposals to maximize the freedom of a hotel room. I figured our words were safely anonymous in a bus full of aged Romanian women, but was brought up short when a lady behind us commented something trivial to her companion... in English. Bianca's face turned so red that her round cheeks looked like apples.

But beyond my desire to flirt with Bianca, and even beyond the desperate hope to merely survive the drive, I wanted nothing more than to sleep. I was beginning to suffer from severe jet lag and a wild two weeks in Romania. I had to tear my eyes off the road because otherwise the adrenaline jolted me awake faster than the hits from curbs and fenders. I twisted sharply to lay my head on Bianca's lap. I don't remember ever actually sleeping, though she claimed otherwise, because when I drifted off my hand thumped to the floor. She would retrieve it and hold it, but that woke me up. The process would repeat, over and over again, all night long.

The flight to Egypt did not offer me any much-needed sleep, either. Every thirty minutes a stewardess made cumbersome announcements in several languages about the need for passenger clearance. First came the passport stamping, then signing customs forms regarding our luggage, then still another for who knows what. It was all a blur to me in my half-sleep/half-dead state. Sheer exhaustion overtook me just as we arrived near the Red Sea.

The airport was a desolate, dusty spot in the middle of a desolate, dusty expanse. A line of busses belched black fumes while waiting for the various tour guides to parcel their charges into the appropriate vehicle. Arab men swarmed around the busses like bees on a patch of dirty yellow flowers. They eagerly offered to carry luggage for a mere one dollar US. I shooed away many, but they refused to take no for an answer during the whole short walk of about thirty yards. A mere ten feet from the bus one overly aggressive man actually tried to wrestle the suitcase from my hand to earn a fee.

The drive through the vast, empty desert was occasionally punctuated by clusters of dirty concrete buildings surrounded by heaps of garbage. In the city of Hurghada itself the buildings were larger and closer together. So, too, were the heaps of garbage. None of this mattered to me. I was abuzz with excitement, not to mention giddy from exhaustion, because as a child I had always dreamt of Egypt. Amazingly, though, I was less thrilled at being in Egypt than being in Egypt with Bianca.

The second Bianca and I entered our room at the hotel in Hurghada, we dropped our baggage and began tearing off each others' clothes. The room had two slender single beds, so we spared one arm each to hauling them together. The other was of course busy unhooking hooks and unzipping zippers. Once the beds were more or less together, we fell upon them laughing and loving and kissing and so much more. The world spun in a heady blur of passion.

Oh, for the anonymity of a hotel room! Oh, to not have to worry about squeaking beds!

But wait, that wasn't the bed squeaking.

It was Bianca.

I paused, suddenly unsure. Other than the crazy, drunken romp in her cousin's bed, I had never been intimate with a woman from another continent before. I assumed things would be more or less the same everywhere—but what did squeaking mean? My answer came when we both dropped to the floor in a crash of tangled limbs.

"OW! You bamboclat!" she blurted, slapping my arm with a wallop.

Lost in my own obsession, I had not noticed that Bianca had been desperately squirming to bridge the ever-widening gap between the two beds, which separated more and more with our bumping and grinding.

"I've been doing all kinds of bloody Nadia Comaneci gymnastics to save us! Where you been?"

Panting, I explained, "I was... I was in the zone, baby."

Fortunately, she just smirked and said, "You sure were!"

## 2

That evening we sat in the hotel lobby, waiting to meet with our tour guide to decide which excursions to take while in Egypt. We waited patiently in a couple of deep chairs, sipping hot tea and snacking on fresh dates. As our guide, Bela, worked through the room and met with clusters of people, the blurry sound of Romanian and Magyar punctuated with Egyptian names lulled me to sleep.

Finally Bela came to us. He was an impossibly skinny man with even skinnier arms in a bright yellow T-shirt. His pimpled features were distinguished only by light brown hair in a bowl cut and large eye glasses, the latter tinted brown, fading to clear at the bottom. He began speaking to Bianca in Romanian, and I tried to piece together what he said. She translated for me as he explained the mechanics of the various excursions to the Pyramids, Luxor, the Egyptian Museum in Cairo, Abu Simbel, and others. We parlayed between Romanian and English for a bit, when suddenly Bela chuckled.

"How about I speak in English?" he asked sheepishly in solid English with a hint of a British accent. He continued, "I am sorry. I am tired and have been talking much Romanian and Magyar. My mind did not switch to English."

Bianca nodded in understanding, leaving me only to imagine what that would be like.

"How many languages do you speak, then?" I asked.

"I speak Magyar, Romanian, Arabic, and Turkish fluently," Bela answered. "And English, obviously. I get by in Italian and German. Anyway, as I was saying, one of the excursions is to spend a day with the Bedouin people. You will tour the desert and oases in American Jeeps, then stay with a Bedouin family for dinner. You will learn about their way of life as nomads of the desert. But really, if I may, it is really like being in a Gypsy camp."

Bianca blanched.

"Not as bad!" Bela hastily added. "We would never allow your safety to be compromised, and we guarantee you won't be robbed. Unlike the Gypsies, the Bedouin people do not feed off others and do seek legitimate income. These tours provide that, and they would not risk it over petty theft. Of course, the United States has nothing like this, so you may find it interesting."

Bela's look made it doubtful, and Bianca's look made it clear: the Bedouin tour was out. We were not here to explore Egypt, anyway, but each other. We opted for an excursion every other day, which left us plenty of time to lie on the beach and on each other. After finalizing and paying for the various tours, we handed over our passports to Bela, who would ensure they were properly locked in the hotel safe.

Later, we sat upon our second floor balcony and watched the sea breeze thrash the palms. The air was salty and seductive, and the vibrantly red bougainvillea fluttered as if they, too, responded to our falling in love. Bianca smoked the day's last cigarette, wearing only my shirt. That was one of those things women did to sink their hooks deeper into men, and it always worked. Well, my ex-wife had never done so, but that reflection was self-explanatory.

I pondered the wonder of Bianca blowing smoke into the air. Despite my cigar indulgence, I never in a million years would have thought I would be attracted to a smoker. The filthy habit had repulsed me since childhood. Growing up in the household of an ex-smoker, that most virulent of lobbyist, I just assumed I would never fall for a smoker. Was I ever wrong!

Bianca defied all my self-established assumptions. How could I sit beside a smoker and not be turned off? It wasn't simply that I understood that in her culture smoking was common, but I was bowled over by sheer chemistry. She liked to smoke? No problem. She liked the lights off? No problem. Every touch resonated on a level deeper than I had ever known or even suspected. Our surface patterns had no relevance next to currents running so deep and so powerfully mixed.

Her touch was electric, but this was far more than lust. Like most men by age thirty, I had indulged in my share of girlfriends and one-night stands; some explosive, most not. Once married, I was happy to end all that foolishness. Then things started going sour, so we tried to spice it up. This happened to coincide with my job doing research for a pornographic website, so we had a... creative... playbook to draw from. I think we did everything that did not actually involve a midget. But our marriage's failure couldn't be fixed by sex: the passion wasn't lost because it had never been.

But the passion with Bianca extended beyond her touch. It was her eagerness for good conversation, her fervor for travel, her zeal for life! It was no coincidence that she taught me the meaning of joie de vivre. This spontaneous trip to Egypt was only part of it. While not many people would just hop on a plane and fly to a different continent, it was not unprecedented. But how many people would shape their entire lives to ensure such crazy trips were possible? Bianca was the most entrancing woman I had ever met. It was chemistry, pure and simple. Or pheromones. Witchcraft?

The night caressed us, and we began to thirst for a nightcap. Unfortunately, gathering a casual cocktail in North Africa was not so easy. Instead we sucked on some juice boxes. The moon neared its zenith and we neared our retiring for the night. Soon our excitement at being in Egypt was replaced by excitement at not having to worry about waking the neighbors.

## 3

The next morning we had a late breakfast, famished after a long morning of finishing up what we started the night before. Unfortunately, the continental-style breakfast had little enough continent and even less style. The orange juice did not come from the overflowing local groves, but from imported single-serving cardboard boxes. The butter was in little plastic single-serving tubs, as was the artificial creamer for the coffee. The bread was nutrient-empty white, and the jams were merely colored corn syrup.

"Are we in Egypt or the States?" asked Bianca. "Check the dish there."

A nearby chafing dish teased with inviting spurts of flavor-tinted steam escaping from the lid. I burned my fingers on it, and was rewarded with a load of boiled hot dogs.

Fortunately, two items were indeed local. The Egyptian yoghurt was thick and deliciously sour with a hint of salt; a worthy accompaniment to the thick pretzels. But it was the huge bowl of dates that was our salvation. The mound of glorious, fat, juicy dates delighted us in a wide variety of browns, reds, blacks, and yellows. Bianca went crazy over the red ones that were crisp and crunchy like apples.

Finally we hit the streets of Hurghada, leaving resorts large and clean and beautiful for streets, buildings, and cars that were not. Hurghada may be brimming with the promise of becoming the Red Sea destination, but it was also overflowing with garbage. Literally. Bianca and I hopped and skipped hand in hand amid waist-high piles of rubbish, but we didn't care. We were lost in each other's love, and it was obvious. We laughed and teased and hugged while skipping over pools of oil on the sidewalks and shattered bits of glass.

Between a tiny office and a rather dubious camera shop was a vendor that caught our eye. We fancied a pair of Egyptian leather slippers, and thought the hawker gesturing for us to enter his shop looked suitably appropriate. He was a young man whose extremely slender build could not be hidden by his flowing, full-length caftan. The tassel of his cap-like fez jiggled with enthusiasm for a sale, and his grin revealed the occasional empty slot beside a number of golden teeth. A thick, pointed mustache finished off his look. We stepped under the sun-faded drapery of burgundy and peeling gold that thrust out from a battered two-story building.

"Something gold for a golden lady?" the man hinted in well-mannered English, nodding to Bianca and then a rack of gold chains. I shrugged and gestured to Bianca, who readily stepped forward. She complimented him on his fine shop.

"Oh, thank you, madam," he said with a bow. "Allah saw fit to grant me many treasures. Some are just for me, such as my children. But others can be yours..."

The hawker's hand swept back grandly to take in his entire shop, which disappeared deep into the building. Masterfully he brought her attention back to the rack of chains. Bianca murmured that they were lovely, but she was more intrigued by the Egyptian leather slippers.

"Slippers?" he asked, turning to me. "Surely a lady would prefer a beautifully hand-crafted dress shoe, several of which I have to offer."

"Not me, my friend," I replied. "Talk to the lady. She's the boss."

He was too smooth to hint how odd that sounded to him. Instead he grinned widely and said, "Ah! A man of prudence."

"Indubitably," I agreed. "I must say, your English is excellent."

He straightened taller and brought a hand to his thin chest dramatically. "I have been speaking the Queen's English since the day Allah saw fit to place her upon the throne."

"Allah saw fit to do so in the 1950s," I pointed out drily.

He smiled sheepishly. "Nonetheless! You may rest assured that the worldwide praise for my goods is not exaggerated."

"Perhaps not the praise, but the price," Bianca interrupted. "Now, talk to me about these slippers."

"But surely, madam," the hawker demurred, "Allah saw fit to grant you such beauty in order to enhance it with some of my fine jewelry!"

Bianca smiled slyly and said, "Allah saw fit to grant me a family with feet."

And they began verbally thrusting and parrying. He was delighted when she countered his proposals with humor. Bartering is an art form designed to make the transaction as much a joy as the item. As an American, I only thought of owning the item. The whole thing seemed to me a waste of time, but to both of them it was highly entertaining. When in Egypt, do as the Egyptians do.

As they debated I wandered the shop. I was unsettled by a man sitting in the deep shadows in the back, beneath a shelf of hookahs. He was much older than the hawker, with a wrinkled hand pinching a smoldering cigarette to lips lost in a flowing white beard. His turban covered his forehead, resting on eyebrows that were huge, ungainly clumps of wiry grey. They knit together as he openly glared at me. I regarded him as he regarded me, one curious and the other apparently angry. It was an unpleasant moment, and I was glad to return to Bianca as she finalized the sale of four pairs of slippers.

"We are agreed, then," the hawker said as he bowed over a pair of slippers. "Four pair, madam, similar to these."

"Exactly like these ones," Bianca said, pointing to the slippers in his hand. "No switching for 'similar' colors or 'approximate' size. We aren't leaving Hurghada tomorrow, man, and I will be back if you switch anything."

"Oh, madam," he replied, aghast. "I would never do such a scandalous thing to one who has conducted herself so magnificently in the fine art of the sale."

"I'm sure," she smirked with a twinkle in her eye.

He pushed one slipper into the other and handed them over with another bow. He did not offer a bag, but snugly pushed all the slippers into each other. Just before we stepped back into the blazing sun, I snuck one last look at the old man in the back of the shop. From this distance I could not see his eyes from beneath the tangle of his monstrous brow, but I could feel them boring into me.

We continued our tour, walking hand in hand through Hurghada's sights, sounds, smells, and waste. Eventually we passed a long, empty lot between the huddled, sand-whipped buildings. The bleached dirt was barely visible beneath masses of garbage piled rank after rank like infantry.

Close to the street were two boys, both naked but for a pair of tattered trousers, torn off below the knee, which coincided with the height of the garbage they stood in. Their faces were still smooth and pretty with youth, but their eyes spoke of hardship more so than their gaunt frames. They stood beside a contraption cobbled together from old, rusty pieces of metal bent into a semblance of a grill. Smoke billowed up from it, somehow even fouler than the odor of the sun baking the garbage.

"Eat?" one called out to us as we passed. "Eat? Cheap eat!"

Both boys looked at us with hope twinkling in their eyes. On the greasy grill lay two small, but plump, fish. Sand was caked liberally over the charred scales. The uneven flapping of the meager flame made the fish half raw and half burnt. Flies buzzed through the black smoke, unimpressed by the pitiful flame. They crawled over the raw flesh and delicately avoided the blackened scales.

"Cheap eat?" the boy repeated. I didn't know what to say, and Bianca squeezed my hand until it hurt. Scattered around the homemade grill were shards of broken glass. In fact, a majority of the garbage was glass bottles. The boys were barefoot, yet miraculously unhurt from walking on the broken bits. Amazingly, or perhaps merely because of their youth, they appeared vibrantly healthy, though the shorter boy had a fresh scrape across an elbow. Bloody, raw flesh was caked with sand, distressingly similar to the uncooked fish they offered us for lunch.

"No, thank you," I said to them. I was tempted to give them all four pair of the slippers we carried, but knew the touristic items were hardly suitable for daily use. There was nothing we could do for the boys, in fact, for they were merely two among millions of desperately poor in Egypt. Had we offered them money, we would have been mobbed by others, so we hurried off. I was deeply disturbed by my first close encounter with the grinding poverty of the Third World.

We headed back towards the hotel when Bianca began swearing. "I need to use the damn restroom," she said. "And I don't want to touch anything anymore in this bloodclot place!"

I replied, "I hate to say it, but see over there? There's a place we could potentially have lunch. Potentially, mind you. But it will likely have a clean restroom, at least."

She followed to where I pointed, then swore some more. "McDonald's? You rasclat! All right all right, they probably have a clean toilet."

So for our first lunch in Egypt we dined on a McArab burger. I loathe fast food, but was intensely curious to see how similar a burger would be to those back home. I discovered that there was no difference whatsoever between a Big Mac in Egypt or in Iowa, and was not inclined to think this was a good thing.

"This is amazing," I said to Bianca. "The pickle tastes identical to the bun. How is that even possible? Isn't it supposed to be, you know, pickled?"

Bianca just threw a French fry at me.

The restaurant was very small and filled with clusters of children hovering around an order of French fries. An apparent businessman in a corner quietly smoked and nibbled his burger while reading a local newspaper. When he put it down and noticed me, his eyes bored into me with as much resentment as those of the old man in the shop. I looked away quickly. Only then did I realize that after nearly four hours of wandering the streets of Hurghada, I had not yet seen one woman.

As we munched our astoundingly tasteless burgers, we explored our Egyptian currency. On the tray, we spread out multicolored bills of various denominations and tried to identify the men depicted upon them. The children laughed at our obvious wonder, and one brave little soul stepped up to Bianca and said in broken English, "I teach people. One dollar."

Bianca smiled and replied, "I pay you with kiss."

She blew him a kiss which he pretended to dodge, and his friends nearly fell over themselves with laughter. When we departed holding hands, they howled anew. We finally swung through our resort and, before returning to the room, strolled past the restaurant. A large tray of ice displayed five huge fish, mercifully rinsed and highly presentable. There were three big, round pink ones and two long yellow fish, all with eyes glassy and crisp to reveal they were caught that morning. We selected two and watched the maitre d' take them away to prepare for our dinner that night.

Not surprisingly, getting dressed and ready for dinner was faster for me than for Bianca. While she did her secret woman things in the bathroom, I glanced at our newly purchased slippers. They were an amalgamation of leathers tanned in different shades of reds and blues, sewn together to neatly conform to the foot. When I pulled them free from each other I barked a laugh. Though the hawker had not switched different colors or sizes, he had given us all left-footed slippers!

I turned on the TV, wondering what kind of shows they aired in Egypt. To be honest, I didn't even know what they aired in the States anymore because I was too busy to watch television. I secretly hoped that through some miracle they would be showing an old episode of *The X-Files*. Did Egypt have soap operas, or some sort of Arabic *Cosby Show*?

Surprisingly, the very first channel blasted English at me. One's native language jumps out when immersed in a foreign culture. A news station was replaying an American speech and, despite Arabic voices talking above and Arabic text scrolling below, I clearly recognized President George W. Bush. His message was also clear: This is a War on Terror. America is right, everyone else in the world is wrong. Oh, and all Muslims are terrorists.

I sat bolt upright and clicked through the stations as my stomach began to knot. It was on every channel. I presumed this was because all the television stations were controlled by Mubarak's regime, but that was far from reassuring. I struggled to find evidence the speech had been tampered with or something, anything, to deny the overtly antagonistic rhetoric I was hearing. Was this why everyone had stared at me so openly today? Suddenly I wished we had stayed somewhere safe, like in Romania. Never thought I'd ever say that!

I swallowed my predicament uncomfortably, then nearly choked when my eyes fell on the table. Spread out and ready for later was the six foot beach towel Bianca had packed for me: a giant American flag.

# 4

Bianca finally exited the bathroom, made up and dressed for dinner. Without a word she took my hand, rather hard, and tugged me out the door. The walk to the restaurant was beautiful, with palm trees again thrashing and the bougainvillea fluttering. It was a warm night, bordering on hot, and the air again smelled salty. Hand in hand we walked in silence. I was so disturbed by W's self-indulgent speech that I didn't notice that Bianca, too, was silent. We passed through the hotel lobby and a voice called out in crisp British English.

"Excuse me, sir? Sir, the tall gentleman with the lovely lady?"

Perhaps half a dozen Arabic businessmen were in the lobby: thickset, graying men wearing silvery suits topped with a fez. All looked distinguished, and all looked at me. I met some gazes and nodded politely, wishing I had actually researched before spontaneously coming here. Was looking a stranger in the eye provocative in this culture, as it was in some others? Now, more than ever, I felt like the ignorant, arrogant American.

But it was not a businessman who called me. The front desk manager, in a suit of dark brown, was waving me over. I reassured myself that he had nothing to say about the inflammatory speech against his religion: surely this was just a routine matter over a credit card or something similar. Yet as I approached, he appeared even more anxious than I.

"Yes, thank you, sir," he said politely. "Come here, please? Thank you."

Well, I thought, here goes.

The manager was a slender, middle-aged man, fairly handsome with chocolate brown skin and a snow white mustache. His teeth were neatly aligned, though stained yellow. When I approached, he lowered his voice very low.

"You, sir, are the American whose passport I locked up last night?"

I hesitated a moment, but saw no reason to make an obvious lie. "Yes."

"Sir, I wonder, have you perhaps... ah... perhaps viewed the news today?"

"If you are referring to the idiotic speech by President Bush, then yes, I have."

His eyes widened, and he was momentarily at a loss for words. I sensed he was surprised to hear someone publicly disagreeing with his own government. In America, that had always been a favorite pastime.

"Yes, sir, well... is this your first visit to Egypt? Yes? Well, sir, I don't wish to alarm you, but I would like to personally offer a word of friendly advice. While it is my role to ensure your stay in Hurghada is as enjoyable as possible, I offer this not as a representative of the hotel, but as a man. Perhaps this week you would care to be, ah..."

He trailed off, unsure and obviously trying very hard to be as inoffensive as possible. His body language spoke volumes. "Perhaps this week you would care to be c-c..."

"Canadian?" I offered.

He deflated in relief, but tried to hide it. "I was to say 'careful', but I think, sir, that we understand each other. Please understand, sir, that I mean no disrespect in any way! Your safety and enjoyment is my business, but a little extra care may be prudent. If asked, which is unlikely, you may find many more amenable to your being Canadian."

"I quite agree. Thank you for your kind thought. But tell me, why is it that everyone likes Canadians so much?"

He grinned and his mustache quivered. "Why, because they aren't Americans!"

Before dinner, Bianca and I had a drink. Though Egypt was a Muslim nation that frowned upon alcohol, it was also a tourism-dependent nation. Thus drinks were available at hotels and resorts for foreigners. More surprising was that they produced their own wine. A bottle of Egyptian Pinot Grigio chilled on a stand beside our table.

We sat on a third-story balcony overlooking the long path to the beach. The wings of the hotel framed the pleasantly palmed and flowered walkway, which extended so far and so straight into the distance that I was reminded of a railroad track disappearing to the horizon. Our table was comfortable: under the stars, lit by the moon, and high enough for the sea breezes to gently cast off the heat of the night. The conversation was not so comfortable, however. In fact, there was no conversation at all. Only the ice in the bucket spoke with a crackle.

I stared at Bianca, who stared at the wine. Not surprisingly, the Pinot Grigio was awful, but I doubted such a trifle would have her so morose. I resisted the urge to dump a Coke in it. Dwelling on my own awkward position after the Bush speech, I was slow to notice that Bianca had actually stopped talking earlier. What had I done to make her angry? After my fairly recent divorce, it was a wonder that I got into trouble so fast!

For the third time I prodded, "Bianca, what's wrong?"

"I'm grumpy and crunchy, that's what's wrong."

"Grumpy and cranky."

"Whatever."

She let it drop at that, and only after I tired of staring neutrally at the moon for several minutes did I try again. "Talk to me, woman. This is, like, a vacation and stuff. Should be fun."

"I don't want to talk about it."

"That much is obvious."

"You wouldn't understand, anyway."

"Shall I get Bela to translate?"

The merest quirk of her lips indicated a possible breakthrough.

"My period just started," she finally said.

"I see," I answered carefully, hiding my disappointment. I sure as hell didn't show that I was secretly pleased that missing sex with me was so catastrophic. Sadly, Bianca was probably the first to feel that way.

"No, you wouldn't understand," she continued. "This is my second period this month. That happens sometimes when you sign off ships."

Delicately I offered, "No doubt because your internal clock gets in tune with all the women you are living with on ships. You all get into a similar rhythm. But now you are readjusting your cycle to home."

She blinked in surprise. "How you know that?"

"I was married," I explained simply.

"So? In Romania the men know nothing of it and ask nothing of it. They no want to know."

"Oh, I'm sure they know when their woman is suffering from PMS."

"America really is different than Europe," Bianca marveled. "But it doesn't change anything. Why this week? We only came here for... well, Jesus Gras!"

"So, I guess the moonlight swim after dinner is out of the question?"

"Yes," she snapped. "And if you make any comment about it already being the Red Sea, I'm sending you back to the room alone right now!"

# CHAPTER SEVEN
## *Arabian Nights*

### 1

THE NEXT MORNING was a long, tired blur of sand and sun. We were actually getting tired of being excited, if that were possible, but that day we were to see a whole host of new wonders.

The Valley of Kings! The Valley of Queens! The Temple of Karnak at Luxor! The Nile River!

The list alone was exhausting, but the drive was worse. Bela bussed us 200 kilometers southwest from Hurghada, intent on a spot 500 kilometers due south from Cairo. The heat outside, in the most lifeless desert on earth, was a brutal 115 degrees Fahrenheit.

Eventually the dunes dropped away to reveal a vast valley. Below us stretched a patchy series of green and not-so-green cropland speckled by rows of dense palms. Down the center of the valley and barring our path was the magnificent Nile River, with life-giving waters blue and oddly placid. Though the Amazon was bigger and longer, the Nile was perhaps the more impressive for flowing thousands of miles through the most arid lands on earth without a single tributary or drop of rain to help it along.

Beyond the mighty Nile's width, beyond its fertile banks and gently rising valley, rose a horrendously ugly jumble of impenetrable mountains. I had thought the dunes of the Sahara were barren, but these mountains were maddeningly monotonous. The same shade of sandstone tan ran from top to bottom, left to right, for untold hundreds of miles. The perfection of color was unspoiled by even a single sliver of darker brown or smudge of darker tan. This was the western side of the Nile: this was reserved for the dead.

The bus chugged slowly across the river and finally rolled onto a dirty road that snaked up into the sun-bleached foothills of the mountains. By the roadside two towering figures observed our progress; the ancient stone broken, marred, yet magnificent. The sentinels sat upon lumpy thrones of stone with arms stiffly resting upon their knees. Both men were faceless but wore the distinctive headdress of Egyptian royalty.

I gasped in recognition and nearly slammed my head into the window for a better look. "Those are the Colossi of Memnon!"

"The what of who?" Bianca asked tiredly, rubbing her purple-shrouded eyes and blinking against the vibrant sunshine.

I hastily explained how in college I had learned all about these two enormous statues of Amenhotep III. Both were sixty feet high, somehow erected 3,400 years ago. The majesty of something so big, yet constructed at the very dawn of human society, was humbling. They exuded sheer power.

"You know, there is an odd story about these that illustrate just how old they are. An earthquake sometime in early BC broke one of them in half. Afterwards the ruined base was said to 'sing' at sunrise. No one could figure out where the sound came from, and all the leading Greek wise men came to investigate, including Strabo himself. The singing was supposed to bring good luck, so emperors came to hear it. When the Romans finally fixed the statue in like 200 A.D., it never sang again."

Bianca just stared at me, waiting patiently for me to finish.

"I never thought I would ever see them in person," I explained lamely. "It's one thing to go see the Pyramids, which are so commonplace an image that they actually lose their magic. But this is the real deal, not some postcard on a refrigerator. This is a remnant from another era, another age, like a secret for the learned, you know? I spent years poring over books with their descriptions and pictures, but never thought they would be so powerful!"

Bianca graciously tried to appear interested at my enthusiasm, but could really have cared less. That is, until Bela rose and repeated everything I had just said. Suddenly it was all new and fascinating when he said it. Bianca excitedly repeated his words back to me, and I just stared at her. Finally I complained, "Jeez, what am I, chopped liver?"

"Yes, dear, you really are very smart," she said with a patronizing pat on my arm. Stifling a yawn she added, "Bela, however, is an authority and you are… you."

I had been upstaged by a man in a bowl cut. Not my finest hour.

The next stop was far, far more impressive. The bus drove right up to an enormous cliff of sun-blasted sandstone that towered vertically for almost a thousand feet. Nuzzling the base of the cliff was a dazzlingly intact temple composed of three tiers of columns collectively soaring about ten stories high. It was huge in scope, in preservation, and history, for this was the Mortuary Temple of Queen Hatshepsut.

When the bus finally came to a stop in a parking lot large enough to make the Superdome jealous, Bela rose and addressed everyone in Magyar, then repeated it all in Romanian. Though the bus's engine had ceased its rumble, the heavy droning of the overworked air conditioner carried on. I could barely hear Bela, nor understand him if I could, so instead watched his skinny arms gesticulate grandly. Those knobby elbows were oddly fascinating. His arms were so thin that I could see no meat at all, nor even thin cords of muscle: just bones beneath a pale drapery of skin. This man was in desperate need of a donut.

After his long, flourishing oratory, Bianca whispered a translation to me in English. "This is the Temple of Queen Hatshepsut. It is considered one of the incomparable monuments of Egyptian history."

"I knew that," I snapped rather petulantly. I was still a bit sulky after she squashed my Colossi of Memnon joy.

"Then I don't need to bother translating anything for you, bamboclat!"

True to her word, as we trudged the scalding hot walk up the entrance ramp, Bela's long descriptions were not translated for me. This was a boon, actually, because it provided me with a less distracted appreciation of the architecture. The first level was a wide colonnade of clean, smart lines. This was the first architectural example of perfect symmetry, predating Parthenon in Athens by a thousand years. The two imposing entrance ramps totaling 450 feet split the vast colonnade in the center, and eventually brought us up on top of it. Before us towered another, even more impressive double row of columns garnished with ten-foot statues of pharaohs and deities with heads of eagles, rams, and lions.

We had half an hour to wander the complex before meeting back up at the ramp. People split off to explore on their own, though a large chunk continued to follow Bela as he narrated the history and import of Hatshepsut's reign and her amazing temple. Bianca was so enraptured by his bowl cut that she nearly forgot to tell me the return time. I let her go and indulged in my own explorations.

In the temple's vast sun court, I mused over broken pillars and shattered colossi. The heat was brutal, but I refused to give up the piles of labeled bricks and stone fragments. I had never seen in-progress archeology before. Alas, after twenty minutes I retreated to the shaded colonnades as well, then moved to the very back of the temple. Here the sanctuary walls rose up some thirty feet, covered entirely by hieroglyphs of birds, eyes, fish, and wavy lines. I got as close as I could without touching them, marveling at the delicate carvings and delightfully noting hints of pigment from millennia ago.

I thought I was completely alone, but soon noticed a nearby niche in the wall was not occupied by a statue, but a man. He was presumably a guard set to prevent anyone from messing with the priceless heritage of his country. His heavy uniform must have been stiflingly hot, but he did not appear to notice the heat at all. How these guys functioned in the summer was beyond me, for it routinely topped 125 degrees. He stared at me long and hard, affectionately rubbing his military assault rifle. I nodded and tried to pass, but he suddenly held out his rifle to block my path. He didn't point it at me, exactly, but the intent was obvious.

"American," he said with a gleam in his eye. His posture was tense, ready.

I pretended not to hear him, but could not take my eyes off his well-oiled and lovingly maintained assault rifle. I had never before been so close to a weapon of that magnitude, and he handled it with the same ease as a teenager did her cell phone.

He repeated the word more strongly and with a peculiar emphasis that I did not understand, but definitely did not like.

"American."

Actually, I was a little surprised he didn't think I was European. I was not dressed in jeans and a T-shirt, nor did I wear tennis shoes. I was wearing Italian clothing that was a gift from Bianca, and I had said nothing in English. Still, I could not deny that I was significantly larger than everyone else in the entire temple complex. Usually I was mistaken for a German, except that I smiled a lot.

"Canadian," I answered with a forced grin. I wanted it to appear natural, so quickly added with faux pride, "Vancouver Island!"

Instantly the man's posture eased. He gave me a quick nod and then ignored me in favor of scrutinizing the sun court. I strode away, taking pains to make it look casual. No doubt he enjoyed the idea of taunting an American, for his demeanor had been unmistakably hostile. I knew in my gut that it hadn't been my over-active imagination. More disturbed than I cared to admit, I was only too happy to meet up with Bianca and the others. That is, until she told me what Bela had just said.

Pulling me close, Bianca whispered fiercely, "Did you know that just five years ago Islamic terrorists killed sixty tourists right here? They were mostly Swiss, but they also killed a five-year-old British kid and four Japanese couples on their honeymoons. I guess they wanted to destabilize the government by taking away tourism, their biggest source of income."

I gulped, trying to swallow the news. Then I got angry.

"What kind of an asshole would tell us that?"

"It wasn't Bela's fault," Bianca answered. "Some Hungarian hag opened her bloody trap... in Romanian, I might add... just to scare the hell out of everyone. Bela had to give the real facts before she made it bigger than September 11th."

"You're serious," I mumbled as the severity of the situation sunk in. If that could happen in the relative calm before Al Qaida attacked the U.S., what would happen now that America had invaded Afghanistan and all but declared holy war on Islam?

"Six terrorists were disguised as security guards," Bianca continued. "They followed the tourists in and stood in front of the entrance to stop anyone from getting out. With everyone trapped in the temple, they had mucho time. They used automatic rifles, and spent forty-five minutes systematically killing."

# 2

It was difficult to imagine anything topping that, but our next stop had the moxie to do so: the Valley of the Kings. It was not a valley, in fact, but a narrow box canyon created by the cliffs of craggy sandstone. We worked our way deeper into it, and the towering walls were so high they seemed to curve over us, ready to fall in. A strange sensation of claustrophobia filled the hot air, despite the gargantuan proportions of stone.

Unlike Queen Hatshepsut's in-your-face temple, the burial chambers of the Pharaohs were intentionally hidden. Though confined to this tight canyon, it took decades of professional digging to find them all, whether modern archeologist or long-dead thief. The entrances were mundane to the eye, but the mind was dazzled by the magnitude of their contents. Even without its treasures, walking into the tomb of King Tutankhamen is awe inspiring. This was not Egyptian heritage, but human heritage.

My enthusiasm for exploring the tombs was immediately doused by the reality of it. I entered three separate tombs, and each depressed me more than the last. What the dry desert air had perfectly preserved for three thousand years was being destroyed by man in a pitiful few decades. The nonstop flashes from cameras were noticeably dulling the delicate pigments of the paintings. Far more destructive were the bodies of the tourists themselves: their breath and body heat created a sauna inside the deep stone tombs. The walls literally dripped with moisture. Before my very eyes rivulets of water washed away precious color and eroded the fragile, millennia-old words of man. Unlike prehistoric cave paintings open to debate, these were words directly translatable. These were the articulated hopes and dreams of men that predated the Bible, soon to be lost forever.

In the afternoon we crossed the Nile River by boat. The battered vessels were maintained as poorly as the pharaoh's tombs: they were dusty and dented, beaten and broken, and faded by the destroying sun. The Nile was easily a mile wide at this point, with waters blue enough to entice a dip. Swimming was not a good idea, however, for pollution had rendered these waters disagreeable. While no doubt millions of Egyptians survived from the Nile's bounty, the famous Nile crocodiles here had been unable to do so.

Still, it was a pleasant crossing, barring the horrendous noise of the motors and the thick plumes of putrid exhaust they coughed up. For in crossing the Nile by boat the wonders of the ancient Egyptians were previewed as they were meant to be. Cleopatra herself viewed the very same thing as I: titanic columns of stone rising above the palms hugging the river's edge. Well, sort of. The Nile had moved a bit in the last three millennia.

So over-the-top were these monuments to an entire civilization, rising from the dirt and smog to cast awe into the minds of men: I feared it was a mirage. But oh, no. Here was Luxor and its magnificently unique Temple of Karnak. Here was arguably the largest temple complex ever built by man, utterly dwarfing the Vatican—and here was where Bianca and I were in mortal danger.

But first: the Arab in the toilet.

After crossing the Nile was a quick lunch, designed to be fast because time was short and the sights vast. Passing on the baloney sandwiches, Bianca and I munched on oranges and fresh dates.

Afterwards I went to the restroom, which was more of an experience than I usually care for in a toilet. The bathroom appeared tolerably clean, but was poorly enough lit that I wasn't sure. Inside were two decrepit porcelain sinks streaked with age and two urinals streaked with I-don't-wanna-know. The doorless stall did not contain western-style toilets, but rather a hole in the floor. Molded into the concrete were two impressions shaped as feet. I presumed this was to assist in squatting while wearing Arab-style clothing. Though I am a man of diverse interests, the defecation habits of the world's cultures do not rank among them.

I was immediately greeted by a tall, skinny Arab man. His face was very lined and very dark, and his smile revealed a complete lack of teeth. He was far too enthusiastic, rushing at me while holding forth a small length of rolled toilet paper. I shook him off and headed towards the urinal. He followed one step behind, babbling in Arabic what appeared to be offers of service. I said 'no' firmly and prepared to do my business.

But he wouldn't leave me alone. He stepped right up behind me and continued to jabber. He shoved the toilet paper over my shoulder and into my face.

"No!" I called forcefully to him, but he ignored me. "I don't want anything. Go away!"

He stood there, waiting for me to do my thing. I stood there, waiting to do my thing. I couldn't. He was literally breathing down my neck, and I was too uncomfortable to urinate. His breath reeked.

"Go away!" I demanded, but he just smiled toothlessly and nodded. Finally I awkwardly fished from my open pants a dollar bill and handed it to him. He nodded and bowed back out of sight.

The Temple of Karnak was just a short walk up a flagstone path from the ancient quay at the Nile. But what a walk! Lining the scorched path were imposing ram-headed sphinxes, numbering over a dozen on each side. They sat regally atop pedestals two yards tall, and their lion-like bodies stretched an impressive ten feet. Between their front paws they protected yard-high statues of kings from the earliest great civilization of mankind. It was almost unnerving to walk down that avenue beneath the primordial gaze of thirty gods.

As imposing as the Avenue of the Sphinxes was, it was nothing compared to the front wall of the temple. This was called the First Pylon, and it was a whopper. The wall was so thick as to appear squat, were it not so staggeringly tall. To the left of the entrance the ancient hand-hewn sandstone rose fifty feet high, and the other side soared to seventy. This defense dominated the view from the Nile, and stepping through its entrance into the Temple was immensely humbling.

Once through the First Pylon, we stood in a giant courtyard lined with columns thick and powerful enough to shrug off thousands of years. Some were carved with deep, glorious hieroglyphics, the delicately cut details leaping out because the slanting sunlight left their recesses dark. Everywhere were statues of kings with arms folded, holding the crook and flail of the pharaohs. All were huge, and many towered thirty feet tall. Pointy tips of obelisks pierced the sky even higher. Everything was simply immense.

Hundreds and hundreds of tourists from all over the planet roamed the hot courtyard. Despite this being a temple, their voices were far from subdued or even respectful. They shouted at each other and children ran through the crowds shrieking and playing.

Bela stood out from the mess of humanity by virtue of his brilliant yellow T-shirt. The reflection from his shirt was so bright in the harsh sunlight that I couldn't look directly at him, for want of sunglasses. Had Bela's brown-tinted glasses not been prescription, I think I would have bullied them from him. After all, I still had to impress Bianca and prove that I was cooler than him. Bela pulled our tour group into the corner behind the unfinished side of the First Pylon. The remains of a mud-brick building ramp on the backside revealed that, in antiquity, the entire wall had been intent on reaching seventy feet.

As Bela delivered his lengthy Magyar/Romanian instructions, I stared at yet another row of ram-headed sphinxes. These were parked beside each other like motorcycles outside a roadhouse in Nevada. All were six feet high and descended from fully intact features to broken faces to shattered bodies and finally to mere pedestals. Though cordoned off, a child jumped the line and sat on the back of a 3,000-year-old sphinx as if it were a 25¢ pony ride outside of K-Mart. Instantly an Arab security guard ran towards him, screaming in outrage. Suddenly terrified, the brat quickly fled. I found his parent's absence gallingly inappropriate, but his wailing, crying flight most satisfying.

The real joy of Karnak, however, was hidden beyond the Second Pylon, which was at the far end of the huge courtyard. This second wall rose sturdily fifty feet into the heat, but beyond it towered the world-famous Hypostyle Hall. Erected by the hand of bygone men, it symbolized the primeval papyrus swamp with a total of 134 columns. The forest of stone trunks was ramrod straight like redwoods, and nearly as thick. We wandered through the maze of dizzying columns, staring up to the lofty heights lovingly carved with hieroglyphics. In the center rose twelve even taller, central monsters rising nearly seventy feet. These dwarfed the other hundred-odd columns that were a mere five stories tall. This awe-inspiring Hall was begun by Amenhotep III, but completed by his famous builder son, Ramses II. Yes, that was the Ramses of Biblical fame.

After we exited the Hypostyle Hall, I split off from Bianca and the main group. Again, the translations were too cumbersome, and besides, I knew exactly what I was looking at. I had studied these ruins for years. As an art historian, I had scrutinized modern photographs as well as both Napoleonic and Victorian-era etchings of them. As an archeology enthusiast I wanted to see the little things, like the piles of tagged stones that had yet to find their rightful place in the jumble of toppled temples.

Fortunately I had a fine direction sense, because the Temple of Karnak was worked on for literally thousands of years and had two main axes at right angles to each other. I quickly left the other tourists and found myself alone with the echoes of eternity. The sun eased lower across the Nile and the shadows grew bolder, eagerly crawling over broken walls and slashing the faces of kings long dead. I wandered to the rear of the Temple and suddenly found myself staring at a wide lake. The vast Sacred Lake was man-made and entirely lined in stone, with steps cut down to its placid surface. A rare cluster of palm trees, the only green anywhere to be seen, reflected in the deadly still surface. I enjoyed solitude with the awesomeness until I could soak up no more.

After a while I returned to the Hypostyle Hall to meet up with Bianca. The sun was now nuzzling the ugly sandstone cliffs to the west. Darkness and silence once again enveloped the great Temple of Karnak as the gawking and squawking tourists departed. In our last few minutes we wanted a picture of us together, but had difficulty finding anyone remaining to help us do so. From out of nowhere an Arab man appeared and offered in sharp, broken English to take our picture for a dollar.

"Not here!" he chirped. "I know better place. Beautiful!"

We followed him through a portal and into a broad courtyard filled with huge, tumbled blocks of stone. Most debris was the size of a bathtub, but many were massive, broken behemoths lying atop each other like a pile of busses. The scenery was impressive, but not at all what we were looking for.

"No, not here," he chirped again. His eyes twinkled with enthusiasm. "Farther. Is beautiful!"

We looked at each other unsure, because the sounds of the tourists had entirely faded by now, and the darkness was growing. Concerned, Bianca asked me quietly, "Do you know where we are?"

"I do. We're not too far, it just feels like it."

Shrugging, we followed him through another portal and into a smaller courtyard, which was still awesome in size and style. In fact, this was one of the most impressive I had yet seen.

The flooring flagstones were swept free from debris and even sand, and all four walls of the courtyard were lined with twenty-foot statues of kings standing before columns even taller. Each king had arms crossed over his chest and held the crook and flail, though many had headdresses, faces, and even shoulders missing. Darkness filled the three-foot gaps between the huge sentinels.

"Wow," I breathed, and Bianca squeezed my hand excitedly. Perhaps not excitedly, I began to realize. We were utterly alone with the stranger and it was getting dark. We could no longer hear anyone else at all, not even faintly.

"No, not here," pressed the Arab. He gestured towards the far end of the deep, dark courtyard to a doorway black as pitch.

"Farther. Is beautiful! More sun there."

I regarded the man more closely. Like every other Egyptian I had met, he was very thin and had dark features with plenty of wrinkles and grey. But his teeth were pearly white and perfect, which somehow smacked of something wrong. Yet he did not appear armed or particularly dangerous. His gestures were overemphasized, but that was common enough when language was a barrier. Still, he seemed a bit too eager to please and was trying way too hard to get us further from the group.

"I think this is a good place," I said to him. Beside me Bianca nodded vigorously.

"No, farther is beautiful," he said, waving his arms in emphasis. "Very beautiful. Not here."

He smiled his predatory grin again, and the uncomfortable feeling that had been growing at his insistence blossomed. There was absolutely no question what was going on. He was leading us into an ambush.

"Take our picture here," I said firmly. "We're not going any farther."

The man met my gaze and I watched the twinkle leave his eyes. The sense of danger flared. I was keenly aware of the countless dark places for thugs to spring from.

"Forget it," I said, then turned to Bianca. "Ready to go?"

"Yes!" she answered.

"No, no," the Arab assured us half-heartedly. "Here is good. One dollar, I take picture here."

We hurriedly posed and he snapped our picture with obvious disappointment. He was so offhand with taking the photo that I was sure he only caught our feet, but we didn't care. He all but hurled the camera back to me after I gave him his dollar. We rushed back to the main group tailing Bela, and left the Temple of Karnak to the ages and thieves.

# 3

Bianca and I took the next day off from touring and leisurely played on the beach—using towels from the hotel rather than the ones we brought, of course. The only thing better than the sun and the surf was the conversation, where I was continually astounded at Bianca's range of knowledge. She would seamlessly transition from classical art and literature to molecular theory. After dinner we walked to an open-air amphitheater by the sea. The air was humid and hot and the moon sweat above. We came to indulge in an aspect of Middle Eastern culture commonly overlooked: the whirling Dervishes. The setting was entrancing, but the real trance was on stage.

As the host described it, Dervishes are Sufi Muslims who use music and dance to reach a state of perfection, or *kemal*. They abandon their egos and personal desires by listening to music, focusing on God, and moving in a symbolic imitation of the planets orbiting the sun. As I would describe it: they spin. A lot.

The music began, and stepping out on stage was a lone man wearing a sleeveless white frock and a felt fez. He was middle aged with a slim build and slimmer mustache. His features were set in deep concentration, in tune with the steady thumping of a kudum drum. He closed his eyes and began to spin. His feet stamped in the very same spot as he whirled again and again and again. As he spun faster and faster, the music built upon itself with traditional Turkish instruments, adding bow fiddles and long-necked lutes.

His frock flew up like a skirt, delineating a circle of clean white in geometric perfection. The droning of the music swelled and he spun ever faster and ever longer. His stamping feet were a blur, and as the music evolved, so, too, did his dance. He waved his arms and suddenly the circle of skirt became a dazzling parabola, radiant in the moonlight. For a whopping twenty solid, mesmerizing minutes he spun ever faster, never once missing a step. It was the single most remarkable human performance I had ever witnessed.

Afterwards we went for a moonlight walk, eventually stopping at a discotheque. The building resembled a small version of the Colosseum in Rome, being a two-story oval structure lined with arches. Pennants snapped above, driven by warm coastal air. Inside, what would have been a sandy stage for bloodsport was instead a dance floor. We were the only two guests in the entire club, so when we crossed the wide, empty floor I tried to spin like the Sufi. I only got about three rotations before I fell into an ignominious heap on the floor.

"You babaloo!" Bianca laughed, tugging on my arm to pull me up.

Above us stretched the open sky: a black tapestry of pulsing stars bisected by the splash of the Milky Way. The DJ switched the music from local tastes to an electro beat. The tempo was upbeat, yet somewhat trancelike, and we began to slow dance. We had the whole dance floor to ourselves, but were rooted right there in the middle, lit silver by moonlight.

The song's lyrics flowed over us, beginning with the longing, yet fortifying dreams of finding each other, then swelling with optimism when they realized that their love alone will make everything all right. With the words 'I'll fly with you,' the music soared into ecstasy. It was insanely romantic, as if the disco—the whole world!—was built just for us, and us alone, open roof designed for us to fly into the night together.

I was completely lost in Bianca, and didn't care that the tempo was too fast for a slow dance. After a glorious eternity, the song faded into the stars. Bianca pulled back, lightly panting, and glanced around as if stalling. She placed her hands on my chest, feeling my heart hammer. Like her heightened breath, my body, too, was not reacting to the speed of our dance.

"*L'amour toujour*," Bianca finally said. "That's the name of that song. Do you know what it means?"

"No," I said.

"It means 'forever in love,'" she explained, somewhat dreamily.

"Strange song to play in a gladiatorial arena," I remarked. "But then, if we had been surrounded by balconies of fans screaming for blood, I don't think I would have noticed."

She pushed back from my chest, but kept a hand out to steady herself. Finally she smirked and said, "We better get that Egyptian music back, or I'm gonna have a heart attack!"

# CHAPTER EIGHT
## *Catfish and Conquest*

## 1

I DON'T KNOW what time we went to sleep that night, but I know damn good and well what time we woke up: 4:30 a.m., for a 5 a.m. departure for Cairo. Of course I was excited to see the Pyramids and the Sphinx, but what really impacted me was witnessing the living culture of the Middle East on that long drive.

Needless to say, it was hot. Without a cloud in the sky, the sun blasted down on the shifting sands of the Sahara, quickly reaching the usual 115 degrees of October. For the trip Bela had hired a local guide who was an expert on all things Egypt. He was a heavyset Egyptian with a flowing white beard and red cheeks. This Arabic Santa Claus excitedly shared with us the magnitude of the desert through which we drove. This corner of the Sahara had one of the only spots on earth where not a single creature lived, not one burrowing insect or even a microbe in the sands. Considering the dubious quality of the bus in which we crossed this most deadly of deserts, I thought perhaps he could have waited for that part until after we safely returned.

But the shiftless sands teased with snippets, and sometimes even pockets, of humanity. After hours of empty dunes, we suddenly came across a blasted tank. This, the jovial Egyptian with a belly like a bowl of jelly explained, was a remnant from the Six Days War with Israel. It was difficult to imagine how any strategic objective could be reached in such a remote and desolate area. But that was nothing compared to the ghostly city we encountered.

Surrounded by nothing but miles and miles of dunes and flat, baked earth, sat a modern series of apartment buildings. They were the same nondescript tan that everything in Egypt seemed to be, and rose easily ten or more stories high. There must have been two dozen huge, skeletal complexes, each with empty, gaping windows that promised a feeble respite from the destroying sun. The Saharan winds whistled through their openings ominously, moaning louder even than our wheezing air-conditioner. It looked as if someone had plucked a Soviet-era series of apartment blocs and abandoned them in the desert. I expected to see vultures and crows circling the dead city, but nothing lived here, not a forlorn palm or even a scratchy shrub.

What was this place, and how did it come to be here?

"This is where the people will live in twenty years," the buoyant guide explained in Magyar, waiting for Bela to translate into Romanian for the guests. "Egypt's population is booming faster than the government can supply housing. Here the people will live when they have filled the cities to capacity. Actually they already have, but as you can see, it is not yet ready."

"Where is the water for these thousands of future occupants?" someone asked.

"Oh, there is no water here!" he laughed, explaining the obvious. "It will be piped in from the Nile. It will take another ten years at least just to bring the water. Only when that happens will the people be moved here."

I seemed to be the only one onboard confused by this. Being American, I had difficulty understanding the idea that citizens would be 'moved' anywhere, especially when there was no promise of employment whatsoever. Because the entire passenger compliment of the bus had lived for decades under the Iron Curtain, however, they understood how true socialism approached problems.

I learned quickly what challenges Egypt faced when we entered the outskirts of mighty Cairo. The ditches lining the road were filled with far more than rubbish and tainted water: there were thousands of men, women, and children. For miles and miles we passed their crude huts cobbled together from discarded carpets and plastic, erected against abandoned tires and who knows what else. They drank and bathed in the water that ran beside the highway in open sewers and ditches draining into the Nile River.

These people were promised housing, but the government had yet to follow through, focusing first on those in the cities. Until then, they were denied homes, jobs, or education and eked out a living in squalor. This was the Third World, and it was without a doubt the most depressing thing I had ever seen in my life. At that moment I vowed to never, ever make the asinine complaint that America was turning 'socialist'. Slippery slope be damned, I believed Americans would have to fall off a cliff before accepting that from our own government.

After seeing all that, I was not much impressed when we pulled onto Tahrir Square and stopped before the imposing Museum of Egypt. Well, until I stepped inside, that is.

Annually some two million visited the museum, which was constructed in 1897 with a staggering 107 halls. The ground floor held all the huge statues—those far too big to be transported anywhere else—and the upper floor housed the small statues, jewels, Tutankhamen treasures and the mummies. The seven main sections were divided in chronological order, from the Old Kingdom, Middle Kingdom, and Modern Kingdom, then through the Greek and the Roman days. The sixth section was devoted to coins and papyrus, while the seventh held the sarcophagi and scarabs. Add to that a photography section and a large library, and I simply had no idea where to begin. I had found the Garden of Eden in Egypt, not Iraq!

What really amazed me, though, was Bela. He had arranged for me a guide who spoke English. While Bianca and the rest of our group trailed off after him and our jolly old soul of an Egyptian, I had my own personal guide! I had never felt so lucky in my life. Bela, bowl-cut and all, was the coolest guy ever. George Clooney oughta give up now.

Abdul was a slender, youthful man who looked Indian to me, rather than Egyptian. He had learned English while studying in London, so he began with exceedingly proper grammar, "Nearly 2000 years before the Romans were building their first mud huts, the Egyptians were constructing pyramids and temples and dams of a magnitude most parts of Earth are unable to duplicate even today."

"Oh, I know, I know!" I answered enthusiastically. "Show me everything!"

He smiled a well-groomed smile and said, "I can do so, perhaps more than you may think, my friend. I am an employee of the museum, and thusly privy to areas otherwise off limits to regular guides and tourists. Would you be interested in such things?"

I slapped my knee and said, "Well I'll be a whirling Dervish!"

Hours later, my head was awhirl with all things Egypt and awesome. Perhaps the most notable sight was witnessing the restoration of an ancient sarcophagus. Actually, none of the original sarcophagus remained, and I gazed upon a modern coffin molded of solid glass. Curators were painstakingly lining it with the millennia-old gold leaf from inside a rotten, broken wooden sarcophagus found in the Valley of the Kings. While less than a third was yet completed, it truly brought home the magnitude of restoring items so absolutely priceless.

Afterwards Abdul gave me a lengthy tour of King Tut's treasures, and my awe was reinforced tenfold. Seeing the golden death mask of the boy king that swept the entire world in Egypt-mania is hard to rival. But that evening, holding hands with Bianca and watching the sun set blood-red behind the Great Pyramid of Giza came close.

Bianca and I spent about two hours exploring the Giza Plateau. The three huge pyramids of Khufu, Khafre, and Menkaure sat before the noble and silent Sphinx. The Great Pyramid is far larger and more impressive than anyone can imagine until seeing it in person. It was cordoned off, which pleased me but no one else. Most tourists wanted to touch the fabled stone of the last remaining Wonder of the World. I did, too, but after seeing the damage wrought by eager tourists in the Valley of the Kings, I was happy to abstain.

But that was only the Great Pyramid. Soaring right next to it, even higher up on the plateau in fact, was Khafre's pyramid. Getting to enter that sure perked me up. Wheelchair accessible it was not, but fortunately everything else was attended to, including a system to keep the human sweat from damaging the hieroglyphs and paintings. Time flew by, and before we knew it the sky burned amber. The sun, now a crimson orb, settled behind the majestic black outline of the pyramids. It was time to go back.

When darkness closed in upon our trusty old bus, crude televisions were set up to show a movie which, to my dismay, was the Hollywood remake of *The Mummy*. It was funny, actually, because it was dubbed over in Magyar with Romanian subtitles. I was used to Dracula with a Hungarian accent, and now the Mummy, too? Midnight neared and we were still on the road. Most were snoozing in their seats, as was Bianca, until a comedy featuring the slapstick comedy of Mr. Bean came on. Her loud chuckles threatened to wake everyone. During a scene where Mr. Bean tripped over a skateboard while sneaking through a parking lot, she burst out laughing so uncontrollably I thought they were going to leave us in the desert.

## 2

Our last two days in Egypt were spent primarily on the beach. The long trip to Cairo had been fulfilling, but exhausting. After a recovery day of napping, laughing, and loving, we had an evening of bad Egyptian Cabernet and a night of stargazing. For our final day we spontaneously joined a small tour for snorkeling and a visit to a private island. Our transport was a moderately old, moderately nice yacht capable of holding about twenty people, though currently only toted half of that. We chugged away from the pier and plowed into the restless Red Sea.

The Red Sea was not red, of course, but was in fact the world's northern-most tropical sea. It boasted some 200 soft and hard corals and was home to an estimated 100,000 invertebrates. I was excited to see some of them, but the extremely choppy sea had me concerned. We sailed for only about thirty minutes before stopping a hundred yards from a rocky, apparently uninhabited island in the Gulf of Suez. Even in the lee that the island provided, the surface was extremely choppy, so only six of us opted to hop in the water for snorkeling. After but five minutes of blowing the excessively salty water out of my snorkel, I wished I had been one to abstain from the excursion.

The water was actually some of the saltiest on Earth. Here, close to the Suez Canal and far from the moderating influence of the main body of the Indian Ocean, the salinity level was a briny forty parts per thousand. No doubt the gorgeous corals preferred it so, because some fifteen feet below the roiling surface was a gorgeous multi-colored labyrinth of coral, polyps, fans, sponges, and other locals. Unfortunately, the fish were as unhappy with the rough water as I, and thusly absent. I split off from Bianca to explore a huge mushroom-shaped rock formation that rose from the deep, but after ten minutes of gagging and spewing salt water I had had enough. I surfaced and looked across the tumultuous waves for Bianca.

After a minute I spotted her a ways away. She happened to surface as soon as I identified her. She spat out some water from her snorkel, then cried to me excitedly, "There's a catfish here!"

A catfish. After all I had seen and experienced, I must admit that I was just not impressed enough by a catfish to struggle all the way over to her. Instead I returned to the boat and discovered that we had been the last two in the water. I joined a couple from France, and we sipped some delightfully fresh-squeezed orange juice with champagne. They spoke English, so we chatted about how we were just happy to be out and about, even if the snorkeling had been a mess. After another ten minutes, Bianca came surging over the landing at the back of the yacht.

She flung some water at me. "Why you not see catfish?"

"Bianca," I said, wiping the brine from my face. "I grew up catching catfish. It couldn't possibly be more satisfying than this juice. Or champagne, I might add."

"Are you lying to impress me?" she retorted. "You no grow up catching catfish: you growed up in Iowa!"

"Yes, and we have plenty of catfish."

She slicked her black hair back and crossed her arms beneath her breasts in a pose of complete defiance. The rocking ship seemed unable to affect that self-affirmed stance.

"With meter-long stingers and everything?"

"Yes, with stingers and everything. I remember once when we got home and were cleaning the catfish in the driveway, one of them stuck Dad. I almost caught him swearing, which was quite a treat for me."

I took another sip, then realized what she had just said. "Meter-long stingers? What the hell did you see in there?"

"A catfish, bamboclat! You know, with the wings and the spiky-tail?"

I blinked. "You saw a sting ray? I've never seen a sting ray before. But... but you said 'catfish'!"

"That's how we say in Romanian. It translates as catfish."

Suddenly the orange juice wasn't so sweet.

Afterwards we beached the yacht beside others on the sand of the private island. It was not particularly large, but the white sands were clean and inviting. We played for a while in the waves among about thirty other tourists. I would pick Bianca up and toss her into the oncoming waves, and all such silly things new lovers do. What I found particularly amusing, however, was the Egyptian crew of the yachts. Four big boats bobbed beside each other, but all the crew had scrambled onto one to better joke and jeer at the tourists. The Egyptian men may not want their own women to be seen in public, even if covered head-to-foot in robes, but they still delighted in all the topless European ladies on the beach. I tried to get Bianca to doff her bra, but to no avail.

After a while Bianca and I wandered into the palms and found a big hammock to nap in. We snuggled together in the shade, our sweat and salt mingling. The sun was blocked by the palm trees above us, but it was still hot and humid. We drowsily reflected on our trip. More importantly, we reflected on our blossoming relationship. Despite the magnitude of what we had witnessed together, by far our favorite moments were the simple ones of togetherness, like that moment. It all went by in a blink, and we were sorry to see our vacation within a vacation come to an end. Alas, we cannot stop the sands of time from flowing.

## 3

Our vacation within a vacation was over. Even worse, the whole shebang was nearing its end. Our return to Brașov was a much faster flight to Bucharest and then a couple hours in the car, so no more autocar drama. We arrived at Strada Lâcramioarelor by late morning. After a relaxed meal of sharing food and stories, Bianca stood up and declared, "I have frogs to attend to."

Curious, I followed her into the living room and saw laid out on the floor two huge, hard-shell suitcases. They were bright green. Defined by rounded edges and sloping angles, they did vaguely look frog-like. Beside them were heaps of shoes in all shapes and colors.

"I pack for up to ten months," Bianca explained lamely. "Actually, one is mostly empty for return presents. Tomorrow I get my tired eyes cosmeticked and my claws sharpened. I need to look young for the guests."

"And another round of potential suitors," I noted wryly.

She did not seem amused. In fact, she seemed sulky. Bianca packed her frogs quietly at first, but as time ticked by, her moodiness grew to something else. Soon she was slamming clothes into the cases with force. I watched her unsuccessfully try to smash the same shoe into a frog three times before she finally hurled it away.

"See?" I teased. "Cobbling issues."

Bianca suddenly whirled on me and snapped, "Why you do that?"

"What?" I asked, surprised at her vehemence.

"You make everything happy. I want to be angry—but you even make my anger turn to happiness!"

"You say that like it's a bad thing."

"I must focus on my real world," she retorted. "My identity. My job!"

A sudden urge overcame me. It was tremendously foolish, but I simply couldn't fight it. I stood up, stretched out my arms and dramatically preached, "Abandon your frogs and anger! If you believe in the laugh, it shall set you free! Let me show you the way to eternal happiness."

I held the moment—too long. My outstretched arms withered under Bianca's glare. It was an epic fail.

"Don't you mock me, rasclat!" Bianca screeched.

"I wasn't," I protested. "OK, I was. Sorry. It's in my nature to combat sadness with humor. You're not mad. You're sad because you're going away to the ships and I'm going back to America."

Bianca sat heavily on the couch and hugged her knees. Finally she admitted, "I enjoy this warm feeling of being so deep and tenderly in love with you inside of me, but I try not to think about our surprising and progressive romance too much."

"Well, then," I said, no longer joking. "Let's talk real world. How do I get a job on a cruise ship?"

Bianca stared at me incredulously for a long time. When she realized I was serious, her self-imposed winter began to thaw. Alas, reality squashed the blossoming hope.

"You can't, of course," she said simply.

"Why not?"

"Americans can't handle ships."

I bristled at her dismissal. Seeing my reaction, she quickly added, "Besides, you're a computer guy."

"A computer business was never my dream," I scoffed. I sat beside her and explained. "When we saw an opportunity, my partner and I went for it. He was already a genius programmer, but I only learned computers because we needed a digital artist. Just a tool, not a vocation."

Bianca looked unconvinced.

"Look, when my partner went nuts—and I mean that literally—he did more than trash three years of hard work. He trashed the lives of my team. Simply put: it hurts too much to use those skills. I don't want to move into a cubicle anyway. Screw it. I'm ready for something different, something new, something wild."

Bianca studied my face, undecided. Finally she said, "OK."

# 4

An hour later we were sitting in the office of Ovidiu, a recruiting agent for Carnival Cruise Lines. He was a slender man with a handsome face, a very handsome wardrobe, and an extremely handsome office. His suite comprised the entire second floor of a brick building, featuring numerous windows looking into a lush interior court. Light filtered in through an angled glass skylight and past his mezzanine entrance, making it look like a bridge over a jungle.

"Americans can't handle ships," he said.

"So I hear," I replied, giving Bianca an amused look. She sat in the chair beside mine, looking relaxed but serious.

"What is it you think I can do for you?" Ovidiu asked. "I am a recruiter for Romanians, not Americans. There are no American recruiters, of course."

"So I hear," I repeated. "Why is that?"

155

"Because none apply," he replied thoughtfully, leaning back. "Why would you want to? The work is very hard, and the money is very small."

Bianca raised an eyebrow, and Ovidiu hastily added, "For an American."

"I'm not thinking big," I said. "It's just a waiter job. I've been in restaurants for a decade."

"Not on ships, you haven't," he pointed out. "Do you know computers?"

"He knows computers," Bianca interrupted, before I could protest.

"Other than doctors, who are supernumeraries anyway, and entertainers, who have their own agencies, the only position I can even think of for an American would involve computers."

"I just want to be a waiter, man," I repeated.

Ovidiu leaned forward skeptically. "Why?"

"My reasons are irrelevant."

"No, they're not," Ovidiu insisted. "Why would they bother with someone who will just quit? They'll want to know your story before they even think of meeting you. And believe me, they'll need to meet you."

"I want to be with Bianca," I explained. "If we have the same job, we can be together. That simple."

"I see," he said, nodding. "Well, in my ten years at Carnival, I've never seen even one American. I would not even talk to you, but Bianca is a good employee and a friend. Again, what is it you think I can do for you?"

"You can think Romanian-style," Bianca answered for me. "Not American-style."

Ovidiu thought for a moment, frowning. "No, that won't work. The bribes are to convince me, and you don't need to worry about that. Really, Bianca, I would sign him on if I could. I can't."

He opened a drawer from his desk and pulled out a pack of cigarettes. We declined his offer, so he casually lit one for himself. He leaned towards me, elbows on the desk.

"You want to know why Bianca doesn't need to bribe me?"

"Suddenly I'm not so sure."

"Bianca is the only one who almost beat me. Almost, of course."

I looked at Bianca, but she said nothing. Her delicate wiggle of satisfaction was corroboration enough.

"As agent to cruise ships, my job is to screen people. If I like them, and there is a job opening, I find the right place for them. Bianca applied for the restaurants. That's the highest paid job, so everybody applies for it first. It is also the toughest, so I don't let them by easily."

He paused, grinned, and offered Bianca a cigarette again. This time she accepted, leaning forward to accept the light with a creak of her leather skirt.

"She said she worked at a certain restaurant. I called the owner and he said, 'oh, of course, she has worked here for years!' That, of course, only meant she could lie and bribe. Romanian-style. Turns out, she only volunteered there for a summer."

Bianca shrugged, explaining, "I needed to learn restaurants."

"I knew she was lying, but couldn't catch her. She was too smart. She had asked all of her waitress friends penetrating questions and listened close. I asked her this and that, and of her experiences here and there. She had an answer for all of it. The performance was amazing."

Bianca laughed, and added, "Until Ovidiu pulled his bloody secret weapon from the filing cabinet!"

Reflecting upon what I knew of Romanians thus far, I presumed this meant a large knife.

"A linen napkin," Ovidiu clarified. "I told her 'You said you know half a dozen napkin folds. Show me.' She wilted before my very eyes, like a Gypsy had spit in her ice cream. I told her to relax, go have a cigarette, then come back. I had her paperwork done by then."

"All that to be a waiter?" I asked. "It's not rocket science."

Ovidiu leaned back again. He casually blew his smoke into the air, then looked me in the eye.

"You have no idea what you're getting into, do you?"

# 5

My final night together with Bianca was a short one. We were to leave Braşov very, very early in the morning, and retired accordingly. I would not see her parents in the morning, so we said our goodbyes before bed. Pops hate goodbyes as much as I, so we kept things brief. I gave Lucky a big hug and a kiss on the cheek. To my surprise, Piti gave me a big hug and a kiss on the cheek. I had forgotten that such an old tradition in Romania. Now I understood how scratchy an unshaven cheek was.

Bianca and I headed into the bedroom together, which prompted a great amount of fussing from Piti. He began barking like a *câine rau* and pointing to the living room's fold-out bed. Bianca tried to soothe him, but he would have none of it. Fortunately, Lucky stepped up and yelled over his protestations. Bianca laughed, then pushed me into the bedroom before Piti could recover his senses.

"What did she say?" I asked.

With a snicker, Bianca translated, "She said, 'What you think they were doing in Egypt?'"

As the door closed, I caught a glimpse of Piti. His eyes stared at nothing, wide with utter shock.

Bianca and I snuggled into the tiny bed, and immediately got down to business. Or tried to, anyway. Every other kiss loosed a horrible screech from the bed. While the nails-on-the-blackboard noise made me cringe, the thought of her parents hearing did so to Bianca. Each time we froze, waiting impatiently in the silence with beating hearts, then eventually began the whole process all over again.

Finally the kissing got too hot, and we leapt out of bed to find a better way to continue. With each step, however, the floor squeaked an alarm. We spun about, assaulted on all sides by turncoats, while kissing and grabbing and laughing and—most importantly—looking for something to brace against. My eyes feverishly passed over the couch-bed filling one wall, windows along the entire length of another, closet doors dominating a third, and the fourth holding the bedroom door and a long, low shelf.

"Don't you have any walls, dammit?" I whispered, half frantic, half laughing. But the joke was on me when we knocked over a shelf and the contents cascaded over my head to strike the floor with a loud clatter. So much for continuing!

Outside the door we heard a muffled, 'Jesus Gras!'

6

We woke at 3 a.m. for the return to Bucharest. We drove more or less in silence. What was there to say? The dream was over. The pain of saying goodbye swamped any enthusiasm for the upcoming battle to meet again.

Eventually I landed back in Nevada. Some homecoming. I was no longer even sure where home was anymore! My first order of business was to feverishly check for an email from Bianca. There were three in just our first day apart. Some were better than others:

"I fight to get my senses back and to re-enter in my cool independent snaky skin. I used to enjoy the pattern of my skin and now I have to get back into it, even if I'm still shivering when thinking of your touch and lips exciting every inch of it. The cold rain stopped just now, but is still gloomy and Brasovy. I ate some M&Ms to feel better because I can't stop thinking of you."

"I still have to pack my frogs, and to take off on thursday night. My dad was upset today because it was such a nice weather, and yesterday, when you left, it was raining the whole bloody day, so Albisoara got wet like a sweaty horny American that I know. We checked a furniture store and we found some nice couch for my living room. Is comfortable and dark brun like a Carpathian bear, and it was inspiring me sensual thoughts of you and me sliding on it. What did you do to me that a couch gets me going?"

"Tommy called me to tell me some more how much in love he is with me and how he can't wait for me to make up my mind and agree for him to protect and spoil me all my life. Jesus Gras, this guy sent his brain fishing. This starts to annoy me. Thanks to your bald English language, I could write him that I went in Egypt with a friend, so nobody can figure out if it's a 'he'-friend or a 'she'-friend. I hope he won't react anti-clockwise direction, when I'll tell him that I fell in love with his co-citizen. I hate to justify my actions! I shouldn't have accepted to spend those days with this guy, but I didn't think he will fall so violent for me. Now I have to walk on egg shells to avoid this bamboclat's heart attack."

# 7

I wasted no time in corroborating that Americans had almost no options to work on cruise ships. All my calls to Carnival headquarters in Miami came to naught, with nary an agency or expert to help. I tried a Canadian agency, to no avail. If I was not an entertainer of some sort, be it musician, dancer, or DJ, I needed to pursue the information technology angle. But that path meant separation from Bianca, so why bother? True, I could potentially start on the cruise director's staff, but the salary was a painful $1000 a month. No thanks. Restaurant or bust.

Even so, I readied my life to switch from turf to surf. I rented the spare bedroom of a friend's house in order to put all my belongings into storage. This allowed me to gather my pennies for another flight. I wanted to be ready for an interview of some sort when Bianca's ship, *Carnival Conquest*, arrived in New Orleans.

*Conquest* was Carnival's brand-new class of vessel, being constructed in the shipyards of Montfalcone, Italy. Bianca signed on while the ship was still in wet dock, as part of a special team selected to give new ships their shakedown. During the transatlantic crossing, they needed bodies to practice on, so the big dogs enjoyed a little executive privilege and played passenger. Thus Bianca could interact with Carnival's senior management. As one could imagine, the stress was very high to please the top tier of a multi-billion dollar, 30,000 employee operation, but the perks were commensurate. Bianca had the ear of some very influential people.

While *Conquest* received her finishing touches, Bianca's duties were light. Delays were not an uncommon feature of the Mediterranean, so the crew had numerous, awkward bits of free time. The proximity of internet cafés meant that Bianca's efforts on my behalf would have been easy to report, had any been possible. The big dogs were set to arrive—but had yet to arrive.

Thus, Bianca did what any sailor would: she lived every second of shore leave like it was her last on earth. Her emails were full of exciting snippets, which only served to whet my appetite further:

> "Trieste. This is an absolutely charming place. All the streets and squares look like museums, they all are so serene and grandiose, that you have nothing else to do but stare and

contemplate, lost in Renaissance thoughts and images. Is strange, you don't feel history, like you do in Romania, but feel art in the highest and the most pure form. Italy is definitely a masterpiece."

"I almost collapsed when I entered in San Marco Square. Is like a dream. You instantly transfer yourself in the past, feeling like wearing cape and mask and spade. The Cathedral, the Doges Palace, the Bridge of Sighs, were miraculous in the setting sun. You and I have to be back here someday. I fell in love with Italy. What you see in pictures or movies, is a pale reproduction of the outstanding reality."

"I love you, my optimist, eternal positive and smiling darling. The day I wrote you the message from Venice, I was already very tired after I slept 5 hours in two nights, and I walked 20 hours in Milan, Venice and Montfalcone. I was missing you, because I was supposed to share all those wonderful impressions with you, and you were so far away, so I got a little bit depressed. But now I'm cool, and confident, so I'm ready to fight for my everlasting love and to wait patiently/impatiently for the time we will meet again. I will enjoy every minute with you, because sailors are used to living the moment, like we did when you came to turn me upside down."

When *Conquest* sailed off for her Atlantic crossing, every person of importance was aboard, but not every thing. Namely, the satellite hookup for internet access. Having exhausted my limited options in America, there was nothing left but to wait for Bianca's progress. I think we both knew it would fall on her shoulders all along. News arrived haphazardly in sporadic emails from borrowed satellite phones and stolen moments at managers' computers:

"I couldn't find the big man's email address, but if he's not onboard I'll talk to him as soon as I reach the States. If you don't mind, I'll introduce you as my fiancé. I know we'll work everything out. Something tells me, you Gemini, that we are meant to succeed together. Kiss you stickily. Bianca."

"Checked with mucho people, but I couldn't get to a conclusion. Some managers say we'll be in New Orleans on Nov 12th and we'll stay 3 nights, other ones say that we'll be there the 14th, and we'll stay 2 nights. I didn't meet the boss yet, I don't know where that guy is hiding. I'm ready to start the offensive. If he won't show up until I lose my sick patience, I'll somehow find and invade his cabin. Don't worry, I don't mean that ship-style."

"You can apply for restaurant, bar or even trainer or cruise director. He'll figure out where he needs you reading your CV. It's confirmed that we'll be in New Orleans Nov 12th between 9am and noon. My love, that will be your turn to strike. Bianca, the fighter."

"Tonight I have to bodyguard the dining room between 2 and 5am. Rasclats! I hope I won't work breakfast afterwards, otherwise me kaput. I saw the boss today passing by, he shook my hand, but he was in a hurry, so I even couldn't ask him when he is available."

"I talked yesterday with Dan, the maitre d' and told him about our sentimental and inter-continental adventure. I asked him his support for getting you on the ship, and he promised to help. He was very happy seeing me so in love and asked me why the hell I don't go to live with you in States, and I said that we are much too adventurous to settle down. Anyway, the ship life will be a challenge for you (me got already used to it). I'm telling you, there are so many temptations on board, that maybe you will tell me thanks for cooperation, I have to check some young hot chicks, which are similar rice on the ship."

"Dan told me to call the Mean Indian, and he asked me when "this Brian guy" comes around. I told him I'm supposed to meet you in New Orleans when we arrive. He said: get a visitor pass for him, and we'll give him meeting with me and Mladen. So, my love, get ready, you are almost in. Those guys I dealt with are the most powerful and influential in the company. Cedric the Mean Indian is first interview and he is the scarecrow. So impress him, my love, as you know to do so naturally, and there is no more obstacle between us. Except your mother, maybe. I'm kidding."

"Is confirmed on 14th you'll have the
appointment with the Gods. I think it was the
right decision to choose the restaurant. You can
get the best money, but I warn you, it's one of
the toughest jobs. You have all chances to get
screwed up bad after only a few months."

# CHAPTER NINE
## *Iceberg, Dead Ahead*

### 1

IN THE MORNING I walked from my hotel in the French Quarter of New Orleans to the banks of the vast, sluggish Mississippi River. Under grey skies I followed the levees towards the cruise terminal, shivering in the cold. Having never been to the South before, I had erroneously assumed it was always warm. For thirty minutes I hopped and huffed in the damp, chilled air outside the gates because port security had surprisingly not received a boarding list for the day. Finally they tired of my badgering and opened the gate, leaving me to ship security.

Getting aboard *Carnival Conquest* was all around hard, even beyond my complete reliance on Bianca. She got me the interview, which had me nervous enough, but when I earned the enmity of the Security Chief I was really pushing my luck. As it turned out, that morning had been randomly selected by the U.S. Coast Guard for the ship's inspection. Even on a ship with established routines, this was a hugely stressful event. On a ship still cluttered and chaotic, it was crippling.

"You're not even on the list," snapped the chief, after several irritated minutes of explaining marine basics to this obvious landlubber. He was a middle-aged Asian gentleman wearing a black sweater over a white uniform. His watch looked like it cost more than my entire three-week vacation in Romania—including seven days in Egypt. "Come back after noon, when the fire drill is over."

I returned at the appointed time, but my name had not been added to the list of cleared visitors.

"I have a meeting with Cedric the... Indian," I protested. "Can't you call someone? I flew all the way from the West Coast to be here today!"

This resulted in numerous impatient phone calls. During each heated exchange, the chief glowered at me more deeply from behind the luggage scanner. Only reluctantly did he let me board.

But where to go?

I passed some plastic flaps into what appeared to be a crew corridor, and soon found the crew mess. It was brimming with people of different colors, screaming in different languages, wearing different uniforms. It was bedlam. I had no hope of finding Bianca in there. Instead, a petite brunette found me.

"You're Brian, *nu*?" she asked, cute round face smiling up at me. She carried a plastic mug filled with coffee still hissing around chocolate soft-serve ice cream.

"I am," I replied. "How did you know?"

"An American in the crew mess?" she asked in answer. I had yet to understand how everyone knew I was American before I even spoke. She continued, "Bianca's working the officer's mess today, so she's busy right now."

I was led by the elbow back into the corridor and into a metal stairwell. The cutie sat on the steps beside a cluster of mugs filled with dregs of coffee and mounds of cigarette butts. "I'm Vio, her cabin-mate. After a quick smoke, I'll give her a call and see what's up. You smoke?"

"No, thanks," I said, leaning against a cool metal wall. I stood a little straighter when I realized that Vio was eyeing me up and down.

"Well well," she said, giving me an apparently impressed nod. "Bianca caught the best fish yet. Even if you don't smoke. But you don't have any money, or you wouldn't be here. Guess that means you're not too smart, either."

Vio finished her cigarette, then called from a nearby phone. She conversed briefly in Romanian, barked a laugh, then hung up.

"Wait!" I cried, but it was too late.

"I know, I know," Vio said. "You want to talk to her. Gotta wait. She's angry because her period just started. We knew it was coming any day now, and she was desperate to avoid another Egypt. When she's mad she won't talk to anybody, so we'll have to wait."

"Oh, come on!"

"No cheeky cheeky tonight, Romeo," she added mischievously. "I'd invite you to my cabin to make up for your disappointment, but she's there. I can already see her wormy apple cheeks burning red as an angry donut's. Meet her at the gangway at two o'clock. You can't wander the ship today because the Coast Guard is here. Big drama, and you don't want any drama before you meet Cedric the Mean Indian. Trust me."

"I can't wait in the mess or anything?" I replied, surprised. "I have to actually leave?"

"Da," Vio replied. "You need to go back to town because I have port manning today, which means I can't get off. So that leaves you to get me a home pregnancy test. Welcome to ships!"

## 2

When I met up with Bianca, she was all business and prepared me for a meeting with the food and beverage manager, preliminary to further interviews. When I arrived at his office, however, I was surprised to instead meet Cedric the Mean Indian. It took all of thirty seconds to see how he earned his nickname. He did not interview me so much as interrogate me. It was the most brutal few minutes of my life, and I barely managed to get in ten words.

Yet somehow it was successful. Cedric arranged for me to meet with the big boss Mladen that evening, who offered me a job not just as a waiter, but as an assistant maitre d'. Because the meeting had been in the dining room during dinner preparation, it was concluded rather quickly. Though always a frantic time, it was even more so that night because the guests were all press getting their first glimpse of Carnival's new baby. During my hasty departure, I was accosted by Dan, the maitre d'.

"Welcome to the club," the salt-and-pepper haired Irishman called on my way out. Dan looked like a man who had seen his share of trouble in the past, but was now a tough, compact set of discipline. Even his pencil-thin mustache looked ready to toe the line. We chatted briefly, and I came to sense that Dan's support had been instrumental in my getting the job. Man, did I owe Bianca!

I wandered the ship awhile, but soon gravitated back to the dining room. I was keen to see how ship restaurants differed from those on land, and differ they did. On the surface the process looked the same, with waiters taking orders and delivering food, but the underlying foundation was structured in a way unique to ships and vastly different than anything I had seen in ten years of restaurants, whether independent structures or part of hotels. It was not just another game, but a whole different sport—not even including the intricacies of dozens of interacting nationalities.

I made my way to the hostess stand to join Dan. We chatted for a long time, dinner raging around us, like officers on a hilltop above the battle. Eventually he left for his office, inviting me to join him at the maitre d' table that night.

When second-seating dinner was finally over and Bianca began tidying up her station, it was 1 a.m. The atmosphere in the dining room was depleted of all energy, like the battleground's last shots had switched from echo to memory. I helped Bianca by folding the linen napkins for the breakfast shift, just a scant five hours away. When Bianca left to safeguard her silverware rack from prowling waiters, I was approached by a Filipino waiter.

"The maitre d' table is ready now," he said. In a surprisingly formal manner, he motioned that I should follow. I then joined a nightly ritual among what could be considered the ship's non-commissioned officers. A round table had been selected in a pleasant corner of the Monet dining room, and there I joined seven others: two maitre d's, three assistant maitre d's, and two hostesses.

Menus were not necessary, partly because everyone knew the selections implicitly but mostly because the kitchen was required to comply with any order. It was assumed I would have steak and lobster, so I was not consulted, but fed. Certainly I didn't argue, even if it was in the wee hours of the morning. Everyone drank copious amounts of wine, except Dan, who sipped from numerous cans of Red Bull. The waiters of the surrounding stations all struggled to finish their duties, while we were waited on hand and foot. I was a bit uncomfortable during the entire 'welcome to the officer's club' experience.

Dan's authority was apparent, as all the others at the table were defined entirely by their differing levels of obsequiousness, with the suction entirely directed at Dan. His charisma was unmistakable, though how exactly it manifested through his curt speech and no-nonsense manner was difficult to put a finger on.

After half an hour Bianca had finished her duties and came to claim me. She was due to work breakfast, of course, but that still gave us a few hours together. Bianca was obsessed about sleeping in a real bed, so we took a taxi to my hotel. She was so exhausted that she drifted off to sleep while smoking on the balcony in my T-shirt. I put her to bed and watched her sleep. I was too excited to relax. Three short hours later the alarm shattered dreams and she stumbled off to the taxi, racing once again to the dining room. This, I would soon learn, was what it meant to work on cruise ships.

## 3

Two months later I signed on to *Carnival Fantasy* in Port Canaveral, Florida. Part of my arrangement with Mladen was a whirlwind tour of the restaurants, starting at the bottom as a waiter and high-tailing it up through the ranks to assistant maitre d'. The beginning was referred to as 'college'. Though intimidating, it was an exciting time. Teaming up with people from all over the globe was a real pleasure, and made the unending hours almost enjoyable. Almost. We worked twelve hours a day, seven days a week—not including homework—bussing tables, washing dishes, and carrying trays. This was all on top of the real challenge: learning ship life.

We had become the property of Carnival. The corporation told us who we slept with and for how long, when we ate and what. This complete lack of free will was the hardest part for me. I had no say in how cold it was, or what I wore to compensate, or even when allowed a bathroom break. If the corporation needed us to work an extra shift after twelve hours already on, we did so. More or less, onboard was on duty.

I tried to keep in close communication with Bianca, but hardly had time for the internet café—and rarely found a free computer when I did. But letters from Bianca were worth the effort. I learned perhaps more about being a waiter on a cruise ship from her grumbles than from college. The letters were an exciting glimpse into how my girlfriend lived her life. Unfortunately, as the weeks went by her words turned more and more sour as the drudgery of nonstop work set in:

"The restaurant college is the most cheerful part of the ship life. I enjoyed it as well. Like you, I was excited to come in contact with people of so many different nationalities. I imagine you are the most bizarre and desirable creature over there. Just don't get too far away, especially in the Eastern Europe corner. It's similar spider web."

"Yesterday we had a crew party up on the Lido deck, and after we ate the food cooked especially for Romanian people, we danced until 3am, and I checked in for breakfast at 6.30. I got old, I think, because in my first contract, I used to party and get drunk almost every night, and I was cool, and now, I couldn't wake up this morning. I was dreaming the alarm clock was ringing, and there was nobody to stop it."

"Now you work midnight buffet? You assistant waiter for a while, then. I wish waiters could work midnight buffet, I'm tired like hell of waking up early in the morning. I'm in the mood to sleep mucho to recover, but only midnight buffet people get more than 4-5 hours sleep. They used to give us breakfast off once at three weeks, but there were some complaints from the guests regarding breakfast service, so the management changed the working system and nobody gets breakfast off anymore. Too bad! Me love you shakily, and I send you slippery kiss."

"My rasclat guests this morning were smelling the glasses I poured water in, saying that they are stinky. I had to change 4 glasses, and all seemed stinky to them. They were yelling at the assistant maitre d' that on this brand new ship everything is stinky, then they go smoke like crew!"

"I have some crappy guests the second sitting, they try to intimidate me, they are giving me hard time eating similar pigs: 3-4 appetizers each, soup, salad, 2-3 main courses, 2-3 deserts, but I'm cool and I have answers for everything they ask. My assistant Adrien saves my life, and I recommended him to Dan for promotion to waiter. What I get for my kind act? The bamboclat got a tattoo in Cozumel on his arm, and now he can barely carry the trays."

"My cabin mate Vio got fixed for some complaints, so she has almost no guests this week. That means no money. You can't play games with Dan, he fixes you like a banana, no matter who you are. So she have no guests for the first sitting, and only 9 at the second one, and those ones are some alcoholic bastards. In the first night of the cruise, they came one hour late, drunk as apples. When she came to sing a Happy Birthday cake for one of them, that one said: 'Can I put the cake on your face?' When she was telling us this story, Vio got mad all over again. Her boyfriend, my assistant Adrien said, 'Don't be upset. Our guest is our master, he is king. You should have said: Yes, put the cake on my face, and as well break the plate on my head, because you are the guest!'"

**4**

I spent one month in school and with practical lessons, which included washing dishes and even a stint in the galley. Mostly I assisted waiter teams, such as the Romanian couple Dumitru and Lowena, who were friends of Bianca's from her early days with Carnival. Back then, Dumitru had been married with children, but fell for the much younger and vibrant Lowena, who was supposed to only be a 'ship squeeze'. Having a new mistress each contract was kind of the usual on ships. Dumitru, however, actually left his family to remain at sea with Lowena. Such stories were common on ships, I soon discovered.

In a blink, it was time to leave *Fantasy* for *Conquest*. Trainees do not choose their ships, of course, but Carnival generally kept family together. In my case, it was all prearranged that I would work under the tutelage of Dan, so I was assigned the snazzy new ship *Conquest*. As an assistant maitre d'-in-training, I was to first work every station as a waiter, then after four months get my officer's stripe and move into the white uniform.

That was all fine and dandy, but my excitement was over finally beginning a life with Bianca. Within minutes of signing on, Bianca found me on the crew deck. We hugged so tightly that we refused to release even for a kiss.

And then she was gone.

Bianca had to run back to her station on the Lido deck. She had snuck off to greet me, but couldn't risk being caught away from her station too long. Such things as life and emotion were completely secondary to bussing tables, even if this early there were only fifty guests aboard, over three hundred clean tables, and forty bored waiters.

Indeed, all I saw of Bianca that whole day was evidence. Our shared cabin was extremely small—perhaps five by ten feet—crammed with two lockers, a sink, a tiny desk covered entirely by a 13" TV, two bunk beds, and a small chair groaning under a box overloaded with gift-wrapped teddy bears. Tommy was apparently back at it. We shared our shower and toilet with two neighbors, and our floor with two frogs. My bunk was shared with my suitcase. Bianca's fixation with a real bed suddenly became very clear. More than 'roteste!' would be needed to get around each other when dressing for work, that's for sure!

Yet despite this apparent proximity, Bianca and I rarely saw each other. She worked in the Monet during dinner, whereas Dan assigned me to the Renoir. This was in order to be a midnight buffet supervisor. Thus while I was working, Bianca was sleeping, and vice versa. Our only overlap was lunch on the Lido deck, which was far too large and crazy for us to ever see each other. Only two short hours between lunch and dinner were available for together time, but those were dedicated to sleep. Such naps were most necessary, because after months of hard labor and only four hours of sleep a night, a body required more rest.

On average, I saw Bianca less than fifteen minutes a day.

In the beginning we found ways to show our affection. The next day, for example, I found Bianca in the Lido's walk-in cooler. I closed the door behind us and kept it locked by retaining a tight grip on the inside handle. With my free hand I grabbed Bianca's vest, pulled her to me, and indulged in some of the hottest, wettest kisses ever. Love among the lettuce! It amazed me how much balm for my fevered soul lay in her lips.

I had no idea I was such a romantic. She whispered how much she missed that, and I did too. It was a fun, yet tender, moment.

It was about all we got.

We worked easily twelve hours a day, seven days a week, and with opposing schedules we may as well have been continents apart. Soon the only sign of Bianca—other than stories by shared friends—were the breakfast trays she snuck into the cabin while I was sleeping. As the days went by, she became less and less talkative. Within a month of my arrival, her entire focus was work and only work. As she struggled harder to wake up for breakfast, and harder to wake up for dinner, she struggled less to head into port on rare time off, and less to find time for me.

My new life moved very fast. Much can happen when your very home moves daily to a new nation. Each week, *Conquest* sailed among New Orleans, the Cayman Islands, Jamaica, and Mexico. The excitement of such locations was quickly stifled when you only see them from the Lido deck during work. Snippets of port would be jumped on, regardless of fatigue or the odd hours. This was what it meant to be a sailor, I discovered.

I saw the whole world in those first few weeks, but not because *Conquest* sailed there. I was now a citizen of Carnival, just one of sixty nationalities working and living in close proximity. A few months ago I was stuck behind a desk designing electronic medical records, but now I could be found at a 3 a.m. Filipino birthday party singing karaoke—using my best Elvis voice to sing Tagalog lyrics, no less. You never know your strengths until you get out of your comfort zone!

My new friends shared with me their stories about life in every corner of the world. There was Robertino, the powerful

Croatian haunted by his service as a sniper in the ugly Croatian civil war; or Ketut, the youngest of six Indonesian boys in his family, who worked to get his sister out of the rice paddy and into school. And then there were the women.

Oh, the women!

Fortunately, I recalled Benjamin Franklin's reminder that 'beauty and folly are old companions.' Bianca, too, had warned me that ships were an adult playground. No problem. I was painfully far from prudish. What was new to me—very new!— was being objectified as a source of financial freedom. I was the only American crew member and, thusly, the only vehicle to a fabled Green Card. I received a great deal of attention from a bevy of beautiful women from all over the planet. This was no doubt a big part of why I was finding joy in my new life on ships, despite the long hours, cramped living conditions, and growing distance with Bianca.

My assistant at dinner, Rasa, a pretty blonde from Lithuania, nightly offered herself for a good time. Even Vio approached me every time she was on the downswing of her on-again, off-again relationship with Adrien. Then there were the literally dozens of women whom I had never even met who found me and offered all manner of... things... for a chance at living in America. A worldwide smorgasbord of babes. A teenage dream come true? More like a nightmare.

Worse, if one could call it such, was my new best friend, Liezle. I had first met this lovely young Slovakian in Carnival college. She, too, had been assigned *Conquest* to join a lover, so we had travelled from *Fantasy* together. As a testament to how insanely gorgeous she was, at the airport she had been accosted by a model scout for lingerie ads. 'nuf said. While we were just friends working together on midnight buffet, we were becoming quite close through a shared disappointment with our lovers onboard. A risky situation, to be sure, in an environment so cold that the need for contact was very real, sexual or otherwise.

And how cold could the dining room be! Pleasing guests with all their foibles day in and day out was hard enough, but the dog-eat-dog world behind the scenes was dehumanizing. At dinner, waiters stood guard over silverware and flatware, lest they be stolen by roving packs of foreign waiters for their own stations. Nationalities banded together in groups called mafias, in order to better protect themselves and their property. This survival of the fittest, this Pancake Darwinism, was never more raw than during breakfast. Waiters squabbled over hash browns like hyenas fighting over scraps stolen from a lion's kill. At sea, all warriors are cold warriors.

Such life took a toll on sanity. Oh, it was maddening! Months of Pancake Darwinism made Bianca live wary, like a cornered animal. She obviously needed some warmth more than ever, but refused to focus on anything but finishing her contract. Words of comfort hastily exchanged while changing uniforms lack oomph. Certainly romance was out of the question, and we couldn't even share something as simple and comforting as a nap together, due to our tiny bunks.

Indeed, Bianca had switched fully into survival mode: all work and no play. Any pretense or appearance of being a wild and free party animal was gone. She was paying the piper for a house for her parents, for lavish vacations, for our torrid love affair across three continents. I wanted desperately to make the latter real every day, and not just a vacation fantasy. But I was new to ships, delighted at the vast differences from land life and still physically and emotionally fresh. Bianca had already spent years working her fingers to the bone, and in order to stave off despondency, had trained herself to shut off emotion when at sea.

5

Finally the time came for Bianca to sign off for a vacation mid-contract. She was a wreck. Her emotions were taut as a bowstring, her body fatigued beyond endurance. Even her hands were split open from the constant cleaning necessary for ship restaurants, requiring a prescription cream to help close the wounds.

We argued over her last lunch off in port. I wanted to spend Cozumel alone with her, and thought it justified considering how much I had altered my life to be with her. She had insisted on lunch with all of her paisanos—fellow countrymen—at their favorite restaurant, La Ceiba. She wanted to thank them for helping her through a tough contract. I reluctantly joined them, but was mostly ignored. They laughed at jokes in Romanian. I spoke English words of endearment to my octopus ceviche.

After lunch the group split, and I barely managed to carry Bianca off for a little personal time on the beach. We lay in the sun but said little. Now that she was alone with me she was quiet, as if she had used up her allotted laughter over lunch. Visions of her silence in Egypt came back to me, but this time I had no chance of luring her into conversation under threat of Bela.

"Do you still want me to go to Romania in June?" I finally asked, referring to our early arrangements to coincide our time off together. Crew were allowed an unpaid work break in the middle of their contract, so I would at least be able to share a few weeks with her while she was on vacation. But I didn't know if I really wanted to go or not.

How ironic! The only thing on this sweat-ship I didn't enjoy was being with Bianca! I felt far more love and affection from our emails when we were apart. I wanted her to get off the ship. Maybe the emails would allow me to return to our fantasy love affair again.

She did not immediately answer. She was saved the trouble when her friends arrived. Suddenly all smiles, Bianca invited them to join us. Lunch replayed. I left.

It all came to a head later that night in the crew bar— Bianca'a last night aboard. I snuck out of my post at midnight buffet and rushed down to the crew deck to find her. I grabbed her, tugged her into a dark corner of the crew bar, and began my interrogation. There was no more time for delay, and no way I was going to let her leave without getting her to talk.

"What is going on in your mind?" I asked roughly. "I don't want to make any assumptions about anything, and I don't want to be disappointed this June in Romania. Was this all a bad mistake? Do you really think it could possibly be the way it was before you ignored me here on *Conquest*?"

"Yes," she answered shortly, "In Romania."

"In Romania," I repeated, rather harshly. "On vacation."

"Not here," she pleaded. "I felt my grumpiness beginning just before you arrived. I was worried this would happen with us."

"Oh, that's nice. Thanks for the warning," I said, mocking her. "Honey, change your life entirely and work like a slave, and maybe there's a small chance I won't turn into an ice queen.' What, are you training to be a judge in Romania? I really am stupid."

"I'm sorry," she said weakly. "I know I'm different on the ships. Is the ships! I turn off all emotion here, is how I survive. I hate the ships and the life so much, and happiness just doesn't belong here. I even yelled at Vio this morning because she's in love with Adrien again and they are so happy and bubbly. And you! You are always happy! Always. I hate that."

I stared at her, incredulous. "You are mad at me? Because I am happy? What the hell is that?"

"You are always so patient and understanding with me, and you never lose your sense of humor. How can you never let anything make you mad?"

"Who says I don't?"

"Come to Romania. Is all planned already, let me make it up to you there. We can rekindle the magic! It was so amazing how we met, our trip to Egypt, please don't let this be the end. Though I... I no blame you."

I sighed. "I don't want it to be the end, either, but this is absurd."

"Come to Romania and let's forget these ten weeks ever happened. It will be your thirtieth birthday. I take you to the Black Sea."

I looked at her, torn. She was saying exactly what I wanted to hear, but was I just being foolish? I did want to go to Romania. I did want to find what he had before. Was it possible? I knew there was only one way to find out.

**6**

The crew bar of *Carnival Conquest* provided a tantalizing glimpse into the seedy, disreputable drinking establishments one imagined near the wharves in a port town. Copious amounts of cigarette smoke tarnished the inadequate lighting, creating dark recesses with dark forms and foreign tongues. One corner was brightened by a cluster of Italians in officer's whites, another a shifting blur of Filipinos in boiler suits, and centered was a large, raucous group of Romanian waiters with unbuttoned vests. These last were the loudest, but who smoked the most was clearly open to debate.

With so little free time on ships, I was at first surprised the bar was so heavily populated. Yet this lack of time was precisely what fueled its patronage. The stress and excitement of working two dinner seatings nightly kept one buzzing far after the final napkin fold. The resulting mix of exhaustion and adrenaline lingered longer than waiters could afford, considering breakfast was at most a mere six hours away. A few shots of alcohol was an easy method of accelerating relaxation.

And cheap, as it turned out. Crew members were exempt from the customs-related headaches guests endured, allowing duty-free liquor to be enjoyed below the waterline. The crew bar, too, offered excellent prices. I was probably the only American onboard offered a bottle of Corona for merely one dollar. Add to this the presence at the bar of the 'crew store'— the only onboard source for buying pre-packaged noodles for the Asians and cigarettes for everyone—and a robust clientele was guaranteed.

I was not a fan of the crew bar. This does not imply a less-than-hearty appetite for alcohol. That would be sheer folly. But loitering at the crew bar largely meant either seeking a new cabin-mate for the night or commiseration with paisanos. I had no intention of hooking up with anybody if not Bianca—despite the outlandish proposals—and I had no paisanos.

Fellow countrymen tended to group together at the end of a tough day. The urge to discuss shared tribulations in one's native language was understandable. Most groups responded to the presence of an outsider with English, of course, but for some reason the Romanians eschewed this courtesy. I had initially tried to join Bianca with the Romanian mafia, but found myself ignored, lonely among others. There was nothing to do but drink.

Because I worked midnight buffet, most nights I ran straight up to the Lido deck anyway. Isolated as I had become in the weeks prior to Bianca's vacation, I felt prying her from boisterous paisanos would be selfish. She obviously needed them. As each day's fatigue cast a shadow deeper into the next, Bianca's joy retreated accordingly. By the end, her smile only showed amid Romanian laughter.

It hurt that I was unable to provide the comfort she required, but I understood. I was a new addition to a difficult routine hammered out ungainly over several contracts. Ship life was tough, very tough, and who was I to waltz in fresh and demand she give up the only thing that had allowed her to cope over the years? When living on the edge, even small pushes must be considered before being enacted. I felt so very, very sorry for my Bianca.

Alone as I had felt among the Romanian mafia, I was not the sole outsider. Surprisingly, Dan joined them every night. He, too, sat ignored among the jabbering, puffing Romanians. He, too, had nothing to do but drink—and he was a recovered alcoholic! The night after Bianca signed off, he waved me over.

"Have a seat," he said, gesturing. Smoke arced from his burning cigarette. The seat beside him was cleared instantly, without his saying a word, as Vio took the opportunity to hop into Adrien's lap. Dan took a slug from a can of Red Bull— probably his twentieth of the night.

"I am ready to clear your work break," Dan said. "You'll come back as a full assistant maitre d', training done. But you know the break won't look good. You sure you want to do it?"

He was right, of course. Bianca had fought tooth and nail to convince Carnival management that I could handle the work load. Now, only halfway into my first contract, I was asking for time off. My reasons had nothing to do with Carnival's big fear —that I would quit—but they had no way of knowing it, nor reason to believe it if they did. I wanted to reassure Carnival that an American could handle ships, but that was not my priority.

"Can I ask you a question?" I said suddenly, "Everyone says you're a recovered alcoholic. You're in a bar with cheap booze, surrounded by people ignoring you. So why are you here?"

Dan gave me a sly grin and said, "Recovered? What's that? I am an alcoholic, whether I drink or not. So was my father, and his father. Hell, we're Irish. I was happy to live in the past. I kept it close, hid it, didn't talk about it. I had a problem. When I finally chose to deal with my past head-on, that's when I overcame it."

Dan smashed out his cigarette and lit another.

"A little advice for you, mate," Dan said, squinting as he took a long drag. "Everybody comes to ships because they're running from something. Everybody, whether they know it or not. Some of us clam up to ourselves, to our loved ones. Others face it. I sit in a bar because the temptation is less than when I'm hiding, alone, in my cabin."

He watched the smoke from his cigarette join the cloud that rolled along the ceiling.

"It only looks bad to those who don't know," he finished. "But they ain't fighting my fight. For me, it's the right thing to do."

"Thank you," I said. "That answers my question. And yours as well."

# CHAPTER TEN

## *In the Hall of the Mustard King*

### 1

DESPITE CONCERNS REGARDING   Bianca's and my initial failure as a couple, I was excited about another visit to Romania. Further, signing off a cruise ship, whether you enjoyed your work or not, was an enervating experience. The awareness of approaching freedom was profound, the anticipation heady. My sense of adventure had been tweaked to such a pitch, in fact, I even delivered a rather humiliating strip tease to guests in the dining room on my last night as a waiter. Sometimes you gotta do what you gotta do.

Bianca greeted me at the airport with a loving embrace and no indication that anything had ever gone wrong between us. I enthusiastically went with it. With three weeks granted for my work break, there would be plenty of time to get to the bottom of our *Conquest* misstep. Even without seeing Bianca's cheeky smile, Romania in June seemed as fine a place to be as any I could imagine. The weather was simply marvelous, with sun and warmth aplenty.

The drive out of Bucharest was far better this time around than my first. Bianca had released her inner angry donut regarding her nation's capital. She was so bubbly, in fact, I secretly wondered if she was sucking up. But when Albişoara chugged out of the plains and into the verdant foothills of the southern Carpathians, I began to understand Bianca's almost euphoric happiness.

The land stretched away in row upon row of richly forested mountains behind field after field of meadows. The countryside was refreshingly unmarred by civilization and filled with green, green, green. Countless acres just sat there, waiting to be viewed and enjoyed, not exploited. Urban sprawl was foreign. This made the cities crowded, but out here the tall grasses rippled in the breeze, making the world shimmer like a mirage. It was so idyllic that I nearly forgot about the weapon in the glovebox.

And we talked. Oh, how wonderful it was to communicate with my Bianca! By the end of *Conquest*, she had become nearly mute. Now she couldn't stop talking about the beauty of summer in Transylvania, how Lucky had planted a million and a half flowers around the house in Sighişoara, and how exciting it would be to help me celebrate my 30th birthday vacationing on the Black Sea.

"I'm so glad my parents are living in the house in Sighişoara now," Bianca commented with a proud wiggle behind the wheel. "The apartment in Braşov was home for a long time, but it will stay empty until we sell it. Besides, you'll like living in the house so much better than in the apartment."

"As long as Piti brings those TV guides with the topless women, I'll be happy anywhere."

"Babaloo," she chided. Then she added with a smirk, "At least in the house we have our own bedroom."

"Oh, before I forget," she added suddenly. "I got your gift for my parents. I wanted it to be something special to celebrate your return. They are very excited, you know."

"We all are," I agreed. "What did we get them?"

"An electric lawnmower."

"An electric lawnmower?" I repeated, surprised. "With a cord? Wouldn't you, you know, run over the cord or something?"

"As careful as my father is?" Bianca replied. "It takes him five minutes to arrange tomatoes on his plate."

Summer Sighişoara was even more awe-inspiring than the countryside. Every drop of sunlight not greedily snatched up by blooming trees gleamed off the cobblestone streets. I was nearly blinded by reflections off the towering white cathedral on the banks of the river Târnava. Albişoara rattled up the bricks to the old town and turned onto Strada Crişan. Bianca's house at the end was blocked from view by a neighbor's cherry tree, which was exploding with ripe fruit. Above all rose the plateau, where even the ancient oaks beamed with renewed life.

Amazingly, I think the parents Pop were happier to see me than even Bianca. They were giddy with excitement, as were we all after several glasses of ţuica. Lucky had prepared quite a feast for our arrival, which was most welcome after so long a journey. We had driven straight through to Sighişoara, which was no small hop after flying from New Orleans to New York to Frankfort to Bucharest on two hours of sleep. We ate similar pigs, then after the sun set went outside to enjoy the stars and —more importantly—the wine. Piti's homemade stuff went down fast, unhindered by any dubious additives such as Coca Cola.

At one point while fetching something, I happened to notice on the refrigerator a number of magnetic letter 'P's. Most had little palm trees and beach scenes with them, but one magnet was a Carnival ship with the letter 'P' in the clouds above it.

"What are these?" I asked Bianca.

She laughed. "Oh, those are for Pop. I send one to my parents each contract from somewhere cool.

Lucky, noting our conversation, stepped forward and said, "Check! Las Vegas."

Sure enough, one letter 'P' was nestled amid the skyline of the Las Vegas Strip.

"Remember how I left Las Vegas early for you?" Bianca asked.

I did, indeed. Just after we first met in Reno, by accident, really, Bianca had cut short her trip to Las Vegas in order to spend more time with me. How's that for sacrifice?

The four of us laughed and shared recollections of our previous time together. Eventually Bianca remembered her parents' gift, and asked me to retrieve it from Albişoara's trunk. I complied, despite extreme lethargy. I was not prepared for the ensuing excitement.

Piti was thrilled beyond belief at the lawn mower. He was so enthused, in fact, that he nearly spun in circles like a Dervish. In one alcohol-induced, frenzied motion, Piti rushed into the house, returned with his cowboy hat, plugged in the lawnmower, pushed it into the dark backyard, abandoned it, jumped into Albişoara, backed her out of the garage, oriented her headlights to illumine the yard, and returned to his new toy. He started mowing. It was 10 p.m.

"Think we should stop him?" I asked. "Mowing while drunk doesn't seem too wise. I know somebody who cut open his foot doing that."

"When Dad's drunk, he does some crazy things," Bianca admitted. "I remember one winter he and my Godfather slid down Tâmpa beneath the funicular."

"That's like a thousand feet almost straight down!"

"Da," Bianca agreed. "And had they no been naked, I think my mother would have been impressed. Instead she had to spoon feed him chicken soup and boiled țuica for a week."

I thought a cold sounded vastly preferable to boiled țuica, but kept that to myself.

After Lucky had successfully hauled Piti back in the house and to bed, Bianca and I sat on her porch swing and listened to the crickets serenade each other. We did the same. I abandoned my impatience to discuss our failed first stab at a relationship. We were too busy talking about everything else in the world. When 3 a.m. came, I was exhausted but not sleepy—New Orleans time was eight hours earlier. But that was not the reason for our late night. Whenever Bianca and I got to talking, hours passed like minutes. Eventually she left, returning in her pajamas.

"Ah, the Thousand Lips Pajamas," I said. "I guess that means the night is over."

With a quirk of her lips, she undid the buttons of her pajama shirt, revealing black lingerie hidden beneath.

"These were a deception," she said, dropping her pajamas to the floor.

At noon the next day, Piti's cucurigu woke us. Sunlight streamed into the bedroom, and I marveled that we had slept through such a glorious, noisy morning. The birds in the trees outside our window were doing their damnedest to simulate a Mötley Crüe concert. After Bianca rose and groggily shuffled away, I lingered in bed, ruminating. The ships were so vastly different from real life that those months felt like a dream. Surely I hadn't left here eight months ago, had I? Somehow, I belonged here and felt like I was home. What did that mean?

Bianca seemed practiced at moving forward as if nothing was wrong, and perhaps I could afford to do so for a short time, too. Would that be so bad, to just relax and enjoy myself for a while? I didn't want to lie to myself. I deplored lying, but was it the same crime when directed inward? How could I justify months of uncertainty disappearing with one look at her rosy apple cheeks? I was such a sap.

But I didn't want to justify anything. I was there, and that's where I wanted to be. I resolved to go with the flow and enjoy myself until I felt it necessary to reign things back to reality.

Which was that afternoon.


# 2


"Câine rau," I said, noting the sign on the metal door before us. As was so common in Romania, the property was completely hidden behind tall, battered walls. We waited before a regular doorway set beside a double-wide metal gate. The street was also double wide, an unhappy combination of old bricks repaired with unsightly slabs of concrete. Unlike Strada Crişan, which enjoyed the ample trees and pedigree of the old town, this area was far more spartan. The moment we buzzed for entry, the quiet of the street was rent by frenzied howling from an entire pack of dogs. Big dogs, from the sound of them.

We heard an irritated shout ordering the dogs to be quiet, then several clicks as numerous locks were undone. Sorin Miere, the Mustard King, opened the door. It was a hot day, so he wore shorts and a T-shirt. His lengthy forehead glistened with sweat.

"Welcome to my factory!" he cried with delight. He rushed Bianca and gave her an exceptionally big hug and mucho kisses—no doubt taking advantage of his wife's momentary absence. Sorin then turned to me, shook my hand, and gave me a kiss on each cheek.

He led us inside to what was actually a small compound. We crossed a large court of brick, defined by a tall stone wall on the left and a large structure on the right. The looming building evidently doubled as both house and factory. The near end was brick and pleasantly dressed with clinging grapevines and hanging flower pots, whereas the bulk extending into the distance was plain concrete. At the far end, several hundred feet away, were large trees shading a huge pen holding back monstrous dogs. They jumped high up their fenced enclosure, snapping and snarling. They most certainly did *not* say 'ham ham'.

"Shut up!" Sorin shouted once again, to no avail. He looked up at me and shrugged his shoulders in defeat.

"They excellent guard dogs," he explained sheepishly. "Friendly after you feed them. We let them free at night hungry."

While the entire complex was not luxurious, it definitely radiated success. Sorin beamed at me when I commented upon it.

"We do fairly well," he said with a modesty proven false by his constant need to giggle. "Come! I introduce you to my parents."

We strode across the bricks towards a smoking grill and a cluster of people. Piti and Lucky, who had arrived earlier, were talking to another couple of their approximate age. Moni and daughter Corina had just arrived from the kitchen bearing heaps of meat ready for the grill. It was the most beautiful sight I had yet seen in this summer-washed country.

"My father," Sorin introduced. "He is Bianca's Godfather. He was colonel in army when Piti was... *cum zici*... sergeant? Yes, sergeant."

A solid man with bold, flowing white hair stepped forward curtly. His girth was impressive, almost rotund, and his bearing that of a man used to being in charge. He shook my hand heartily, then grabbed my head and forced it down to kiss both my cheeks. Mrs. Miere was a shy, petite woman who could easily have been Lucky's sister.

"Wow," I commented. "A colonel!"

"Bah!" he said, gathering my sentiment. Via translator, he dismissed his rank with a comment that 'everyone has a superior officer, including colonels.'

Then Colonel Miere proceeded to step back and overtly scrutinize me. Everyone went quiet. Finally he said something to Piti that made everyone laugh. It's always unnerving when everyone is laughing at you and you don't know why.

With a wary smile I asked, "What did he say?"

Sorin stifled his giggles to answer. "He said 'if everyone is as big as you, is good we never went to war with America.'"

Only then did I realize that everyone around me was lucky to reach even five foot six.

Despite protestations that he was 'a normal guy', the colonel began barking orders. Bianca was ordered to give him a kiss. Moni was ordered to place the meat on a table. Piti and Sorin were ordered to grill it. All the women were then ordered into the kitchen to prepare food. Corina was ordered to bring me a beer. Everyone complied with alacrity.

Before grilling, I observed Piti preparing the grill in a manner I did not recognize. Using a long fork, he had stabbed a slab of something and was running it lovingly over the hot grate. Fat dripped into the coals with a satisfying pop and sizzle.

"What the hell is that?"

"*Slanina*," Sorin answered. He referred to a series of odd-shaped slabs of mottled white and dark gold. One side had been scored to make them look like fatty little combs.

"Is smoked fat."

"I beg your pardon?"

"Smoked fat of pig," he repeated. "Goes good on grill. Excellent with eggs, also. Like your... bacon, but no meat."

I stared at the slabs in wonder. They were indeed nothing more than a thick slice of skin with a couple inches of fat still attached. How most Romanians could remain so skinny while eating pure fat was a marvel.

I was particularly fascinated by the meat. There were piles of chubby, linked sausages and mounds of long, coiled sausages that easily measured over two feet had they been unfurled. The largest stack of skinless sausages I did not recognize at all.

"What are those?" I asked Sorin.

"Ahh," he said. "*Mititei.* Very good."

He looked at me helplessly for a moment. His limited English had evidently reached its end. Before he could find a way to respond, his father took over.

"Corina!" he barked forcefully. The dogs in the pen had nuthin' on the colonel.

Seconds later Corina came out of the house and pounded across the bricks to stand at attention. Colonel Miere obviously ordered her to fetch Bianca. Also obvious was that he need not have bothered. Bianca heard him clearly from inside the kitchen, where Corina had been. Bianca approached, holding a sweating bottle of beer and asked, "What is it?"

The colonel instructed her to 'educate Mr. Brown about mititei.'

"Oh, you'll love them," Bianca said, complying. "They are sausage rolls of lamb, pork, and beef. They are mixed with paprika, dill, salt, garlic, and... soda of baking I think you call it. We mix them with love and chill for a few hours before grilling so they fatten up. They are eaten with mustard and beer."

"Mustard, of course!" I agreed, giving Sorin a grin.

Eventually we settled around a long table under a shady tree. It was heaped with all manner of wonderful things: tomatoes beading refreshingly cool, grilled meats steaming deliciously hot. I chose a seat beside a half wheel of chalky, semi-hard cheese, but was interrupted by the colonel, who directed where everyone was to sit.

"Piti, Lucky!" he said, thrusting a finger to the chairs at his right.

"Sorin, Moni!" he followed curtly, pointing across the table.

"Bree-ahn, Bianca—"

"Colonel!" his wife snapped.

He stopped in mid-sentence, ran a sheepish hand through his white mane, and quietly sat down. Corina giggled. Sorin looked like he wanted to, but after a glance at his mollified father, wisely kept himself to a smile.

The whole meal was fantastic, but the mititei were absolutely divine. I had multiple food-gasms of the highest order. Afterwards I seriously considered asking for a cigarette. I couldn't stop talking about those mititei. They were unlike anything I had ever had before, both juicy and almost puffy-plump. Bianca, pleased at my enjoyment, heaped different mustards on my plate in which to dip the sausages. I particularly liked the one with horseradish.

Bianca recommended, "If you like the horseradish mustard, before taking a bite of mititei, nibble on a puppy."

She placed a clove of garlic on my plate.

"What's this?"

"A puppy."

"I don't want to eat a puppy," I whined. "The Hell Hounds are mad enough."

"Babaloo, that's what we call one little garlic. If you no want, eat a red."

"What's a red?"

"A red," she repeated, gesturing to a tomato.

"You call them reds? How creative. Why not call a banana a yellow?"

"No, she calls you a brown," Sorin joined in, snorting with laughter.

"And what you call oranges, eh bambo?" Bianca finished. "You can't eat only meat and cheese, is not good for you."

"She says to the giant among Lilliputians," I added wryly, finishing her sentence for her.

The banter continued, while the colonel observed that he was not surprised I enjoyed the mititei so much. Since the renewal of hostilities in the Persian Gulf, a sizable American military force had been stationed in Romania. Many of the soldiers expressed a preference for mititei, claiming it surpassed even their love of cheeseburgers. While distressingly unpatriotic, I certainly understood the sentiment.

After dinner, the men settled into the cigarettes and the women settled into the kitchen. I offered to help with the dishes, but was roundly refused. There was simply no fighting the established gender roles. Instead, Corina asked if I would play badminton with her in the courtyard. With a stomach groaning under the weight of smoked pig fat and raw puppies, I doubted I could handle her youthful zeal.

But I readied myself to be trounced by a child, sitting on a bench and tying my shoes a bit tighter. I snapped a lace. Immediately I looked around. Fortunately Bianca had not seen it. The colonel had. He threw up his hands and joked disparagingly to Piti something about 'bringing Rambo to my house.'

After twenty minutes of playing badminton with Corina, I was mercifully relieved by Bianca.

"Order my father to take over in ten minutes," Bianca said. "My godfather will get a kick out of you giving orders. But not to him, of course. Oh, and could you also ask my father to bring me lemon for my tea?"

As I walked over to Piti and the two Miere men, I nervously mouthed what words I knew in their language. I wanted to try my tongue at Romanian, but didn't have a clue how to order anyone anywhere. Fortunately I knew how to ask Piti for lemons.

Or so I thought.

Romanian words tumbled from my lips. I thought they sounded pretty good, and stood up a bit straighter. Piti did, too. He positively bristled, in fact.

A yawning silence answered my statement. Even the dogs stopped barking. All three men stared at me, mouths agape. I looked back quizzically.

"*Lamâie!*" Bianca shrieked from across the courtyard. She dropped her racquet to run over and cover Corina's ears. "It's lamâie! Not lamooyay."

"Lamooyay," I called back, not hearing any difference. "That's what I said!"

Bianca's face turned red, as if she were having a heart attack. She was anything but incapacitated, however. She stormed forward, shouting accusingly, "It's the 'A' with the hat on it! You no hear the difference?"

Sorin erupted in giggles powerful enough to knock him from his seat. The colonel looked confused, whereas Piti just stared into space, dumbstruck.

"All right," I demanded. "What's so funny about me mispronouncing 'lemon'?"

Rather than answer, Bianca's eyes fell on Piti. She squeaked and scampered away.

"You wanted to ask Piti for lemons for Bianca?" Sorin asked, spluttering with uncontrollable mirth.

"Yes," I snapped impatiently. "Was my pronunciation really that bad?"

Sorin glanced to make sure his daughter was out of earshot, and explained, "Your accent was very good, in fact. Your Romanian was perfect."

"Well, what then?" I asked, vexed.

"You ask his OK for oral sex with his daughter!"

### 3

"I suggest tour of my mustard factory now," Sorin said, giggling. "You are lucky Piti is retired, or he would probably shoot you."

"I think escape is a great idea," I agreed.

"Is nothing much," Sorin said of his factory as we walked towards the back of the family structure. "But is enough."

He led me through room after room, each with concrete floors and several with drains set in the center. Mostly they were large and empty, as there was nobody working today. Each room had some sort of large machine dominating one wall and a long line of laminate counters. He illustrated the various machines used for different levels of grind, from fine for the mustard seeds to loose for the horseradish. It all looked quite simple, actually. The plastic jars were purchased in bulk, of course, then filled by hand and labeled accordingly. One chamber was devoted to exploring differing product lines of soda.

"I have five... employees," Sorin said. "One is delivery man. Twice a week I deliver also, and my father takes over here."

"I'll bet the employees like it better when you are boss," I teased. He snickered in agreement.

"Is this the premium, or something?" I asked, referring to a plastic-wrapped stack of flats loaded with jars ready for delivery. They were labeled with MIERE across the front.

"Why you ask?"

"It has your name on it, but the others do not."

Sorin laughed. "Oh, no, is honey mustard."

I frowned. "I don't understand."

"In my language, my name means 'honey,'" he explained.

I started laughing. "You mean I've been terrorized by Colonel Honey?"

We poked our heads into the final chamber, a large store room, and were surprised to see Piti and the colonel. They waved us over, and the colonel barked at Sorin. He nodded enthusiastically.

"He says tell you he gave you one case of mustard with horseradish. Is in your car."

"Oh, that's not necessary," I replied. "Very kind of you, though."

"Is done," Sorin said. "Besides, Piti likes. I don't think you will get any."

The colonel was musing over a wall of heavy shelves loaded with numerous plastic bottles. I recognized them as the same bottles as the sunflower oil Lucky used for cooking her fantastic meals.

"You produce sunflower oil, too?" I asked.

"No," Sorin said, growing excited. "We produce țuica."

"Hot damn!"

"The best țuica is always made at home," he continued. "My father is... expert. We distill in our house in Moldova. I hope to show you sometime."

"Suddenly I'm scared."

"Yes!" Sorin agreed. "We sell also, of course, but save the best for family. Some is very, very... powerful. Danger in good way."

The older fathers were busy admiring the various shelves, and only then did I see they were labeled. I gathered that the newer 'vintages' were on the bottom, but as the levels rose, so, too, did the age. The higher shelves had an increasingly smaller number of contents, with the very top graced by only three dusty bottles. The colonel pulled up a stool and lumbered up to grab one of these last.

He dropped down with a pant, and called to me in his usual, forceful manner, "Mr. Brown!"

The colonel presented the bottle to me, stating something with a voice that was probably as kindly as he was capable. There was still a hint that sounded more dangerous than even homemade moonshine.

"For you," Sorin translated. "Is ten years old."

"Oh, no, no," I demurred. "I couldn't. There's only three left!"

"He says is because you are the first man of his Goddaughter's that he... approves."

I took the bottle and thanked him. It was not easy to swallow for guilt. Here I was accepting a 'welcome to the family' gesture, when it remained to be seen if I was going to walk away from the entire affair.

# 4

"We need to talk," I said.

"Not now," Bianca replied hastily. "The train is almost here."

"On the train, then."

"No, bamboclat, when we get to the Black Sea!"

"Fine, fine," I said, acquiescing. I glanced around the bustling train station and asked, "Where is the restroom? I want to go before we get on the train."

"Oh, no!" Bianca cried, scandalized. "Can't you hold it?"

"I'm a boy-person boy, Bianca," I replied sarcastically. "Being scared of public restrooms is a girl-person thing."

"Is not that," Bianca pleaded. "Number one or number two?"

"Are you my mother now?"

"Will you shut up?" Bianca snapped. "You no seen public toilets in Romania. They horrible, papa! There is so much wonderful things to see in my country, but the structure is so bad that people take one look at the public toilets and leave. They no talk about Peleş Castle or the monasteries of Moldova: only the communist public toilets."

"Can't be worse than those in Egypt," I soothed. "I'll keep my expectations low."

Bianca sniffed indignantly.

Inside the entrance to the men's room, I was accosted by a fat, hairy woman of undecided age but decided filth. Darker skin hinted at her being a Gypsy, corroborated by an utter contempt for personal hygiene or unsoiled clothing. She sat heavily upon a tall, broken stool like a bloated frog on a sick mushroom. She was actually inside the men's room with me.

The woman croaked something to me not in Romanian, but the Gypsy language Roma, then reached out a claw holding a damp, crumpled roll of toilet paper bereft of an inner cardboard tube. I ignored her and poked my head into the only stall.

The horror... the horror!

Because Romania is firmly a part of the West, I was shocked to see that there was no toilet at all. Instead was a creepy, filthy hole in the floor. Arranged around it, Arab-style, were two impressions indicating where your feet should go in order to squat over the hole, should you be wearing a kaftan. Both patterns were filled with urine.

Not surprisingly, there was no toilet paper.

I returned to the grotesque woman reluctantly. With great dread I stared at the hand waggling toilet paper at me. Her fingernails had not been trimmed since the revolution. Surely not washed, either. I grimaced as I held out a US dollar with my fingertips.

She greedily snatched the money up in a blink, then began unfurling the thin roll of paper. With one eye clamped shut, she squinted with the other at her work. How she could peer past the huge, hairy mole above her eye was a mystery. Finally she tugged off three delicate squares of paper—so thin as to have only one side—and handed them to me.

Pride be damned. I fled.

For the first time, I was glad Bianca didn't want to talk. For the next several hours I was unable to speak.

5

When imagining Romania, most people do not picture seaside resorts and spas. This is no doubt due to the overbalancing emphasis on vampire pop culture. In fact, Romania's Black Sea coast has been celebrated since Roman times. Ample archeological evidence supports this, and so does the big-ass statue of the Roman poet Ovid. As we all know, he was exiled in 8 A.D. by Emperor Augustus and died in what is now Constanța. Duh. Lest we forget, Ovid was the wise man who observed, "A woman is a creature that is always shopping." Another duh, but he was the first man with the guts to actually say it in public.

Romania's main Black Sea resorts filed along nearly fifty miles of sandy beaches, dispersed among towns named after Roman gods, cool names like Venus, Jupiter, Saturn, Neptun, as well as Olimp—presumably for Mount Olympus. The resorts lining the coast were spacious and modern, with even a few Art Deco-designed hotels thrown in the mix. After enduring block after block of bloc, this was most refreshing.

Still, while reminding me of Miami Beach, the Black Sea most certainly was not. Everything was a percentage less perfect: the sand generally not as soft, the weather generally not as warm, the surf generally not as calm, and—most distressingly—the bikinis not generally as small. I was assuaged on the latter point by the fact that most of them did not include tops.

A friend of Bianca's, having retired from Carnival after earning a position as head chef of a hotel in Saturn, got us a great deal. Saturn was a tired mid-fifties town, less impressive than the heady luxury of Olimp, for example, but our Romanian-style discount more than made up for it. Our room was on the top floor overlooking the sea, which broke with alarming strength not twenty yards outside our balcony.

Early on the morning of Friday the 13th, I was awakened from my slumber by Bianca—in only her bra and panties—attacking me with an entire cake.

"Happy Birthday!" she cried, juggling the cake awkwardly to prevent it from sliding out of its sagging cardboard box.

"What the...?" I began groggily, then leapt out of bed as the box slipped from her grasp. The cake plopped upside-down onto my still-warm pillow.

"Jesus Gras, woman!" I exclaimed, hopping about naked in an effort to keep my bare feet off the cold tiles.

Bianca burst out laughing.

"I turn thirty on Friday the 13th," I muttered indignantly. "And wake up to my lover trying to smother me to death."

"Sorry," she said, laughing. "I wanted to surprise you."

"You sure did!"

"Eh," she scoffed. "Romanian box. Damn it, I wanted to show you his face. He was beautiful."

I stepped closer to examine the ruined cake. The crumpled mess revealed a yellow cake with chocolate frosting.

"Well," I commented, "The bottom looks great. I've been guilty of judging by that alone."

I scooped up a finger-full of frosting and streaked it across her bare belly.

"Bamboclat!" she cried, grabbing a handful of cake and smashing it against my chest. Heavy gobs of chocolate dripped messily from my rather aggressive chest hair. I grabbed Bianca and threw her on the bed. The resulting food fight was far more satisfying than, say, those at grade school in the cafeteria. Afterwards, we lay in the begrimed bed and waited for our panting to subside. Like the sheets and pillows, we were covered entirely in chocolate and crumbled yellow cake.

"I hope you liked your birthday present better than my cousin did on her birthday," Bianca commented.

"You know what I want for my birthday?" I asked dreamily, staring at the ceiling.

"What?"

"You to pay the extra tip for the room steward to clean this up."

# 6

The days were quite hot, which implied much considering I just came from the Caribbean. The Black Sea itself, however, was excruciatingly cold. We were just catching the very earliest of the season. So less time was spent on the beach and more in the cafés. This suited us both just fine.

A striking difference between America and Romania was in the nature of the outdoor cafés. Extending for miles, even linking up the towns, were dozens upon dozens of prime patios overlooking the waves and beaches, surrounded by lush gardens and mature trees—and all of it was damn near free. In America every square foot would have cost a fortune, with the premium spots no doubt hosting expensive restaurants or exclusive clubs. But here they didn't even serve food, and gladly let us stay all day for the price of a Coke. No doubt everything had been built 'for the people' under the communist regime, but I thought someone would have figured out after a decade of capitalism that these were unclaimed gold mines.

The afternoon grew late. We walked along the beach, holding hands on one side, and sandals on the other.

"So," I said. "When I return to *Conquest*, are you going to study to become a judge?"

"What?" Bianca asked, confused.

"On *Conquest* you were colder than Oana the Ice Queen."

Bianca smirked and appeared ready to unleash a jibe of her own, but suddenly thought better of it. She spent several moments to gather her thoughts. I waited patiently, occasionally pushing her further up the beach when the surf surged too close.

"I care for you very, very deeply," Bianca said at last. "I am moved more than you know by you coming back to me. I thought for sure that... that when I left you on *Conquest* you would go ship-style."

"Ship-style?"

"Bang all the chicks."

"Oh, I'm too old for that," I scoffed. "Though it's not like I didn't have temptation."

"You will," Bianca said, staring at the sand. "Is not that you are a man. Is that you are on ships. I know ships, and you don't. Nobody can until they live it. Everyone cheats on ships at least once. Everyone."

"Bianca—"

"Just don't tell me about it," she interrupted. "Just come back to me, here."

"You're blowing me off," I said sternly. "You want me only on your terms, is that it? I want to have a life with you, not a string of vacations. Great sex isn't enough to bring me around the world. Well, not more than twice."

Though she still stared at the sand, I spied a hint of her smirk.

"Look, Bianca," I said more softly. "Every time I see you it's as natural and wonderful as the first time, and not a minute seems to have passed—even though its been months. That is something special, something worth fighting for. We have three weeks together here, but then I have four months on *Conquest* as assistant maitre d', and two months vacation while you're on *Glory*. When I return, as assistant maitre d' I can transfer you to my ship. We know that. The question is whether we both want that. I do."

I paused and looked her in the eye.

"I'm not sure you do. On *Conquest* you weren't ready. It was all crazy fast, I get it. But that was a long time ago. Time's ticking away, Bianca."

Finally Bianca did not shy away.

"One of the things I love about you," she said slowly, "is that, like my parents, you are understanding and patient. They stuck by me thick and thin, when I left for Belgium with my ex."

"You never told me you lived in Belgium," I said, surprised.

"Ten years," she admitted. "My ex was not very kind to my parents. He actually mocked their commitment to me, that they would still talk to me after our... situation. But in the end I left him, and they were still there for me. And like them, you stood by me despite my coldness, despite all things thrown at you."

"But that's what it's all about," I pressed. "I am a simple man, Bianca. Long distance relationships don't work because the whole point is to be together. True, we can't be—yet—but we have a clear path and a set timeline. So until that time, I need communication. When we were on *Conquest*, I never got a single 'stay by me, I love you.' I know you were struggling to survive, but I was there for you. But I won't wait for anybody if they take it for granted."

We scrunched awkwardly over the loose sand. The tide had risen too high to walk on the sea-smoothed edge, and the surf was too cold to endure any more surprise splashes.

"I will do better," Bianca said, squeezing my hand. "I love you, and don't want ships to come between us. Ships gave me and my family a life. Ships brought us together. I won't let them take us apart."

# 7

My transatlantic flight back to New Orleans went by in a blink. All I could think about was Bianca. Particularly, I replayed over and over each morning we woke up together. Her face wrinkled from the sheets and pillows, she woke with a smile and a laugh. Sometimes it was only in her tired eyes, but it always radiated from the inside out. I loved her intensely, and also felt loved. She cared deeply, and what little time she had to give, she gave completely.

I had never lived such a wonderful dream as those last three weeks. They were beyond magical. They were prophetic. How could I endure six months without her? But this was ship life, the life we had chosen. Our vacations were perfect because we paid the piper.

We paid him dearly.

# CHAPTER ELEVEN

## *The Barry White Omnibus*

### 1

RETURNING TO *CONQUEST* was a nightmare. Prior to my leaving on the work break, it was agreed I would return as a full assistant maitre d'. I had the approval of Dan, of course, as well as his boss, the food & beverage manager. However, during my absence they had both signed off. Regardless of promises—including that of *everyone's* boss, Mladen—the new food & beverage manager refused to promote an American into a position of authority, however menial. This was not a supposition: Gunnar told me to my face. Dan's warning had been prescient.

Gunnar and I hammered out an arrangement that the rest of my contract would continue as part maitre d'. That meant a strange half-waiter, half assistant maitre d' hybrid. There were no rules for such an awkward position, and Gunnar devilishly overlapped the two roles in order to undermine my success at either. A setback, to be sure, but I was confident I would win him over.

I was wrong.

Gunnar was Machiavellian in his efforts to get rid of me: he even arranged my schedule to deny me all access to meals, then sent out spies to catch me sneaking food! The upside was that I finally got skinny. I kept a positive attitude through it all, knowing it was just a delay. Further, without having to fret over Bianca's odd behavior, I was able to pursue my own path more freely. I made many friends and enjoyed adventures I had previously only dreamed about.

Yet in the end, despite my best efforts, Gunnar's position never wavered. He refused to have on his record the promotion of a man who he assumed 'would just quit.' His words. International politics swirled around me, whether I liked it or not, as various managers chose sides over this would-be precedent-setting American. A final confrontation resulted in an agreement that I would return from my vacation to another ship, where that food & beverage manager would grant me the stripe of a junior officer. I asked for it in writing, but was denied.

So while I recuperated a couple months with family, Bianca slugged it out with Dan and the rest of the Romanian mafia on a ship prior to an assignment opening Carnival's latest ship in Montfalcone. Our emails kept the fire blazing:

"Reposition cruise, no passengers tonight. After dinner we went to the disco, then we made a crazy Romanian party in a bar, dancing on the tables. At 5.30am we were dragging our sick bodies to the cabins. Lucky me I started at 1pm next day. Lucky everyone, I had a morning face that scared all the mirrors in my cabin."

"I'm still shivering thinking about our nights in RO. I miss you and I want you more and more. I hope I'll be able to keep under control this magnificent feeling, otherwise I will explode, because it keeps on growing since Reno, Brasov, Sighisoara, the Red Sea, the Black Sea... is more and more deep and intense. I'm glad actually to have it, because it gives me joy and power, and some kind of path. It's so fulfilling!"

"I was freezing yesterday in the cabina, and I was missing the way you used to hold me in your arms. It felt so good to fall asleep snuggled against you. Jesus Gras, Brian, once I'll get you, I'll never let you go again. I love the way you love me, the way you smile, you talk, and all I want now is to dive in your dimples."

Returning to Miami, ready for my next assignment, the bottom dropped out. Gunnar had ensured I was demoted to waiter. I tried to go over his head, even storming the home office of Carnival to speak with Mladen himself, but was rebuffed. Carnival policy was total support of on-sight officers while at sea, end of story. To get me out of their hair, I was assigned to *Carnival Legend*, the toughest ship in the fleet: eight day cruises out of New York City, with four days at sea. Even veteran waiters fought to stay off that hell pit. Thus they ensured I would quit.

It was the worst time of my life.

**2**

Only on *Legend* did I truly understand what Bianca went through on ships. My existence, too, became all about survival. I, too, did things I wasn't proud of.

Management was intent on getting rid of me. The foreign employees did not want me setting a precedent and having Americans take away their jobs. Carnival Cruise Lines was a US company, after all, that rarely hired Americans. Thus my side jobs—those extra duties assigned to all waiters—were uncharacteristically harsh, designed to humiliate. When another man was merely required to gather the salad tongs from around the restaurant twice a week, I was forced to scrub and mop several levels of escalators, including walls and even ceilings —every night.

I worked fifteen hours a day, every day, cruise after cruise. Only once in eight days did I receive a lunch off. The hundred hour work weeks kept on coming. I stopped counting after fifteen weeks.

Not only was management out to get me, but fate was, too.

When I finally changed side jobs to something less labor intensive, the Norovirus struck. Suddenly we had special cleaning day and night. My fingers were already cracked and split, so repeated bleaching was simply par for the course. Dozens of crew feigned illness, desperate for the two-day quarantine that allowed merciful rest. Waiters jumped like rats from a sinking ship. One friend requested a transfer to *Inspiration*, two others requested *Fascination*, while yet another left for *Paradise*. I witnessed my friend Xenia crying from the stress, while my partner Ramona—literally nearing an emotional breakdown—had cried herself to sleep for a month.

Everyone was overworked and under appreciated. Ratings for guest satisfaction in the dining rooms plummeted.

*Legend's* response was *more* work.

Because the guests were not having enough fun, waiters were forced into joke and trick training, with additional hour-long sessions learning knock-knock jokes and how to fold paper napkins into little birds. This move was not exactly the morale booster Carnival anticipated.

Lack of proper rest and nutrition, coupled with inane guest requests and pitiful earnings, turned me feral, like a wild animal. Pancake Darwinism made me surly, even aggressive. I stopped talking to everybody and only kept counsel with my diary, into which I poured endless profanity and disdain. Cynicism replaced smiles, laughter lost long ago. I became a zombie, trudging through hour after grueling hour of menial labor for what seemed like no reason at all.

Astoundingly, life got worse. I will never forget the day I snapped.

In the few minutes between breakfast and lunch, I ran to the crew internet. Hoping for an email from Bianca, I instead found a message from home. I happily clicked on the email, figuring it would be filled with soothing, Grandma-stories about my nieces. It wasn't. There had been a suicide in my family.

I simply couldn't believe that my cousin had committed suicide. Upon reading the words, I could no longer picture his face. Instead all I saw was my uncle. I knew how much my uncle loved his soldier son, how proud he was of him. My uncle was a joyful man, and it was easy to imagine his excitement when arriving at their Texas lake house for a planned visit with his son. Oh, the anguish he must have suffered when not seeing his boy, but a note and a missing rifle. I had nearly choked when I read that he finally found my cousin on the other side of the lake. How long had he searched the woods for his only son, how much pain did he endure?

Though not the soldier my cousin had been, I was a fighter. How awful that it took something so terrible, so final, to remind me of who I was. But my awakening was nothing so clean and inspiring as a light bulb brightening over my head. Oh, no. It took the form of burning anger, of violence.

In a daze I returned to the dining room for the lunch shift. Waiters rushed around everywhere, but to me everything moved in slow motion. Time seemed to have changed. Time was precious, I suddenly realized, and I was wasting it working like a slave and not getting any closer to my Bianca. Our plan to come together had failed, and I wasn't doing anything about it. I was trapped, and approached the toil by selfishly complaining and hating the universe. I should instead be trying to find a solution. My smoldering anger flared brighter. I was furious at my cousin for his selfish act, for his not trying to find a solution.

I looked at the clock and realized that over half of my set-up time had elapsed. Whether I liked it or not, I had another mind-numbing lunch to plod through. My partner had not yet checked in—again. He had been late too many times, frequently arriving after even the guests had, and was worthless even after he finally arrived.

I marched over to the assistant maitre d' and forcefully demanded a new partner. He blew me off. As if on queue, my partner, a skinny Jamaican named Roy, sauntered in smugly. Like always, he knew I would do all the set-up in his absence just to make my own life easier. To the manager, Roy absurdly protested that he was never tardy, and even called me a liar.

"Eh, rasclat!" Roy called, "Why you give me hard time? You lie!"

Despite my aversion to confrontation, I found myself poking my finger into his chest and yelling, "You shut the hell up!"

I stormed off towards our station. Roy followed, shouting insults at my back.

"Why you make drama with boss? I never late, mon! You always late! You the trash!"

I was almost shaking with emotion, my disappointment and rage at the world overcoming me. I didn't want it to win. Everyone else had already foreseen the outcome of my internal war: the balcony above filled with spectators and a circle formed around me and Roy.

"You blood clot!" Roy screamed. "I could kick your ass right now!"

I don't actually remember pushing Roy over the table. I will always remember him tumbling across the broad circular surface, flailing legs knocking aside glasses and plates. He dropped off the far end in a cascade of falling silverware.

Cheers and jeers exploded throughout the dining room. Roy struggled to his feet and rushed back to reengage with me, but I was ready. I grabbed a handful of his vest and brought my arm back to hit him in the face. Suddenly a huge man leapt into the fray and pulled us apart.

"Stop it!" a Croatian waiter shouted, getting between us.

"You want some, eh mon?" Roy screamed. "I give it!"

"Shut up!" the Croatian boomed. "Look at his face, man! For Christ's sake, he's gonna kill you!"

So it was over before it started. Roy backed down, then limped away, shaking his head. Still seeing all through a red haze, I stared at the waiter whose table we had destroyed. He also happened to be Jamaican, and cowered as he rushed to fix his station. He quivered, wide-eyed and terrified. He was scared of me, I realized. What kind of animal had I become? What was it about working the sea that made people so vastly different?

The assistant maitre d', of course, just reminded everybody that lunch was in five minutes.

Ship life.

It was the lowest, most awful moment of the lowest, most awful time in my life. Only then did I understand how men could be so cruel to each other, how we could be conditioned to do anything.

Bianca led me back to reality, back to sanity. She may have shrugged off my help when she was down, but when I was lost, her love and hope guided me through it all. She was amazing. Her next email, sent before my blowout, finally reminded me of who I was:

"Thank you for offering to send me your ear, my artist, but no Van Gogh sensibilities for me! You know by now, I hate creepy stuff, so you should better have some absinthe and, if you can't find Gauguin, pick up another artist to channel. Me lovesick over you, and I took the masochistical risk of looking at our pictures of Egypt. My mother developed them and sent them to the ship. I stared ten times at them and I haven't had enough. So, don't you worry, my love, I'll make love to you with the same passion even when we'll be two disgusting mummies talking Hungarian. Check how me adapt to your creepiness."

Bianca's letter was nothing dramatic, but merely a response, a snippet of our dialogue. But this was not the dialogue of a monster, of a man engulfed in violence and cursing the world. Our dialogue became my lifeline, pulling me out of the pit. Her emails vacillated between commiseration and encouragement. They were reminders that some annoyances were universal and to stop granting them significance greater than they deserved. Mostly, though, they were documentation of the reasons I needed to find a better path for us:

"Another day on ships! I got bingo the first sitting. The sons of a bitch, 16 of them, conquered my station, with mucho fricking kids, who were drawing on my table cloths with butter, dressings, ketchup and other semiliquid items, shouting and moving similar worms. Bamboclat, papa, I swear I'll never have kids, God forgive me! But when I saw those caring sick mothers smiling with patience and comprehension watching the bug's flic-flacs I felt like throwing all overboard."

"My guests are fat bitches. Today they shot my brain with their incomparable stupidness. They came late and asked everything from that sick menu. I had to take their horrible pictures with 4 cameras, then they asked extra appetizers, then dressing for Caesar salad (1000 island dressing!), then 2 lobsters each. One of them was sick so she asked me bring sea sick pills, for being able to eat mucho more."

"Luckily, the 4 cows never showed up again, I won't get any money for the 2 days they scrounged my brain, but better like this than driving me nuts. A day before yesterday I got kicked by the revolving door, so half of my plates were on the floor, making the noise of the century. Dan was there, but he didn't say anything, because just few min ago my guests were telling him how I was the best waitress they've ever had. But the next day he was about to break my neck, because he caught me washing the soup spoons in the hand wash sink. Meow!"

"Of course my garbage guests were unhappy with everything: why the iced tea is so strong, why the steak is so hard, why the dessert is not good, why they didn't have the water, iced tea and bread in time. Next day, I spent two hours extra in the dining room, to make sure everything is prepared. Things went perfect until main course time, when we got short of ice and iced tea, and we couldn't find anywhere, all waiters were running similar headless quails. And for everything to be well done, my babaloo assistant, switches the trays in the galley and she brings me 8 lobsters instead of 8 prime ribs. Upside down, papa! I had just 10 min to set up the tables for the second sitting. I run with the show plates to the dish wash, when I come back, my silver rack was gone. Somebody stole it. I had to steal somebody else's butter knives, and I had no silver for main course, so I left the appetizer silverware for the whole dinner."

"There are so many couples on this ship, most of them married, and they seem so happy and complete. Most of them met on ships and got married, and share everything. I didn't use to care about couples until now, but now, when I have you and I need you so much, I see them otherwise. Christmas is coming, and I make deal with you. You celebrate with me Christmas and put M&Ms under my tree, and I promise to dress every Halloween as the sexiest vampire you've ever seen. But don't scare me too bad with your creepy stuff."

## 3

I have always believed the definition of luck is when opportunity meets preparation. So it was with my fateful meeting with Daniel. He was the hotel director of *Legend*— second only to the captain himself and arguably more important. But Daniel was one of only four Americans onboard, and the only one in management fleet-wide. Though numerous levels above my station, he befriended me out of sheer loneliness. Most importantly, however, Daniel helped me abandon the dead-end of restaurants and apply as an art auctioneer on ships.

The auctioneer hiring process made Carnival's methods look porous, and to get into the seven-day auctioneer screening of Sundance at Sea, I had to go Romanian-style. Thus, while slaving literally 100 hours a week on *Carnival Legend*, I lied, cheated, stole, and bribed my way into Sundance's good graces. After a gift of a duty-free $100 bottle of cognac, my resumé passed from *Legend's* auctioneer up to his fleet manager. She reviewed it and granted me five minutes on her next visit, which was weeks away. After schmoozing her successfully, which did not involve shagging her ship-style as I had been advised, she recommended me for a phone interview with her boss.

All was set for me to leave *Legend* and become an art auctioneer, but for one horrible, heart-rending catch: my contract had to naturally expire. No resigning. No quitting. No firing. Sundance did not want to 'poach' employees from Carnival. I would be stuck as a whipping-boy for many, many more months. I honestly did not think I could make it without walking away from it all.

Then a miracle happened.

Out of the sheer, blue sky the maitre d' asked if any waiters wished to sign off early. Amazingly, Carnival had too many crew members in Miami queued for a ship, and would void anyone's contract if they would just leave immediately—as in a couple of days. There were only a few spots available and, upon hearing the announcement, ran to the restaurant's balcony and cried at the top of my lungs that if anyone got in my way they would be utterly destroyed.

So in a couple of days, I stepped off *Legend* as a free man in Port Everglades, Florida.

In fact, the miracles were just beginning.

Bianca's ship, *Carnival Miracle* was scheduled to arrive from its maiden transatlantic crossing in Jacksonville, Florida that very night!

I was in a rental car in a flash, and fretted the entire 350 miles up the Atlantic coast. The weather fought me tooth and nail, but after surviving the last thirteen months at sea, I'd be damned if I let a tropical storm stop me.

Port security did, though.

I waited hours in a cold, driving rain well after dark, about two hundred yards from the ship. There was no way to communicate with *Miracle*, for the port itself hosted brand-new features that did not yet include telephone or even radio. Even worse, as had happened in *Conquest's* maiden crossing, the new ship's internet was not functional. I didn't even know if Bianca received my emails stating I'd be waiting outside. I resolved to wait all night, to not leave that spot until either she left *Miracle* or *Miracle* left port.

Then I saw a flicker of movement far in the distance. Someone was walking down the empty road, passing into each globe of light, only to drop back into darkness. After several painstaking minutes I finally recognized in the backlight a waitress in uniform.

Bianca ran the last hundred feet through the icy drizzle. We crashed into each other and embraced for a long, long time. I could hardly breathe, though from the crushing hug or the emotion I didn't know. I didn't care. Sometimes even Hollywood ain't got nuthin' on real life.

## 4

My driver refilled his Styrofoam cup of red wine again, only this time also enjoying a slug straight from the bottle before nesting it near the parking brake. Music from Barry

White, the paragon of booty music, crooned from a cassette to romance us. Minutes crawled into hours in the stifling Bahamian night. Wine was downed and yawns were stifled. Duncan, the taxi driver, finally set aside his *Playboy* magazine and inquired once more about my strange quest.

"When's this woman of yours getting off?" he asked.

"Probably a little after midnight," I answered tiredly.

"Heh, getting off," he repeated crassly, like a teenager happily discovering his own crude joke. All in one he chuckled and sipped and chortled until it turned to a gasp. Apparently his latest dousing of wine had gone down the wrong way.

"You aren't worried about cops or anything?" I asked him.

"What, you another uptight American scared of everything?" he asked, dismissively. "Ain't gonna drive off no cliff, mon. We at sea level. Lighten up, yeah?"

"I'm light, I'm light!"

"So, you flew to another country for four hours with this babe?" he continued skeptically. "She's not free 'til after midnight, and back on board working at five thirty in the morning? Are you crazy or just stupid?"

"A question for the ages," I sighed. "But really, what's an extra few hundred miles when you've fought to close a gap of several thousand? And last night? Well...."

"She's that good in bed?"

"Romance, Duncan," I chided with a sigh into the wet night. "Romance! After months of being apart we had one glorious tryst. Imagine it, a cold night with bitter rain and thrashing wind. A lonely road cuts through the forest, lit only by misty globes of light in the dark. From opposite ends we ran to each other for our first kiss in a thousand miles. It was the single most romantic moment of my life."

"She must hump like a champion," he slurred knowingly.

I glanced up at the massive beast silently rising into the night beside us. Towering fourteen stories high, *Carnival Miracle* blocked out the stars that drunkenly wavered above. Her white flanks glowed brilliantly, courtesy of powerful flood lamps that also revealed insects the size of baseballs. They blazed by as little meteors, swirling and spinning as if inebriated by the air.

The stars looked drunk, the bugs looked drunk, and then there was my taxi driver. Ship life.

Duncan was a middle-aged Bahamian, skinny as a rail yet mature and strong in appearance. Gray crawled behind his ears, up towards the flat top he hacked into place. I opted for Duncan's van out of the long line of competitors because he appeared the most fun-loving and flexible, and I knew I had a long wait. I got far more than I bargained for.

I noticed the stack of *Playboy* magazines in the front passenger seat were all from the 1970s. Had they not been so dog-eared, I idly wondered if they were worth some good money, like an attic full of baseball cards sold on eBay. While of course I greatly appreciated good pornography, even I would have shied away from placing it so openly on the front seat while trying to capture a fare.

"Ah, romance," Duncan continued blissfully. "I love romance. I romanced myself five children, so I understand. Yeah, like Barry White's 1970 song 'Walking in the Rain with the One I Love'."

Before embarking on a whole new, crazy scheme to stay afloat by going to auctioneer training, I was able to steal one more night with Bianca. Last night *Miracle* had overnighted in Jacksonville, and tonight it was overnighting in Freeport,

Bahamas. I had already driven seven hours to see her for four, so why not hop a plane to the neighboring nation for a few more? We had to communicate our plans, synchronize our schedules, and, well, other stuff.

"Yeah," Duncan reflected. "So last night you two banged all night, and you wanted one more go around before you leave for Idaho, eh mon? 'I Can't Get Enough of Your Love, Babe'. 1974."

"Iowa," I corrected. "I'm from Iowa."

"'I'm Gonna Love You Just a Little More, Baby'," Duncan continued. "1973."

"I guess that's one way of putting it."

"I can think of lots of ways to put it, mon, if you know what I mean," he sniggered into his wine. "Sounds like she can, too."

"You have a noble soul," I commented drily to Duncan. "Yes, we had last night together, but it wasn't all like that. I mean, we hadn't seen each other for almost half a year. We didn't want to go straight to the hotel, but the only bar nearby was doing karaoke. After all I had gone through, I couldn't bear to hear a drunken redneck crooning Meatloaf's 'Paradise by the Dashboard Light'. So we bought a bottle of vodka and took it to the hotel."

His voice dropped low, switching into Love Doctor baritone. "'It's Ecstasy When You Lay Down Next to Me', 1977. So then you got naked and gave her your love potato."

"I don't even know what my love potato is," I answered. "I'm from Iowa. Idaho has potatoes. Iowa grows corn."

"So you corn-holed her?"

"We talked, among other things."

"Talked?" he asked, incredulous.

"Yes, we talked. We conversed as two intelligent human beings. What, are we mere animals?"

"I'd like to go animal-style on a European chick hot enough to fly to another country for. I love white chicks."

"She does have a brain, you know. That's what first turned me on to her," I added with pride. "We were walking together, talking about science when I mistakenly dismissed krypton as not being an element, but merely fiction from Superman. To refute me she listed, from memory, all the noble gases in descending order on the Periodic Chart of the Elements. I mean, that's hot, don't you think?"

Duncan looked at me blearily, unsure if I was serious. "With sweet talk like that, I bet the bitches line up at your door."

My thoughts drifted off to Bianca and our previous night in Jacksonville. So long had passed since last seeing each other, we both took it slow. We had to get used to one another all over again, to rediscover each other. I sat on the balcony, sipped vodka, and watched her laze on the bed. She frolicked and rolled happily, smoking a cigarette and shooting vodka. Long months of separation began to melt away as we got more and more into each other, as we always did. We teased ourselves, letting our vibes slowly entwine. When we could no longer contain our desires, the world spun in a heady mix of euphoria, fate, fatigue, and vodka. I actually shuddered with emotion as I recalled the tears in her eyes when we first started kissing.

"So she likes butt stuff, then?" Duncan mused aloud, breaking my thoughts.

Suddenly a lone, statuesque figure appeared in the gangway, mercifully taking the conversation away from the direction it was going. Bianca wore a tight blue dress that hugged her curves and split high to reveal long, strong legs. Her round face was nearly hidden beneath a tussle of jet-black hair that snapped in the ocean's breeze. Bright red lips smirked devilishly as she descended the gangway towards us. Duncan whistled in admiration.

"Whoo boy, she can talk 'bout gas all night!"

Bianca hopped perkily into the taxi beside me with a grin.

"'I'll Do for You Anything You Want Me To'," Duncan boomed before I could say anything.

"Huh?" Bianca said, her attention pulled away.

"1975," he clarified.

"Meet Duncan," I offered wryly. "After all my trouble in getting here, I get upstaged by the taxi driver! If he had a bowl cut, I'd be doomed."

## 5

Duncan careened across the dark, empty island towards Freeport. Bianca and I hugged in the back of the van, not from affection but fear for our lives. The drive from the port to the city was less than ten miles, but I began to doubt we would make it. Eventually we calmed and sat quietly holding hands. Duncan paid far more attention to the action behind him than to the road in front. His brows rose with each kiss we snuck, illuminated by the dashboard lights and reflected in the rearview mirror.

"Go!" Duncan boomed to Bianca as she began kissing my neck. She stopped and glared at him.

"Excuse me?"

"So!" he lamely amended, "You were a passenger and looking for some below decks good times, or what?"

"We met in an Old West ghost town," she answered, still annoyed.

For the first time, Duncan was taken aback. "Really? This I gotta hear."

Suddenly he reached into the back and began groping blindly. The van rocked back and forth as we careened from lane to lane. Huge mangrove trees jumped out at us, glowing monstrously in the headlights, but the van swerved to safety at the last moment. I felt our luck running out as he continued to fish for something in the back. Surely he wasn't trying to cop a feel of Bianca—right?

"What is it you want?" Bianca snapped.

"Coconut milk!" he called hastily as he wrenched the steering wheel with both hands to jerk us into the wrong lane. A huge lizard rushed back into the trees, happy to get off the road. Bianca opened the cooler hiding in the dark and retrieved a dripping bottle half-full of a watery, cloudy liquid. Duncan produced a flask of gin from beneath his *Playboys* and topped off the bottle with it, even as the van bounded high into the air after striking a huge crack in the pavement. The thought of a gin/coconut milk cocktail after red wine in Styrofoam, churned aggressively by the van, made my stomach roil.

"*Ce pui mei!*" Bianca muttered exasperatedly in Romanian.

"Bianca!" I cried, surprised. "Did you just say 'who fucked my chicken'?"

"What? Oh, no, no. Well, close. You use a verb for the nastiest word in the language, we use a noun. So instead of 'what the F' we say 'what my dick.' *'Ce pula mea'*."

"Oh. Wow. I'm sorry: I thought you said chicken."

"I did. Instead of saying *pula*, sometimes we say *pui*. It's like you saying shoot instead of shit."

"Wait wait wait," I cried, holding up a hand. "Are you telling me that in Romanian, the word for penis is pula... which is a feminine noun? No wonder the guys are all so macho: they're compensating!"

"'Don't Make Me Wait Too Long'," Duncan said, interrupting. "1974's *The Very Best of Barry White* album. With the Love Orchestra, of course."

"Huh?"

"Oh," I interrupted, "Didn't I welcome you to the Barry White Omnibus?"

"This a van, mon!" Duncan protested. "Now, tell me how you met and how sweet it was."

"Well," Bianca began, "I was visiting my friend in Reno, Nevada."

"'Let Me In, and Let's Begin With Love'," Duncan interrupted. "1981."

"Will you shut the hell up?"

"'Relax to the Max', babe," he defended. "The stage is yours."

"Thank you."

"1981."

After a final glare, Bianca squeezed my hand and began her narration anew. "My girlfriend from home lives in the States now, and I was visiting her after a contract with Carnival. She worked for Brian's computer company back then. I was only there for a couple days, and they coincided with a big music festival they bought tickets for months before. She knew I didn't like soul music, but didn't want to give up the concert. So she brought Brian to entertain me."

"Soul music?" Duncan interrupted yet again. "Who?"

Bianca couldn't recall and looked to me for an answer. I slid deeper in my seat, frightened to launch a whole new line of love talk.

"James Ingram," I peeped.

"What?" Duncan exploded. "James Ingram? Love that American soul, baby! 'It's Your Night'. 1983. Great stuff."

"Whatever," Bianca snipped, refusing to relinquish the direction of conversation. "We didn't listen anyway. It was a huge outdoor show on a golf course, and we walked around the whole thing twice as the sun set over the desert. It was beautiful. We talked and talked, and next day Brian gave me personal tour of a ghost town he wrote a book about. It was like a movie with that actor, what's his name? The American who shoots everybody."

"That ain't all of them?" Duncan asked, confused.

"Clint Eastwood," I supplied painfully.

"Yeah, that one," Bianca agreed with approval. "A Clint movie, like those ones from Italy. This was high on a mountain with super steep sides that were nightmare to be in high heels. I saw a tumble weed! Anyway, Brian was so funny. He kept saying how old it all was. The buildings were, like, only one hundred and fifty years old!"

"That ain't old?"

"My hometown has no beginning: it's always been there. Anyway, we shot whiskey in a saloon, toured haunted hotels, saw silver mines, and even took a train ride through the desert. I saw rattlesnake! He narrated the whole time about history and the ghost hunts he did for his book," she boasted. "That's when I started to like him. He's so smart."

"Uh, sure," Duncan agreed dubiously. "He got a brain, you know. He talks 'bout comic book gas."

"She left to see Vegas for a few days," I supplied. "But after only one day came back to Reno to see me instead. Did we ever even go to sleep before 4 a.m.? I don't think so. Anyway, when she flew back to Romania, she called me while waiting for her connecting flight. That's when it clicked in me, that I needed to see more of this woman."

"Damn right," Duncan agreed. "'I Just Want to Make Love to You'. 1967."

"Hey," I protested. "That's not a Barry White song. That's Isaac Hayes!"

"How did you know that?" Duncan asked, flabbergasted.

"Would you believe I saw him in concert once? Upon reflection, I believe we were the only white people there."

"It's official: you are 'The Man'!" Duncan celebrated. "Barry White. 1978."

# 6

Bianca and I walked hand in hand through the silent, dark lanes of the International Bazaar of Freeport. The uneven bricks beneath our feet, pooling water from earlier rains, proved a formidable barrier to Bianca's high heels. She clung tightly to me for stability, but my head was swimming with joy and we stumbled together, laughing the whole time.

"So," I said as we passed the faux Roman section lined with columns peeling white paint. "I will be back at sea soon. I have a week's training in Pittsburgh to learn the job of art auctioneer, and then I will be an auctioneer's associate. It will take time to get my own ship. Perhaps my next ship, when I'm an art auctioneer's associate, we will meet up with *Miracle*."

"Oh, I hope so! These meetings are so wonderful, but they really need to happen more often. I miss you so much."

"Me too."

The Roman section soon morphed into a Moroccan theme, splendid with the intricate geometry of Islamic art. Ads for duty-free alcohol were everywhere, a stark reminder that we were far indeed from North Africa, as if the ivy creepers hugging the walls weren't reminder enough. I could only imagine how a conservative Muslim would handle the poster yelling, "Go Mount Gay!" It referred to my favorite Barbados rum, Mount Gay, but I sensed a tasteless joke was hiding in there somewhere.

"It's not guaranteed that I will be an associate, of course," I continued. "But I will make it happen. After a few months as associate I should have my own ship as auctioneer. Then you can come on board as my assistant. Imagine: we can finally get you free of the cabins below the waterline—and have a real bed! Auctioneers live in guest rooms, eat guest food, and live the dream of cruising every day. You won't slave 80 hours a week at hard labor anymore, and we'll be together."

"Oh, make it happen!" she begged. "I can't wait."

We moved from Morocco to France. The streets were particularly dark here and many corners were black. A closed restaurant, Café Michel, offered us a table to relax. We could almost hear the echo of the Parisian hand-accordion as we sat by the café-style awning hanging over the cobbled streets. Toulouse-Lautrec posters advertised the wild bordellos of the French night scene. Altogether the sights, sounds, and sensations of the Caribbean were raw and powerful. There was something electric about the tropical night air that I had never found anywhere else in my travels. As the beat of a nearby dance club thumped, Bianca smoked a cigarette and we discussed our situation, our hopes, dreams, and plans.

"Until you become an auctioneer," Bianca said quietly, getting serious, "we must focus on our jobs. No promises but that we'll be together. Me too seasoned, me know ships. We are not ready to be together yet."

Parting and planning for the next effort at togetherness, again!

"All right," I agreed. "Look, working as a waitress pays for your family's retirement, and allows you several months a year to see them. I get it, and will never jeopardize that. It will take me months before I can safely pay you the same, but I will make it happen. So when I start this thing, I gotta focus. It's got to be just me and my career. No work breaks or anything. No distractions. We communicate better through email anyway!"

"Why you say that? We communicate fine in person," Bianca said, sliding her hand across the table. Instead of taking my hand, she began to play with my beaded bracelet. She spun it around my wrist and teased it with her fingers. A chill tingled across my body as I suddenly recalled her touches past.

"We've fought for over a year now," I finalized. "So what's another few months while I get my ducks in a row?"

"Why you have ducks?"

"No, no, it's an expression. I need to get my affairs in order."

"Affairs?" she gasped with alarm.

7

Auctioneer screening felt like an extension of *Legend*, though the brutality was entirely mental and emotional. I endured a strangely focused enmity from the trainer, the self-proclaimed Lucifer, who made half the trainees cry and the other half quit. Had I not just been through hell on the high seas, I would have thought his verbal abuse completely and utterly contemptible. Well, it *was* completely and utterly contemptible, but at least I understood his reasons. And, honestly, his creativity with insults was pretty impressive.

Despite such tribulations, I did reasonably well. This was less from my being talented than my being aged. Most of the competition for the highly sought and highly lucrative position were barely out of high school. By the end of the week I had secured a post to train under the recent Rookie of the Year. The ship was *Majesty of the Seas* or, as auctioneers knew it: the Widow Maker.

That's when things got interesting.

If I had thought Carnival's approach to human rights was cold, then Sundance at Sea treated its auctioneers with the icy breath of Death. After only two weeks on the Widow Maker, the recently young and vibrant Rookie of the Year—now ulcerated, impotent, and alcoholic—got screwed by Sundance and denied his desperately needed vacation and sent to another ship in need. In order to squeeze more life out of the poor bastard, I was promoted by default to associate and they brought in a new auctioneering couple.

He was a Brit, she was a Turk. Charles and Tatli were both likable, but again alcoholic and dysfunctional. We missed our sales goals with an alarming frequency, while they seriously discussed either quitting Sundance or divorce: which came first they soon stopped caring. Yet I was miraculously promoted again, making me the first of our trainee class to gain a big ship —a return to *Carnival Conquest*, no less! But such was the domain of Bill Shatner, the strangest auctioneer yet, who gleefully added perversion to his alcoholism.

Those were some weeks!

I focused on the job, but our huge success rested on Bill's shoulders, not mine. I resolved to watch and learn as much as I could from Bill, when he wasn't dragging me to the crew bar or another Mexican brothel. It was a rather unusual manner of training, to be sure, and not nearly as interesting as I would have thought when I was a teenager. I could refrain from such extracurricular activities easily enough—I've never been a big 'let's go bang a prostitute' kinda guy—but what proved more troubling was avoiding the advances of the crew.

Auctioneers enjoyed immense privileges onboard, thusly adding even more to the promise of a Green Card. Oscar Wilde said it best when observing that "by persistently remaining single a man converts himself into a permanent public temptation." Indeed, for a while, I thought surely I was going to be kidnapped by the dance captain. Tina was beautiful, of course, but had the IQ of an ice cube. The whole situation was so outrageous that I never took it seriously.

But one outrageous factor I had to take seriously: ships are lonely places.

It had been many, many months since I had felt a warm touch. Everybody seemed to be sleeping with everybody— ship-style—but what was really lacking was simply human contact. Why was there no middle ground? The bonfire of temptation flared ever higher and hotter, exotic and enticing. I didn't want to burn in the fire, but I didn't want to remain in the cold, either. There were times when I thought I should just 'do what I gotta do' and get it over with. I didn't want that and knew it wouldn't ease my loneliness. Bianca's words of experience rang in my head the whole time, 'No promises but that we'll be together.'

Bill finally went on vacation to Thailand. The promise of cheap hedonism was too much to bear, and he never returned. I took over as auctioneer. Sundance allowed me one cruise to prove my mettle, though under the direct observation of Lucifer himself! I had thought his abuse was unwarranted on land, and now I was going to get a full, personalized dose on international waters!

Lucifer lived up to his name. As soon as he arrived, he disappeared into the crowd. I had no idea where he would be or when, but he was watching, waiting for a mistake. When I didn't provide one fast enough, he actually resorted to sabotage. I was fighting for my career, for the fate of my lover, and yet my very own trainer was inciting a riot at my art auction! The stakes were high, but with the assistance of a lecherous fireman named Greg Gregg—quite a story there—I secured my place as an art auctioneer.

What a whirlwind life had become since meeting Bianca!

Our initial discovery of each other had been a bolt from a clear blue sky, and despite our passionate wishes and tremendous efforts to come together, fitting me into her established ship routine had failed. As a couple we regrouped, slowed down, and began our lettered courtship. During my tumultuous demotion on *Legend*, her love had screamed off the page. She hopped from *Glory* to *Miracle*, Carnival's latest and greatest, whereas I dropped from Carnival entirely. But within weeks of that I was back at sea on *Majesty of the Seas*, ready to make a new go of it all.

The roller coaster ride of the art world resulted in my being the first of my class to become an associate, the first to be assigned a big ship, and first to be offered my own ship. Because my fight was alone, it felt like it lasted years. It had actually been about six months. While I fought the slings and arrows of outrageous fortune, Bianca sank back into her ship habit long since established. Her emails grew not distant, but less intent. She was more or less content with her lot. I was not. Every time Sundance stresses threatened to derail me—a weekly occurrence—I remembered her bleaching menus at midnight, dreading the breakfast shift. We were coming together, oh so slowly, but were closing the gap.

Finally, after two years of ups and downs, I had found a way to bring us together. I was given my own ship, *Sensation*, and could bring her aboard as my assistant. I sent Bianca the necessary art books to get her up to speed. She was a born saleswoman and smart as whip. Now, at long last we would work together, for a common goal, side-by-side.

Together we would rock the fleet!

# Part 2:

## SHIP HAPPENS

There is nothing more enticing, disenchanting, and enslaving than the life at sea.

— Joseph Conrad

# CHAPTER TWELVE

## Fish Pills

## 1

*SENSATION'S* DEPARTING auctioneer met me on the gangway. He was a small, sweaty man with abundant, curly red hair covering his forearms. He looked exactly like Robin Williams. We shook hands, and he welcomed me aboard, saying with a glint in his eye, "I'm Robin."

Seeing my raised brow, he grinned and explained, "When they tagged me with that in training, it stuck. I use it in auctions, and they love it. So as far as I'm concerned, I'm Robin."

"Perish the thought I'll be forever branded Buzz Lightyear," I opined.

We had been walking up the gangway, but he stopped short so suddenly that I nearly ran into him. He turned about and regarded me skeptically. Finally he said, with a pronounced Australian accent, "You're a Yank? Ain't no Texan, are you?"

"I'm from Iowa," I replied, to which he loosed a sigh of relief. He did not explain the odd question, but continued onward. We strode down the I-95, ducking beneath leaning towers of plastic-wrapped bread and cases of paper products. A cluster of Indonesian waiters hunkered around a plastic coffee mug drafted into ashtray service. Robin said nothing until we reached the purser's office.

"You got the handover notes I sent?" he finally asked. "Good. Uncle Sam said you were on *Ecstasy*, so you know *Sensation*. Same class ship. We don't have to bother with much, then, other than the inventory. We're due for a new load of art, so our supply is very low. Should be easy."

We took the guest elevators up to deck five and strode quickly down the passageway. About midship he unlocked a door to an interior cabin and announced, "Here's the cabin."

Not surprisingly, the auctioneer's cabin on *Sensation* was the most dispensable guest cabin available. It was rather small, with two separate bunks pressed against two different walls. That was a surprise that I did not care for at all. What really struck me, however, was the smell: the room reeked of fish.

"I heard you are here with your girlfriend," I said. "What's with the separate bunks?"

I had learned over the course of my years at sea to take beds very seriously. While I no longer shared my bunk with my luggage, as I had as a waiter, I was keen to start sharing an actual bed with Bianca. That little bit of normalcy had become literally my only criteria when it came to judging accommodations.

Robin was about to answer when a very tall, attractive woman entered from the bathroom. She was six feet tall and, while pleasantly slender, still built solid. Her long hair was naturally blonde, but the last six inches were dyed black. She wore a cowboy hat and boots over snug blue jeans.

"He stinks," she stated in answer to my question. "He belches all night, so I want as much distance as possible."

"Hey, you can tell me," Robin said to me. "Are all Texans so loud-mouthed, or did I just get a gem?"

"She certainly looks like a gem," I replied. I offered my hand to her and introduced myself. Her grip was indeed as hard as diamond.

"I'm Vanessa," she said. "You like cod liver oil?"

"Are you asking me on a date?"

She gestured broadly to the room. "We've got plenty for ya. I'm sick of 'em. If I smell one more damned pill, I'm gonna puke. Lover boy here don't eat no food, jus' lives off cod liver oil."

A quick glance proved that she wasn't kidding. I counted no less than four bottles of cod liver pills of varying sizes. A fifth bottle lay on its side on a bunk behind where Robin sat, looking suspiciously as if it had dumped its contents between the cushions. The largest container, a family-sized jar with a wide mouth, was currently open. The smell of heavy fish oil almost visually emanated from it.

"Aren't you supposed to refrigerate those once opened or something?" I asked in wonder.

"Bah!" Robin replied. "You Yanks always worry about stuff like that. Gimme a break. How you won the West beats me: I don't think you'd last one week outback."

"So'd you tell him yet?" she asked Robin.

He ignored her query, instead turning to me to say, "It's a pretty decent ship, overall. You should do OK."

"Tell him," Vanessa ordered suddenly, pretty lips parting in disgust that she had to force the issue.

Robin reacted strongly, rearing up and out of his seat in anger. In a flash both were glaring at each other, faces flushed and postures frozen in defiance: she tall and leaning willowy-strong over him, he looking up to meet her with bulldog neck tensed and fists clenched.

"You shut up!" he spat with surprising vehemence. It was strange seeing Robin Williams seething with anger. I waited for the punchline. When it came, all I could manage was a groan.

Vanessa snatched up the nearest bottle of fish oil pills—the family-sized jar without the lid—and hurled it at him. Delicate globules of smelly fish oil sprayed wide, bouncing off Robin to clatter off the walls, the desk, the bed and everything else until they found every last corner.

"Damn you, woman," Robin snarled, reaching for her. She gamely bounced back, but this was no game. She retreated nimbly and reached out to place her hand on his head. Robin swung at her, short arms pumping the air, but comically his reach was too short to touch her. They exchanged all manner of insults, voices rising until she screeched and he bellowed.

Finally he muscled his way past her amusing defense, and gave her a solid slap across the face. The sound was shockingly loud. Violence in person is completely unlike anything in the movies. It was immediate, intimate, horrible.

"Oh!" she cried in surprise, hair flinging wild.

I leapt in between the two of them, now shouting myself. I had no idea what was going on, even as I sensed this was not an unusual occurrence between them. Indeed, before I could interfere they both whirled upon me as one.

"This is none of your business, Yank!" Robin bellowed.

"I can handle this myself!" Vanessa echoed. She was already returning her attention to her adversary, adding, "I'm from Texas!"

Vanessa then delivered a tremendous blow of her own, a wallop that sent Robin reeling. Before he had a chance to recover, she shoved him onto the bed. Next came a sharp crack, a head hitting the bulkhead, and Robin collapsing. He gave a low moan, and instantly Vanessa was atop him. They began madly kissing, passionately rolling across the tiny bunk, and grinding cod liver pills into my future mattress.

I stared in awe, completely forgotten—as was, apparently, the handover. Though strangely keen on remaining and watching, prudence prompted a departure.

The handover was indeed fast, what, with the reduced inventory and the ship tour scuttled by angry sex. But *Sensation* was a *Fantasy*-class vessel, which I knew well both above and below decks. *Sensation* was a bit worse for wear, but when sailing from New Orleans it was no wonder. The Big Easy was not a town exactly known for hermetically-sealed, clean fun.

The cabin seemed to present the most immediate concern. It was small and ugly and stank. The room steward was thrilled beyond belief when I gave him orders to remove all the fish pills, even if they did continue to pop up for weeks afterward. The best thing about the cabin, other than free room service, was that it was directly beside the art locker. So close, in fact, that I felt safe creeping in my underwear into the hall on those nights the fishiness kept me awake.

## 2

One of the more annoying tasks cruise ship department heads are subjected to is the stage talk. On day one, the cruise director presents the cast of characters to the guests—twice—in the main lounge. Speaking before a large audience is arguably the greatest universal phobia of humankind, ahead of even claustrophobia. Because crew members lived in tiny metal boxes under the ocean, the latter was rarely an issue for very long. As an auctioneer, speaking was my job, but I suffered the usual jolt of nerves when literally under the spotlight. It's brighter than most people think.

Half a dozen of us were crammed between the thick red velvet of the stage curtain and a coarse, cream-colored secondary. We ducked beneath ropes, stepped above speakers, dodged props.

"Would it were not so, would it were not so," chanted my neighbor repetitiously. He was a very young, small man with hair gelled into short, artistic swirls. His mannerisms were undecided—clothing American, language Shakespearean, accent utterly undefinable—but his manner was most certain: he feared an oncoming cardiac arrest. Just watching him made my own heart palpitate.

"I abhor this!" he cried anew. "Ohmygod, is there a mirror anywhere? How's my hair?"

"Right here," answered a rail-thin man with pale skin and black hair. He tapped a small mirror mounted behind the curtain. A pronounced soul-patch relaxed beneath his lips. Indeed, his every fiber oozed complete calm. "At this distance, they won't see any details. Stay chill, brother."

"A tragedy—indeed!—set to befall me upon the stage," the young vendor promised. "I'll swoon, verily."

"What do you do here?" I asked, trying to take his mind off the stage. "Where you from?"

"I'm the new tattoo artist," he answered hurriedly. "Stefan, from Bulgaria."

I exchanged a surprised glance with the thin man.

"We have a tattoo artist?"

"He's from Bulgaria?" he asked in return.

"Airbrushed tattoos," the youth explained. "I have a kiosk on the pool deck. And to answer your unspoken question, sir, my mother was English with a great appreciation for Shakespeare. It gives me comfort."

"You don't look that comfortable," I said doubtfully. "I mean, come on. This is nothing compared to performing Shakespeare."

"Perform?" he squeaked. "Who ever said anything about performing? I can recite Shakespeare all day, but I'd never dream of performing it. I have bad stage fright."

"You know, Stefan," I said. "I'll tell you a little secret. A friend of mine was a standup comedian in New York City. He opened for some big names, even Jerry Seinfeld. I asked him how he handled looking out at all those thousands of people, and you know what he said? You can't see them! The lights are right in your face, so it's just you doing your thing. You won't even know you're on stage."

"Just don't trip on your way out," someone teased from down the line. "They remember that."

"But soft!" Stefan growled, fighting his fear with anger. "I took the simplest job I could find to get me beyond the Black Sea, and now they want me to recite King Lear upon the boards for thousands! I should have applied at McDonald's."

"I hear you, brother," offered our chill companion. "But you get used to it. Really. The cruise director doesn't call us out in any order, so you can go right after me. Just say your name, job, and country. Wave. That's it."

Stefan's indignation flashed anew. He looked ready to hyperventilate. "But... must I not introduce the next person? I have to introduce the next person! There's a next person that needs introducing! O, woe is me to have seen what I have seen!"

"Don't bother," came the calm instructions. "You have enough to deal with. If you can remember Shakespeare, you can remember your name and home."

In an effort to buck himself up, Stefan brought a hand to his chest and quoted, "Cowards die many times before their deaths; the valiant never taste of death but once."

"*Henry V?*" I asked, absolutely floored by the erudition of this strange man.

"*Julius Caesar,*" he corrected before swooping into a mumbling chant of Shakespeare, like some sort of prayer. Instead of twenty Hail Marys for remorse, he was reciting iambic pentameter for repose.

The cruise director's dialogue moved towards vendor introductions. Max, the flamboyantly gay assistant cruise director with curly blonde hair and pock-marked skin, stuck his head through the curtains and gave me the nod. I stepped up to the curtain, but our thin companion placed a hand on my shoulder to stop me.

"I'm Marc, by the way," he said. "When you're done waving, just introduce me and hand me the mic. I'm from Zanzibar."

"You're from where—?"

But Max was already tapping me on the back with the microphone. I had volunteered to lead because I heard somewhere that people generally remember only the first and last in line. I took the microphone from Max and strode onto the stage. I thought I was in control, but my knees began shaking when I looked at one thousand faces in the dark. Even the balcony was full! So much for the bright lights theory.

Man oh man, is everything different with a white-hot spotlight on you. Fortunately for me—and to the chagrin of my friends and family—once given the cue to talk, nothing could stop me. I talked my talk, grinned my cheesy grin and waved my cheesy wave. Once finished with my obviously perfect and awe-inspiring performance, I joined Max at stage left. He immediately began gesturing very suggestively with his eyes.

"Geez," I said quietly to him. "Can't you wait until backstage to flirt?"

"You forgot to introduce the next one!" he snapped, even as he smiled to the guests.

I felt like an idiot. Fortunately, I was well-practiced at such a feeling. Still convincing myself that I was all smooth and stuff, I moved to salvage the situation. As I brought the mic to my lips, I suddenly realized I forgot where Marc was from. Eyes burned into me hotter than the spotlight, and I just stood there, mouthing the air as if I had swallowed a bug.

Finally I croaked, "Marc... Zimbabwe!"

Mild applause meant that I was off the hook. I felt horrible for blowing Marc's introduction, but he was still cool as a cucumber. He strode onto stage and effortlessly did his own little song and dance.

"Yes, good evening, ladies and gentlemen," he said. "I am Marc, the port and shopping guide, so you'll see a lot of me this week. As my colleague has so eloquently observed, I am indeed from exotic Zimbabwe."

He gave me a sly grin.

"And I would like to introduce you to a newcomer on *Sensation*, Stefan from Botswana!"

The applause quickly faded into an awkward patter, because no one came onstage. Instead we heard a faint scuffling followed by a loud 'WHUMP!'

The curtain billowed out, revealing arms and legs thrashing upon the floor. The crowd started laughing, then burst into applause as the terrified tattooer scrambled out from under the curtain. Stefan all but sprinted to the center of the stage, hands sweeping over his gelled hair, over-eager to make up for his embarrassing loss of mojo.

Poor Stefan's pains were not quite over. He spoke at great length, having apparently found his composure—but not his mic. It was too far from his mouth. No one heard a thing. A great, yawning silence descended upon the lounge. Stefan sensed something was wrong, but did not know what it was. He overcompensated by talking faster and faster. Fortunately, only those of us onstage heard his awkward rambling.

Max finally ran up to the hapless youth and, with comedic overacting, pushed the microphone closer. He pretended to chastise Stefan greatly, and the audience laughed appreciatively. From the stage, however, I noticed that Stefan did not take this well at all. His stage fright flashed into anger. Again overcompensating, he brought the microphone too close and his words were deafening and breathy, with a hint of a snarl. Had he quit then and there, his exit would have been somewhat graceful. Alas, when machismo reigns, misfortune follows.

"Sorry I forgot where you're from," I whispered to Marc at stage left.

"Stay chill," he replied with a sly smile. "I'm from Canada. My trick to deal with nerves is to think of a different place every time, keep it fun. Last cruise I was from Angola. But I think I may have thrown off Stefan. Our boy isn't doing too well."

Indeed. Stefan had forgotten where Marc said he was from.

"I HAIL FROM BANANA REPUBLIC," Stefan blurted, almost eating the mic. His face was visibly red now, no longer from embarrassment, but from anger. "I MEAN BANGLADESH, DAMMIT! I COME FROM THE LAND DOWN UNDER."

The crowd rippled from Stefan's curse.

"You're from Botswana," Marc whispered helpfully.

"I AM FROM BOTSWANA!" Stefan repeated with emphasis.

"Where the tall corn grows," I mischievously added.

"WHERE THE TALL CORN..." Stefan began repeating with gargantuan volume-enhancement. Finally he caught on and stopped. At long last, fuming, he stalked off the stage.

Our duties done for the night and the ice broken, I invited Marc and Stefan to join me for a cigar in one of the lounges. Stefan surely needed an intravenous alcohol drip. We had a grand time, and when I finally returned to my cabin, I was excited about *Sensation*.

It didn't last very long.

3

The storms were atrocious. Never had I encountered seas so rough as those that night. *Conquest*, which had also sailed the Gulf of Mexico route, had once outrun a hurricane with less turmoil. 100,000+ ton mega-ships rocked no more than your average shopping mall—albeit on Black Friday—but even taking into account the smaller size of *Sensation*, the pitching was unheard of. It was awful. And it got worse. And worse again. The rocking was so bad, in fact, that I backed up all the data on my personal laptop to CDs and kept them in a plastic baggy beside my life vest. Descending from multiple generations of Boy Scout Masters had taught me 'Be prepared.'

Carnival handled the crisis well. Hallways and common areas blossomed with barf bag stations like flowers in spring. The stewards needn't have bothered, though, because few folks left their cabins. While the bars were full—requisite to any Carnival cruise—the dining rooms were ghost towns. Room service was so overloaded that waiters were pulled from the restaurant to assist at all hours, day and night. Shows were cancelled, due to unsafe tilting of the stage, and shops were closed, due to the floor being covered with smashed bottles of perfume.

This gave me the brilliant, if misguided, idea of cracking open a bottle of cologne in my cabin to combat the smell. I now enjoyed a heavy fish musk.

And the art auctions? Who would risk vomiting for that? Too many Jean-Claude Picot prints already induced gagging. As the cruise rocked and rolled ever onward, my emotions were as turbulent as the angry sea upon which we pitched. I recalled a former colleague of mine, Charles, who had once said that having a bad auction tears you up inside. I understood all too well.

My first auction could have been considered a success. If I spun it really hard. And didn't look at any numbers. Or told Sundance about any of it. And jumped overboard.

Still, this was my first-ever auction on my own with all-new crew, and we worked together smooth as silk. My art movers were the Filipino cover band, and they were brilliant. They even worked my check-out line, because *Sensation* was one of the last ships without an associate. So the few people that trickled in, barf-bags in hand, were dazzled by a robust performance. The numbers, however, were anemic.

I had expected to reach half my goal with the first auction. Hubris, no doubt. But it was not a particularly high goal, by Sundance standards. By day three of five, I still only hovered at around half that. I sold only one lousy CP—the designation for a high-caliber work. Worse, it was by Jean-Claude Picot. Insult to injury.

My disappointment was acute, painful. If I failed on this cruise, I jeopardized everything I had worked so long and so hard for. Even optimists sometimes hit a wall, and I felt in my gut things weren't going to improve this cruise. I had learned long ago to trust my gut, because even if it led to mistakes, the path was always right for me. But I sensed disaster looming ahead. Was I really so weak that the first time my name was on the line I panicked? But it wasn't the first time I was in charge. That had been on *Ecstasy*, and I passed with flying colors.

What was missing?

The answer, of course, was Bianca. I saw no end of ways she could help make a killing. She was the star salesman, not me. When she joined me on *Sensation*, everything would be easier. Therein lay the next trouble.

The very first email I received from Bianca after signing on was bad news. She had discovered some transfer paperwork details not yet completed. I expounded my frustrations in reply. I fancy myself as a great communicator, though that is not nearly as good a thing as I think it is. There's room to argue that unloading your burden onto others is selfish. But we all need to vent every now and then, and that is what understanding friends and family are for, right? Is it not a privilege to help someone in need? Alas, I'm an idealist, and this ain't no ideal world. The moment I hit 'send', regret blossomed. I could have at least waited until the first cruise was over before whining!

To punish myself, I undertook the odious task of defrosting the refrigerator in my cabin. Though it was only a small dorm-style fridge, Robin had ignored it until two solid inches of frost coated the insides. Hours ticked by in my nasty, smelly little world. I watched gelid fish pills drop in soggy, misshapen plops. Self-flagellation would have been preferable.

Perhaps I had been spending too much time with Stefan and his sudden bursts of iambic pentameter, because that night I quoted Hamlet in my diary: *There is nothing good or bad, but thinking make it so.* It was as close to optimism as I could muster. Looking at the words made me feel better.

It didn't matter. Unbeknownst to me, on *Sensation* I had already made the most naive mistake of my life.

# CHAPTER THIRTEEN

## *Barf Bags*

### 1

BY MORNING OF the last day of the cruise, I had given up all hope of reaching my sales goal. I wasn't even close. No angel investors promised to swoop in and buy a Picasso. Only in the final hours of those hateful first five days did *Sensation's* brutal gyrations ease. We had reached the continental shelf near the Mississippi delta.

It was over.

I had failed.

Strangely, I felt calm about my failure. In the last two years I had learned how to read guests, and knew this was a damned odd cruise. Indeed, not a single department made their ship's goals—not even the bar, which was simply unheard of. Sundance would not care, of course, but I had done all that was to be done. It just didn't work. Further, I had reviewed the numbers that Robin and Vanessa had pulled in, and noted they averaged only a handful of CPs a cruise. That was a terribly disheartening fact that, ironically, gave me hope. Next cruise I would succeed where Robin had not, and this awful cruise would be forgotten.

Marc had become a good friend already. He, too, was judged on sales, though how that worked was curious because he didn't sell anything. According to some sort of arcane algebraic function, he, too, had missed goal. As usual, he was unperturbed. I didn't think anything could crack that man's cool. Then again, he was not under threat of firing, failure, and heartbreak. I was.

"You realize, of course," Marc said, "the cure to your problem is a cheeseburger."

"You are a man of wisdom, my dear doctor," I agreed. We hit the pool deck to fill his sensible prescription.

As *Sensation* eased up the Mississippi, the view from the pool deck revealed a misty sun settling over the swampy woodlands. Oil refineries, ablaze with orange lights, punctured the lush canopy. Their thick smoke pushed and swirled into the dark blue sky like milk added to a bath.

"You know," I began slowly, directing Marc's attention to the tattoo artist with a nudge. "I think Stefan's a little... overzealous... in his work."

Stefan laughed and laughed with a trio of skinny teenage girls in bikinis. They were bubbling excitedly and pointing to various places on their bodies they thought a tattoo would be cute, or, of greater importance, look adult. Stefan eagerly joined in, observing nooks and crannies that he had no business whatsoever in acknowledging on fifteen-year-old girls.

"Yes," Marc agreed with his usual gravitas. "He's rather creepy, isn't he?"

Stefan motioned for us to wait, so we watched him apply his fake tattoos. Dropping to a knee before a girl, he proceeded to spray her slim thigh with a solution from a water bottle. She wiggled with the chill, bringing giggles from her friends. With great ceremony and great wads of paper towels, Stefan patted her thigh. Long after she was dry, he kept his hand pressed to her prepared skin. Eventually he looked up and gave her what he no doubt thought was a reassuring smile. I was distinctly reminded of the Big Bad Wolf regarding Little Red Riding Hood. Fortunately, Stefan managed to avoid drooling and licking his chops.

Finally he brought out the airbrush, which in fact looked much like a modern tattoo gun. Now he focused upon his work with care and pride, and soon enough the girls bounced away, all but squealing over a blue dolphin jumping over a kneecap.

Stefan packed up and joined us. Wiping excess paint off his hands, he confided, "I love my job!"

"Perhaps a bit too much," I observed.

"Can one desire too much of a good thing?" Stefan scoffed via Shakespeare. Suddenly, almost comically, we all paused as a colleague sauntered towards us. Boys will be boys.

"Now that," Marc commented with surprising warmth, "is far from harmless. She's downright lethal."

"A goddess, I say!" Stefan agreed. "Her name is Oana. I don't know what she does onboard because she won't talk to me. I think she has a desk up on the Promenade. Alas, she does not love that does not show her love."

"What does that mean?" asked Marc calmly.

I marveled how he was unintimidated even by Stefan's overwhelming speech. When this Bulgarian spoke, I felt the need to cite my *Highly Selective Thesaurus for the Extraordinarily Literate*.

"Oh, how this love of spring resembleth the uncertain glory of an April day," he answered. "Which now shows all the beauty of the sun, and by and by a cloud takes all away."

"In English, please," I said.

He looked sideways at me and said, "That is English."

Stefan began wringing his hands in dismay over the whole thing, and finally answered, "She is Romanian, and God forbid she lower herself to talk to a Bulgarian. Romanians are frequently like that. Bulgaria is the only country in Europe that makes them look good, so they turn their noses up. I tried to impress her with the fact that my mother is English, but it didn't help."

He held open his palms and looked ruefully down at the spattered paint. "Guess I look like a peasant working the fields."

"Is that so?" I murmured. Oana was a petite brunette—which summed up most Romanian women—and cute as a button. She moved with a perkiness that was refreshing, for I was all too used to seeing Romanians tired and worn from life in difficult circumstances.

Tired of being verbally upstaged by Stefan, I decided it was time to dazzle my new friends with my unstoppable charm. When Oana stepped into line behind us, I said to her in Romanian, "Hello, beautiful."

Oana gave me a surprised look. I thought she would be pleased to hear her native tongue. I was sorely mistaken. With each following question, her adorable countenance stiffened further and further. Had I been a wise man, I would have learned from Stefan's stage mess and bowed out while I was behind. But I kept trying, asking a few more simple questions and exhausting my limited Romanian.

"And good evening to you, sir," she replied with a pronounced emphasis on her choice to speak English. With a coolness reminiscent of that other Oana, the Romanian judge, she eyed each of us up and down. When she finally reached Stefan, she ever-so-slightly sniffed. She then assiduously ignored us.

"Perhaps you should increase dosage to a double cheeseburger," Marc suggested thoughtfully.

"American girls are easy," Stefan agreed. "I'm stickin' to them."

Chuckling at my own humiliation, I quickly changed the subject. "I'm glad we don't have to pay for the burgers, because after this cruise I'm broke."

"I heard that, brother," Marc agreed.

"I've made a killing!" Stefan gloated. "What you guys lack is passion for your work."

"I'd suggest you tone down your love of duty," Marc commented drily.

"This morning my auction brought in only a thousand dollars," I lamented. "Why, yesterday I had a sidewalk sale that had just two people. Two! One guy literally debated with his wife for thirty minutes before grudgingly buying a $50 print. I barely reach 50% of my lowest goal. One more cruise like this and I'll be fired. Seriously. Is this cruise discounted, or what?"

Marc gave me a funny look, and asked, "You mean you didn't know?"

"Know what?" I said, suddenly nervous.

"This *was* a discounted cruise—highly discounted. One of *Sensation's* stabilizers is broken. We're gonna rock like this every cruise until dry dock, good weather or bad. The cruises are all but given away so they can at least get some onboard revenue."

Suddenly it became clear what Robin and Vanessa had been arguing about. He didn't want to tell me what I was up against! You can always count on Sundance culture for colleagues to leave you flapping in the wind.

## 2

The next cruise, only four days long, set out into seas worse than the previous. I seriously began to entertain the idea that we had found some sort of rip in spacetime and were now sailing below the 66th parallel into the Antarctic Circle.

Like most experienced seafarers, I could handle the rocking and rolling of heavy swells. What was intolerable was the banging and jerking that literally ripped the art displays off the walls.

Setting up the first auction was stressful enough under the specter of self-doubt, but worse was also having to deal with the Filipino band fighting over the barf bags. As they squabbled, my art carts rolled across the deck like loose cannons, threatening untold thousands of dollars in damage to art that I was liable for.

In the middle of that headache, I was ordered by security to drop everything and go gather each and every art display from all over the ship. Though guests were denied the open deck, that didn't stop a continuous stream from curiously poking their heads out the door. Invariably the wind ripped the door from their hands to blast through the interior of the ship, brutalizing furniture and shredding displays. A dozen frames were scratched beyond repair and four works of art—totaling some $10,000—were destroyed.

Yet hope blossomed when people actually showed up at the auction. Why, there was a whole crowd of 'em!

Alas, to say these folks were not art buyers was a gross understatement. I did not sell a single work of art. My God-awful $600 in revenue came merely from shipping costs for the free giveaways. Auctioneers raffle off artwork as an incentive to boost attendance, but guests must ship it home. The logic, of course, was that once an art tube was already opened and paid for, up to six works fit inside. Those on the fence may be more inclined to fill it. But nobody was on the fence. Nobody was even near the property! Filling empty invoices for $30 in shipping costs was a staggering waste of time with no reward. Indeed, *I* paid for all those 'free' works of art out of my own pocket!

Venting in my diary, I accused the world, blamed fate. I was poetic. I was crass. Above all, I was honest:

November 21, 2004

This is a new cruise after a sickening first cruise. I had an auction today and sold... 600 bucks. I am so disgusted I can vomit. They all came for the free art only. I am tearing apart inside realizing that this perfect situation could go so terribly wrong. I am so worried about losing this job, I can hardly sleep. Last cruise was awful... but nothing was as bad as this! I still have 3 days to make it happen, and I will do everything I can... but I already am doing it right. I know I am.

If I lose my ability to have Bianca in my life because of this goddamn ship and these goddamn people... I am sick at the thought. I think of her every moment of every day, and I can't handle the thought of not having her. Screw my ambitions for a career, I need her. Why else am I doing this? And I may not get her if this keeps up. Obviously she is not interested in me for the money, but how else can we live together? How? How else can we have the funds and the flexibility to live in two countries at once? She'll never abandon her family and come to America. I must make this work! It's blowing outside, and I am spending the whole night locked in my cabin, stewing miserably. I just ordered room service, three roast beef and bries on baguette. I have a tumbler of Mount Gay Eclipse on ice, and I'm going to gorge myself and get drunk. I don't care. I have all day tomorrow to make tomorrow night work. Getting this weather with these people on this broken ship on my first cruises is proof that life is not fair.

November 23, 2004

Yesterday's auction was a failure. I woke up this morning at 5AM, due to stress. I feel it in my every pore, so this is what it's like! My hands are so shaking that I can hardly type. I feel the tight, bunched and tense muscles in my shoulders, and my stomach is trembling. This perfect, perfect, perfect opportunity is slipping away through my very fingers! It's been two years, and now more than ever I can't live without my Bianca. I owe her so much for opening my eyes to life and love, but cannot ask her to take any undue risk with me. If I can't provide what I promised and what she needs (read: comparable money), I'll have to call everything off on *Sensation*. I hate letting money influence my life. Romanians say that 'money can't buy happiness, but helps with everything else'. What am I doing wrong? I follow every guideline for success… some auctioneers just tank on certain ships… we all know that.

I smoked a nice cigar on the open deck, a beautiful morning with the sun rising with splendor out of pink clouds off the steamy coast of the Yucatan. I felt myself growing sick with worry, though, and had to shakily make my way to the cabin. I sat and tried to release the stress through tears, but none would come. I shivered in turmoil while I listened to the song that I always associate with Bianca… 'Lamour toujour'. The words, music, memories, and all associations with bliss made it impossible to cry. There is just too much happiness to live and work for. I feel like I am in the darkest place in my life, but that's just drama. It was so much worse just 9 months ago when I was broke and working like a donkey as a waiter for nothing but disrespect and disdain.

Love is a frightening thing as much as a blissful one. I have never felt fear before in my life, never, until the thought of not having her. This self-imposed torture cannot be rationalized, like I always, always try to do. I am such an unemotional man, everything that I have used in the past to help me through tough times is crumbling at the thought of a trembling touch of her hand. Her laugh is a balm, but more than anything I just want to hold her! How does someone else fill a gap that is in me, and so personal? Am I half a man? How can I grow old without her?

The only failure I can imagine in my life would be to lose her. I could be fired, forced off the ships to live a life of cubicles and mediocrity, and I would be fine if I had her. Life cannot be mediocre with her in it. I wish I were a poet. I am a wordsmith, yet utterly incapable of expressing my feelings for her, my needs, wants, desires, passions, hopes.

One stalwart person had attended the second art auction. Me. That's right, even my art movers had succumbed to sea sickness.

Four days. Three auctions. Two gone. One left. Zero sales.

## 3

If I didn't do something fun, I was going to die of stress before the last auction.

Costa Maya was a modern port of call, a cluster of Carnival-sponsored shops and restaurants on the rugged eastern coast of the Yucatan peninsula, south of the touristic heavyweights of Cancun and Cozumel. The shore was blocked by a length of rocky shoals stretching to the horizon, behind which spread untold miles of low jungle. Out there, the Mayan civilization had flourished.

Walking the length of the pier, I stared down at the shoals that had kept this coast rustic since time immemorial. Atlantic surges exploded upon the three-dimensional labyrinth of sharp, black rocks, shattering and spraying into the air. The wind whipped the foam and mist away before I got wet, leaving only the sting of salt for my nose and eyes. Yes, this was indeed how I felt!

I wandered the slender ribbon of sand that separated the rocks from the jungle. The beach, if it could be called such, was dotted with tiki huts assigned to block the tropical sun for pairs of lounge chairs. Further away loomed several gargantuan thatched roofs, and across the distance traveled faint music. For the 238,000[th] time—once for each mile to the moon—I heard Jimmy Buffet's 'Margaritaville'. Nobody needs that. I stuck to the water's edge.

Eventually I spied a white canopy sheltering a small area set amid the ragged rocks. Usually touristic spots were in-your-face obvious, but this was subtle, like a gem waiting to be found amid rubble. I followed the narrow path through the sharp rocks, up and down and around, and eventually reached the small, shaded section. On a platform of smoothed rock, barely six feet from the surf bursting and battling violently with the shoals, was a massage table!

I was greeted by a small woman of Mayan persuasion. So petite as to appear childlike, she was probably too young to even catch Stefan's eye. A Spanish-style dress flowed to her ankles. White cloth on chocolate skin—like the contrast of surf on shoal—was a vivid, thunderous wonder to behold. She patted the towel-shrouded table.

"Twenty dollars," Chiquita said proudly, accent strong. Small teeth flashed beneath a flat Mayan nose. "One hour!"

I handed her a bill and said, "Here's fifty. Make it two hours and gimme all you got."

Bad move. The sheer tonnage of this girl's power could stop a team of oxen dead in its tracks.

Chiquita began by pummeling my back. While I assumed she used her fists, I wondered if perhaps she had secretly switched to clubbing me with a giant fish. I was nearly beaten unconscious. Then the real brutality began. Her fingers pinched with more strength than any human had any business possessing. The platinum, mechanized fingers of Schwarzenegger's *Terminator* squeezed my flesh into quivering slabs of pain.

Chiquita broke apart my tensed shoulders as though cracking an egg. She pushed her thumbs into my body as if kneading stone into dough was no problem. She walked on my back, grinding her heels as if extinguishing a cigarette. I knew some people paid for such things, but never thought I'd be one of them. The world faded.

# 4

Light. Blinding light. The sound of surging waves. Peace.

I was dead. I knew it. I had gone into the light.

A figure approached from above, light flaring behind, to glide gently down to my level. Then a kind, gentle smile. She was beautiful. An angel? No, a purser.

"Brian?"

She spoke my name from far, far away.

"Brian? Yes, I thought that was you. Are you all right?"

Clarity struck, overwhelming me. The sun followed suit.

"Unh?" I grunted, squinting up the gangway. The afternoon sun bounced brilliantly off *Sensation's* gleaming white hull.

"You've been standing at the bottom of the gangway for five minutes."

"Oh, hi Farida," I stammered. "Yes, yes, of course. I'm fine, thank you."

"Security didn't know if they should call the port authority or the doctor," she added, placing a concerned hand on my arm. "You were dragging your shirt in one hand, and the other was fondling your... well, the other is fondling your breast."

I dropped my hand immediately. Lamely I explained, "I was checking for my nipple. I thought it'd been rubbed off by Chiquita the Barbarian."

"Have you been drinking?" Farida asked, wrinkling her nose.

"No, but I wish I could. I think it would be a bad idea right now."

"Come," she said, taking my hand. Even in the blasting heat of Mexico, her brown hand's immense warmth was soothing. I realized dimly how long it had been since I had felt a caring touch. It helped more than the massage.

"You need an iguana!" Farida declared, tugging me along behind her.

"Don't we all?" I asked, trying to rekindle humor.

Fifteen minutes later I had an iguana on my head. His name was Kukulkan.

I was saved.

# 5

Farida, though living in South Africa, was an Egyptian Arab. She had the sweetest demeanor ever. So sweet, in fact, I only referred to her as Sugar. Her polar opposite was fellow purser Harald, from some remote island in the far north claimed by Denmark. His skin was remarkably pale, and his demeanor every bit as cold as the shores he called home.

"You look like shit," Harald said with a Scandinavian's lack of pretense.

Farida silenced him with an accusing glare, then made a point of smoothing her black tube dress.

"Uh, ya, you look like you need a walk on the beach," Harald amended, trying to accede to Farida's wishes. It was obviously difficult for him to be positive. "Relaxing and all that shit."

Farida placed an excited hand on my arm and said, "My dear friend Susana, the internet manager, is Mexican. She said only ten minutes from here is a bit of real Mexico!"

"Susana is Mexican?" I asked. "Her last name is O'Reilly, she's whiter than me, has freckles and red hair!"

"Yes," Farida bubbled. "The world is an amazing place, isn't it? We just need a taxi."

"And a driver that won't take us into the jungle and rob us," Harald grumbled.

Farida gave him an exasperated look.

Soon we were on a sandy beach, surrounded predominantly by locals. Happy brown children played in the surf, while parents bartered for cups of chopped fruit, upon which they shook chili pepper. Farida led us to a cluster of tiki huts blocking the hot sun, where we were surprised to meet Marc.

*Sensation's* two pursers, the port & shopping guide, and art auctioneer all settled into chairs sitting crookedly in the sand. The surf surfed, the breeze breezed. Drinks perspired. Three of us relaxed. Harald bitched.

"At least nobody here is smearing shit all over the walls," Harald observed with as much cheer as he could muster.

"Oh, Harald..." Farida sighed.

"You mean that rumor is true?" I said, surprised. Actually, unfortunately, not surprised.

"Ya," Harald snorted. "Who do you think had to deal with the complaints? Some animal smeared his shit all over the public toilets. Twice. I thought we were uncivilized on the island, but the peasants this cruise make me sick."

"Stay chill, brother," Marc murmured, eyes still closed.

"Hector will be here soon," Farida said brightly, swirling the ice in her tequila sunrise. "He likes to wander the beach and let the children play with his pet iguana. Susanna says he always walks by the tikis here to see if tourists want a picture with him."

I was eager to talk with Farida about Egypt. I shared with her my extreme pleasure in touring her homeland with Bianca. Talking about good times made me feel better.

"You fell in love!" Farida said dreamily. "How wonderful. She is joining you on *Sensation?*"

"If I can keep the ship, yes. That's why I'm so stressed."

"That's so romantic."

"Farida would be jealous," Harald added. "If you were black."

"Don't worry, Sugar," I said. "Someday some lucky guy will sweep you off your feet."

"I love living in South Africa, the men are so beautiful! But I miss my family," Farida admitted. "Father would be so angry with me for drinking this! But how can one visit another culture without tasting what it has to offer? I realize now that in many places of the world alcohol is central to their culture."

"I would have died long ago without booze," Harald agreed, rubbing his short blonde hair into a tussle. "What else to do on a winter night that lasts months? Can't count your money because you don't have any, and can't have sex because there's only one woman for every ten men on the island. But there's ten beers for every man, so alcohol kept me warm at night."

Farida smiled. She was radiant when she did so, her whole being emitting pure joy. "Back home I couldn't have imagined cold and dark at all! Marc, you're from a cold place, too, aren't you?"

"Canada," he agreed.

"You know, Marc," I said, "I've been wondering about your secret. How is it that you are always so chill?"

He shrugged and answered, "I'm a firewalker."

"I beg your pardon?"

He chuckled.

"Yep. That's most people's reaction. Surely you are aware that people have been doing it for millennia? Yet Western science has no satisfactory explanation. I like to explore, and there are plenty of mysteries right under our nose. My sister and I taught seminars on how to do it."

"That simple, eh?" Harald said peevishly.

Marc nodded and said, "That simple. You mock, of course, but it's true. Most people simply dismiss what they cannot understand, or what their dogma says is not so. When your feet are naked on top of coals at 1500 degrees, you learn to not let other people's issues bother you."

Now those were words of wisdom!

Hector arrived. Children emptied the waves to give him a noisy, bubbling escort. As Farida had promised, a three-foot iguana lazed upon his broad shoulders.

"After you, Sugar," I said.

"Oh, no no," Farida replied emphatically. "I don't want to touch it!"

"How about you, Harald?" I asked, but his sour face was answer enough.

Hector, all smiles, kindly asked for a donation in exchange for a picture with Kukulkan. I handed him five dollars, and before I knew it had an iguana on my head. Though named after the Mayan God of War, the iguana, like all reptiles, was surprisingly warm. The greatest joy, however, was that we finally convinced Farida to strike a pose with the animal. Her look was priceless.

Yes, indeed, sometimes all you need is a good iguana!

# 6

The last auction came. I was ready to give it my all. I had implemented every course of action I could possibly think of, breaking my bank to squeeze every bit of advertising possible.

My worst fears were realized.

I sold nothing. Zip, zilch. Nothing. Nada. Bianca would say '*nimic*'. Piti would say 'Jesus Gras!' I was unable to say anything.

Only a dozen people showed up, for word had spread among the passengers that the free art wasn't free. This was not merely supposition, but based upon the flood of comment cards denouncing me as a liar and promising to spread the word. No idle threats, apparently.

The cruise from hell. Revenue was down across the board. The spa began offering $160 treatments for $60, but had not a single taker. Even the bar sales were down 50%. I didn't think that was even possible. Marc, too, had missed his sales goals. Even Stefan spoke of 'taking arms against a sea of troubles and, by opposing, therefore end them'.

*Sensation* had been struck by a squall on the first day, setting the tone for the whole crossing of the Gulf. While the ship proverbially battened down the hatches, guests literally began looting the gift shop! And the asshole that spread feces on the toilet stalls? Still anonymous by the last day, he had graduated to smearing it on the doors of people's cabins, too.

I had done all that I was trained to do, all that I could. I just didn't care anymore. I was a burnt-out husk of a man, ruined by failure, not to mention sore from the expulsion of stress through bruises. I felt like I had gone through a combustion engine. Two near-miss failures in a row was enough to get demoted and lose my ship, but two catastrophic failures would surely get me fired.

# 7

During the stage talk at the beginning of my third cruise on *Sensation*, I was a zombie. Marc, inspired, announced that I was from Haiti. Still numb to the world, I emailed Bianca with the news that I had failed. I didn't know what was next. Was there still a chance that Sundance would only demote me, rather than cast me adrift? I tried to sound as cautiously optimistic as possible, but made it clear that I was currently unable to provide for Bianca the life promised.

Two days later the dreaded response from Sundance came. My personal and ship email accounts both screamed in bold letters:

"CALL ME ASAP - Gene"

One does not receive notice to call Uncle Sam without flinching. This was not a reference to the U.S. government, but a nickname for Gene, the Sundance manager of fleet operations. While he did, in fact, look like Uncle Sam, the name also came from the fact that he was generally a force for good, even if not hesitant to throw his weight around. *Sensation* was at sea somewhere in the Gulf of Mexico, but I did not want to wait until regular cell phone reception resumed near Mexico. I swallowed the excessive cost to use the ship's satellite phone and received Gene over a crackling connection.

"You seem to be having some problems," Gene began simply.

"Yes," I replied.

"Failing goal twice in a row is inexcusable, and bringing in literally zero is unheard of. Were you sick? Take a pill and get on with it. I have two dozen new trainees looking to replace associates looking to replace auctioneers. Get it?"

"I have lots of excuses, but I won't bother you with them," I said. I resisted the urge to mockingly thank him for his support. One does not joke with Gene like that and stay employed. "That said, if you read my reports you'll see that revenues were less than 50% for every single department, including the bar. If you want verification, I can put you in touch with the hotel director."

Silence answered me, punctuated all the more by the static.

"Brian..." Gene began, but I interrupted him.

"If you have to cut me, then cut me. But I'll bring in the money. Give me this cruise to prove it. I'll double my goal."

"Every auctioneer says that," he scoffed. "You all know it's two strikes and you're out. Unless you really do double your goal. But what are the chances of that, really, Brian?"

"Try me," I said flatly.

There was a long pause at the other end of the line. Finally Gene said, "Well, you need to if you want to maintain the average on that ship," Gene said. "Robin routinely doubled his goals. In fact, I have his last two cruises in front of me. He sold $28K and $35K."

"I'll do it," I promised.

"I'll make you a deal," Gene said. "If you double your goals this cruise, I won't tell the owner, Frederick, about this. If he finds out on his own, you'll be fired. Hopefully for you, Lucifer isn't checking. He would tell Frederick. He still hates you."

He hung up. I sighed.

Gene was lying, of course. He was trying to scare me into selling. Unbeknownst to him, I knew exactly how much Robin had ever sold, and it wasn't anywhere near double goal every cruise. The numbers Gene had cited were, in fact, the two highest Robin had ever pulled in over the entire year. Indeed, Robin had frequently missed goal, and that was even from the superior home port of Tampa Bay. Most auctioneers were careful to hide all such documentation—competition for ships being so fierce—but Robin was delightfully sloppy. He had left on the sales laptop every file and report from the last ten months.

Uncle Sam was just playing the Sundance game. Why use a carrot when you want to use a stick, work the animal to death, then just get a new one?

But I could play the Sundance game, too. What I withheld from Gene was that in yesterday's auction, I had already surpassed all my goals.

# CHAPTER FOURTEEN
## *Wood*

## 1

AND, JUST LIKE THAT, life on *Sensation* completely turned around. I did, indeed, double my goal on that third cruise. And then the next. And the next. I could only surmise the root cause of those first nine nerve-shattering days. Perhaps Carnival thought onboard revenue would remain high during all-but-free cruises. If so, they were quite wrong. They did fix the heavy discounts, even if they didn't fix the stabilizer. Regardless of all, I made a point of forgetting the past and focusing on the future. It was easy enough, because as sales improved, so did life.

With plenty of sea days providing ample time for now successful auctions, my evenings were open to publicize as I saw fit. Hitherto, as an associate auctioneer, I was under another's direction. But now I was the auctioneer, able to enjoy more freedom and flexibility than literally any other position onboard.

Because my art gallery was not positioned ideally on the Promenade deck, I instead made rounds to all the different vendors. Being seen and interacting with the guests was paramount in my line of work. I would make an appearance at the internet café, run by the charming Mexican Susana, who was also working my auctions. Next came the Formalities shop, run by the laughing Hungarian Ildi, who was delightful, if perhaps a bit anxious. I tried to hang out at the excursions desk with the Romanian Oana, but she remained aloof. Mostly, however, I loitered at the centrally located desk of the port & shopping guide. Canadian Marc being my best friend onboard was obviously a nice perk.

After my rounds, most evenings I enjoyed running on the sport deck. The track was an awkwardly tight loop with 11 laps to a mile, so to gauge myself I set my watch alarm. Letting my mind wander freely was easy when flying on the open deck a hundred feet above a black ocean.

That is, until *she* showed up.

A pretty, lithe blonde sweating in spandex before me on the track was wonderfully distracting. And she was always before me, because no matter how hard I ran—pardon the pun—she outpaced me. I was an accomplished runner, but she was much better.

I had no idea who this woman was, but secretly hoped she was a Steiner. I also had no idea that she would be the cause of the greatest trouble I could imagine. But she wasn't the only pretty lady who got me trouble, though for entirely different reasons. The next day I was completely blindsided.

After the second winning cruise had returned to homeport, I decided to head into New Orleans and reward myself with some oysters. I was striding past the guest elevators near the gangway when a shout startled me out of my wits.

"Brian!" a voice shrieked.

I leapt back with a gasp. I frantically searched for the verbal assailant, but saw no one.

"In here," the voice pleaded. I recognized the accent as Oana. Her voice emanated from a guest elevator, past a large box gripped firmly by the doors.

"You scared the hell out of me," I chided. "What are you doing?"

"I need your help."

That much was obvious. She had been trying to wedge a narrow, but exceedingly long, box into the elevator when the doors closed on her.

"I'm trapped," her voice continued through the half-closed doors. "On homeport these doors only work with a room steward key."

I pushed, prodded, and pulled the box until we together managed to stand it upright inside the elevator.

"Thank you," Oana said, panting from the exertion. She had been unloading supplies, based on her dusty jeans and sweaty T-shirt. Her curly black hair was wrestled back awkwardly by two overwhelmed clips. "Can you help me carry this to my desk? It's heavy. A steel rack for flyers."

"Of course. How did you get this thing so far on your own?"

"Marc," she spat. Her cute face grimaced. "He helped me carry it all the way from the marshaling area. The steward keyed the elevator for us and left, when Marc suddenly ran away."

"Ran away? That's odd. He didn't say anything?"

"Something about wood, I don't know. You Americans are strange."

"He's Canadian. Americans are perfect," I reminded her.

"North Americans, then," she corrected, rolling her eyes. She blew out the last of her exasperation as the elevator began its climb. "I'm sorry, by the way, about the other day when I blew you off. I thought you wanted to get in my pants."

"Well, duh," I said with a smile. "But that isn't my primary objective. I have a girlfriend. She's Romanian, too."

"Everyone has a girlfriend," she sniffed. "On ships that doesn't matter."

"It matters to me."

She harrumphed as the elevator opened. Together we hauled the box down the Promenade to her desk. We set it down with a heavy thump, then waited to catch our breath. Chief Officer Nino walked by, dressed smartly in his white uniform. Oana gave him a friendly wave and a smile. I called out a simple greeting as well, then began opening the box by sliding a pair of scissors down its length.

I paused, however, when I sensed something was wrong. Oana was standing rigidly at attention. I glanced up to see the XO staring down at me. He was a slender, clean-cut Italian man of late middle age.

"You are in a guest area wearing shorts and sandals," he noted stiffly.

"Oh! Yes, I'm sorry," I said, rising. "I was on my way to port when Oana asked me to help her move this. We'll be done in just a moment and I'll take the nearest crew door."

He was not at all satisfied with my explanation. Indeed, Nino looked even more annoyed. He stepped so close that he violated my personal space.

"If I see you even one more time dressed this way, you know what I will do?" he threatened. "I will give you a written warning. A few of those and you are out of Carnival forever."

I blinked in surprise. I could not fathom why he was so angry.

"And you will refer to me with respect," Nino continued coldly. "When you see me, you will not ask 'how are you', but say 'good evening, sir.'"

"Yes, sir," I replied, mustering all the meekness I could. It was hard to swallow my growing irritation.

The XO continued to stare me down for a long minute, then abruptly spun on his heel and stalked away.

"Let's get this finished," I muttered irritably, turning to Oana. She stared at me with huge, round eyes.

"I'm sorry, Brian..." she stammered. "I had no idea I'd get you in trouble with this!"

"Forget it," I snapped. "It wasn't your fault. I may have warranted a rebuke, but his presentation pissed me off. He could have ordered me to dress appropriately, but instead he threatened me! What the hell is that? Is a polite 'how are you?' so informal as to warrant a written warning?"

I released my fuming with a huff, then chuckled. "No good deed goes unpunished!"

# 2

After stage talk that night—Marc being from Burkina Faso and I from Micronesia—we decided to watch a football game. American football was, of course, hardly acknowledged by the vast majority of the crew. Soccer was the world's sport of choice, which I found rather trying. I enjoyed playing soccer during my school years, but watching it was dreadfully boring. Piti was to thank for my 'come to the gridiron' moment. After enduring eight mind-numbing hours of soccer—boasting a whopping two goals—I longed to unravel the complexity of American football's seemingly chaotic violence. Doesn't everyone watch football for intellectual stimulation?

We met in the aft guest lounge, where we could enjoy the game and a cigar. Almost immediately, however, I noticed that the usually unflappable Marc had become, well, flapped.

"Is everything all right?" I asked. "You look positively jumpy."

Marc, who had been scanning the main Promenade entrance, turned to look at me with surprise.

"I'm sorry, did you say something?"

"Marc," I said. "You're freaking me out. You act like somebody put a hit out on you."

"Actually," he admitted, "I'm being chased by a lumberjack."

"Oh, is that all?" I said with a puff of smoke. "Happens to everyone sooner or later. You being Canadian, I would have thought sooner."

"This guy from New Jersey keeps asking me about lumber prices in Mexico," Marc explained. "In the middle of my talk about the shops in Cozumel he interrupted me three times about it. He even came up on stage, man! I'm terrified he's going to ambush me."

"Well, the Garden State is renowned for its meddlesome lumberjacks, but I've got your back. Stay chill, brother."

Marc smiled and sipped from his beer. "You mock, of course. Seriously, dude, this guy is a weirdo."

"I wish I had a good forestry joke to lighten the mood," I said wistfully. "Something clever... about *log*arithms, maybe. Oh, wait, I know! What's brown and sticky?"

"What?"

"A stick."

For a long, long moment Marc regarded me skeptically. Finally he muttered, "No wonder your girlfriend isn't onboard."

Oana entered the lounge just then, saving me from what would no doubt be an equally embarrassing parry/riposte. The moment she saw us in the corner, she waved.

"Someone's looking for you!" she called as she bounced over.

Marc fled.

"Wha-?" Oana asked, startled, as she sat down beside me. "He's been jumpy all day."

"I hadn't noticed."

She smoothed the hem of her flowing dress of bold silver stripes. I, too, remained in my stage-talk formalwear: a double-breasted olive suit with a yellow Picasso tie. Wasn't this how everyone watched football?

"What did the XO want?" Oana carefully pried.

"Oh, no," I groaned, setting down my drink. "Now what did I do?"

"Oh! He said he was looking for you a few minutes ago at my desk. I assumed he had already talked to you."

"Did he look pissed?"

Oana frowned. "I seriously doubt he had been drinking."

Chief Officer Nino entered the lounge and spied us immediately. He walked straight over and, quite formally, asked if Oana would kindly give us a moment alone. I rose as Oana departed, but Nino motioned for me to remain seated.

"I just wanted to tell you," he began slowly. "Regarding earlier today... that I was already most upset for other reasons. I did not mean to be so harsh."

I blinked a moment, trying to process what I had just heard.

Very, very graciously I replied, "Thank you, sir. It's extremely kind of you to take the time."

He nodded, then departed.

I was utterly stunned. A first officer... apologizing? *Sensation was* a ship of miracles!

But as good as life had become on *Sensation*, it was not without frustration. Responding to my initial email of dismay on that first cruise, Bianca had complimented my patience and maturity regarding how seriously I took my promise to support her. During that time, Bianca was again on Dan's crack team that opened the new *Carnival Valor* in Montfalcone. That came with the usual snippets of tourism and partying, followed by a week of intermittent internet.

Because I rued that sorrowful missive, my subsequent emails had been short. My world had collapsed concurrent to a very rare—and well deserved—perk of her hard work: plenty of time off in port. Only long after she babbled about why Italy was the greatest place on earth did she offer me words of support. No doubt she didn't realize the magnitude of my dilemma. How could she, if I was not fully forthcoming? Still, I couldn't help but dwell upon four lines raving about Italy for every one line expressing enthusiasm to join me on *Sensation*.

The reasons for delaying our joining on *Sensation* were twofold: her paperwork and my failure. The latter issue, at least, appeared to have passed. When I expressed cautious optimism about retaining *Sensation*, Bianca offered to apply for a transfer to *Sensation's* dining room. Just to be with me, she said. This offer implied her willingness to sacrifice the privileges of working on Dan's team. She was making an effort.

But was she? We both knew I would rebuff her offer. Sundance could—and often did—transfer auctioneers with only a few days notice, frequently to a different cruise line altogether. Bianca had no chance of keeping up with me via the restaurants. Even if she could, she would continue to work 80 hours a week and we'd never see each other. I sensed this was something different from her, and not actually a real gesture. In a Machiavellian manner, she was even setting me up as 'the one who gave up on us'.

Wow. Working as an art auctioneer had really gotten me thinking like a schemer! Why was I second-guessing my Bianca? We had enough obstacles without adding head games to the list!

But on came her subsequent email, and her tone had indeed changed. She claimed she was getting all kinds of confusion about what to do. Her friends and coworkers were pushing her hard to accept a promotion to hostess, and then have me follow her around from ship to ship.

I was incensed.

Becoming a hostess would cut Bianca's income in half. A hostess was lower than the lowest manager on the restaurant totem pole, whereas art auctioneer was an elite position onboard. I had gone through too much for us to take such a preposterous stall lightly. And stall it was: she was obviously hesitant to join me.

I structured an email with my rebuttal of each concern she listed, in order. I was even audacious enough to instruct her to print it out and read it with some M&Ms or whatever ritual she needed to focus, because what I had to say was important.

Bianca and her friends were limiting their progress, and thusly lives, to their own narrow experience: the restaurants. It was all they knew. They were defining success as an easier schedule, easier duties, and perks such as nice meals and wearing nice dresses. That was all crap. Such things were taken for granted by auctioneers as the least of our benefits. As a hostess, it would be the pinnacle of success. The only advantage of her suggested path was stability: an understandable concern, but a high price indeed.

A week passed.

Finally I received an email thanking me for my clarity of thought and helping her through a tough time of indecision. A bit aggressively, I pushed my advantage and made it clear that I had waited a long, long time for her and worked hard to give her this opportunity to break free of the restaurants. *Sensation* was on its way to becoming a success, though I didn't have enough track record yet to call it that. I thought of my bad times as the worst-case scenario, but her words implied she thought my good times as the best-case scenario. True, ups and downs were aplenty, but here I was: an auctioneer in record time.

If the foundation of her resistance was stability, I wrote, then get in writing that Carnival will hire her back if she so desires. After all, Dan was the senior maitre d' of Carnival Cruise Lines and would bend over backwards to keep her.

I was trying to stay positive, but losing my patience. It had been two years!

## 3

That night I ran. Oh, did I run! I thundered down the track, desperately trying to release my frustrations into the night sky. It, too, was turbulent. The black distance was not complete, for the low horizon flickered red, as if a volcano was erupting just beyond sight. Random bursts of lightning would flare intense yellow, momentarily revealing miles of choppy sea, before returning to a fitful, purple slumber.

Alas, my aggravations were compounded when the pretty blonde runner showed up. She wore spandex shorts and a T-shirt pulled up to reveal her middle. At first, my focus was entirely on myself, my troubles, my pace. I pushed hard, burning muscles commanding all attention. I forced the highest long-distance speed I could muster. After a while, however, I noticed that she was using me as a mere pacer. She ran at my side for a few laps, then kicked into a higher gear and left me in the dust.

Unconsciously, I sped up. She did the same. Soon we were both flying around the track at full throttle, scattering sea gulls and guests inclined towards a light jog. What had begun as just me outrunning my emotions became a fierce competition between silent strangers. I lost track of how many laps we ran. I never lost track of how many I came in second: all of them!

Then I had a blow-out. A calf muscle spasmed and the pain forced me to immediately limp off to the side. My breath sawed roughly through my throat, my heart thumped jarringly in my chest. The victor finished her lap faster than ever, then gracefully pulled over to where I sat on the deck, panting and pooling sweat.

"Well done!" she complimented generously. She was glistening beautifully with sweat, but barely panting. Bitch.

Her face was very pretty. She smiled encouragingly to me. Taking advantage of the break, she loosed her hair from its ponytail and gave it a wild shake. She paced back and forth, keeping her muscles warm. Deck lights outlined the sharp, tight contours of her middle. Each perfectly-defined abdominal muscle popped out in relief. She had the sexiest six-pack I had ever seen.

I wheezed, "Please tell me... you're some champion... somewhere..."

Still smiling, she said modestly, "Not exactly."

"Then... at least say... you're half my age."

She scrutinized me a moment, then said, "Probably. I'm twenty-one."

That didn't make me feel any better. I was only thirty-one.

"I ran for national team of Serbia," she admitted, accent thick, English unsure.

"At least tell me you're a Steiner," I joked, finally catching my breath.

"I am," she said as she reached out a hand and helped me up. "How you know?"

I chuckled as I limped back to the track. "You must be new if you don't know the joke about Steiners."

"Oh," she replied, suddenly blushing. "We not all sleep around."

"More's the pity," I teased.

We cooled off our muscles by walking—me limping— down the track. We talked for a long time. Her name was Vela, and this was her first contract. Her English was poor, yet she was already taking advantage of the ship's free language classes to learn Spanish. Unlike most of the spa staff that I had met, Vela was not here for a 'good time'. She exuded focus. She was incredibly sweet. She was entrancing. An hour passed, the brisk air long ago cooled our steaming bodies. The sea storm made the night electric—or was it for an entirely different reason? A thing for Vela was the last thing I needed right then.

Or was it?

"Would you like to join me for a drink?"

## 4

The next day was a blur. Homeports usually are. A delivery of art materials occupied most of my time. I took supreme care to avoid entering guest areas in my 'unloading clothes'. What really made the time fly, however, were the bits and pieces of Vela.

Off and on, all day, if we didn't visit briefly in the mess or in the corridor, we talked via phone calls and pages. It was fun. I enjoyed being social in such a manner for the first time in a long, long time. We were playful about it all. Like teens. Stefan would have been proud.

But when I saw her on the Promenade handing out flyers, Vela was all woman. As a representative of the Steiner salon, she radiated confidence with a face and hair made-up to salon perfection. A white dress hugged her statuesque curves lovingly, and her every move made the sequins shiver. Her every move made *me* shiver! She was busy when I passed by, but managed to glance up from her crowd of gawking admirers to mouth the words, 'call me'.

I felt a tingle of excitement. Yes, I really did feel like a kid again!

Later that day, after the stage talk, Marc remarked on my different behavior.

"You seem high as a kite," he observed. "Sell a Picasso or something?"

"Oh, no," I replied, chuckling. "I've just had a good day. Or, I should say, I had a good night."

He raised his eyebrows inquisitively.

"No, no, nothing like that. I mean, not really. I met someone, that's all. I've been running with a pretty Steiner girl for a while, and I asked her to join me for a drink. It was innocent."

"Innocent?" he repeated dubiously. "And what did you do, then? Play scrabble?"

"We talked about my ghost book, if you must know," I defended gamely. "I'm a smart writer and stuff, which is why chicks dig me. Didn't you know?"

"You dog," Marc accused with a grin. "Trying the old, 'scary story' line, eh? Movies work better, so you can put your arm around them in the theater. Remember, dude, you told me how you met your girlfriend. I see you're sticking with pick-up lines that work."

"I-what? It wasn't like that at all!" I protested. "We just talked."

"Mmm hmm," Marc hummed doubtfully.

"Come on, lots of people are interested in ghost stories. I don't bring it up to show off."

"Mmm hmm."

"I bring it up to get them interested, yes, but about something different, about history."

"About you," Marc noted with a smirk.

Just then, Farida approached. I nearly leapt on her for assistance—that is, until she handed me a dog-eared copy of my ghost book. I gaped at it, struck speechless by the timing. I had forgotten that I gave her the only copy I had onboard.

"Hello boys!" she said. "Brian, here's your book back. I enjoyed it very much, thank you."

Marc gave a suggestive grunt, waiting patiently for me to confess.

"Oh, you've heard the story, haven't you Marc?" Farida continued, oblivious to what she had stumbled into. "When Brian met his girlfriend, he gave her a personal tour of a haunted Old West town! You've read his book haven't you?"

"Why no, I haven't," he replied, snatching the book from my nerveless fingers. Giving me an expressive look, he added, "Funny thing, that. But you know, guys don't talk about such things to other guys."

"What an amazing first date that would be, don't you think?" Farida continued dreamily. "Like stepping into another world. Sunsets over mesas... tall, dark, rugged men... women who drank whiskey with the men...!"

She spun off, swept away by thoughts of romance.

"See, that proves my point," I said, trying to salvage my situation. "I'm not trying to get on Farida, am I?"

Marc muttered flatly, "Tell me you wouldn't get on Farida."

"Oh, no," I stammered. "Am I, like, one of those creeps now? Who don't respect women?"

"Yep," Marc said, perking up in triumph. "One of those creeps."

He folded his arms behind his back and stalked away, leaving me alone. And creepy.

## 5

One of Marc's duties was coordinating with port shops. Prior to the recent advent of the position of port & shopping guide, the cruise director had been responsible for recommending—or more importantly, not recommending—options in port. This had resulted in the illicit flow of monetary bribes to a ship figure who already exuded enormous influence. A single cautionary word would cause sales to plummet, so it was paramount for shop owners to keep cruise directors happy. The ever-vigilant Carnival stepped in, created the new position, and thusly ensured bribes remained safely in the corporate coffers.

This did not mean that savvy entrepreneurs were unable to offer perks, however.

In Costa Maya, Marc and I were chatting with the manager of Diamonds/Tanzanite International. I was relaxed after a secondary encounter with Chiquita the Barbarian. After prostrating myself humbly before her and begging for a gentle touch, she had restored my shredded calf muscle. Marc was relaxed because, well, he was Marc. Yet it was not to last.

"Oh, no," Marc suddenly groaned. "He's here. No, don't look! He'll see us."

Both the manager and I immediately spun about. Marc groaned.

A sweating, middle-aged man in glasses approached us. He ran his hand through damp, thinning hair before extending it to us.

"I've been looking for you!" he exclaimed triumphantly to Marc.

"Oh, hello again," Marc greeted as nonchalantly as he could.

"Have you looked into the Home Depot list I asked about?" the man excitedly asked.

Marc stalled, saying, "You see, my normal duties require a lot of face time with the various business owners here."

"Yes, yes, so they do!" the sweaty man continued. "My point exactly!"

He glanced around the shop approvingly, then set his shiny eyes on the manager. Juan was a slender, handsome youth who dressed very well. His English was marvelous. Juan gave Marc a wry smile.

"Why, indeed he did work his local contacts regarding Home Depot, sir," Juan said smoothly. "But I cannot fathom why you would choose to go there. Would you not prefer to support local business? It is in our best interest to make you happy on more than one front, and you will find us far more... flexible... than an American corporate mega-store."

"Why yes!" the man agreed enthusiastically. "That's what I've been telling Marc all week. That is precisely why I asked him for a complete list of stores selling lumber."

"Lumber, you say?" Juan asked, flashing another glorious smile. "Why buy retail when you can do so much better? I'm so glad that Marc brought you here, my friend. He truly knows his business. My father owns the largest furniture factory in the Yucatan. He has connections to lumber."

Juan grabbed the New Jersian by the arm and led him away, saying, "We must both truly thank Marc—in writing!—for connecting us so far above and beyond his normal duties..."

Marc stared at me, completely dumbfounded.

"Well done," I complimented. "My comment cards either ask me to sell cheaper art or say I smell like fish. You, on the other hand, have just been guaranteed a glowing review of your brokering of a Mexican lumber deal!"


## 6


After another week, I finally received an email from Bianca. My soaring hopes were immediately quashed. What she wrote left me agog. She wanted me to take a work break from Sundance and take a cruise on *Valor* so we could talk—*in two months!*

I stared at the email, unable to identify the flurry of emotions sweeping through me. Part of me was sad. She commented that I sounded different, while she was the same. Yeah, I was different. I had a sorrow in my soul from months —nay, years—of unsuccessful toiling to be with her. I was angry at her indecision and had quite literally told her I was running out of patience. A poor choice of words, obviously. Maybe she read that it was too late and I was moving on, when I merely meant that it was time to make it happen!

Especially after the last week, I had never been more certain of what I had with Bianca. I couldn't tell her why, of course. With every moment I spent with Vela, I honestly couldn't stop comparing it to my time with Bianca. It was exciting, yet paled in comparison. Such an admission would offend both of them, of course. Yet adding to my confusion was the fact that my last letter to Bianca was before I had even met Vela.

I wanted to send a soothing response, assuring her that our future was my focus. But I couldn't. I was too angry. As she said, she was the same—handling the situation only on her own terms.

Her proposal was almost as insulting as her suggestion that I follow her on her hostess career. Sundance did not offer work breaks. I had told her that several times. Even if they did, asking for one would be career suicide with so many hungry auctioneers fighting for *Sensation*. She obviously was not listening to me, nor trying to understand my life—the lifestyle I chose entirely to be with her, the lifestyle we both agreed was our path to being together. Apparently, in our many long months—years!—she had changed her mind.

So she wanted me to take a cruise on her ship, did she? So I could spend thousands of dollars for her to dazzle me in her spare time like I was Tommy the Teddy Bear? What the hell had become of our dream? Had time and real life finally killed it?

## 7

On the next cruise, I again surpassed all my goals in the first auction. Work was going splendidly. So was life on *Sensation*. Vela and I had seen each other every day for a week. The chemistry was good. Very good. But more than that, Vela was an incredibly sweet young woman. It was refreshing that she simply wanted to spend time with me.

When the port of Cozumel came around again, Vela joined me for some sun and sand in the morning. As it turned out, too much sun. We both soon returned to *Sensation* red as lobsters. With her afternoon shift still an hour off, Vela came to my cabin. For the first time, I was happy to have the fish smell. It was terribly unromantic, and that suited me fine. Sort of. I just didn't know anymore.

We played around, easing our hot skin with some well-placed ice. Play is where we stopped, however. After a while, we lie beside each other and just enjoyed each others' company. Sometimes a warm embrace was more powerful than sex. As a teen, I would have protested that idea mightily. As a teen, I was naive.

In the dark cabin, I started to drift off to sleep. I awoke at Vela's touch. She traced her fingertips lightly along the features of my face. Her touch was very delicate, the sensation soothing. I wondered what she was thinking, but didn't ask. I just enjoyed.

Eventually she asked quietly, with a hint of amusement in her accent, "Am I the youngest woman you've been with?"

I chuckled.

"Technically, my dear, we haven't actually 'been' yet. I assumed you would have noticed something like that."

"Maybe we can work on that," she said, teasing her fingers through my chest hair. "After work I have Spanish class at ten tonight, but I'm free afterwards. Do you want me to come over?"

"More than just about anything," I said.

# CHAPTER FIFTEEN

## *Thumbprint Rage*

### 1

THE NEW YEAR of 2005 started with a bang. The first good news was that in the final cruise of 2004, I had the highest sales of the year on *Sensation*. In just a few weeks, I went from zero to hero, as they say.

The second good news, received first thing on New Year's Day, was even better. At long last, Bianca had obtained in writing a promise that Carnival would hire her back if she were ever so inclined. No more concerns about worst-case scenarios: even if I was suddenly killed in a tragic blimp accident or something, Bianca would be able to care for her family.

Yet such glorious news came with a caveat. She still insisted on transferring to *Sensation* as a waitress—though right away—so she could transition more slowly to being my assistant. She wanted to transition more slowly after two years?

I was not particularly happy with this plan of hers. I recognized she was making an effort, but it seemed to fly in the face of all that we had been conversing about over the last two months while I was on *Sensation*. Apparently she felt the devil you know is better than the devil you don't. I had found in life that jumping in with both feet forced adaptation faster and more completely. Easing in a little at a time brought baggage and hesitation, which led to resistance. But that was me. This was about her.

So I agreed.

I was so eager to get Bianca onboard, I nearly overlooked the obvious. What about Vela? Assuming I had a ship squeeze was one thing, but actually meeting her...? I wanted, I needed, Bianca in my life immediately, but was I setting myself up for a drama?

The subsequent email changed everything. The menacingly bold letters of a Sundance order wrote:

"HANDOVER TO PREVIOUS AUCTIONEER
ON JAN 10 - Gene."

I had lost *Sensation*. A bang? More like a thermonuclear detonation.

# 2

When *Sensation* returned to homeport, Marc and I went out into New Orleans. We strode through the French Quarter, admiring the architecture and history, feeling the dirty vibrance of the Big Easy. Marc had not yet seen the old town, and was exhilarated at the 'anything goes' attitude. That is, until he heard the Anglicized pronunciations of the French street names. After finding locals pronounced Burgundy Street as

"Ber-GUN-dee", he began to question such freedom of expression. His spirits were saved at Café Maspero by a steaming mound of expertly fried shrimp tumbling over the sides of a po' boy sandwich.

"What do you think about Ildi?" Marc asked, as we sat at a thick wooden table amid the bustle and swirl of the lunch hour.

"I think she's wonderful," I replied. "Her laugh is contagious, she's capable and attractive. However, I sense that she's a bit, I don't know... desperate? Is that the word?"

Marc nodded.

"Yep, that's what I thought, too. Whenever I talk to her in Formalities, she's almost giddy in the hope that I'll ask her out. I think that would get old pretty fast. Maybe even scary."

We ate in silence for a while, but finally I felt the need to talk to a friend.

"I'm starting to get in over my head, I think," I commented.

"Vela?"

"This is going to sound bad, but I truly feel this is the last opportunity I will ever have with another woman, because next time I get Bianca I'm never letting her go. We've hit the point where we need to make it happen or go our separate ways. I refuse to let the latter happen. *Sensation* has been weird from the beginning, not just for me, but for Bianca and me—a hiccup in our relationship that I don't think really represents our true state of affairs. I think when I failed at the beginning I fed her greatest possible fear. I sent her a letter that first week when I wasn't selling, and she's been backpedaling ever since."

"So 'next ship', eh?"

"Sorta like saying 'I'll start the diet tomorrow', isn't it?" I agreed. "But whether I like it or not, Bianca and I do have a 'don't ask, don't tell' policy. I can do what I want. Just because I chose not to since the beginning doesn't mean I can't play around now. But I'm a little scared to open Pandora's box, you know?"

"Well," Marc said simply. "Most of us have a 'ship squeeze'. It's part of the life."

"It is," I agreed. "Bianca's best friend, Flaviu, had a different girlfriend every contract for years, despite a wife and kids at home. Then suddenly he thought it was love. He divorced, lost his kids, and married his new squeeze. He managed to go almost two whole contracts without sleeping around. Now he has two ex-wives."

I paused a moment before continuing.

"I'm not saying I'm like Flaviu. He's a chauvinist pig. I blame both of them for that mess, because obviously his new wife knew he couldn't stop sleeping around. I'll never be like that. But I just might kick myself if I don't play at least a little on ships. It's like going to college but not living in the dorms: you don't really get the whole experience. I fought the idea for a long, long time, but now that the opportunity is almost over...."

"Don't know what you've got until it's gone," Marc intoned.

"Figures, the first time I entertain the idea of playing around, I actually fall for her! Vela is beautiful, obviously—"

"A body to die for," Marc agreed, interrupting a bit too eagerly.

"But she's a nice girl, too. Focused. I've never met a woman with such a balance of fitness, ambition, and kindness. It's quite a turn on. Yet whenever we're together, I think only of Bianca. As good as it is with Vela, it's just not the earth-shattering stuff I have with Bianca. Strange. I am seriously entertaining the idea that this Romanian cast some sort of spell on me."

"Much of your dilemma has been taken care of for you," Marc pointed out. "You are leaving in a week, like it or not. Regardless of your feelings for Vela, you both know you're parting. Do whatever feels right."

"That's the problem. What feels right anymore? It all does! I've never had difficulty telling right from wrong before."

"That's because there actually is no right or wrong here," Marc observed. "You are free to do whatever you want, but are still warring with whatever is the reason for your self-denial. Is your concern losing Bianca? Is it hurting Vela? Or do you think you are unworthy of having what you want?"

"I wish I had some 1500 degree coals right now for clarity," I sighed. "You know, after hot moments with Vela I feel like a little kid. I'm so full of energy and excited and happy, I feel fifteen years younger. How can that feel wrong?"

"Somehow I doubt that fifteen years ago you were a little kid," Marc noted wryly.

"I've never been good at math," I admitted. I chuckled and teased, "The only math that matters here is that I'm thirty-one and Vela's twenty-one."

"You dog," Marc mumbled over a mouthful of French fries.

"But you know what I write in my diary? Every comment totally reinforces the wonderful relationship I have with Bianca. Or used to have, or had on vacations, or whatever you call it. My time with Vela is great—probably as good as it gets for the normal realm of us mere mortals. But my chemistry with Bianca is sublime! I'm telling you, everything I've been expounding over the last two years is being proven, ironically by another woman! Every fiber of my being resonates with Bianca, and I think of it even when I'm lying with Vela. All things are going so perfectly with Vela, yet it still pales in comparison with that fantastic woman I have fought so hard for."

"So why," I finished, "Why can't I stop with Vela?"

"Yet you will," Marc said, "But whatever you do, don't ever, ever tell Bianca. You would only be serving yourself, not her."

I stared at my shrimp. They had gone cold and weren't so tasty anymore.


# 3


I stared at the dark ceiling. My heart had finally settled back to a normal beat, but instead my mind raced. One woman I couldn't keep my hands off. Another I couldn't keep my mind off.

What really made me mad was that Bianca was going right down the same old path: planning her life on her own, hoping for a meeting somewhere to pretend she was happy. When I told her I lost *Sensation*, she almost excitedly asked me to take a cruise on her ship! That way she would not have to rearrange her life at all. Like her insistence on remaining a waitress, this was a last-ditch effort for her to keep her long-term plans with Carnival, not me.

Ships were no longer helping us. They were keeping us apart. Worse, it was almost impossible to make plans with Bianca while she was at sea because she shut down all sense of hope. After my disaster on *Legend*, I truly empathized. Waiters were in many ways like a shell-shocked soldier: until they got off the front line, even if for just a while, they couldn't remember normal life. This only reinforced that to really be together, Bianca would have to join me. I wanted to make Sundance work with her, but she wanted me to make it work for her. For the first time, I was beginning to seriously question our relationship.

I had changed my entire life for this, and wasn't going to give up on us—not until I had a tangible reason to. Doubts were natural. Separation made them inevitable. What was needed was focus. I had lost it for a moment on *Sensation*. But did Bianca ever have it?

So I was confused, angry, and impatient with Bianca. This led me into the arms of Vela, where I was merely confused. No, this was just a last, wild fling before settling down. It was the settling down that I wanted! If that was to be denied yet again, was it so wrong to want to spend some time with a lovely, intelligent woman?

I rolled onto my side and kissed Vela on the cheek. She smiled at me drowsily.

"All I have to give is a few more days," I said. "I would like to spend them with you. Nothing more, nothing less."

"Nothing more, nothing less," she agreed.

# 4

I was exceedingly annoyed. *Sensation* closed access to the gangway at 3:30 p.m. on home port. I checked my watch for the hundredth time. It was 3:20 p.m. The tall, brown-skinned security chief ordered the crew gangway to be pulled up.

"Wait!" I cried, "It's not 3:30 yet!"

"Close enough," the chief replied. "All crew are aboard, all visitors are off."

Three Filipinos disassembled the X-ray machine and pushed it aside. Two Indians muscled the metal plank inside the shell door. One American swore and stormed off.

My fleet manager, Roger, was supposed to have personally met with me to discuss my future with Sundance. His clearance as a guest had been last-minute, and I had figured perhaps his arrival would have been, too. My life was hanging by a thread, and he didn't have the decency to call? That was his job! Screw him.

I went to the open deck, snapped open my cell phone, and angrily dialed Uncle Sam.

"Why Brian!" Gene said cheerily after I introduced myself. "What can I do for you?"

"You can explain," I said rather shortly. "Roger was supposed to come aboard today and do so personally. I'm too busy polishing the paperwork on *Sensation's* highest sales of the year to deal with a no call/no show."

"Highest sales of the year?" Gene asked.

"Yes. Check your inbox, it's all there. I have increased my sales four cruises in a row now, and this last one exceeded anything achieved by the last auctioneer."

"How do you know that?"

"I have my sources. I have doubled goals for weeks running now. That's something Robin never pulled off, as you well know. Why are you pulling me off *Sensation* when I am breaking records?"

Gene was silent a moment.

"Your numbers were good, but not great," Gene admitted reluctantly.

"Improving every cruise," I reminded him sharply.

"Look, Brian, we had no ship for Robin. He's the senior auctioneer. Don't worry, you'll get another ship."

"When?"

"I have you signed up for the advanced training class the last week of February. We'll decide then."

"I've only been at sea two months and am still fresh. Give me another ship."

"Not until advanced training. That's a good thing, Brian, believe me. Some of the others in your class don't even have their own ship yet. February was the first opening. Assuming you get the seal of approval from Lucifer, you'll get a ship."

"I don't need any further seal of approval," I pushed. "My numbers speak for themselves. Besides, Lucifer hates me for reasons that defy explanation."

"True, but some of us like you. See you in Feb."

He hung up. So did I. I nearly threw the phone overboard. If I had to pass another damn test under the scrutiny of Sundance's evil trainer Lucifer, I was doomed. Would the drama never cease?

In fact, it was about to get a lot worse.

Farida insisted that I have a going away party on my last night aboard *Sensation*. To that end, she invited all of our group to gather for a drink after duties permitted. A few of us were not allowed access to guest areas, so Farida took the liberty of designating my cabin. A guest cabin, to be sure, but still quasi-legal for all. This would have suited me fine, except for one thing: Vela wanted to see me on my last night onboard.

Barring Marc, no one else knew about my involvement with Vela. I couldn't bear to have my friends know that, after months of talking about nothing but Bianca, I had a ship squeeze. Farida nearly swooned with envy at the thought of our international romance. Oana, though secretive about her own past—she came to ships to avoid a marriage proposal—had ties to the Romanian mafias on other ships. And Ildi's advances, though directed at nearly every male with a pulse, had only been kept at bay by my pleading unwavering faith to Bianca. Simply put, I was leaving and saw no reason to complicate everything for everyone.

The lies began.

I warned Vela that I would be unavailable on the last night, due to overwhelming handover responsibilities. In particular, I told her I had to do a full inventory of all thousand works of art still onboard. That was true. I told her it had to begin at 9 p.m. That was not true.

Vela immediately offered to assist me, commenting excitedly that she got off work at 9 p.m. It was hard not to cringe. Cowards are supposed to cringe, after all.

Lying sucked. No wonder I never did it before. I felt hollow inside. How could anyone get used to that awful feeling? Who the hell would even want to try?

# 5

In the beginning, I forgot my inner turmoil at the party. The best parties were always organic. Planning may take minutes or months, but the real thrill comes from people: arriving separately, bringing their own special contribution—whether entertainer, listener, or merely a warm body—interacting, then perhaps leaving together. My favorite dynamic about ship parties was the irrelevance of race, color, or creed. The friends laughing and hugging and eating and drinking in my cabin that night covered half the globe. We were white, black, and brown, Christian, Muslim, shamanist, and atheist. I loved that about ships! A good party also usually has a surprise of some sort. Ours began surprising, all right: it began with the laying on of hands.

Marc and Farida arrived first, a little after 9 p.m. But Farida immediately sat on the floor, propped her back against the bed, and rubbed her temples.

"I have the worst headache," she moaned. She looked up at me apologetically and added, "I'll try to be cheery, though. I promise."

Trust Sugar to apologize to someone else for being in pain!

"Would you like me to take it away?" Marc asked gently.

"Whoa, slow down there, tiger," I interrupted. "I know that sex is the best way to cure a headache, but the party hasn't even started yet!"

Farida slapped me on the knee.

"If you don't object," Marc continued. "I can probably make it go away with some energy work."

"What do you mean?" Farida asked, frowning.

"A form of energy work," Marc explained. "You know I'm a fire walker, but that's just part of my exploring energy."

"Are you serious?"

"I explore lots of things," Marc said simply. "I spend a lot of time in the presence of shamans. I lived months in Sedona with spiritual healers before joining ships. There are lots of labels, but it's really the same as anything else. Praying to God, communing with the Great Spirit, working with universal energy: they're all just different ways for humans to interact with something greater than themselves, and thusly find comfort. It's a lot more simple than people seem to think. If you prefer, we can get you some aspirin."

"No, no," Farida replied, enchanted. "This sounds interesting. Oh, I just love ships! So many different ways of approaching problems."

"Shall I leave?" I asked. "I'd like to watch this, though."

"Stay," Marc bid. "Let's all just be quiet for a minute or two."

Farida sat cross-legged, while Marc moved to sit on the bed behind, legs straddling her.

"Lean forward," he ordered gently.

Farida closed her eyes, with a hint of an excited smile. Marc ran his hands up and down her back in a light form of massage. His features were exceptionally relaxed—as usual—but soon took on a look I had never seen in him before. Though there was no pinching of the brow or any other such indication, his face exuded extreme concentration. He had definitely entered into a place that was different. I would not use the word trance, because he seemed obviously in control of himself.

Marc's hands moved over Farida's back in what could only be called a searching pattern. Then suddenly he made motions like scooping something off her skin and flinging it away. This continued for about two minutes, and the room began to feel distinctly heavier. Then suddenly Marc opened his eyes and helped Farida sit up with a gentle tug on her shoulders.

She blinked a moment, then stared up at him with wide, incredulous eyes.

"Why, Marc," she marveled, "My headache is completely gone! Brian, did you see what he just did? It really worked!"

"Wow," I admitted. "Just to be sure, had you tried sitting quietly before you came here, or already taken aspirin or anything?"

"No pills, and I lay down for half an hour in my cabin," Farida explained, still squawking excitedly. "It didn't help my head at all!"

"It wasn't in your head," Marc said simply, pouring himself a glass of red wine. "You should probably work on your posture."

Suddenly a pounding rattled the door. In popped Harald with a bottle of liquor.

"I'm here, bitches!" he stated. "What, there's no food? What kind of shitty party you guys throwing here?"

So much for positive energy.

Harald inhaled deeply through his nose, then only reluctantly loosed it with a satisfied sigh.

"Ahh..." he said. "I love the smell. Reminds me of home!"

Romanian Oana arrived shortly thereafter. Hungarian Ildi brought several bottles of champagne. Mexican Susana brought her new boyfriend, Canadian Michel. Junior, a Jamaican head waiter friend, came by later. Indeed, the door was left open because people came and went throughout the night. Junior left to serve the maitre d's table, for example, and Ildi had paperwork. Fortunately, she returned with even more champagne. The two that should have left, ironically, stayed the whole time. Susana and Michel really needed to get a room for themselves.

Ah, but they were in love! They were also a study in opposites attract: she was a rigidly methodical computer manager, he was a spontaneous jazz musician; she was only arguably under five feet tall, he was undeniably over six feet; she preferred hot weather and jalapeños, he liked cold winters and cheese curds. But love conquers all. They laughed and hugged and rollicked all night. There was love to spare, in fact, and everyone glowed in their presence. They gave us all hope. Certainly they were a reminder to me of what I was fighting for.

A highlight of the night was reliving our recent trip to Cancun. I had rented a car in Playa del Carmen, and in crammed Marc, Farida, Susana, Michel, and our Bulgarian friend Pavlina. We played tourist: lunched, shopped, saw the sights. Farida even tried her hand at driving. Backing the car out of the parking spot had been so stressful for her—and entertaining for us—that later she joined me on a bungee chair for a wild fling a hundred feet into the air, calling it 'small potatoes'. This last statement was made in honor of my being from Iowa, she said. Hey, she was trying.

The trip had been a delight from start to finish, and ranked absolutely as one of the best days of my entire ship career. The activities were not so special, but the people sure were.

Making the memory even more special, Michel revealed a presentation he had created by consolidating the photos and video from our cameras. Seeing highlights from everyone's perspective was enlightening. All three of my trips through the buffet line were documented by friends who marveled at how Americans ate. Marc's post traumatic stress was revealed when we drove past a Home Depot. We were all impressed by Susana dancing with our waiter, as if we were in a ship dining room. Finally a video caught us all singing Christmas carols while I unsuccessfully tried navigating Mexican streets.

We laughed so loud, it was amazing the neighbors didn't call security.

The alcohol began flowing even more freely, which made cramming nine bodies into my cabin more agreeable. Marc was particularly pleased at being pressed into Oana all night. Lucky bastard.

By midnight, it was time for room service. We ordered four roast beef and brie on baguettes, four shredded chicken fajitas with mixed greens, four focaccia with basil, grilled zucchini and garlic aoli, and four simple turkey on white bread sandwiches. We were ready for action! Apparently the kitchen was not.

"Would you look at this?" Marc called upon opening the lid off the first plate. "The sandwich guy must have some personal issues: look at these thumbprints!"

He held up the plate for us all to inspect. Pressed deeply into the soft white bread of a turkey sandwich were the undeniable thumbprints of an overly aggressive chef. Marc illustrated for us a likely scenario regarding how such foul play came to be. He pantomimed an angry man slamming together sandwiches, face filled with fury over such a large order at midnight. Coming from Mr. Chill himself, it was hilarious.

"What would make a man turn so violent towards a sandwich?" Marc mumbled as he devoured the prosecutorial evidence.

"You've never worked in ship restaurants," Junior noted.

"Hear hear!" I agreed heartily, offering a toast.

The phone rang. I was in the far corner, and rushed to pick it up. Before I could get near, however, Ildi snatched up the receiver.

"This is the Goddess!" she answered drunkenly.

She frowned a moment, then suddenly burst out laughing. "She hung up!"

"How do you know it was a she?" asked Oana. "Maybe it was security. We're getting pretty loud."

"Of course it was a woman," Ildi teased. "Who else would call Brian after midnight?"

I slumped back into my seat. Such a perfect party. Ruined by my lies.

# 6

The party ended about half past 1 a.m., because most of us had to get up early for home port duties. I myself had a 6 a.m. handover with the returning auctioneers Robin and Vanessa. That did not mean I was ready to retire, however. There was one very uncomfortable mess I had created that needed clearing up.

Vela was not in her cabin when I knocked, but her cabin mate informed me that Vela had spent most of the night in the crew bar. I checked there next, but Vela was nowhere to be found. Ildi was, though: getting wildly drunk with a waiter. I wasn't sure if I was happy for him, or worried for him.

Five minutes later I found Vela running on the track. She flashed past me like a bullet, chewing up miles in record time. As always, she had her hair pulled into a pony-tail, a T-shirt yanked up, and spandex shorts. She was a sweat-glistening goddess. This was who she was: a competitor, always training, always bettering herself. I was fortunate my path had crossed hers so briefly on her way up. She saw me step onto the sports deck, but manifestly ignored me.

Vela deserved to keep me hanging. I waited patiently, wallowing in guilt. I felt like a kid who stole candy just to see if it was exciting or not. Only it wasn't candy. And it wasn't exciting. What, would I have preferred to find it thrilling? Of course not! This affair, probably like all of them, was a lose-lose scenario. For every 'Susana and Michel', there were countless 'Brian and Velas'.

Vela blasted away another three laps, then slowed to a walk.

"So," she said, panting. "Party over?"

"Yes," I said simply.

"Your 'inventory'?" she asked, somehow making a pant sound accusing.

"Starting soon."

"You'll get no help from me," she said flatly.

"Look, Vela," I said. "The party was thrown by my friends. It was a very surprising and happy thing. We kept the door open because everyone was invited to come in. Is that how you knew I had a party? You walked by the door?"

She nodded, staring down at the track beneath her shoes. She finally caught her breath.

"You should have come in," I said.

That much was sincere. The insincerity followed.

"A friend said I missed a call while in the bathroom. I figured it was you and called your cabin. You weren't there and, well, the party kinda took over."

Vela stopped pacing. She let out a sigh, then a sniff, then untied her hair to give it a violent shake.

"Look, Vela," I said again meekly. "I'm sorry the last night worked out so poorly. Nothing has worked out this contract. The first two weeks were the most stressful of my life. Meeting you was a wonderful surprise, even if we both knew it would be short-lived. I asked you for a few days, and you accepted. I'm sorry I screwed up the last one so bad."

"It's OK," she said graciously. "We had fun. Nothing more, nothing less."

We embraced tightly for a moment, when suddenly Vela pulled back. She looked down, aghast at all of her sweat soaking into my silk Tommy Bahama shirt.

"So we can hit the shower now?" I teased.

I was answered by a towel thrown in my face.


# 7


The handover was a goddamn mess.

For some reason that defied explanation, the port authority required that I leave the ship by 9:30 a.m. Handovers invariably run out of time when departing auctioneers leave in the late afternoon! The good news was that *Sensation* was Robin and Vanessa's old stomping ground, so we could dispense with everything but the inventory. The bad news was that at 6 a.m. only Robin showed up. Vanessa had left him to his fish pills.

The really bad news was that Robin had no idea how to conduct an inventory on his own, as apparently Vanessa had always been in charge of paperwork. He moved slower than molasses in winter, and complained more than even Harald.

The really really bad news was that after three laborious hours of dealing with Robin's lackadaisical efforts, the computers went dead. We were unable to print and mutually sign off on the ship's inventory. We photocopied an old paper report and hurriedly ticked off the expensive works I had sold, but I was legally liable for any mistakes—mistakes that could cost me many thousands of dollars.

The really really really bad news was that *Sensation's* new accountant had erred on the end of cruise reports and had to redo them later in the week, so I was unable to even leave with the necessary documentation. There was literally no possible scenario worse for a departing auctioneer, and everything was entirely beyond my means to remedy.

Stress. Lack of time. Pure, utter hell. I heard Lucifer's ugly laughing in my head.

I was still fighting with documentation when security found me and ordered me to the gangway. On the way, I passed Farida. She ran over to hug me, and I scooped her up with one arm and carried her like that halfway to the gangway because security wouldn't let me loiter.

Just before I was escorted to shore, I stopped. The rather large Indian chief of security barked at me to keep going, or the port authority would have to report my delinquency to the U.S. Coast Guard.

"Wait!" I cried. "I left some vital paperwork in the art locker on deck two."

"Have them mail it," he replied curtly. "Nobody messes with Coast Guard."

"Five minutes," I insisted. "I'll be back in five minutes."

"No way," he said resolutely. He thrust a strong, brown finger towards the gangway.

I turned and ran back into *Sensation*, shouting over my shoulder, "Can't deport me: I'm American anyway!"

I rushed into the elevator, but didn't stop at deck two. I went up to the salon.

The reception area was swamped with guests inquiring about the spa, the massages, the facials, the whatever. Vela sat amidst the bumbling crowd, shining radiantly in her sequined best. When she saw me, she jumped up from behind the desk, pushed through the crowd, and gave me a big, powerful hug. Powerful, indeed: I felt my spine crack! Only then could I leave *Sensation*.

Half an hour later I was staring out the open facade of the Cigar Factory in the French Quarter. Across from me was the little triangular park flanked by the streets Decatur, Conti, and North Peters. Beyond a parking lot flowed the Mississippi. The little park was lined with shrubs that directed my gaze to a towering public statue. Resting upon tiers of marble were three bronze figures: the lowest a morose Native American, above a Bible-toting Capuchin monk, and boldly strutting above both was the founder of New Orleans, Jean-Baptiste Bienville.

This was my favorite spot to kiss Bianca, other than our brick lane under the old citadel in Sighişoara. I felt numb, and not because of the January drizzle. In the blink of an eye, *Sensation* had become a place of comfort. I had stayed longer on other ships, but had never before been emotionally engaged. I made real friends on *Sensation*. I hadn't thought that was possible on ships.

Now I understood why Bianca insisted on remaining emotionally closed at sea. I would miss them all mightily. Well, not Harald so much. I could see them all in my mind: Oana's alternating cute smile and cold shoulder while passing hours at her desk, or Ildi's hyperactive but highly contagious laugh in Formalities. I warmed at Farida's beaming enthusiasm and adventurous spirit—whether luring me to an iguana, joining me on a bungee chair, or at our dinners on the open deck sharing appreciation and wonder at the mighty sea at night. Susana, the sweet but fiery little thing, with tall and droll Michel. I felt my heart pound while running with Vela, my head swim at her intoxicating, feminine smell.

And Marc? He was my best friend of all on *Sensation*. Hours of relaxed conversation about politics and literature, of philosophies and faiths. He was as curious and accomplished an explorer as Stanley or Shackleton. Stay chill, brother.

Life was charmed for a while. *Sensation* was the first ship I had worked where leaving was a time to cry, not to fly. I was so sick of saying goodbye. I hated ships for that. Ships were life times ten. They brought wonders beyond imagination, then took them right back. It was our lot to be thankful for the moments. I was sick of moments. I wanted more. I vowed the next ship was Bianca or bust. I couldn't handle saying goodbye anymore.

The only plus was that Bianca was on vacation in February, so I could spend some time with her in the real world. Before I went another round with Lucifer, I had to find some answers in the Carpathian snow—like whether or not I truly knew who I was fighting for.

# CHAPTER SIXTEEN

## *Carpathian Snow*

## 1

WINTER IN THE CARPATHIANS was magical. It was the stuff of dreams, an idyllic wonderland that, as the carols romanticize, actually included horse-drawn sleighs. Though cloudy, the forested hills glowed with the clean face and crisp, undulating lines of untrammeled drifts. Snow was plentiful but light, not heavy and wet; winds were gentle and tinged with pine, not bitter and cutting. Indeed, the air was content to loiter just below freezing, loathe to hinder anyone's life beyond merely maintaining that softening blanket of snow. Around every curve of the road was another cluster of snow-capped cottages, windows warm and orange. I wondered if Thomas Kinkade had ever visited.

My arrival in Romania had been timed to coincide with Bianca's end of contract. I had been warned that she slept for the first couple days, but assumed she was exaggerating. Hardly. She did indeed sleep for two days, with nary a wakeful moment. She didn't even eat, but only woke enough to give a kiss to her dear father and a hug to her dear mother. Then back to bed until her subconscious told her it was time to live again.

I smiled when I saw a new refrigerator magnet among those lucky letter 'P's, mounted as they were in palm trees and cruise ships. I had sent Bianca a big brown letter 'B'. Silly, yes, but it's the silly little things that make life fun, like jumping into a pool totally clothed—or, better yet, totally unclothed. I also spied Lucky munching on M&M's I had sent, customized brown with Romanian text. That had not been so easy to accomplish: they had to verify that *frumoasa mea* and *te iubesc* —'my beauty' and 'I love you'—were not obscene or some terrorist code. My delight was doused when I next noticed the art books I sent her so long ago were still wrapped in plastic.

Why did life always give conflicting signals?

Living in the Pop house—even if temporarily without Bianca—still felt right, though. More than ever, in fact, because I was picking up some Romanian. I discovered that the thrust of a conversation could be gathered from a relatively small grasp of the language. Further, even Romanians commonly confused their own language's cumbersome grammar, so my horrendous conjugation was no barrier to their understanding.

The first morning, while sipping coffee together on the three-season porch that was working overtime, I was surprised to catch Piti musing with Lucky about what my father did for a living. Aligning bits and pieces comprehensibly—though obviously incorrectly—I managed to answer that my father had designed radios for NASA's lunar missions. Piti thought that was delightful. I thought the communication was.

The next morning the parents Pop were ready to take our conversation to another level. Piti fretted impatiently while

Lucky leisurely poured my coffee and presented a thick slab of *cozonac*, my favorite Romanian pastry with walnuts and cinnamon. She gave me a wink, and together we overtly ignored Piti's restless wiggling. With grand flourish, Lucky offered me nearly everything in the kitchen. I carefully considered each and every item, only pretending to notice Piti when țuica was offered.

Piti was so eager to talk that he nearly leapt out of his chair. Finally, exuberantly, he opened his mouth to speak... but said nothing. His white brow plunged when he realized he had forgotten his prepared English. Grumbling, he thumbed through the Romanian/English dictionary to refresh his memory. Lucky laughed and gave him a kiss on the cheek, which irritated him even more. He swatted at her like she was a fly.

"Bianca..." Piti finally said, eyes squinting through reading glasses, "*Foarte*... focus... Piti *și* Lucky. Bianca *nu*... focus... Bianca."

I set my coffee down, nodded, listened.

"Check!" Piti continued, motioning to signify our surroundings. "*Casa*... garden... *bun, destul*. Eh... good, enough. *Merci mult* Carnival. Boot..."

"But," I corrected kindly.

"But," Piti repeated with difficulty. "Bianca *nu*... marry. Bianca *nu*... children. Sheeps..."

"Ships."

"Sheeps," Piti repeated, unsuccessful with the short 'I'. "OK. America OK. Piti *și* Lucky OK here. Da?"

He was trying to say Bianca had done enough for them and should live her own life. I quite agreed. I reached over and took the dictionary from Piti. I flipped through the pages, but surprisingly didn't find the word I was looking for in either the Romanian or English sides. I improvised by using a word I happened to remember from a long ago walk through the countryside.

"Bianca... *magaruș*."

Piti's white brows shot up in surprise, then immediately knit in confusion. I had called his daughter a little donkey. I chuckled and flipped through the dictionary. It did not translate the word stubborn or obstinate, but rather had recalcitrant. Go figure.

"Aha! *Incapaţinat*," I explained. "Stubborn. Similar magaruș."

Laughing, we marched onward to understanding. Piti and Lucky were worried that Bianca's life was passing her by. They wanted her to have a family of her own—already long overdue in Romanian society—and if that meant in America, they would be happy for her. They would miss her, of course, but already did nine months of the year. They wanted my help convincing her that she had already provided all they would ever need for the rest of their days. She needed to finally forget about Catalin.

"Catalin?" I asked in Romanian. "Who is Catalin?"

Piti and Lucky shared a surprised look. With a sour face, Piti scanned the dictionary. Finally he pressed his finger to a word and showed Lucky. She shrugged.

"Aah," Piti replied. "Husband."

2

On day three, Bianca finally stepped out of the bedroom. She was alive again after the dark and deadening winter of Carnival and, like a bud waking to late-spring sunlight, soaked up the warmth, released stored hope, unfolded. She was so rejuvenated, in fact, that I felt guilty bringing up the ships at all. Returning to Transylvania, I had figured Bianca's and my roles were reversed from our previous 'Romanian recalibration'. During that summer on the Black Sea, Bianca had felt culpable for failure. This winter in the Carpathians, it was my turn. She was concerned about me losing my spot on *Sensation*. I was concerned about losing my integrity. But now there was a whole new element to get sorted out—and fast. Who was this 'husband' of Bianca's?

But first: the corpse and the clown.

Rival cousins Radu and Adi were at each other again, only this time I started the whole mess. Who would have thought taking the two sets of cousins out to dinner would create another revolution in Romania? We were all at Cristina and Adi's apartment when the subject of where to dine was discussed—though discussed was hardly the word.

"Hotel Sighişoara," Adi called enthusiastically. "Best place in town."

"The Stag House," Radu challenged with an ugly, toothy grin.

"Nu, nu," Adi continued, blowing off Radu's suggestion. "Hotel Sighişoara is an important landmark that once housed the city council."

"Over a century ago!" Radu countered. "Who cares about that? The Stag House is an important landmark that holds the Romanian-German Cultural Center now."

"I'm tired of your Germany!" Adi exclaimed, flapping his arms in exasperation.

"And I'm tired of your kitchen cupboards!" Radu shot back.

"Good! Go back to Germany and buy another computer. They sell brains, too?"

Two days later, they were still at it. They hadn't paused for a minute. Radu had even taken a day off from work to keep the argument going. He loitered at the train depot all day, harassing Adi as he conducted trains. Finally Adi couldn't take it anymore and had the *poliţia* escort him away. Radu had been so angry he raged all night long. Poor Laura. She looked like she had worked a full contract in a ship dining room: her eyes were sunken even deeper than Radu's. While the ladies and I shivered in the dark of the old town's Citadel, Radu and Adi stayed hot by maintaining a fire of verbal abuse.

"What time is it?" Radu sneered to Adi. "Check your little pocket watch, train-boy. Can you blow your whistle for us?"

"I work for a living!" Adi roared. "I work hard and come home to a loving wife. In Germany all you've got are your two hands!"

"Can I get out of here?" I begged Bianca.

"Oh no you don't," Bianca laughed. "Cristina and Laura have had to deal with this for two days."

The sisters nodded in unison with comically long faces.

"OK, bambo, I save you this time," Bianca said. "Go to the shop over there and buy two packs of Marlboros, two Snickers, and two Cokes."

I frowned at her. "You mean now?"

"Da. In fact, add six packs of menthols."

"Sounds like an interesting plan you've got brewing."

"Romanian-style," she agreed.

So I ran off to the nearest *magazinul*, as Romanians call their little corner stores, trying to remember the list and pondering the strangely intense debate. Adi and Radu both championed buildings central in the old town of Sighişoara. Both structures were built 600 or more years ago, and both offered the same food. Yet these two men were about to come to blows. Obviously this was about more than which restaurant.

While in line at the store, I was particularly self-conscious. The only winter coat I had was a bright yellow ski jacket, which lit up the black and grey of Romania as brightly as the Vegas Strip lit the desert. Encumbered with my goodies, I waited at the end of a long line and listened to the comments whispered disdainfully in Romanian.

"Typical American: he comes to our country and buys Snickers, Coca Cola, and American cigarettes. He probably only eats at McDonald's, too."

At that point, I would have suggested a McDonald's if Sighişoara had one!

When I returned with the designated items, Radu and Adi were arguing so fast in Romanian I couldn't pick up a word of what they said. Their body language was clear enough.

"Aah!" Bianca said, taking up the goods. "Now we can get to the bottom of this!"

"And what exactly is the bottom of this?" I asked. "Why is this such a big deal?"

"You need to understand," Bianca explained. "This is the first time in over a year they have gone out to dinner. This is a big deal."

"I'm happy to hear that, but it doesn't explain why they're behaving like children."

"Machismo," Bianca said, wrinkling her face. "It's easy to ignore that the rich American is paying, but they still need to feel in control. That's why us women can't say anything. But we can get around that if handled right."

Bianca gave a can of Coke to both combatants, then continued to pay off Radu with the Marlboros and Adi with the Snickers. She gave a long, almost pleading speech in Romanian. Radu sulked. He tried to look cool by lighting up a Marlboro with overt affectation, but only looked like the zombie of James Dean. Adi, on the other hand, beamed like a child. He gave one candy bar to Cristina and wiggled with excitement as he stuck the other in his pocket.

"There!" Bianca said, returning to my side. "I tell them you are really into creepy stuff, but are too shy to ask to be next door to the house of Vlad the Impaler. That means the Hotel. I bribe them so they save face."

"Yeah, OK, but why a can of Coke before dinner?"

"For the wine, babaloo," Bianca replied, surprised. "They can't order it in the restaurant or they will look like peasants."

"And the menthols?"

"For us girls," Bianca replied, distributing the cigarettes to her cousins. "It's your apology to them for the last two days of hell."

Bianca pocketed two packs of the menthols and added, "This for my services."

The arbitrated Hotel Sighişoara proved to be an excellent choice. The cellar, which was promptly set aside for our party, was pure medieval awesomeness. The walls were built entirely of roughly cut, but highly polished, ancient stones. Each had been expertly fitted and mortared, and as they stacked upward they curved inward, creating a rounded ceiling. Like a long igloo of rock. Wrought iron wall sconces of huge dimension—obviously age-old and having once held torches—were capped with electric globes to provide light. They were strung together with heavy, dungeon-worthy chains. Occasional wooden shelves jutted from the curving walls to hold displays of antique musical instruments. In one corner was a narrow table laden with ornately curved candelabra and flickering candles, while the point of interest at the other side was a four-foot opening in the stone blocked by a thick iron gate. The floor was planed planks of ancient oak.

Dinner was wonderful, though of course not on par with Lucky's culinary prowess. It is a well-known fact that the best food in Romania comes from the home—no doubt due to the superlative ingredient to be found there. Love is tangible. Our evening progressed in the expected series of food, dance, food, dance, with drinks throughout. Though the cellar looked archaic, the sound system hidden among the foundations was anything but.

Things turned amusing when Radu became wildly drunk. He began freaking out whenever anyone touched his face. It began with an act of kindness after he had messily devoured some food. Laura tried to wipe clean the excess mustard off his cheek in motherly fashion. Radu slapped her hand away with a ridiculous amount of bluster. Eyes glinting with mirth, she began playfully poking at his sunken cheeks. His knee-jerk reactions were comically excessive. He bellowed like a stuck pig, he flailed his hands before his face, and even hopped about the room.

Adi was only too happy to get in on it. While talking to someone else, and even looking away, Adi would reach over and slap Radu across the face. The resulting explosion of profanity shook the heavy oaken tables far more than Radu's wriggling and kicking like a five-year-old protesting bedtime.

Indeed, the real delight of the evening was Adi. He got roaring drunk. His manner of play was endlessly entertaining, whether locking himself behind the iron bars in the tiny coatroom—which was no doubt originally designed to hold munitions—or unsuccessfully trying to climb the stones up to the ceiling. He fell three times in rapid succession, and the fourth time gripped the chains and iron sconces for additional purchase. Luckily I managed to haul him back to the ground before he did some damage. When no one else seemed concerned about breakage, I remembered sheepishly that the chains had been specifically designed to hold people—against their will!

Eventually Cristina hauled him back to the dinner table, where he pouted and plucked at his long-cold food. The moment of forced calm was not to last. Like so many disasters, it began with ABBA.

The upbeat piano of 'Chiquitita' brought Adi to his feet with a leap. He rushed to the corner, swaying and blearily regarding the table laden with candelabra. None of us could figure out what he was planning. Then with one grand sweep of his long arm, he cleared the table of all its many contents. Dozens of candles and intricate holders tumbled to the floor with a crash, candles spinning, hot wax splattering. Pools of wax congealed instantly on the cold stone, and smeared into the cloth of Adi's pants. This did not stop him from grabbing the nearest chair and dragging it before the now-empty table. He plopped down heavily—nearly falling over into the pile of candles—and proceeded to play his new 'piano' to the song.

While I tried to keep Cristina from fainting, the others began roaring with laughter. Bianca sidled up to the table to provide the accompaniment to Adi's piano. She crooned into an empty beer bottle, slinking across the table-top in her most seductive lounge manner. She pouted and sulked during the lows, but the end of 'Chiquitita' was so upbeat she was compelled to rise and dance on the table.

Regretfully, the song ended. Adi leapt to his feet and ran over to a shelf displaying an antique gramophone. He stuck his head into the huge flower-like horn and bellowed, "Repeat! Repeat!"

His face got stuck.

Adi flailed his arms and began rearing back. Gasps sounded about the room, but fortunately Radu was nearby. The gawky, pale man was amazingly fast enough to stop Adi from completing his motion. The century-old machine had nearly shared the fate of the candelabra! But the danger was not over, for Adi kept flailing his hands. He placed a hand roughly on the age-old spindle of the machine for leverage and began pushing.

"Stop, idiot!" Radu shouted as he tried unsuccessfully to unhook a small clasp that had fallen and caught on the back of Adi's shirt collar. They wrestled for several agonizing moments, then safely extricated Adi's face from the horn. They kept slapping each other even as they fished for Adi's glasses in the huge horn. While Radu carefully replaced the gramophone on the shelf, Adi grinned widely at us, proud of his adventure.

"'Thank You for the Music!'" he hollered in English, quoting another ABBA hit.

"More like 'S.O.S.'!" Cristina muttered, burying her face in her hands in defeat.

3

Bianca and I walked home from the restaurant, holding hands through a lazy ballet of dancing flakes. I had thought Sighişoara was stunningly beautiful in summer, but it was utterly mesmerizing when frosted. Gaslight glowed on ancient stone, and the frozen streets of the old city, while empty, seemed not lonely, but patient.

Though tired and more than a little drunk, we both felt a bit sobered by the time we reached the end of Strada Crişan. Bianca unlocked the gate and we shuffled into the courtyard, luminous with new-fallen snow—then stopped dead in our tracks.

Fresh footprints in the snow. Leading to the house.

A rustle, and movement, in the shadows of the three-season porch.

"Son of a bitch!" I whispered harshly, starting a rush for the porch. But Bianca latched onto my arm and tried to haul me back.

"Wait!" she whispered. "Stop!"

"You're being robbed!"

"No," she whispered. "I don't think so. Just wait a minute, please?"

"But your parents are in there sleeping!"

"No, that's my father."

I stared at her, incredulous. "It's three o'clock in the morning. You don't mean he's been..."

My eyes followed the tracks back from Bianca's house to the neighbor's yard.

"He's been with the neighbor lady?"

Bianca led me to the porch swing in the courtyard. Mechanically pushing off the shroud of snow, we sat, we rocked. She explained.

"It saddens me," she said, watching the snow increase the density and speed of its flurry. "It saddens me how it hurts my mother, but he always comes back."

I was shocked. Piti was cheating on Lucky? They looked like the happiest, most loving couple I could imagine.

"How long has this been going on?" I asked quietly.

"A long time," Bianca answered. "All along. My mother cannot provide him what he needs. She knows he loves her more than anything else in the world. She knows he always comes back."

"Until he doesn't," I muttered, unimpressed.

Bianca was silent for a moment. Eyes blinded by the rush of snowflakes, her voice shifted to a far-away place.

"Only one thing ever kept him from coming back," she intoned. "The revolution."

She squeezed my hand. I listened, enthralled amid revelations and snow.

"We were living in Braşov when it happened. We were having breakfast when my godfather called. He was a colonel in the military and my father a sergeant, of course. I remember hearing his voice through the phone. He sounded serious. A lot more serious than the Braşov revolt two years before. My father was out the door in two minutes flat. Before he left, he insisted that we stay inside. Don't go out for food, water—nothing!—until he called. Don't even answer the door unless it's Colonel Miere. Not even the neighbors, he emphasized. As he ran down the stairs, he shouted that he would come back for us no matter what happened.

"We didn't hear from him for three days. No calls, no messages, nothing. That whole first day we thought it would just be another attempt halted before it got started. That had happened a few times before, but they never got very far. Father said he knew those would fail because they were isolated, far from the capital. This time the television didn't mention much, of course, other than a small riot in Timişoara, far to the west. My mother and I were glued to the contraband radio my father smuggled in from relatives in Hungary. It was a bloodbath in Timişoara.

"On the second day, I remember the fuzzy announcement that changed everything. This one was different. This revolution started outside Romania. Poland, Hungary, Czechoslovakia: all the Eastern bloc, it seemed. We couldn't hear any more because the signal was so faint, and outside became so noisy. When I looked out the window and saw the line of tanks roaring down the street, I knew. We were so scared. We cried every time we heard the machine guns outside. We heard them a lot.

"By day three, we were so hungry. We had nothing in the kitchen because the rationing had been getting worse and worse. We didn't even have cooking oil. But we knew there was no food in the stores, nobody in the piaţas. We were too scared to even talk to the neighbors, because the secret police were everywhere, everyone. I remember once my godfather saw the *securitate* file for my father. He couldn't show it to him, of course, but told him about it. Father was a good soldier, but even *his* file had over one hundred pages."

Bianca sniffled, blinked back tears and melting snowflakes. Suddenly I remembered my first visit to the capital city Bucharest. I had asked our driver to show me Ceauşescu's huge Parliamentary Palace—the largest building in the world after the Pentagon—but he instead passed right by it and parked in the middle of traffic across the street. Next to a cemetery. He crossed himself and whispered thanks to those buried there. These were the men who stormed the Parliamentary Palace and Intercontinental Hotel—students, salesmen, normal people like me. Ceauşescu, the twenty-two year communist dictator, ordered his soldiers to shoot into the crowd with automatic weapons. Soldiers who did not obey would be shot.

That could have been Bianca's godfather. That could have been Piti.

Most of the soldiers did not obey. Yet many did. The securitate sure did. Protesters were massacred: shot from various buildings and even crushed by tanks driven into the crowd. More than enough to fill that cemetery across the street. Perhaps it was his barbarity even until the end that made his execution so hasty. Ceauşescu and his wife were convicted of genocide and immediately shot—the very second they stood against the wall. Three soldiers did it. Hundreds had volunteered.

"At the end of the third day," Bianca continued, "Piti came home. He said it was over. He never said another word about it. He never told us about even a single minute of those three days."

"So you don't know if he stayed in Braşov, or was sent to the capital," I mused gently.

"It doesn't matter," Bianca said. Then she added defiantly, "He always comes back!"

And Catalin didn't, I thought.

Bianca froze.

"What did you say?" she asked sharply. She dropped my hand, leaving me holding cold night air.

Horrified, I realized that I must have said my thoughts aloud. I felt like the biggest asshole on the planet. I tried backpedaling, because the last thing I wanted to do was bring up our current mess after Bianca's heart-wrenching memory.

"I didn't mean to say that," I said gently. "I'm sorry. It's just that maybe only now do I understand why you obsess so much over 'coming back'. I thought maybe—"

"No, no, you got it all wrong," she huffed. "I don't know who you've been talking to—"

"I've been talking to your parents, honey," I said gently.

"Me not ready to talk about Catalin," Bianca dismissed crisply. "Is not what you think. Just leave it at that."

"But how can I now that it's out there?" I said. "Piti said something about him being your husband!"

Bianca stared at me with huge eyes.

"He said that?" she screeched. It echoed through the night.

"In a manner of speaking," I explained, taken aback by her reaction. But suddenly overwhelmed by years of secrets, I blundered forward. "We were trying to communicate while you were busy recovering from the slave labor I'm trying to save you from."

"I don't need saving from you or anybody," Bianca said flatly. "Nu, we were never married. Obviously you misunderstood."

Snow fell. Chill crept in.

"I will tell you about it," she promised quietly. "Nu now, OK? Is late. Me tired."

She was right. It was late. We prepared for bed in silence, minus a squawk when slipping between the cold sheets. Bianca's body pressed into mine for warmth, and soon her measured breath indicated sleep. It was not so easy for me. The chilly pillow swallowed my head, but I didn't feel like closing my eyes. I was disturbed by the revelations of the evening, and angry that I made her bad memory worse.

I would never truly comprehend what Bianca and her family had endured before and during the revolution. Nor could I forgive the machismo that let men justify so freely trouncing on loved one's feelings. But I did understand the audacity of being judged by people completely ignorant of the reality one lived in.

Above all, I understood that these people were deeply wounded and needed time to heal. They deserved patience. The least I could do was give it without conditions.

# 4

The next afternoon, Bianca and I took a walk through wintry old town. The snow still fell, but was clearly tired of doing so. The flakes were fat and hesitant, taking their time to reach us. Our large umbrella blocked their lethargic attempt. Bianca snuggled onto my arm as we made our way to our kissing spot below the citadel.

"You're shivering," Bianca commented after an icy-lipped smooch. "Why you no zip up your coat?"

"Can't," I grunted, wrapping myself a bit deeper into my coat. "I broke the zipper this morning."

"First shoelaces and now zippers!" she chirped.

"I am a man of enormous power," I intoned, lifting my chin and gazing to the horizon.

Unbidden, Bianca removed her gloves to better loosen my scarf and clasp the buttons beneath. I knew better than to protest. Suddenly she snapped her hand away and winced.

"Ow!" she said, shaking her hand to ease the pain. "These damn hands."

"What's wrong with your hands?" I asked, holding them up to look.

Her fingertips looked shredded, with deep splits in the skin revealing raw, angry skin beneath. I had noticed her taking great care with her hands, but had assumed it was from the dry, winter air. There was no doubt she had been hiding something far worse.

"Just from the bleaching," she dismissed, trying to pull her hands free.

"Bleaching the damn ship all day!" I exclaimed, "This is really bad, Bianca. Why didn't you tell me?"

"And have you as worried as my parents?" she retorted. She tugged her gloves back on with a wince, and said soothingly, "I'm getting a special cream after you leave. Best doctor in Brașov."

"That's hardly a confidence booster."

"Like your confidence needs a boost!" she teased, breaking free. She rewound my scarf with an affectionate pat, snatched the umbrella and quipped, "Keep your hands off the umbrella. He's twenty-five years old and I don't want you breaking him, too."

We continued our walk, conversing hesitantly. I wanted to talk about heavy stuff. She did not.

Eventually we found ourselves strolling through a piața. Dozens of tents had been set up and peasants and vendors were selling everything imaginable. We stuffed ourselves on samples of cheeses from all sorts of animals' milk, and samples of sausages from all sorts of animals themselves. Of course, a Romanian piața was not limited to edibles by any means: there were clothing vendors, tool makers, black market CDs, DVDs, you name it. I wondered if I tried hard enough if I could find an AK-47.

"I can't imagine selling outside all day in the winter," I commented. "I think I could handle physical work, but to stand there all day? I would freeze!"

Bianca said nothing.

"Bianca?" I asked, sensing that something was wrong.

We stood before a makeshift tent cobbled together from several tarps of different colors and materials. Three six-foot folding tables, arranged in a U-shape, offered up dirty plastic bins half-full of scratched CD cases. Bianca stared at the writing scrawled in marker across the recordable disks.

"What? You want a movie or something?"

Now it was Bianca's turn to shiver.

"It *is* freezing," she muttered in a far-away voice. "Freezing standing there all day. Everyday. For nothing."

"You worked in a piața like this?" I asked, surprised. "Like when you were younger or something?"

I was imagining a first job, such as I had done during high school for extra money. I had no idea how ethnocentric the idea was. Bianca soon educated me.

"After the revolution," Bianca answered in tight snippets. "I worked in a piaţa. I sold dubbed cassette tapes."

"My black market girl," I teased. As usual, I was very slow to realize how inconsiderate I was being.

"I set up before sunrise every day," Bianca continued in a drone. "And worked until after dark. Twelve hours, thirteen, I don't know. Similar ships. But when I got home I had to make the tapes—all night. Every forty-five minutes I had to wake up to flip the tapes and record the other side. All night long. Every night. Every day. Every forty-five minutes. I was so tired. I was so cold.

"You see, before we had to leave Belgium, my ex used all of our remaining money to buy recording equipment and the latest cassettes from western musicians. He thought maybe they would sell OK in Romania, now that the doors were open and everyone was looking west. But after the revolution nobody had any money. Nobody had any money, not even for cheap illegal copies. We were starving."

"What was he doing during all this?" I asked.

She shrugged lightly and said, "What he could. We didn't know anybody in Timişoara. He didn't get anything done."

"Why didn't you move back to Braşov, where you had family?"

She didn't answer. The haunted look in her eyes hardened into something very different.

"I vowed in that fucking stall that if I ever get out of this, I will never be poor again."

**5**

So much for the easy 'Romanian recalibration'.

The night before I left for America, we could no longer delay talking about our future. We had enjoyed a month of long days of brisk walks, long evenings of dinner and drinks, and long nights of play. There had been revelations. It was time for resolutions.

Bianca and I rocked gently on the chilled porch swing. The night sky was supremely black, the stars crystalline, the air crisp.

"So," I said.

"So," Bianca agreed, star-gazing.

"Let's keep this simple," I said. "You were a goddamn mess on *Conquest*. I was a goddamn mess on *Sensation*. We're even. Shall we make the next ship the success story?"

"Even?" she mocked. "Life is not so equitable, Mr. Brown. And you don't even know if you'll have a 'next ship'."

"Thanks for the vote of confidence."

"You're always chasing butterflies, Brian," Bianca chided. "You make everything sound so positive, but you're just denying reality. You told me that you passed all these tests, yet here you are again, having to impress this Lucifer blood clot. You obviously haven't convinced him you have what it takes."

"Have I convinced you?"

She stared at the ebon sky.

"Well that's just great," I replied sarcastically. "You know, I'm doing my best. My best to understand, to provide a life for us."

"I expect nothing from you," Bianca said. "I only hope."

"You know, Bianca," I said, taking a stab at explaining my thoughts. "You claim you won't marry someone for money. You turned down Tommy the Teddy Bear and who knows how many others. Do you really feel like it's your job to do this all alone? Isn't the whole point that you go through life's challenges together?"

"Oh, Brian," Bianca said, shaking her head. "You really are a dreamer, aren't you? 'All you need is love?' is that it?"

"I'm not that naive," I said, bristling.

"We're both adults," Bianca pressed. "I expect nothing from you, and will thank you for the time we've had if you find someone else who can give you what you need."

I stared at her, incredulous.

"So 'come back to me' has now become 'thank you for your time.' Lovely. When did that happen?"

"I just... I just don't know what the future holds anymore," Bianca admitted.

"Neither do I," I said, "but that doesn't mean I'm scared of it and hedging my bets. Look, I came here expecting to get an earful. I'm getting it. But you don't really want to give up on us now, do you? We're finally getting past some barriers here! Let's keep trying."

"But what if you fail again?" Bianca asked.

"Well," I said after a moment of thought, "if I can't impress Lucifer one last time and get another ship... and you don't feel able to move to America with me... I guess I'll thank you for our time together."

# CHAPTER SEVENTEEN
## *Tadpole 23*

1

I SUFFERED NO ILLUSIONS about my return to Pennsylvania for advanced auctioneer training. It was gonna suck. Auctioneers, as a rule, continuously preened themselves and strut like peacocks. When faced with others of their kind the posturing became absolutely unbearable. Even my huge ego was flaccid compared to those blowhards.

The weather was equally repulsive. Winds roared out of the mountains, snarled around the bridges, then hunted down each soul unfortunate enough to be outside. The skies were locked in slate gray. The cold was sharp. I longed for the gentle, soothing snows of Sighişoara.

Sundance's formula for auctioneers was different from that of trainees. The transportation from the airport to the hotel was no longer designed to impress, for example. Rather than being chauffeured in a Lincoln Town Car, I was shuttled in a brand new Chrysler 300—a sweet ride, to be sure, but a far cry from a driver in coat-tails. At the hotel, however, the prominent status of auctioneers was reinforced with a private room boasting a hot tub.

At 9 p.m., we met in the lounge. As with any pack of animals, the established hierarchy was readily apparent to a trained observer. The outskirts of the lounge were filled with milling, nervous trainees: all very young and very attractive, mostly male. The crowd bunching near the bar consisted of returning auctioneers, rising in prominence as they neared the altar to alcohol. The sycophants stood thick indeed around the bar's four chairs, for those seated were preeminent.

The two far chairs were occupied by a long-established auctioneering couple, Jim Nabors and Scarlett Johansson. Their Sundance monikers had been selected with care: he the spitting image of Gomer Pyle, and she the stuff of men's fantasies. The two near chairs, however, held the men of the moment.

First was the auctioneer dubbed John Goodman: a huge man with a straggly goatee crawling down the rolls of his thick neck. He must have been six and a half feet tall and well over three hundred pounds. But the second man, of average height and build, clearly dominated all. His swagger made that clear, even if his grooming did not. His clothing was a sloppy, unkempt mess, as was his brown hair. He had big ears and an ugly mouth.

It was time for my performance. I was more nervous about this moment than I expected to be at any time the entire week. I pushed my way up to the bar. The braggarts paused their blustering to gauge if I was so worthy. All eyes were on me.

"Give me a double rum on the rocks!" I ordered with bravado. Then I turned to the seated, hyena-like man and greeted coolly, "Lewis."

Upon hearing the messy man's real name, rather than his Sundance moniker, the demeanor of the altar defrosted. Old auctioneers nodded. New auctioneers whispered.

"I'll be damned," Lewis—otherwise known as Lucifer—said derisively with a slight British accent. "It's Buzz Lightyear!"

"That's the Frog Prince to you," I replied. Waiting a dramatic half second, I added, "As I recall you told Frederick himself."

The room fell into stunned silence. A woman somewhere gasped. A tray dropped in the distance, complete with clang and crinkle of glass.

"What?" rumbled John Goodman, "A new guy outsell me? Impossible!"

"No, no sales at all," came the icy response. The uneven, toothy grin was replaced with a sneer. "But something far worse."

"Worse than no sales?"

"Yes," he answered. "He once proved me wrong."

Lucifer's puffy eyes met mine and he added contemptuously, "Something he'll regret for the rest of his very short career."

## 2

The introduction was coordinated by Gene, who once again channeled Uncle Sam. While his age, build, and particularly features were akin to those of the proverbial Uncle Sam, his dress was even more so. Gene wore an American flag: the pattern continued neatly from his windbreaker, down across his jogging pants, to even his tennis shoes.

About thirty bodies sat facing each other in a circle: most wide-eyed trainees, the rest returning auctioneers. Beside me sat the only person who was neither: Hot Cocoa. The Brazilian beauty with the dark skin and raspberry lips had been a fellow trainee last year. She had intended to remain a permanent associate, but asked to join advanced training in a bid to become an auctioneer after all. Her name was Mariana, but the awe-filled moniker I gave her in training had caught on.

"My name is Gene," the patriot said, "who you all spoke to over the phone. My role is manager of fleet operations. I welcome you all to Sundance. It's an exciting time for us, with growth exceeding everyone's wildest expectations. That's because of people like you!"

"Those that survive," Lucifer interrupted from behind the circle.

"Yes," Gene agreed after a pause. "This will be a challenging week. I wish I could lead you, but we're growing so fast that I simply no longer have the time. So let me introduce the man who is now in charge. His name is—"

"Lucifer!" the slovenly man interrupted again. He strode to the center of the circle. His swagger was profound. So was my nausea.

"Pond scum!" Lucifer said sharply as he glanced over the circle. "That is what you are. You aspire to be more, yes, but most of you will not succeed. I am happy to say that our drop-out rate is now over 50%. That's not the failure rate, you little amoebocytes, but the drop-out rate. Many who tough it out still don't get in. This will be the hardest week of your life. It is not only my job to make it so, it is my pleasure.

"It is my duty to help you crawl out of the primordial ooze and become something greater. A few of you may evolve into tadpoles, at which point you will be released to the big pond. More will fail out there, but some will survive to become frogs. You see a few frogs in attendance here. Keep your place in mind: returning auctioneers are not here for you, but their own advanced training. They will not help you unless I order them to."

"Now," Lucifer continued. "Names! In the past, Gene did a name game where we labeled you by the celebrity you most resembled. He thought that was a fun way to break the ice, yet emphasized that you have more important things to remember than people's names. That's a load of crap. Most of you will not make it, so it's a huge waste of time."

Gene looked up from his BlackBerry and clucked his tongue at Lucifer.

"However," Lucifer sighed, with obvious reluctance, "I defer to Gene's age and expertise, and will give you all the benefit of the doubt. I shall present you with monikers that assume you will see week's end."

"You!" Lucifer said, thrusting a finger at a handsome young black man. "You are Tadpole One."

The youth looked too awed to be offended. Lucifer strode around the circle, pointing rudely to each trainee in turn, designating them Tadpoles One through Twenty-two.

"So now, trails of slime, you are free for the night. I suggest you study the books you were assigned to bring. If you did not bring them, then pack. Tomorrow at 8 a.m. meet here in auction attire. That includes gavels. If you don't have a gavel, then pack. You may now go soil yourselves."

Cocoa leaned in to me and whispered, "He hasn't changed much, has he?"

Before I could reply, Lucifer stepped up before us. His hands were stuffed in his pockets, with one untucked shirttail covering a forearm.

"Hot Cocoa," he greeted, bending towards her with a smarmy smile. "I'm glad you're here. We needed a woman among the exalted ranks, and you look sexier than ever."

"And you're charming as ever," she replied sarcastically.

Lucifer grinned hyena-like, eyes glinting lasciviously. I couldn't fathom how Cocoa kept her cool. I never before realized the unique challenges supremely hot women had to endure in the workplace. I had always assumed it gave them an edge, but suddenly I wasn't so sure. Still leaning forward aggressively, Lucifer swiveled his head towards me. He reminded me uncomfortably of a praying mantis.

"Buzz," he gloated. "Your savior, Gene, wants a word with you."

Then he was gone.

"Correct me if I'm wrong," I said to Cocoa, "but aren't returning auctioneers supposed to get special treatment?"

"Oh, you've always gotten special treatment from him all right," Cocoa laughed. "That's why I like hanging around you: he usually leaves me alone."

"At least I'm good for something," I muttered with a smile.

"He's always hated you," she said. She placed a reassuring hand on my arm and added, "I hope, for your sake, Gene has good news for you."

"The understatement of the year, my dear."

I went straight to Gene, who was still busy checking emails on his BlackBerry. I waited respectfully for him to finish.

"Oh, Buzz!" he said, finally putting his phone away. "We need to talk. We have a list of complaints about you."

I stared at him, stunned. "A... list?"

"Five, to be exact," Gene supplied. "We'll talk about them in the morning, OK?"

"Not on your life!" I quickly responded, eyes wide. "You can't keep me stewing all night after telling me that!"

Gene paused a moment in thought, then shrugged. "All right, then. The auctioneer of *Sensation* wrote a very long and detailed email about how you left the ship in shambles."

"No way," I retorted. "I left things better than I received them. Way better, if you count aerating the damn cabin. That's a major rule in Boy Scouts, you know, and I come from a long line of Scout Masters. I want to know exactly what Robin said."

"I'll read you the email," Gene said, again citing his smart phone. He searched for what felt like ages. Finally he brightened and said, "Here we go! First, he said you didn't provide him with an end of cruise report from the ship."

"Yes," I agreed. "There was a new ship's accountant who messed up. It took him two days to get the reports, which were emailed to me. Robin should have emailed them to you, as well. If you don't have them, I'll forward them to you immediately. I keep everything."

Gene regarded me thoughtfully. His doubt was poorly hidden, but eventually he gave another shrug and said, "No, if you sent them I'm sure I have them somewhere. The second complaint is that you did not sign a proper handover inventory."

"Yes," I agreed again. "The sales computer crashed while we were doing it. We printed an inventory and manually checked off all the high-end works I had already sold. You'll recall that there were a lot of them. We both signed off on it. I sent in Sundance's copy the very next day."

Gene looked at me a long time in silence. It was most unsettling, because Gene had been my biggest ally during training. Without his support, Lucifer was going to destroy me.

"Third complaint," Gene continued suddenly, "You left without giving him a full ship tour."

"Are you kidding?" I squawked. "*Sensation* was his ship for the previous ten months! Further, I was ordered to leave the ship by 9:30 a.m. due to Coast Guard regulations. I was actually escorted out by security, in fact. The ship's purser can even verify it. You got anything tangible, or is this—as Lucifer would say—all a load of crap?"

"Fourth complaint," Gene said tersely, "You left him with no employees to do the paperwork. And I have indeed noticed a very high amount of paperwork issues since you left. So has Frederick."

Gene looked at me accusingly, letting the magnitude of his final words sink in. Frederick could—and did—fire his auctioneers on a whim. However, I wasn't scared. I was furious. With each point Gene rattled off, it had been more and more difficult to contain. Finally I exploded.

"This *is* a load of crap!" I boomed. "The internet manager from Mexico, Susana O'Reilly, was in charge of checkouts. She's a genius."

Gene looked at me with open disbelief, like I claimed the dog had eaten my homework. He asked sarcastically, "A Mexican named O'Reilly?"

"You think I would make up something like that on the fly?" I countered. "You know what this is all about, don't you?

Robin signed on without his girlfriend, Vanessa. Her name was on every single report. The problems with the paperwork are because he doesn't know how to do anything, and never did! He couldn't even figure out how to do a paper inventory, Gene. I had to teach him how! The guy's blaming his complete incompetence on me."

"Vanessa was not with him?" Gene asked, surprised. "Now that you mention it, I do remember her name on the reports."

Gene pocketed his BlackBerry, then said casually, "Well, I guess that clears up that, then. Don't worry about it any longer."

He acted like nothing had happened at all. I was still fuming.

"What's the fifth complaint?" I asked, trying to keep my voice cordial.

"Hmm?"

"You said there were five complaints," I pressed. "What what the last one?"

"Oh, yes, well," Gene said idly. "He claims you stole several bottles of fish oil."

### 3

Advanced training was relatively easy. Then again, compared to what the trainees were enduring, so was engineering a suspension bridge. Three tadpoles were booted on the first day because they had not brought everything asked of them, and another had already left in tears—a high school football star who couldn't handle the verbal abuse. Two more quit on day two, and day three saw the end of five more. Twenty-two had become fourteen.

At lunch on day five, I passed Hot Cocoa at a sushi restaurant. She sat ramrod straight in a chair opposite Lucifer and John Goodman. Auctioneers usually lunched together, but I was surprised she hadn't fled upon seeing only those two present. She was already regretting it. John reached across the table and placed his beefy hand on hers. Cocoa winced and extricated her hand immediately. However, she placated him with a smile from her knockout lips.

"Buzz," she cried out in relief, "I've been looking for you all day!"

John looked at her in surprise, and rumbled, "But *I've* been with you all day!"

"I was just going to brag to my classmate," Cocoa soothed, "about how I've been learning all day from one of the highest earners in the fleet!"

John nodded imperiously, expecting to hear nothing less. Lucifer, on the other hand, waved his hand dismissively.

"Bollocks! He's all piss and wind," he mocked. "He learned everything from me."

Such conversation was precisely why I rarely dined with other auctioneers. John's obsession with his own success was distasteful. Almost hourly he had interrupted Lucifer's lectures to inform the trainees, the returning auctioneers—really anyone who would listen—about how he had solved yet another issue that plagued the rest of us. His solution was invariable: sheer bravado. Of course I was loathe to socialize in any way with the odious Lucifer.

But with Cocoa's expressive eyes begging me not to leave, how I could abandon her? Reluctantly I sat down.

"Don't bugger about with Buzz," Lucifer ordered Cocoa. "He got lucky once, but his sales are crap."

"But you said Buzz was the first one in our class to get his own ship!" Cocoa replied.

"Yeah, and first to lose it, too," Lucifer cackled.

"I broke the ship's record the week before I got yanked," I pointed out.

But Lucifer was not listening. He was busy leaning into the aisle to accost our waitress. Though she was at another table, he certainly didn't let that slow him down.

"Hey!" he barked over their conversation. "Bring us some California rolls. Two each. We're in a hurry."

"I'm sure it was only a matter of scheduling," Cocoa said to me reassuringly, patting me on the arm. John's gaze followed Cocoa's movement. When she stopped, his focus returned to her ample cleavage.

"Dusty said that happens sometimes," she continued.

John snorted derisively and said, "With the big dogs, schedules don't matter."

"That's right," Lucifer agreed. "You don't hear the big dogs whining about such things, do you?"

"He wasn't whining," Cocoa protested.

"Don't worry about it," I said lightly. Then, intentionally ignoring the two men, I asked, "So, tell me Cocoa, weren't you originally planning on being a permanent associate?"

"I was," she agreed. "But Dusty—you do remember him, don't you, the auctioneer you handed over to on *Conquest*? Dusty pushed me to step up and try for my own ship."

"That's a rather altruistic move for an auctioneer," I observed.

"Yes," Lucifer barked. "Dusty is a relic. He won't last much longer. The new system has associates on every big ship now, and if he keeps that crap up, he'll be replaced himself."

"He's a nice man," Cocoa defended lightly.

"Sure he's nice," Lucifer snapped, "If you got a body made for *Playboy*."

Abruptly he shouted to the restaurant in general, "Where's my beer?"

"I know Dusty," John added. "He was good for his time. Invented a lot of good gimmicks that made me a fortune. You handed *Conquest* over to him, Buzz?"

"I was associate for William Shatner," I replied.

"Well don't worry about *his* schedule," Lucifer commented. "He never made it back from vacation in Thailand. With all those cheap whores, we'll never see him again."

"What about Charles and Tatli on the *Majesty of the Seas*?" I asked Lucifer, regarding the couple I worked with as a tadpole. "Have you heard anything about them?"

"They were having lots of problems, all right," Lucifer said. "I was sent to *Majesty* to teach them what they were doing wrong. They're OK now."

Fortunately the food arrived to occupy our attention. While conversation was mercifully stopped, Lucifer's vulgar eating habits were equally unpleasant. He used his fingers to messily dunk slices of a sushi roll into the soy sauce. The black liquid gushed over the sides of the dish and stained the table cloth. He gobbled each portion down grotesquely, chewing with his mouth open and smacking soy-stained lips.

"Did I mention I made over three hundred thousand last contract?" John asked Cocoa as he reached across the table and helped himself to her wasabi.

"Yes," she answered with a fake smile. "Twice."

"Are we going to be performing in advanced training, or what?" I asked Lucifer, trying to overlook his revolting etiquette. "I was told we would be judged anew, yet I fail to see how. We're not scheduled to auction."

"Fail, yes," Lucifer agreed. He answered with his mouth full, revealing mutilated bits of food caught in his uneven teeth. "You should be used to that. On day six I'll pair the auctioneers with new kids. They'll present what you write. You'll be judged on their performance."

Cocoa dropped her chopsticks with a clack.

"You're judging us by someone else's performance?" she asked, aghast.

"Yes," Lucifer chortled into his beer. "So you better suck up now. I'm in Room 324."

Cocoa didn't take the bait, but only snorted, "You wish."

Lucifer then looked to me, and added with heavy insinuation, "Better suck up or I'll pair you with some git too stupid to know he's already on his way out."

Desperate to recover some lost ground, I asked him, "Did you ever actually tell Frederick that I'm the Frog Prince? That was the deal when I proved you wrong on *Ecstasy*."

Both Cocoa and John stopped eating to better observe Lucifer's response.

"I did," Lucifer said, inadvertently spitting a sesame seed on the table. "But don't gloat yet, little man. Being in Frederick's sights is a double-edged sword. You think he can't keep track of all one hundred auctioneers and eighty associates? MIT consulted *him*, for Christ's sake. He's the one who pulled you from *Sensation*, not me. He sees a zero even once and he'll pull an auctioneer, no matter what. Even John here got pulled from a ship once."

John was so surprised at Lucifer's admission he momentarily altered his gaze, which of course had once again found Cocoa's cleavage. After he harrumphed, he quickly returned to his ocular duties.

"Proving me wrong is sufficiently difficult," Lucifer offered, "that I gladly held up my end of the bargain and told Frederick you're the Frog Prince. But I think you got lucky on *Ecstasy*. You losing *Sensation* proved me right. Tomorrow you'll have your one and only chance to show me you shouldn't be demoted to Tadpole Twenty-three."


# 4


That night I received an email from Bianca. It was short, and I was glad for it. Rather than sending me well wishes, she demanded to know why I hadn't written to her with news of my having successfully secured a new ship. She ordered me to be a man and demand a ship immediately. She always used that word, 'demand'. At first I suffered a flush of anger, but soon swallowed it in favor of sadness. She simply had no clue what my world was like. I secretly wished to see how she would handle all the arrogance and verbal abuse.

Ultimately, however, there was little I could say to her. How could I tell her my career—and thusly our very relationship—was to be determined not by my own performance, but that of some kid I didn't even know?

# 5

The morning of day six, the auctioneers met for breakfast. Uncle Sam and Lucifer gathered us around a large table laden with pastries and coffee pots.

"As most of you know," Gene began, "I like to pull aside the experienced ones to ask their opinions of the trainees. Sometimes classmates see things trainers do not. I'm not talking about only class behavior, but also what you've seen after hours. If someone can't handle their alcohol here, for example, they will never survive a ship. Now, we're not rating anyone yet, but I would like a simple yes or no for each trainee: would you want them as your associate or not? So let's start with, er, Tadpole One."

A chorus of nods indicated general approval of the black youth.

"I quite agree," Gene said. "He's a promising young man. And Tadpole Two?"

"Which one's that?" Jim Nabors asked.

"The tall one."

"With the red hair?" asked Hot Cocoa.

"No, that's Tadpole Five," Lucifer corrected. "Tadpole Two is the big, dumb one."

"But he's got the freckles, right?" asked John Goodman.

"No, that's Tadpole Twelve," Lucifer corrected again, with lessening patience. "Tadpole Two is the big dumb one who should stick to rugby. Has a broken nose."

A chorus of negatives arose.

"And Tadpole Three?" Gene asked.

"Is that the Scot?"

"No, the Scot's the really bad one," Kurt Russell said. "The worst."

"Yeah, the Scot sucks," agreed John. "I think he's Twenty or something. But Three's OK."

"The Scot is Tadpole Twenty-two," Lucifer seethed. "Honestly, you people make a fortune and can't tell apart a couple dozen stupid kids?"

He was answered by a circle of shrugs.

"I just made an executive decision," Gene announced. "Next month we're going back to the name game."

Lucifer gave Gene his boss a sour look, but Gene just smiled back.

"Now," Gene continued. "Everyone remembers Tadpole Four. She's the one that looks like Jennifer Aniston. Who wants her on their ship?"

All hands shot up around the circle, but one. Cocoa merely crossed her arms beneath her generous bosom, and glared.

# 6

"Tube worms!" Lucifer boomed, "Today we're doing groupings."

Lucifer was actually addressing a classroom jam-packed with both trainees and auctioneers, but the latter knew that the barbs were not meant for them. Well, most of us, anyway.

"Grouping is a technique enabling you to sell an expensive work by first building up to it with smaller, unrelated works. You can use a crappy Jean-Claude Picot landscape to sell a

Picasso. It works because you educate the audience without lecturing them.

"Rembrandt is a good example. Most of the audience knows shite about him, except his name and that he did paintings. They don't know he was the world's greatest copperplate etcher, and did more of those than paintings. So when you show them what looks like a fat, black postage stamp and ask for $3,000, they blow you off. They assume his paintings are worth untold millions, and anything less is a fake. You can't waste ten minutes lecturing them about what they're looking at because they'll fall asleep. They're drinking free champagne, for Christ's sake. So how do you educate them?

"The secret to grouping is to offer a different artist's work that can also teach the audience about Rembrandt. He was famous for his chiaroscuro, of course. So find a painting with a strong sense of chiaroscuro and use that to educate the audience about chiaroscuro. It doesn't matter if you sell it or not, because you just prepped your audience to buy what you want them to. Do that with a few different works, and when you finally bring up that big Rembrandt, the audience can now properly appreciate what they're looking at."

Lucifer sat upon a stool, self-satisfied, and asked, "Any questions?"

"What's chiaroscuro?" a hesitant voice asked anonymously.

Lucifer bristled, and the room fell silent.

The hyena-like smile returned quickly, and he said, "Ooh, you maggots make this too easy! The idiot who asked that want to identify himself, so I can fire him?"

"Let's get to the fun part, shall we?" Gene interrupted. "Each trainee will be assigned an auctioneer, who will teach you how to group for the work we assign you. Together you will select two works, each from a different artist, to group with your assigned work. Trainees, after lunch you will present for the class your grouping."

The tadpoles looked about, edgy over who and what they would be assigned. All knew their futures were at stake. Most auctioneers yawned, but not me. I truly did feel like Tadpole Twenty-three. While we waited for Gene and Lucifer to finalize their list, I met the worried gaze of Hot Cocoa. So I wasn't the only terrified auctioneer. I gave her a reassuring smile.

Finally Lucifer announced the pairings, starting from Tadpole One and moving up numerically. The list seemed endless. At long last two trainees were assigned to Cocoa: Tadpoles Nineteen and Twenty-one—Twenty having since dropped out. They were tasked with grouping for a Picasso etching. Cocoa wiggled happily in her seat, delighted to have an undisputed master artist who had excelled in every aspect of art, ever. They would have an easy day.

That left only one trainee yet to be assigned, and only one auctioneer yet to teach him.

"Tadpole Twenty-two," Lucifer called out, trying not to gloat. "Buzz Lightyear."

A bulky, almost brutish youth with red-blonde hair moved over towards me, tipping over a few chairs in the process. His hip nearly ejected Scarlet Johansson from her chair. Upon reaching my side, he gave me a shy smile that belied his physical attributes. He fidgeted mightily, desperate to hear which artist he would be assigned. I was no less anxious.

"The final artwork you are assigned to sell," Lucifer said slowly, teasingly, "the last of the class, is a color lithograph from Norman Rockwell."

A chorus of rueful groans rose from the class. Mine was among them. The lumbering tadpole looked at me with huge, terror-filled eyes, and stammered in a thick, Scottish brogue, complete with rolling R's.

"A dinna kin! Who the bloody hell is Nor-r-r-man R-r-rockwell?"

# CHAPTER EIGHTEEN

## *That's Americana*

### 1

ORDINARILY, HAVING AN entire morning to create a block of groupings would be more than enough time. But Norman Rockwell was not your average artist.

And Tadpole Twenty-two was not your average trainee.

"A hae nae thochtie aboot yer R-r-rockwell. A'm fre Scotland!" the brutish man protested in what I suspected may, in fact, have been English. I could understand Romanian better! "Can ye gie's a haund?"

Seeing my confusion, Tadpole Twenty-two forcibly calmed himself, then repeated slowly, "I have *nae* idea *aboot* Nor-r-r-man R-r-rockwell. He is American, aye? Can you help me?"

"Of course I can help you," I said. "That's why I'm here. Now, what's your name? I don't want to keep calling you Tadpole Twenty-two."

"Ma name is Hamish."

"Why of course it is."

The thick youth stared in befuddlement at a printed copy of the artwork he needed to present. He shook his head sadly, red-blonde mane shivering in disgust.

"A dinna kin..." he began, but paused. Once again he forced the words out slowly. "I don't understand this Norman Rockwell picture. What's on the minda this fat old copper here, bringin' a wee girlie to a pub? D'ya like ice cream, little girl? B-r-r-r, I think it's creepy."

Such was the state of the world, when the illustration of a friendly small town policeman at an ice cream parlor laughing with a little girl immediately conjured fears of pedophilia.

"Stay chill, brother," I said. I had caught onto Marc's catchphrase, but my own lack of excitability was less from confidence and more from despondency. "That's a classic image of his. This was fifty, sixty years ago. It was a simpler time, OK? It's supposed to be sweet, and you act like it's one of Dalí's illustrations of Dante's *Inferno*."

"I've heard o Dalí!" Hamish said excitedly. "We can yuse him!"

"I don't see how," I commented, moodily. "The only thing melting in this picture is the girl's ice cream."

We sat beside each other, staring silently at the image.

"Maybe we be goin' at this wrong," Hamish said after a while. "What's the best work ye ever sold?"

"Hmm? Oh, I sold a Picasso etching once, for about $60,000. But I wouldn't consider that the best work I've ever sold."

"Really?" he asked, intrigued. "What was, then?"

"Before I worked for Sundance, I sold an exceptionally unique watercolor from 1937. It was the original design painting for the Dwarf cottage in Disney's *Snow White and the Seven Dwarves*."

"Another bloody landscape," Hamish groaned to himself. "Nae help there. A'm shagged."

Suddenly an idea popped into my head. I couldn't believe it. Could the grouping really be that simple? With a huge grin I clapped Hamish on the back and asked, "How's your embarrassment gene?"

Hamish leaned back, unsure, as if I was in a cop outfit offering him ice cream.

"We weren't there when you trainees did the test," I explained. "You know, to see if you get embarrassed in front of groups. I hope you don't, my friend, because if you can handle it, you're gonna knock 'em dead."

Hamish regarded me skeptically.

I pulled him close and said, "Your accent is part of the plan, but make sure you actually speak English and not Scottish, OK? Now, here's what you're going to do..."

# 2

The afternoon was excruciating. I sat beside Cocoa, and together we watched tadpole after tadpole rise reluctantly to the front of the class and stiffly regurgitate a list of focus-points. Because the order was in tadpole enumeration, the entire afternoon had to pass, snail-like, before the time came for Cocoa's team to present. About halfway through, I had to remind her to breathe. But Tadpoles Nineteen and Twenty-one had the most self-evident material of the day, and Cocoa had properly led them in the right direction. The two presenters took turns elaborating on stylistic details or influences, as appropriate, and ultimately received a complimentary applause.

"Last one for the day," Lucifer called. "Next up is Norman Rockwell. Look, I'm tired, so don't stall by padding your lame presentation with an imitation auction. I've heard enough fake 'sold!'s to last a lifetime. If you little barnacles sold even one-tenth of the works you pretended to today, you'd be up here teaching and not me. Just keep it to your presentation of each work."

A few scattered whispers and random coughs filled the room as Hamish rose. His thick frame bumped into several people as he wormed his way through the crowded tables, prompting apologies along the way.

"Ho ye! Sairy! Sairy!"

At long last, Hamish stood at the front of the class, towering over a portable podium that held a sales computer. The projected screen behind him remained blank, and Hamish gave me a nervous, almost pleading glance. I smiled and nodded encouragingly.

"Before a show this first work," Hamish said. "Can anyone tell me what is the one and only art form originally and totally American? That's right, tis only one, but it's changed the world."

Hamish paused for dramatic effect, searching the crowd for an answer. No one had it, so he brought up his first image. Laughter rose from the crowd as they beheld the cartoon character Wile E. Coyote falling off a cliff.

"Animation!" Hamish presented with a flourish. "That's right! Most historians agree that American Winsor McCay brought animation tae life in 1914 wi' *Gertie the Dinosaur*. Certainly the whole world agrees that Walt Disney made animation an art form worthy o the ages. And what's behind that American magic?"

Hamish pointed at the screen behind him and cried, "This!"

"An original production cel o Wile E. Coyote. Every second the Coyote chased the Roadrunner took twenty-four o these cels: all painted by hand. They were photographed in sequence tae make a short film—we all know how it works. What we dinna all know is that in the old days, the tools tae creating these animation marvels were considered just that: tools. Once used, cels like this one were thrown away by the thousands—and now their rarity makes them *worth* thousands!

"Ye can own a piece o history. Not some dusty old trinket or faded letter, but something that brought joy tae yer parents' childhood, tae yer own childhood, tae yer children's right now, and wull be there tae make yer grandchildren laugh. Ye think Wile E. Coyote won't survive that long? He can survive a drop from this cliff, can't he? You bet he wull! But the original artwork from the original artist's hand that brought him tae life? You can bet they won't."

Hamish paused to tap some keys on the computer. He was doing very well. Many trainees were jotting down notes. But the real challenge lay ahead. The next work would make or break him, and Hamish knew it. He tried not to look at Lucifer, but instead took a deep breath and readied for the plunge. The next image popped up.

"Whit's this?" Hamish asked enthusiastically.

The answer was so obvious that nobody bothered. I worriedly held my breath. This was Hamish's moment, which meant it was my and Bianca's moment. Did Hamish have it in him?

"It's bloody Fred Flintstone!" Hamish exclaimed, bringing chuckles from the class.

"Aye, ye all know that," he continued. Hamish began talking faster and with more enthusiasm. He almost began jumping up and down, working himself up to a moment that was going to make him a hero... or get him fired.

"This one's an original animation cel from 1961. Tis already fifty years auld. But nae like the so-called 'classier' films from Disney or Warner Brothers, Hanna Barbera cartoons were made special for television. They began an entire era: an era o Saturday morning cartoons. Who nae remembers sittin' afore the tele watchin' cartoons in yer pajamas? Did ye lay on the living room floor like ah did? From the past, ye say? Nae! How many of ye even now enjoy a cup o coffee while yer kids do the same thing ye did on Saturday mornings?

"This ain't just some throw-away tool from fifty years ago, mates, this is a piece o Americana. A'm from Scotland, and ah grew up watching *The Flintstones*. The whole world did—the whole world does!—don't let anybody else take away yer heritage. This is *your* history, this is a part o *your* life!"

Hamish burst into song.

"Flintstones... Meet the Flintstones," he sang, "They're a modern stone age family..."

Hamish raced back and forth in front of the class, waving ecstatically to get the crowd to join him. The trainees were hesitant, of course. It had been a long, stressful day, and everyone was tired. But not anymore. Hamish kept right on singing.

Something magical happened.

The whole classroom woke up. Students slouching at their desks perked up, and trainers began sharing huge grins.

Suddenly the entire classroom was roaring along with their energetic maestro.

"FROM THE... TOWN OF BEDROCK,
THEY'RE A PAGE RIGHT OUT OF HISTORY.
WHEN YOU'RE... WITH THE FLINTSTONES
HAVE A YABBA DABBA DOO TIME,
A DABBA DOO TIME,
WE'LL HAVE A GAY OLD TIME!"

"That's right!" Hamish boomed, panting with excitement. He had the entire room in the palm of his hand, and he knew it.

"Dinna let some fool from Scotland steal yer heritage. This is Americana. Think yer too adult tae have cartoons on yer mind? Keep it in yer heart—keep it in yer home!"

Striking while the room was hot and bothered, Hamish immediately clicked onto the final work. Up flashed the familiar image of the little girl sharing ice cream with the town sheriff in an ice cream parlor.

"We've been talkin' aboot American tradition. How's this? We all know this image, don't we? Tis a classic from Norman Rockwell: famous for comforting images that make us smile. But it's more than that, ain't it? His was the hand that graced the cover o *The Saturday Evening Post* for forty years. That's right, forty years! He painted over three hundred covers o America's favorite magazine. But where'd he get all that inspiration, I wonder?

"From you! Everyday people, everyday places, everyday things. These are Americans," he emphasized. "Washington, D.C. cited Norman Rockwell as a *Great Living American*, saying tae him—and I quote, 'Through the magic of your talent, the folks next door—their gentle sorrows, their modest joys—have enriched our own lives and given us new insight into our countrymen.'"

Hamish slowed down, and looked over the class. His face became serious, his words intimate. Everyone listened with rapt attention.

"This is more than just a classic image," he finished gently, earnestly. "This is a happy moment o yer life, or yer parents' life, or even yer grandparents. This is something special. This is Americana. Don't take it for granted. Life is about moments, and what better moment tae remember? Whit's better than always having a smile on yer wall? Ye don't want yer children tae forget about this simpler, happier time, do ye? This is Americana. This is yer gift to them."

Hamish paused, then quietly said, "Thenk ye."

The room burst into applause. Gene actually rose to his feet to clap. John Goodman nodded deeply in approval. I was so thrilled, I hugged Cocoa—not that I ever needed a reason to try that. Hamish blushed so profusely that his cheeks nearly rivaled his hair.

Until Lucifer stalked to the front.

His head was slouched forward, his arms tight behind his back. His face was silent and hard as stone.

"You can sit down," Lucifer said gently to Hamish, with a slight, yet still imperious, wave of his hand.

Lucifer opened his mouth, but paused. The room waited, silent, expectant.

"This pains me to say it," Lucifer finally said, "but that was excellent. It was perfect. Tadpole Twenty-two: I know you didn't write one bloody word of it. I don't care. I am going to steal all of it. That was fantastic."

A satisfied breath of relief flushed through the room. Lucifer eyed the assemblage before him, then added briskly, "You idiots better write the whole thing down, or I'm firing every last one of you."

Gene stepped forward and added with a big grin, "That goes for auctioneers, too!"

3

The next morning I woke up very early, as was my natural habit—or curse, depending on how one looked at it. The returning auctioneers had partied late into the night, but I had retired around midnight. Without having even set my alarm, by 5:30 a.m. I was slipping quietly down to the lounge for a cup of coffee. Like every morning that week, Gene was already in the lounge working before I arrived. Despite being a large man, he looked small amid the huge gathering of logbooks, sheafs of papers, a laptop, and his BlackBerry.

"Good morning, Gene," I said, raising my coffee in salute.

"Always the early riser, eh Buzz?" Gene greeted kindly. "Didn't party with the auctioneers?"

"Enough," I answered. "But I'm a morning creature, as you know. I love the calm before the storm."

Gene smiled and nodded.

"Ship assignments today?" I prodded.

"Yes," he said. He grinned somewhat mischievously and added, "The trainees all earned a spot, though they don't know it yet. Even Hamish. Well, unless they implode delivering their mock auction this afternoon."

"Oh, I'm sure Lucifer will delight in tormenting them until the very end. But auctioneers don't have to wait that long, do we?"

Gene chuckled. "No, you won't. This is one of the best parts of my job: giving ship assignments. Brian, I'm putting you on a ship that I think will suit your talents perfectly. You're getting the *Seven Seas Mariner*. You know it?"

I shook my head.

"The *Radisson Seven Seas Mariner*," Gene emphasized. "It's a six star ship. Congratulations."

I blinked in surprise. "I didn't know they even came in six stars."

"Well, a very few do, and you're on one," Gene said proudly. "You see, I know you're not one to let alcohol get the better of you, which is important because the cabin includes a fully stocked mini bar."

I was thrilled beyond belief, but didn't dare let on that alcohol got the better of me all too often. Feigning indifference with supreme effort, I said, "Is that so?"

"It's a luxury ship in the true sense of the term," he continued, beaming. "You'll have your own private balcony and the galley is staffed by Le Cordon Bleu."

"You're kidding!"

"You've earned it," Gene complimented. "The clientele, of course, is well-to-do and highly educated. No singing 'The Flintstones' to them. But what better auctioneer than the only one who was also an art historian? I think this just might be the ship you've been looking for!"

## 4

Blood smeared on the artwork. Nibbled bits of flesh clung to the computer. An auctioneer trembled, hyperventilating. A nightmare?

No, a handover.

With great pity I regarded the *Seven Seas Mariner's* departing auctioneer. I looked down at her raised rump, lost in loose skirts of thick green fabric, while her head and shoulders were thrust beneath a low shelf in the art locker. She scratched and hissed like an alley cat. Somewhere down in that shadowed recess, a small frame cowered.

"You're freaking me out, Alanis," I chided gently. "Will you please calm down?"

A squeal of triumph signaled success, and she wriggled back into the open. On her knees in the tiny, crowded art locker, she tossed back her head and fingered wild locks behind her ear. She rearranged her woolen shawl and sniffed indignantly.

The auctioneer dubbed Alanis Morrissette could have been quite pretty. Should have been, in fact. She had lustrous black curls and big brown eyes behind horn-rimmed glasses. Her mouth was also bold, with large, perfect teeth behind curvaceous lips. Those lips were bright red, but it was not from lipstick. They were stained from the blood welling up from self-inflicted wounds. She was so thoroughly dominated by nervous mannerisms that it was impossible not to judge her by them. Her body was wracked by shudders. Those huge white teeth were always masticating a finger, to the point where all ten fingertips were ruined stumps of flesh. They left bloody streaks on everything she touched.

"Freaking you out?" Alanis squawked. "Freaking *you* out? We have only six hours for this handover and you're talking about *me* freaking *you* out! What about the inventory? What about the paperwork? Oh my God!"

"Stay chill, sister," I soothed, glancing at the laptop. "According to the computer, we're almost done and we have loads of time."

"Loads!" Alanis repeated, finding a way to somehow be even more aghast. "We were supposed to have a load of sales materials today. Oh my God! Is it here? Did you see a pallet on the dock for us? I already signed for it, but I didn't verify anything!"

Alanis shivered again. It was painful to watch, and my heart ached for her. I felt a kinship with Alanis because she had been a fellow tadpole just nine months ago. We had even been assigned homework together. She had been a nervous girl then, but had since become an old wreck of a woman.

"You're going to have a heart attack by thirty if you keep this up," I commented. "Now, relax and breathe, OK? Let's just talk about some of the simple stuff. Like what are *Mariner's* ports, for example?"

"What?" she screeched loud enough to make a banshee proud. "You don't know the ports? Didn't you read the handover report? He didn't read the handover report, oh my God!"

"You never sent it, dear," I said gently.

Fear flashed across her face. "Oh my God, I forgot to send it! Does that mean I forgot to cc it to Sundance? Or did I forget to cc it to you? Oh no, what if I didn't send it to either of you?"

"It's OK, it's OK," I soothed again. I wanted to reach out to her, feeling a strange desire to stroke her frazzled hair as if she were a hyperactive longhaired house pet.

"It's awful here," she muttered, losing herself in a low moan. "They won't let us do any of the things we were taught. None of them. I had to watch my butt every minute with that damn chief officer."

Upon hearing those words, I had begun chewing at my own fingernail. Sheepishly I lowered my hand.

"I can't believe I lost my first ship," she sulked. "They cut me after only two months."

"Me, too," I consoled.

"Really?" she asked. A bit of torn cuticle dropped from her trembling lip. "But you were the first of us to get a ship. They sacked you, too?"

"Two months," I agreed.

Alanis began chuckling silently. I knew she didn't mean to be rude, but something was very, very wrong. Her quiet chuckles swelled, and suddenly Alanis was lost in raucous, unbalanced laughter.

"But he'll be watching your butt now, that's for sure!" she cried. "The Flaming Dutchman!"

She laughed so hard that she buckled forward, gasping for breath, huge lips almost comically gulping the air. Her body shook and she clutched her middle. When she raised her head again, she was snuffling back tears. Strange how laughter looks like crying with no sound. What was it about working on ships that made so many people cry?

Alanis suddenly snuffed out her hysteria as thoroughly as if dumping a candle in water. She peered at me strangely. I stared back, brows raised, unsure what to say. I was thoroughly confused and more than a little intimidated. Her behavior was highly erratic. I had seen it before. I had seen it all too often on ships.

Suddenly Alanis gripped me in a tight, earnest embrace. Though surprised at first, I soon squeezed back. We embraced a long time. Eventually Alanis pulled back. She stood tall, pulled her curls behind her ear again, and became resolute.

"Thank you, Buzz," she said. "You know what? Screw the handover. Screw it all. Sign my name on whatever needs it. This whole experience has been awful from the beginning. I'm done with it. I'm never going back to sea again."

She stalked off, leaving me alone in the silent, crowded locker.

I smiled. A hug was a powerful thing, but this one was particularly so, for a unique reason. We had not conversed, or even seen each other, in nine months. Even then, we had only known each other peripherally for a few stressful days. We did not even know each others' names. But we had shared something that few people would ever understand. She knew she would not get a hug like that back on land.

Strangely enough, at that moment I thought about *Moby Dick*. Understanding had blossomed while hugging a sobbing colleague in that cramped, dark little art locker. During my school days I had slogged through the novel and learned the usual: namely that Captain Ahab's quest for the white whale was the quintessential tale of revenge. I had figured the sea was integral to the story because the book was really an exhaustive lesson about whaling.

As a landlubber, it was impossible to comprehend life at sea. The magnitude of humility was profound. No amount of human effort could withstand the sea's caprice. The mental fortitude required to cast your lot into such a vast, uncaring void was staggering. Ahab's crew had regarded him with awe —not from fear over his recklessness, but because he actually dared to match wits with the sea, dared to demand from it something he wanted, rather than take what was given and count his blessings.

We, too, dared to demand against the sea.

Perhaps, when deciding to join ships, we were assuaged by man's modern marvels to feel physically safe. But the enormity of what lay beneath our daily toil, literally and figuratively, was something no one could understand until endured. It had broken so many Carnival waiters I knew: Camilla, Ramona, and Xenia, to name a few. It had broken me. And certainly the auctioneers Shawn, Charles—now Alanis—had all cracked under the inherent loneliness of those who dared.

But what of Bianca and I, who dared the greatest thing of all?

## 5

I stepped into my new cabin. My breath caught, hung in midair. My leg, too. I stood there, poised to step, but frozen in the doorway.

The mother of all cabins. I had thought that on *Conquest*. I had even thought that on *Majesty of the Seas*. But this... this was superlative.

And it was mine.

It took me a moment to absorb all I was looking at. I was used to tiny metal boxes with tiny metal bunks, but instead beheld a chamber that sprawled past a king-sized bed. There was even a sitting area with a couch. Opposite that was a large, ornate wooden entertainment center graced with a minibar and refrigerator. A comfortable desk was lit with a green-hooded lamp. Beyond all that luxury was something even greater: a full-sized, private balcony overlooking the sea.

Stunned, I explored past the walk-in closet and into the bathroom. I began laughing as uncontrollably as Alanis. The bathroom was equally gorgeous, boasting an actual bathtub! Mirrors were everywhere, as were fine brass appointments and glass shelving laden with spa-worthy toiletries. I made a mental note to collect the complimentary shower caps for my mother.

Though still in a daze, I returned to the sitting area to look over Alanis's handover notes. I was eager to see what was necessary to keep this most amazing cabin in the history of the universe. My eyes scanned the pages nervously, but brightened when I realized Alanis had only offered three auctions over an entire fourteen day cruise. With five days at sea, there was no excuse for not working each of them. But then I began asking myself why she wouldn't have done five auctions, when she was stressing and failing so badly.

The answer suddenly occurred to me—and scared me.

There were only 700 guests on *Mariner*. Each art auction on *Carnival Conquest* hosted half of *Mariner's* entire passenger manifest! So a numbers game was a afoot. I had to think outside the box. Fortunately, I identified several opportunities for art history lectures and gallery functions. I'd find a way. I had to.

After digging deeper into her documentation, as well as scanning her sales materials and personal notes, I formed a theory regarding why Alanis had choked on *Mariner*. Like her predecessor—who apparently had run the same number of functions and also been booted after two months—Alanis had stuck to an auctions-only attitude, and sunk. I also sensed that her hyperactive, stressful personality may have been toxic to the rich folks.

Eager to test my hypothesis, that evening I put on my best suit and readied to wander the ship. Even as I was reaching for the door, a knock upon it surprised me.

Who could possibly be calling upon me? I had only been onboard a few hours and had met no one other than Alanis, who had signed off. I opened the door and was pounced upon by a very beautiful, very young brunette in a sparkling sequined evening gown.

"You're Brian!" she said energetically, stepping forward. "I'm Karrie with a 'K'! I'm from Texas!"

I retreated under her assault of enthusiasm. She had particularly pretty lips, urgent with lipstick fire engine red. But her smile was engaging and honest.

"I see," I said, stammering out a reply. "I'm Brian. Oh, yes, you knew that. How did you know that?"

"I worked for Rachel!"

Was everything she said so buoyant? She said everything with such wholehearted zeal that by comparison I looked almost dour.

"Who's Rachel?" I asked.

"You know, Rachel," she repeated, flashing her radiant smile anew. Her teeth twinkled as much as her dress. "The auctioneer, silly. I used to work for her. I'd like to work for you, too! You didn't bring on any other staff, did you?"

"Uh, no," I said replied, brain struggling to recall the handover notes. Karrie with a 'K' was extremely distracting.

"I'd be happy to keep you on. Oh, that's right, you're one of the two singers for the shows."

She presented herself with a flourish, arms spread, and said, "Ta dah!"

"Would you, uh, like to come in?"

"Love to!" she said, skipping past me. She bounded across the cabin and immediately slid onto the bed. She rolled luxuriously back and forth over the comforter, sequins shimmering in satisfaction.

"Make yourself at home," I commented wryly from the doorway.

"I just love your bed," she purred. "Oh, what I wouldn't give for a real bed! I like my cabin, sure, but I don't have a real bed."

"If you were older, I'd be tempted to offer it any time," I quipped lightly.

"And if you were younger, I'd be tempted to accept," she shot right back, grinning.

"Already?" a gruff female voice called from behind me. I spun about to see a petite woman with short-cropped blonde hair gazing up at me with baby blue eyes. She wore a black dress with frilly cuffs and a plunging neckline. Like Karrie, she was also pretty, but in a more mature manner. She had strong features, a strong voice, and even strong mannerisms.

"You certainly move fast, mister," she teased, poking me in the chest. She had strong fingers, too. Her voice was engagingly sassy and gruff.

"This isn't what it looks like!" I said quickly.

Karrie stopped her frolicking, half rose from the bed dramatically, and raised a hand with all the aplomb of the

Supremes. With a crystalline voice, she sang, "*Stop! In the name of love.*"

I looked back and forth between the two women, completely at a loss.

"It's mingling time, silly!"

"You ready to go, mister?"

"Are you, uh, the other singer, then?" I asked, trying to keep up.

"That's right," she said, offering me a very firm handshake. "I'm Laureen."

"And that's Karrie with a 'K' in my bed," I commented. "I'm starting to really like this ship."

Karrie bounded past us and back into the hallway. She spun spritely, then danced her way down the hallway.

"Is she old enough to be away from her parents?" I asked Laureen.

Laureen laughed. She hung onto my arm and pulled me down the hallway.

"You ever been on a six star ship before?" she asked. "No? Well you're in for a ride. Let me fill you in."

# CHAPTER NINETEEN

*The Burning Spot*

## 1

LAUREEN NUDGED ME through the lounge, this way and that, via my arm. She laughed and smiled at everyone we passed, interspersing bits of wisdom and warnings of expectations.

Into my hear she said, "This is the main lounge where Karrie and I schmooze nightly—hello Frank!—it's usually enjoyable, but not always fun and games—Mrs. Redding, great to see you again!—unending cocktail conversation can get a little maddening by the end of a contract."

"I can imagine," I muttered, somewhat awed by what I was witnessing. We waded through the dark recesses of a lounge that radiated outward from a large, circular bar. Every cluster of low-backed seats was brimming with well-dressed men and women of obvious means. Unlike the lounge scene I was familiar with in Las Vegas—where everyone was young and sexy and they knew it—these were classic gentlemen and ladies, replete with waxed mustaches and tails, real fur and frills.

"You do this every night?"

"Every single," Laureen agreed. "We have a daily three drink allowance. You, on the other hand, better be Mr. Moneybags or you're in trouble."

"I'm in trouble," I agreed.

A pair of nearby ladies overheard me, and tilted their heads conspiratorially with a click of pearl necklaces. Laureen trilled an overtly loud and high-pitched laugh.

"Oh, Brian, darling, you are marvelously amusing!"

As soon as we passed, she gripped my arm tighter and whispered huskily, "Don't do that again or you can kiss this cruise goodbye. If you don't act like you belong, they'll avoid you like the plague. Can't be seen relating to the little people, now, can they?"

"I'm sensing that my predecessor may have had difficulty with this."

"She did," Laureen agreed. "And her sales suffered for it. But stick with us girls, Bri Bri, and we're gonna change all that!"

Laureen released me in favor of an appletini, and soon Karrie, Laureen, and I were tag-teaming the guests. The singers swept the old men off their feet, of course, which left me to dazzle the little old ladies. I was decidedly nervous over such a proposition. Fortunately, flirtation came naturally, and it in fact turned out to be a lot of fun. It also exercised my memory in unexpected ways.

Mrs. Mowry, for example, the widow of a prominent oral surgeon in Seattle, found my having earned the dentistry merit badge in Boy Scouts simply delightful, but surprisingly spent a great deal of time testing my dental knowledge to see if I was, as she said, 'trying to fleece an old lady.' Mrs. Greenblatt, on the other hand, claimed to be related to Grenville Dodge, the progenitor of the Transcontinental Railroad, so I interrogated her to see if she was pulling my leg.

Eventually the girls pulled me from Mrs. Miller—third ex-wife of a Gemini-era NASA administrator—and informed me it was time for dinner.

"We'll be late," Karrie bubbled. "Can't have you late to your first table!"

"My first table?" I asked, confused.

"Come on, mister," Laureen said, once again hauling me away by the arm. "I see I've got my hands full with you."

We strode into the exquisitely decorated dining room, where I found it difficult to not ogle over the delectable displays of food. After a decade in the fine dining business, I was not easily impressed by food presentation. *Radisson Seven Seas Mariner* impressed me.

"This has to be a mistake," I said, shuffling my feet to slow the girls' tugging me to the hostess stand. "What kind of masochist would want to dine with a salesman?"

"Art auctioneers are officers," Laureen explained with amusement in her growly voice. "And all officers host a table. No choice, mister. We have a choice though, don't we Karrie?"

"We do!" Karrie answered spritely.

"We do," Laureen repeated. "But I think we'll take pity on you and join you at your table."

The maitre d' directed us to 'my' table, where we found two couples already waiting at a round that sat ten. Wine was served prior to the first course, and the girls and I chatted idly with our assigned guests.

Suddenly a heavyset, bald man rushed up to me. He was visibly agitated and sweating profusely. His upper lip glistened with perspiration and with every fidget, his head flashed with reflected light.

"I'm Randy Young from Chicago," he bellowed, holding out a clammy hand.

"Hello, sir! My name is Bri—"

"Where's the Chief Financial Officer?" Mr. Young interrupted. "I need to sit with the Chief Financial Officer. Are you the Chief Financial Officer?"

"Uh, no," I stammered, glancing to Laureen and Karrie. "I assume he'll be here soon if he's not already..."

"It would absolutely be our pleasure to bring Andre to you, Mr. Young," Laureen said, smiling. Mr. Young glanced away nervously, and Laureen caught my attention by emphatically nodding her head towards a slender man in officer's dress uniform on the far side of the dining room.

"Yes, I see he's already arrived," I agreed, pretending to be on the ball. "If you would excuse me, Mr. Young, I would be happy to ask him to join us."

"I'll do it!" Karrie offered, already spinning away.

The Chief Financial Officer, Andre, was a small Dutch man with light brown hair and a shy smile. He formally introduced himself to Randy, just as the beginning of dinner was announced. We all sat down, more wine was poured, and dinner began. As an appetizer I enjoyed a medley of iced seafood, followed by a baby spinach salad, a lemon sorbet, and finally a divinely prepared Chilean sea bass. The food was magnificent. The wine was magnificent.

The conversation wasn't.

Randy never shut up the whole damned dinner. Not once did he let anyone else say a word. Even the food didn't slow him down, as he was only too happy to talk with his mouth full. Oh, how I longed for the gossip of the little old ladies—their manners had been impeccable!

During the appetizer Randy droned on about his newly successful accounting practice, and how his mastery of numbers had pulled him from the streets. A real rags-to-riches story, he claimed. Over the salad he branched off into his hobby of tracing his family tree—not easy when none were men of means—yet the traces of his forebears had convinced him that they, too, were number-savvy heroes. For dinner he moved on to his favorite sport, and we were 'spellbound' by descriptions of his bowling prowess—complete with a mock demonstration of his release, wherein he accidentally knocked a tray out of a waiter's hand. Plates broke, shrimps flew, but the man played on. By dessert, I was mercifully too drunk to really focus on his personal mastery over bowling statistics, specifically his quantifying of home-lane advantage.

While he demanded the attention of the entire table the entire time, he never once actually spoke with Andre, whose presence he had so excitedly demanded. I presume he merely wanted to brag to 'someone of numbers'.

"You originally from France, or what?" Randy finally said to Andre over dessert. "Andre's French, right?"

The Chief Financial Officer blinked back to consciousness.

"Why yes it is, Mr. Young. My mother is French, though I was raised in Rotterdam."

"That in France?"

Andre smiled blandly as he answered, "The Netherlands, Mr. Young."

"I know some French," Randy asserted. "When I rescued my dog—hey, art guy, you listenin'?"

"Hmm?" I said, suddenly leaning back from Laureen, who I had just requested throw me overboard. "Oh, of course Randy. I'm rapt with attention."

"Rescued him from a couple big dogs in the burbs outside Chicago," Randy continued, puffing up with pride. "He was just a little guy, you know, and was in danger of being torn to pieces. There were two German shepherds among the pack, I remember, and he was just a little bichon frise. You know, those useless little fuzzy French dogs? And I thought, what's a little Frenchy gonna do when faced with these big German bad-asses? If you can't play with the big dogs, and all that. Little Frenchy'd probably roll over and die rather than fight, right? So I jumped into the brawl and kicked some ass—er, butt, pardon—just like America at D Day. I threw my bowling bag at one, scaring it off, and charged the other. Everyone else scattered."

Randy was too caught up in himself to notice Andre's eyes flash with each continued inference to World War II.

"So I called him Le Mutt," Randy continued, beaming at his own cleverness. "He's not a very good dog, though. Slobbers a lot and doesn't listen."

"Like my ex-wife," I observed.

Andre's irate gaze turned away from Randy and leveled on me.

"Oh, would you look at the time!" Laureen called loudly. She rose from her seat, effectively cutting off the conversation. Everyone else fairly leapt to their feet.

"We have a rehearsal tonight," Laureen apologized to the table, tugging on my arm.

"Tonight?" Karrie said, frowning.

"Yes, dear," Laureen replied sweetly, though her eyes rolled expressively, "Remember there's a new schedule for this cruise."

"Since when? Oh, yes, of course!" Karrie said, finally getting on the same page.

As we hurried out of the dining room, Laureen muttered, "I used to like bowling..."

The three of us regrouped at my cabin, taking full advantage of my balcony. The sky was clear and the stars beckoned above. It was a wonderful evening, all things Randy aside. We chatted and got to know each other over a bottle of sparkling water—all of us having had way too much to drink. Eventually Karrie departed, citing a late-night date.

"At this hour?" I asked. "I know I talk as much as Randy, but my topics of conversation are scintillating and titillating and other big words, too."

"Somnambulistic," Laureen quickly growled. "Monochromatic, unimaginative—"

"Thank you, Laureen," I interrupted. "But really, Karrie with a 'K', should even I fail to entertain, you don't need polite excuses. Just run. That's what most pretty ladies do."

"No, really," Karrie said. "I'm seeing a shoppie. He gets off at midnight. Anyway, I'll see you tomorrow at the lounge."

"Ugh," I said, my head swimming. "Another round of all that?"

"Seven days a week, mister," Laureen sassed.

Karrie left, and a moment of silence settled over Laureen and I. The wind from the sea fluttered over us, damp and chilled. The quiet was not uncomfortable, however. For some reason, Laureen and I felt like old friends. Perhaps we were just both mature enough to not feel obligated to fill every moment with distraction. We just leaned on the railing and enjoyed the moment.

After a while I turned around to look back into my cabin, which glowed warm and inviting. I stared at the huge bed and sighed.

"That bed is perfect," I muttered.

"That was the worst come-on ever," Laureen chided, slugging me in the arm.

"What? Oh, no no," I replied, chuckling. "If I were to make a move, you would be powerless to resist my Casanova-like smoothness. Duh."

I turned back to viewing the waves slosh below us.

"I'm sorry," I said, "I was just thinking about my girlfriend. She's obsessed with a real bed."

"I heard *that!*" Laureen exclaimed. "She on ships, too? When she coming aboard?"

"After two months," I said. "I have that long to sink or swim here. It works out well, though, because after two months we go into dry dock. That's three weeks long, as I recall. Anyway, when *Mariner* returns to sea, so will we. Together."

"Sounds like you got it all worked out."

"Not really," I admitted. "This ship is our last chance for a life together. We've been working at it for two years now, and still haven't found a way. It's *Mariner* or bust. I must make this happen. I can't be distracted by all the fine wine and gourmet dinners. My girlfriend is slaving away eighty hours a week! It's just not fair."

"Fair?" Laureen said gruffly. "Ain't nuthin' fair at sea, mister. You just gotta do the best you can and hope everyone else does, too."

## 2

The next morning I spent organizing my art gallery. It was not a gallery, per se, but much better. A section of wide, comfortable corridor along the starboard side of the ship had been designated for my art, with floor-to-ceiling windows providing perfect light. Walking down the corridor, a guest was flanked on both sides with easels presenting my best, rarest, and most expensive art. At the end waited my desk, whereas at the beginning was the harpist.

Yes, a harpist.

Ethel was not just some chick in a toga plucking a lyre, but rather a master musician brandishing a six-foot single-action pedal masterpiece of polished wood. Her touch made the very air shimmer. When playing aggressively, the air in my chest actually throbbed as far away as my desk. Ethel was surprisingly young of age but old of soul, and when not entertaining guests in the adjoining lounge, she was sneaking their finger-sandwiches.

"Hey, Bri Bri!" a husky voiced called. I looked up from my files and saw Laureen and Karrie standing over my desk. Both were dressed for the port, Mexico's Cabo San Lucas.

"Your horny gorilla girls are here to claim you!" Karrie said, bouncing excitedly in her red bikini.

I blinked at Karrie.

"I beg your pardon?"

"Our favorite drink here in Cabo is called a horny gorilla," Karrie explained. "This is one of the only party ports, so let's get a move on."

"I see. Well, I have work to do, so I must regretfully decline."

"You've got plenty of time, Bri Bri," Laureen said brusquely. "And from what I just overheard in the hall, sounds like you'll have Hot Man eating out of your hand by the end of the cruise."

"Very Hot Man," Karrie emphasized.

"Ugh," I said, "Don't remind me. This morning Van den Hoffer tore into me in front of all the other officers. Turns out I was supposed to be at a revenue meeting. Of course, it wasn't in my handover notes. So not only did Hot Man have to call me at my desk, he reprimanded me for not being prepared to explain last cruise's poor sales. That I signed on yesterday didn't seem to sway him in the least."

But Karrie wasn't listening. Instead she fanned herself off, eyes dreamy. Finally she whistled in admiration at the vision in her mind. Laureen seemed to share Karrie's reverie, saying, "Wish he'd tear into me."

"He could reprimand me all day," Karrie said.

"And all night!" Laureen agreed. "He's so damn gorgeous."

"I wish he was our horny gorilla," Karrie continued.

Laureen slapped her thigh and cried, "Call me Faye Ray: he could carry me off any time!"

"Will you two stop?" I pleaded.

"Oh, like you didn't notice," Laureen said. "Certainly he noticed you."

"What's that supposed to mean?"

"We overheard him in the hallway," Karrie said brightly, raising her eyebrows suggestively.

"And boy oh boy, does he like you," Laureen finished.

"The hotel manager?" I asked. "You mean he's gay, then?"

Laureen sighed and said wistfully, "All the good ones are."

"Ah, now I get it!" I said, understanding blossoming. "Alanis said something about the Flaming Dutchman. The hotel manager's name is Van Den Hoffer. She didn't seem to get along with him too well."

"You won't have that problem," Karrie said helpfully. "I think he was just playing hard to get with you this morning."

"All right all right," I said. "Enough of all that. It's flattering, but I've got work to do. Before you leave, I have a quick question for you both. My handover notes say you helped with paperwork, but don't mention any payroll for art movers. Who did Alanis have move her art onto the block?"

The girls frowned in unison. "Block?"

"Yeah, you know. The easel at the front of the crowd."

"Crowd?"

I frowned at them, suddenly nervous. "You do know what auctions are...?"

"Oh, she never had enough people for an auction!" Karrie said.

## 3

The next day my auction could have been considered a disaster. Only a dozen people showed up, after all. But these weren't just warm bodies filling chairs: these were imminently qualified art enthusiasts. I operated the auction like a gallery sale. It was a huge success. The goals for my two week cruise were entirely met by tea time!

The next cruise, things were even easier.

At the end of my third cruise on *Mariner*—having once again cleared all my goals within the first days—I learned something profound.

The anatomy of a conch is a curious and unnerving thing.

"Yeah, mon," said the Bahamian in the conch shack by the sea. "Take da skin and eyes right off, den trow dem in da water. Dey live by demselves for two more days."

"Donny," Laureen chided with her best gruff voice. "You pullin' my leg?"

Laureen leaned over the counter to get a better look inside the shack. In Donny's hands was a large conch shell and a knife. Between his legs was a five-gallon bucket filled with seawater.

"No, uh, gills or organs or anything?" I asked, leaning forward beside her. "Just the skin? Living?"

"Yeah, mon."

"Lemme see!" Karrie called from behind us. She unsuccessfully hopped to see over us.

Before our astonished eyes, Donny demonstrated. Experienced fingers pulled from the shell a floppy, purplish alien-slug-thing. Using his knife, he expertly cut something slimy off of something else slimy—conch skin and eyes from conch body, presumably—which he then tossed over his shoulder. Through the open rear of the shack it flew, to plop back into the Caribbean Sea.

Donny was a thick man of middle years. The majority of his hair was going grey, and the majority of his teeth were going away. He and his wife, Monique, were proprietors of The Burning Spot, one of a long row of conch shacks lining a pier nestled beneath the huge bridge leading to Paradise Island.

The Burning Spot was a fascinating study. The shack was the size of a regular garden shed, though the entire back was open to the sea. From the ceiling dangled all sorts of oddities mixed in with daily use items. Funky ornaments made of seashells swung in the breeze, bumping into grill brushes and spatter guards. Painted carvings of fish and sharks swirled through wriggling lengths of plants that drooped from hanging pots, making the interior look like some sort of underwater diorama filled with litter.

The front wall of the shack folded into a counter, over which Laureen and I draped ourselves, beside a pile of conch shells strung together and heaped several feet high. As we watched Donny continue to intimately manipulate the conch, I pressed into the stack of conch shells.

"Gaaaaah!" I suddenly bellowed, stumbling backwards into Karrie and nearly knocking her off her feet.

"Hey!" she cried. "Watch it, cowboy!"

"Some cowboy," Laureen laughed huskily. She poked me, teasing with a voice usually reserved for small children, "Was it all slimy and icky, Bri Bri?"

"I-I just got tentacled!" I protested. "These things are still alive!"

Donny and Monique laughed hysterically. Monique buried her face into his broad shoulder, overcome with mirth.

"If their skin can stay alive for two days," Laureen observed haughtily, "Whatcha think a whole one can do?"

"I thought they were just shells," I muttered. "For decoration."

"Decoration's over dere, mon," Donny said, gesturing above him with his dripping knife.

In the sheltered corner hung an old and tired pom pom, heavy and limp, some strands stuck to a cast iron pan. There was obviously a story there, but I wasn't sure I wanted to hear it. Watching Donny laugh maniacally holding a sharp knife in one hand, and a slain alien in the other, brought to mind all sorts of B-rated horror movie imagery.

"Donny catch dem every mornin'," Monique said, popping open our bottles of beer.

"Cheerleaders?"

Monique laughed heartily. She had huge, brilliant teeth and a wonderful laugh. "He wish! He jump right off de back here before sunup. Dey come to de pier every day, like de cruise ships."

"And people order lunch when they're sticking things out of their shells and wriggling at them?"

"You did," Monique answered.

"She did," I corrected, returning Laureen's poke.

Drinking a Vitamalt—the sweet unfermented beer-like beverage that was all the rage in the Bahamas—we watched Donny's progress. He was freakin' me out. From the bodies of the conchs he pulled weird, half toothpick-sized slivers of what looked like gelatin. Each such find brought delight, and he promptly popped them in his mouth. He loved 'em. I didn't have the stomach to ask if they were conch anatomy or parasites.

Yet despite the grisly performance, the results were worthy. We took our three bowls of chilled conch salad to a crooked wooden table in front of the shack, and readily devoured the contents. The conch salad was delicious. The minutes-fresh meat was firm and bright. Mixed in were chopped tomatoes, onions, and peppers, the whole doused in copious amounts of freshly squeezed lime juice, then a pinch of salt and pepper. We snarfed it down in a blink, then had a hearty debate about ordering more of the same or something different. Variety won, and we ordered some grilled snapper, which was also caught that morning.

While we waited, debating the merits of Vitamalt, Karrie noticed a guitar hanging from the ceiling.

"Donny!" she called. "Gimme that guitar and let's get this party started!"

And so the party started. Karrie strummed the old, beaten guitar, and the two girls sang song after song. Everyone was having such a good time that other customers began leaving the other conch shacks in favor of The Burning Spot. Donny and Monique were flooded with extra business, but certainly didn't let the long lines increase their speed. That would have been most un-Caribbean.

The weather was warm but not hot, the breeze lively but not gusty. We were in the Caribbean dream. When Karrie began taking requests from the small crowd, Laureen and I hung back and sipped our Vitamalts.

"I am tempted to say it," I commented hesitantly. 'I really am, but don't want to screw things up."

Laureen brightened in faux-joy, clasped her hands over her heart, and fluttered her eyelashes melodramatically.

"Oh, Brian!" she gushed, "I love you, too!"

I chuckled, but that was more of a stall. Finally I blurted it all out, lightning-fast, "I think I'm being rewarded for all my hard work!"

I squeezed my eyes shut and tensed, waiting for reality to crush me.

"I'm still here?" I asked, peeling an eye open and peering about. "I wasn't struck by lightning or anything?"

"This is the life," Laureen laughed. "You're not going to jinx yourself. You're not dreaming."

"It's just so hard to believe," I explained. "After storming through so many ships—let's see: *Majesty of the Seas*, *Carnival Conquest*, *Carnival Ecstasy*, *Carnival Sensation*, and now *Radisson Seven Seas Mariner*—I guess I had just gotten used to worst-case scenarios. But this is the end of our third two-week cruise. We cleared my goals in, what, the first three days of each? Amazing! One more cruise like this, and I'll finally be able to bring my girlfriend aboard. It just doesn't seem real, you know?"

"We all feel that way when we get on *Mariner* the first time," Laureen said.

"I mean, I actually swam in the Panama Canal!" I continued. "These ports are unbelievably awesome, and too small for the big ships to reach. And every night getting to paid to drink and socialize with two pretty ladies? This is too good to be true."

"Relax, mister," Laureen said. "Sounds to me like you've earned a rest and a little success."

"Maybe you're right," I said. "Years at sea have gotten me looking over my shoulder for disaster. But I'm still haunted by what was said on my first night."

"That your ex-wife drooled a lot?"

"No," I laughed. "That life at sea isn't fair. Something's gotta balance the scales."

4

And something did indeed balance the scales. My life was a slice of fried gold, but Bianca's was a fruitcake—one of those nasty Christmas ones:

"Here I am, my love, in sunny Jamaica. I was supposed to go to the beach today, but there is some kind of new disease on the ships, so we had to do a hell of a special cleaning, washing and sanitizing everything in both dining rooms. Jesus Gras! Two more hours of fun, taking everything off the tables and carrying to the dishwasher. And we have to check in for dinner one hour earlier, too, to set the stations back up. This nightmare will last at least until the end of the week. Me go now to feed the beasts."

"It's now an official epidemic of I don't know what disease, called "Northwalk" or something like this, which screwed our asses big time. Apparently one bastard who ate raw oysters in New Orleans brought it on the ship, resulting in over 150 cases of sick people, crew members and guests, which means emergency. Every damn day special cleaning, and crew not allowed into ports. We were making plans, the Romanian geese, to go out in Cozumel but had lousy lunch in the crew mess instead. Then back to dining rooms to turn them upside down again. Every day this cruise we double clean everything in the dining rooms, and check in early for extra work on top. This evening again special cleaning after dinner, and tomorrow US inspectors will be on top of us, to decide if we can sail or not."

"God, how I need to talk to you! I can't use the computer as long as I would like, because there are only 3 of them working and the line is long. I love you and your messages. I still clean dining rooms and cabins, lots of people sick, I don't know what the hell is going on, I heard we'll skip Cozumel and sail back to New Orleans where we'll stay two days to clean over and over again. I just finished to sanitize my cabin again, after yesterday they kicked us out from the cabins to sanitize. I'm sick and tired of this nightmare, believe me, darling. I got to go now. I miss you like crazy!"

"I was pretty low spirited today, because I was tired and lovesick and homesick and sick and tired, but I'm tough, my love, don't worry about me, I had harder times than this."

"I don't know what to do. I need to find a replacement hand cream with antibiotics, because my hands are very spoiled. I hope I'll find the way to cure, otherwise I'll be forced to take an unpaid work break and risk not being hired back. I almost can't use my right hand anymore. The hard water and powder kill me. Me go. Why the hell I love you so much, you handsome dimple-cheeks bastard?"

Reading about Bianca's life was almost physically painful. I wanted to bring her to *Mariner* immediately, but she kept citing our agreed-upon two months of success before leaping.

How could she be so stubborn in the face of all this? I wanted to shout at her through the email!

But I only needed one more successful cruise to meet our self-imposed conditions, and then it would be dry dock. From there, we would finalize the paperwork for her to leave Carnival and become my partner. After so long, Bianca was so close that I could almost smell her perfume!

# CHAPTER TWENTY

*Bahama Boom*

## 1

PARTICIPATING IN THE DRY docking of a cruise liner was a rare opportunity, a part of the nautical lifecycle few could ever see. Thus *Seven Seas Mariner's* dry dock in the Bahamas promised to be a great experience. It wasn't. Well, maybe it was, but all I could think about was my approaching rendezvous with Bianca.

After dropping off all the passengers in Miami, *Mariner* sailed to Grand Bahama Isle, then moved into a labyrinthine, natural breakwater outside of Freeport. The shore was sandy and extremely pale, with several finger-like berths jutting into bright, healthy blue water. A huge cruise ship from Royal Caribbean filled the largest berth, its exposed hull the smooth, dull white of bleached bone. The entire site was industrial, with rusted steel and debris rising up from the crystalline waters and welding sparks dropping down into it. It was unpleasant seeing such Caribbean perfection being marred.

*Mariner* pulled into a tight berth, entering steel walls with the same ease as parking a car between painted lines. I sat on my balcony during the whole process, smoked a cigar, and watched the action. There was little enough of it. Because my balcony was on deck four, the top of the wall was my height, nary eight feet away. A crane, on rails atop the wall, rolled noisily back and forth, finally stopping directly before my balcony to drop me in shadow. The noise of the shipyard was unbearable, with the crashing of metal on metal, of heavy machinery, craning, and welding.

I wanted to see the water drain from around the ship, but after hours of waiting in vain, the sun set. Orange lights snapped into life, turning the rusted metal walls to maroon and giving the pale sand outside an eerie glow. In the distance, rain freshened the salt of the Caribbean. Lightning flashed along the deep, dark horizon. It was a beautiful, silent display of nature that helped take my mind off the noisome work of man.

In the morning, *Seven Seas Mariner* was high and dry. The floor beneath the ship had been submerged upon our arrival, but had of course been firmly attached to the two metal walls. The giant U-shaped berth had risen, over the course of many hours, by the release of seawater ballast from tanks within the structure. Once the berth's floor met the hull of *Mariner*, the two rose together. There was nothing exciting about any of it, though later, while standing beneath the hull and seeing 48,000 tons balanced perfectly upon the slender keel, my heart went pitter-pat. Had *Mariner* lost her balance, my hard hat wouldn't have helped much.

Power onboard was minimal, and the air conditioner was shut down. Fortunately, most of the crew had signed off. Alas, I had to remain in order to secure several million dollars worth of art onboard. The empty, dark corridors were like a ghost ship. The few of us remaining scurried about the dark like rats too stupid to abandon ship, but then pleasantly surprised that it hadn't sunk after all.

The entire first day I worked at removing all the paintings and prints displayed on the walls of *Mariner* and locking them in a specially designated holding area. The hotel director, Van den Hoffer, 'supervised' a bit more than he had to—whether he was interested in the art or in me was difficult to surmise. Though only hovering in the periphery, he was most distracting. He was the most beautiful man I had ever seen. Why, even I couldn't stop looking at him. No wonder the girls were so gaga.

After securing the art was complete, there was nothing for me to do but stay out of the way. Dozens of men worked on dozens of projects simultaneously, from carpenters redesigning rooms to upholsterers redesigning furniture. Just about the only place I wasn't in harm's way was in my cabin.

My first visit to the beach left me so badly sunburned that I couldn't go outside for a week. Day after day for two weeks I paced in my cabin, feeling trapped, thinking I would have actually slit my wrists had I been stuck in a crew cabin in the bowels of the ship. The heat was stifling, but whether amplified by sunlight through the glass balcony doors or the surrounding acres of steel in the Caribbean, I couldn't tell. Despite the temperature, I had to keep the balcony door shut in order to dull the harsh sounds of construction. I felt sorry for the crew, who were forced to sleep on the pool deck in lounge chairs and listen to that racket all night.

Trapped in my metal hell, I feverishly anticipated my and Bianca's imminent rendezvous. Her ship *Valor* was docking for just one day in nearby Nassau—near the very end of the dry dock—but one day with Bianca was worth a year's wait. I knew that all too well!

## 2

I liked to think of my seven seas rendezvous with Bianca in Hollywood fashion. I was the hapless guy who realized too late that he'd made a mistake, who then rushed off to catch his lover before she left him forever. I would magically appear right where I needed to be to prevent her from taking the vows, or boarding the plane, or whatever other Hollywood invention of the moment. But sometimes Hollywood is full of crap.

I didn't have the deep pockets of Richard Gere in *Pretty Woman*, who showed up in a limousine with flowers to win Julia Roberts forever. But all I had to do was hop from one Bahamian island to another. I even had time on my side: the flight wasn't until the morrow. How hard could that possible be?

Turns out, pretty hard.

The first hurdle in getting on the flight from Freeport, Grand Bahama Isle to Nassau, New Providence Island, was communication. *Mariner's* internet was down, and nobody aboard had a cell phone that worked in the Bahamas. Finally I borrowed a cell phone from a local welder, but discovered the airline would not accept credit cards over the phone.

Thus the second hurdle: cash. Ships frequently ran on a cash-only basis, but I had just paid out everything I had to my employees before they left for vacation. The purser was gone. My friends were gone. In fact, almost everybody was gone!

But not my room steward. Alas, Ricardo drove a hard bargain: he demanded a credit card as hostage until I paid him back. Further, he needed 100% interest. The irony was that he had only twenty dollars!

I ran outside of the shipyard to where a limousine waited. Oddly enough, aged and sun-blasted limos were commonly used as taxis in the Caribbean. The driver informed me that the nearest ATM was in the airport, but twenty dollars wouldn't get me there—taxi drivers extorted the crew mercilessly. He drove me as far as my money lasted, then abandoned me on a lonely, sandy road lined with wild canes and bamboo. The airport was one mile farther down the road, he said. It was almost 100 degrees outside, with a merciless sun, and humid as hell. My sunburned flesh ached even beneath two layers of protection. When I finally arrived at the airport, sore and soaked with sweat, there waited the taxi driver at the end of a long queue of empty limos—he had driven straight to the airport anyway!

The ATM only took Bahamian bank cards. Hurdle number three.

I tried dealing with several taxi drivers, even at the risk of violence. Talking to drivers deeper in the queue was serious business. I had seen fights, and even an actual riot, over cabbies not getting fares properly. But I needed someone to take me gratis to a bank in town, where I could then pay him. But it was Saturday, and banks were closed. Even if the ATMs took US plastic, they were all inside the buildings! Striking out with the taxis, my walk back to *Mariner* through the torrid heat was awful. Worse, during my absence, the ship's water had been turned off.

Proverbial hat in hand, I returned to room steward Ricardo. I begged him to gather friends to gather money so that on the morrow I could get successful transportation to the airport. After promising him the sun and the moon—and after two hours of collecting among the crew—I received the necessary money. Amazing, how such a paltry sum of thirty dollars caused such distress!

The next day I got to the airport and paid for my ticket with a credit card. When I landed in Nassau, I was thrilled to see an ATM that took non-Bahamian bank cards. Alas, it only dispensed a maximum of $100—all Bahamian. That didn't seem like much of a problem at the time.

Enter hurdle number four.

I had already booked a room at the British Colonial Hilton. This was good, because everything in the entire city of Nassau was shut down for Sunday night. I didn't want to eat at the Hilton, because they were in the midst of Conch Week, wherein every single entree featured conch. I was sick of conch. But the only restaurants open, namely the Greycliff and Chaz, both wanted $70 a plate: cash only. By the time I returned to the hotel, even their restaurant had closed. After hours of wandering, I found a small local café that sold me red beans and rice.

Yet, in the long view of things, that ordeal was the least I had endured in my quest to be with Bianca!

3

I had gotten used to the long gaps in my life without Bianca. I hated them. Use did not make them any more tolerable, nor pass any faster. That said, when immersed in the work of preparing for our life together, I was preoccupied.

Not so, in Nassau.

Having arrived at the huge pier extra early, steaming coffee in hand, I watched *Carnival Valor* ease through a pink haze that lingered long after dawn. Watching something so huge move so fast so silently was always a bit eerie. Then again, only a foghorn could cut through the noisy bustle of the port and cries of sea gulls.

After three months, I was finally going to see my Bianca! But not until the mooring lines were secured. I watched the Bahamians rush about the pier, securing the heavy ropes expertly transferred from the seamen on deck. They moved with an alacrity surprising for the Caribbean. Maybe my luck was finally shifting away from the constant worst-case scenarios I had endured all during dry dock.

Maybe not. One last hurdle awaited: a Disney cruise ship was coasting past the reefs and vacation houses towards the pier. If the Bahamians didn't finish with *Valor* fast enough, the Disney ship would dock and shut down the pier while it, too, properly secured its mooring lines. That would mean yet another delay.

Worst-case scenario prevailed: the Disney ship docked. Nearly an hour passed before I saw bodies coming down the gangway from *Valor*. The first several hundred were guests, of course. Before I finally saw Bianca saunter down the gangway, the sun was blasting from directly overhead.

Bianca wore a snug dress of some bizarre purple and white stretchy material. It hugged her curves tightly, which is what I wanted to do. Those curves were a bit spare compared to three months before. She had dropped a lot of weight—weight she didn't really have to lose. But her cheeks were still round and rosy, and her smile pronounced. Unfortunately, so were the dark patches under her eyes.

"You look fantastic," I said as she gave me a big hug.

"They give you free cocaine on that magic ship, too?" Bianca said, smirking. "You really are a rock star."

"You do look good," I reaffirmed above her objections. Glancing her over again, I added delicately, "You do look tired, though. If you want, we can take a nap before lunch. I have a room for us at the British Colonial Hilton, as requested."

With grand flourish, I bowed deeply and held out my hand for her. Instead of taking my hand, Bianca frowned.

"As requested?"

"In a manner of speaking," I clarified, rising up. "Remember in Egypt you commented that you always wanted to stay at the best hotel in a foreign country, where royalty and celebrities go? I got us a room at the British Colonial Hilton. Filmed two James Bond movies there, don't you know, and it has the only private beach in Nassau."

Bianca smiled briefly, but it never reached her eyes.

"How about lunch?" she piped instead. "We could go to Hard Rock Cafe."

"The Hard Rock Cafe?" I asked, blinking in surprise. Bianca was not one for a quickie before lunch in a new place, but I had thought she would at least want to see the hotel and maybe relax with a smoke or something.

"But you and the Romanian mafia go to Hard Rock Cafe every time you're in this port," I protested.

"It's where I'm most comfortable," she said simply.

Though unsure of what she meant by that, I acceded to her wishes. A few minutes later we screamed our orders to the waitress, barely able to be heard over the thundering music. I reached across the table to take her hand. She kept her hands folded in her lap.

With that rebuff, the odd vibe I had been getting from Bianca flared into the first full warning bell. Lunch was all right, but Bianca seemed... nervous. The second warning bell tolled upon entering our room at the British Colonial. I pulled Bianca close for a kiss. She did not resist, but was obviously hesitant.

"What's wrong?" I asked, pulling back. "You've seemed edgy all morning."

"Look, I don't know how to say this, so I'm just gonna say it."

We sat on the bed and faced each other.

"The timing isn't right for me to join you yet."

I stared at her, stunned. I didn't say anything. Bianca knew me well enough to know that meant something was seriously wrong.

"It's just the timing!" she repeated. "I still want to join you."

I continued to stare at her, waiting for an explanation. She hurried to offer one up.

"There's nobody else or any such thing. Ask anyone. Besides, you know how cold I am on ships. The timing isn't right."

"The time is now," I said. "Look at your hands!"

I grabbed her wrists and forced her to show me her hands. Every finger was split open or uneven with cracked scabs.

"How long do you think you can hide this?" I demanded. "Are you really that scared to join me? Being a waitress this long is killing you!"

"I'll be going on vacation in just two weeks," she defended. "I'll be OK."

I eyed her warily, and asked, "Two weeks? You never told me that! How is that possible? You're still in mid-contract. We had it all planned, Bianca. After dry dock you join me, we finish the contract together, then vacation in Iowa so you can finally meet my parents."

"They need me to open the next ship," she explained, pulling her hands away. She acted defiant, yet she wouldn't look me in the eye. Instead, she dropped her gaze to the comforter. "I get a short break—just a month—then open the *Liberty* in Montfalcone."

I was shocked at what I was hearing, but deep inside, anger brewed.

"You're ditching me for another chance to see Italy on Carnival's dime!" I accused.

"It's not like that," Bianca said quietly. "It's about timing."

"Timing!" I snapped. "How much more goddamn time do you need? Another two and a half years?"

"What's your worry?" Bianca shot back. "You're happy drinking and dining and dancing with your two babes every night."

"Are you kidding?" I asked, raging. "Don't play that game with me! You know they're just friends, and you know damn good and well how long I've been focused on us!"

Silence descended. Anger was in the air, a desire for hurtful words. I bit my tongue.

Finally Bianca spoke.

"It is about timing," she said in a quiet, subdued voice. "I'm just not in the right mindset."

"You're not ready to share your 'big secret' with me," I clarified sullenly. "Even after all this time. Incredible."

"It's just a little more time," Bianca said. She began to sniffle and her eyes darted about the room. "I almost lost you once on *Conquest* because I couldn't adapt. I'm scared I'm going to lose you again and it will be all my fault. I need for you to be you. I need you to be patient and understanding, more than I can ever be. Just a bit longer. After nearly three years, what's another few months?"

"So what do I get?" I quipped. "Some extra foot rubs, or something?"

Bianca's eyes grew wide at my harsh statement.

"Why you so mean?"

"Why are you so selfish?" I retorted. "It seems that this is all about what you want, on your terms. After communism and Catalin, you never had control over your life, and now that you have it, you refuse to lose it. Since you can't control how I'll react to whatever your 'big secret' is, you won't tell it. Don't control our relationship. Participate in it!"

"I don't expect you to understand," she whispered.

"I don't understand," I agreed. "Do you understand what we're talking about here? I return to a life of fine wine and gourmet dinners, nice clothes and luxurious ports, relaxation and lots of money. You go back up to your elbows in bleach, hands split open and sleep deprived—but you get a peep at Italy for free! And better yet, you get to keep hiding. Oh, by the way honey, if you're still able to type with bleeding fingers, maybe you can keep telling me that you love me. I'm sure that's enough to make me wait another three years."

Looking her in the eye I said, "I won't. Why should I?"

Bianca looked at me with wet eyes, but she refused to break into tears. We sat and looked at each other, minds spinning. I was too stunned to think that this was the end, though I felt in my gut it could be. I refused to give up on us quite yet. But for the first time, I feared she had already done so.

"I don't understand," I said gently, if earnestly, "but I accept. Acceptance is what love is all about. Think about that when I'm gone."

## 4

I was in a daze during my return to *Mariner*. I simply couldn't believe that after so very long struggling to be together, Bianca had said 'no'. Was what I had thought fantastic actually just fantasy? One thing was for certain: I would take the plunge for Bianca at any time, and had done so repeatedly. She had not reciprocated. But then, how could I blame her for fearing she would sink under the burden of her own baggage? She had failed us once already, she said. Doubt inevitably pulls one under.

How had I not allayed her fears after all this time? What was I not doing?

But some fights one had to fight alone. What I really needed to figure out was whether Bianca had lost her internal struggle or hadn't bothered to engage in battle at all. I ruminated on that while the plane was delayed. It was more than a little annoying when a twenty-minute flight was delayed by an hour. We sat in the broiling heat in our little metal box on the tarmac. Alas, such things were to be expected in the Caribbean.

One irate American was apparently new to the Caribbean, because he complained loudly the entire time under the false impression that this would improve performance. He was exceptionally rude to the flight attendant, to the point of screaming obscenities, all while his two children stared, wide-eyed and trembling. Finally the plane was cleared for takeoff, just when the asshole decided he had waited long enough. He yanked his children out of their seats by the arms and drug them through the plane to the exit. Once before the sealed door, he shrieked like a madman at the attendants, the captain, anybody, to let him out. When a beleaguered flight attendant tried to comfort his crying children, she suffered another round of verbal abuse. He was finally let off the plane, but then demanded his luggage. They had to unload half the passengers' baggage to retrieve it.

In all, we were delayed an hour and a half. Just as the flight roared into the air, I thought my annoying distractions were at an end, and I could stew peacefully. It was not to be. A little Bahamian boy climbed atop the back of the seat before me and stared at me with big eyes.

"Daddy?" he asked, looking at me quizzically.

I glanced up at the boy and snapped, "Not bloody likely, kid."

Upon landing, I went to an internet café before returning to the ship. After two and a half weeks without internet, I was suffering from withdrawals. I needed to reread some of Bianca loving emails, and maybe glean from them something useful. Instead I received an email from Sundance:

"ZERO SALES UNACCEPTABLE. HANDOVER TO NEW AUCTIONEER IN TWO DAYS - Gene."


# 5


I had lost my ship of dreams because I hadn't closed any sales—while *Mariner* was high and dry and gutted like a fish! My mind, already dizzy because of Bianca, blazed red-hot with indignation. At that moment, realization formed in my mind, clear and crisp like a beacon in the night.

Ships destroyed lives.

I called Gene on the spot, screaming at my cell phone over the café's droning calypso music.

"Gene!" I cried angrily. "What the hell, man?"

"You've been warned," Gene replied faintly over the poor connection. "Another cruise with zero sales? It doesn't look good for you, Brian. I'm sorry."

"You should be apologizing," I snarled. "We're in goddamn dry dock!"

"You're in dry dock?"

"Haven't you read any of my reports?," I replied, rather nastily. "You just look at the damn numbers and skip everything else, don't you?"

"I see," Gene said slowly. "Well then, I guess we'll have to fix that at the next advanced training. We could get you in by the end of summer, I think."

"What?" I exploded. "No way! You guys screwed up, not me. I'm kicking ass on *Mariner*!"

"Well," Gene said smoothly, "You're numbers are OK, but I wouldn't—"

"Unbelievable!" I cried, cutting him off. "Cut the crap, man! You say that to everybody. My numbers are orders of magnitude better than the last few auctioneers, and you know it."

Gene was silent a moment, then said, "The ship is going to another auctioneer. He'll be there in a few days."

"Then I demand another ship right now!"

"...demand, Buzz?" Gene repeated. His voice was soft, which indicated danger.

"This is the second time Sundance screwed me," I emphasized, throwing caution to the wind. Bianca may have been wrong about a number of things, but suddenly I realized she was right about one thing.

"I want a ship now. I'm not going on another three month unpaid vacation because of your screw up."

Gene was quiet for a moment, and I suddenly realized that I had gone too far. One always speaks with Uncle Sam with extreme respect, yet I had been raving like a lunatic. A long minute passed. I listened to the clanking tones of the calypso. Had he hung up? I didn't want to be the one to ask. I felt like a dork.

"All right, Buzz," Gene finally said. "I have a ship for you. It's another small ship with lots of money, but it won't be open for a month. You'll board in Athens."

"Good!" I said, and hung up.

I sat and stewed for awhile. The calypso music was sounding more and more garish by the moment, and my head began to hurt. Life was changing too fast!

Yet one good thing came from the whole mess: before I signed onto this new ship in Greece, Bianca was going to be on vacation. I wanted to call her immediately, but she was at sea on *Valor*. Thus I wrote to her, 'No more Hollywood rendezvous, woman! Meet me in Athens when you get off *Valor*. If you aren't there, it's over.'

I didn't care about ships. I didn't care about my career. I never wanted to go to sea. I never wanted to be an art auctioneer. Those were only means to an end, just a way to get Bianca in my life. In the beginning, finding a life together across the continents had seemed impossible. So many barriers blocked us! But together, haphazardly, we made a door. It was right there in front of us, ajar. But she just wouldn't step through it.

'Just like old times, my love!' Bianca wrote back. 'Romance abroad. We've made love on the Red Sea, the Black Sea, the Caribbean Sea, so why not the Aegean Sea?'

I tried to feel stern with her. Bianca was doing it again: pausing at the threshold, reliving our controlled snippets of perfection. I wanted to use my brain, to criticize her for not stepping through. Cobbled together bits and pieces of perfection were not enough of a foundation to build a life upon. But my body kept getting in the way. Despite my disappointments, my heart beat faster at the thought of holding her on another far-flung tryst. The feeling was heady, euphoric. I shared her desire to abandon everything for just one more visit to rapture.

But I wasn't going to Athens for another honeymoon. I was going there for a new ship. And if she wasn't going to be on it, then neither was I.

# CHAPTER TWENTY-ONE

*The Oracle of Delphi*

## 1

IN ATHENS, BIANCA greeted me with a big hug and a kiss. She couldn't stop laughing with excitement and enthusiasm. Looking wonderful in tight jeans and a brown leather jacket, she seemed as natural and warm and happy as always—when on land, anyway.

Surely my disappointment in the Bahamas had just been a bad dream, a manifestation of my greatest fear. I refused to believe that this bouncing, radiant woman had played me for years. The entire transatlantic flight I had imagined how we would discuss what happened. I must have rehearsed speeches grand and small a hundred times. Yet when I saw those round cheeks flushed with genuine joy, all thoughts of heavy talk vanished. I felt like a dog that forgets everything the moment a squirrel happens by.

Bianca, of course, did not mention the Bahamas. She was almost giddy to share with me a surprise: she had booked us on a special, week-long tour of Greece. She promised an awesome week exciting our minds, our imaginations, and at night, our bodies. Our transportation was a huge, modern tour bus. The predominant language spoken was Romanian, indicating that Bianca had booked the trip from home.

The first day we drove north for what seemed an interminable time. Bianca kept our itinerary to herself, thinking the surprise would be welcome. After uncounted hours in the bus, I wasn't so sure. We left the main highways and began snaking through very rural, but very beautiful hills. They extended into the distance, green and steep.

The distant plains rose up into a fan, which at its peak was pierced with a startling series of rocky pinnacles that thrust up from the earth like fat stone fingers clawing the sky. It was one of the most unusual rock formations I had ever seen.

Our bus ascended a most bizarre series of curves towards the strange stone upthrusts hundreds of feet high. Perched upon their pinnacles and hugging the cracks and crevices so very, very high up were ancient monasteries. From the plains so far below they just looked like tiny shacks, but were in fact massive stone complexes.

"These are the monasteries of Metéora, which is Greek for 'suspended in the air'," Bianca explained. "The old monks would wander up into the mucho caves to reflect. Over time they climbed all the way to the top of the pinnacles and made the monasteries. Some are still reachable by the rope and pulley system they created centuries ago. Imagine being pulled up in a big net like a fish. Really!"

After parking the bus, we ascended winding walks carved into the sandstone. Half walkway and half stairs, the path itself was miraculous and wonderful to behold. Precarious drops threatened at the edges every which way in a 3D labyrinth of ancient brick and air. We crossed a rope bridge over a chasm thirty-foot wide, its depth unknown. All this, and yet the monasteries were still hundreds of feet directly above us! We had yet to reach the stairs that curled upwards around the outside of the cliffs.

The ascent was a lung-bursting climb. Bianca paused halfway up for a cigarette.

"Perhaps now is not the best time for that," I observed with a smile. "Remember, I saw your medical file for the transfer as my assistant—which you declined."

"My lungs are fine," Bianca quickly scoffed, taking a deep drag of her cigarette.

"I saw lots of delicate white streaks," I teased.

"Those white things are cool," Bianca stated matter-of-factly. "Come on, marathoner, let's go."

Finally we stood before the entrance to one of the monasteries. The brick walls were scrubbed clean to look brand new, and funneled the approach into an antechamber that sheltered a massive wooden door. But what really caught my eye was the view. The plains spread out below to infinity. It was awe-inspiring.

Before approaching the entrance, Bianca pulled me aside.

"Only Greeks and Romanians are allowed inside this one," she whispered. "Our religions are brothers, but that's not the reason. Apparently centuries ago a Romanian nobleman gave mucho money and troops to the Greeks, so they still honor us. So polish up your Romanian and don't order lemon with your tea."

I cleared my throat and readied my best Romanian accent. I felt like a spy. Brown... James Brown. In fact, I recognized these monasteries from the climax of the James Bond movie

*For Your Eyes Only.* If the ascent nearly killed 007, I could forgive Bianca for having a rough go of it.

Inside the small antechamber were dozens of skirts hanging from pegs. An old Greek woman supervised as Bianca pulled one over her jeans. After Bianca gave her skirt a flourish, the old woman nodded. We entered.

"What's up with the skirts?" I asked in a whisper.

"They're still civilized, babaloo," she replied. "Only women in skirts are allowed in."

We passed through a corridor of stone, which opened into a courtyard surrounded by walls of both brick and sandstone. Flower pots were everywhere, lining the walks and hanging in rows across the walls, filling the area with radiant color. We turned a corner, and what did I see? Why, half a dozen Chinese girls shrieking in their native tongue, of course.

Bianca's eyes widened in shock. I burst into laughter.

We spent the morning poring over books from hundreds of years ago, and parchment fragments from thousands. It was an amazing, humbling morning. But that is not what made it so special. The memory I will always cherish was after I bought Bianca a coffee and she started henpecking me. With a smile, she demanded I hold this, that, the other thing, now get me a cigarette, now take my picture, don't let my coffee get cold, babaloo! I fired right back at her, and we laughed and squabbled back and forth. As much fun as that was, I think what made it so memorable was being caught bantering by two little old ladies from the bus. In Romanian they remarked, 'young love.'

If only it were that simple!

But, true to Bianca's word, things just got better.

We visited the tomb of Phillip II, the man who united all of Greece under one flag. This was what allowed his son to move onto even greater things—hence the name Alexander the Great.

We stopped on the plains of Marathon, where I simply had to get out and run a bit in honor of Pheidippides. The apocryphal story tells of how, after the battle where the Greeks defeated the Persian forces of Darius I, Pheidippides ran from Marathon to Athens with the news. Upon declaring 'we have won', he dropped dead from exhaustion.

We paid homage to Leonidas at Thermopylae, where his three hundred Spartans held off forces of literally hundreds of thousands of Persians, an event that inspired the blood-spattered, testosterone wet dream movie *300*.

But our touring the history of battle actually got bigger, if that was possible, for we next went to Mycenae. We drove through a hilly area forested with orange and lemon trees, with rockier areas sprouting copious groves of olives. Perched on a saddle between two small mountains was the ruined palace of the great Agamemnon, famed king in Homer's masterpiece on the Trojan War, the *Iliad*.

I nearly had a heart attack when I looked up at the entrance and beheld the fabled Lion Gate, some 2,300 years old, which had been the focus of one of my college papers. I thought the battered stone was more beautiful even than Brad Pitt playing Achilles in *Troy*. Bianca did not agree.

I was really and truly getting my geek on as we passed more and more mind-blowing places. Epidaurus, Mt. Olympus, Sparta. Bianca nodded with approval at my joy, like a parent observing a child's first visit to a carnival.

After a few days exploring the Peloponnesus, we crossed back over the Corinthian canal to visit Athens. We enjoyed a long, fascinating day exploring the Acropolis and its museums. That night we dined on a rooftop cafe, drinking Metaxa brandy and toasting the Acropolis, whose white marble glowed gloriously above us. The next morning we moved into the Aegean to see some islands. We ferried between Poros, Hydra, and Aegina, each far cooler than the last.

It was all so awesome. Yet it was also something else: a tactic. Bianca was using the past to distract me from the future. But the isle of Angistri changed everything.

2

Via an early morning ferry, we arrived at Angistri, where we planned to stay for a couple of days to relax. Our hotel was a charming little pad right on the beach with a couple dozen rooms and a couple dozen stray cats. During the day they lazed on the outdoor dining room chairs, as well-fed and well-groomed an any well-to-do tourist. A vine-covered trellis blocked the sun from above and the fluttering bougainvillea softened the breeze from the sea. Our room was small and simple, though the balcony was large and ornate. While not overlooking the sea, the balcony did offer an excellent view of a large Greek Orthodox church, complete with whitewashed walls and five blue domes.

After settling in, Bianca and I wandered to the beach to play. The sand was exceptionally rocky, but the waters were crystal and gorgeous and strangely invigorating. There was something magical about the Aegean Sea, as if Poseidon still slumbered within and released a bit of divinity into everyone taking a dip in his sacred waters. The Aegean sun, too, possessed the supernatural: no matter how long we basked in it, we didn't get burnt.

After some sun and a light lunch, Bianca and I rented a motor scooter to explore the island on our own.

"I've never had a passenger on a scooter before," I said honestly. I didn't feel the need to share that I had never been a driver for one, either.

"No problem," Bianca said, slipping in behind me. "My ex had a motorcycle in Belgium. We rode together all the time."

"Great," I said, revving the motor to hide my sarcasm. Being a scooter, of course, meant it was merely a high-pitched whine.

Because only one road led to the far side of the island, getting lost was out of the question. I almost ran off the road a few times, but convincingly blamed the undulating, hair-pin curves of the road. When it snaked through towns I almost hit the walls, which were always whitewashed and brilliant with flourishing bougainvillea. Outside the villages, we cruised through forests of low pines, the terrain quite dry with rugged hills and rocks. Eventually we cruised along the edge of majestic cliffs that dropped into sparkling waters. We sped along, smelled the pine, viewed the beauty, felt free and young and in love.

Indeed, the best part was feeling Bianca's arms around me and her warmth at my back. She leaned into me with total confidence. It was truly the happiest single time in my entire life, that silly little ride across a Greek island.

Until I crashed.

Fortunately, Bianca had already gotten off the back. While she was scouting out an isolated beach, I decided to play off road for a bit. That lasted all of thirty feet. I hit the gas and went straight into a bush. The back brakes, I had already learned, were mostly nonfunctional, so I had to make do with the front brakes. I think in my shock I gunned the motor, too. The scooter dumped me into the bush and flipped over on top of me. It was not my finest moment. I was just glad that Bianca hadn't seen the crash, or how lamely I kicked the scooter off me. I had all the grace of a turtle on its back.

Several minutes later I came puttering back to the beach, bleeding and battered and scraped, including my face. Upon sight of me, Bianca burst out laughing.

We relaxed on the nameless beach for a couple of hours. There was no sand, actually, but an unbroken ribbon of smoothly polished black stones too large to be called pebbles. The lapping of the translucent waters was so gentle, the breeze its brother, and us soaking up the sun made for a magnificent afternoon. We watched the sun set over the mountainous islands across the sea. The drive back, with a busted headlight and wobbling front rim, brought us back to reality.

Dinner was wonderful, with the vines and flowers lit by torches and tables lit by candles. As we dined on grilled lamb, cats brushed by our legs and purred for a bite. Bianca and I shared a table with the two elderly ladies from the tour bus we'd seen at the monestary.

"What happened to your face?" piped up one as she adjusted her shawl. She asked in English. With a New York accent. My jaw nearly hit the floor. She hastily explained, "My sister and I lived in Brooklyn for decades."

"We got out before the Iron Curtain," agreed Sister Two. "And returned after the fall of Ceaușescu."

"Such a shame," murmured the Sister One. Sister Two nodded.

"The Iron Curtain?" I asked, still trying to recover from my surprise.

"No, dear," answered Sister One. "Your face. You used to be so pretty. What did you do?"

"Uh, I crashed on a scooter. To be honest, it does kind of hurt."

"Of course it does, dear," said Sister One. "We've got a cure for that though, haven't we?"

"Yes we do," agreed Sister Two, as she pulled open a large handbag. I suffered a sudden flashback of the peasant woman I sat beside on the plane, nearly three years ago. If this New York Romanian pulled out a large knife, I simply knew I would faint. Instead, she revealed something even more dangerous: a round bottle of țuica.

We four toasted each other. Two of us choked, and not the two I thought it would be. The drink was ghastly powerful and as close to pure alcohol as I'd ever come across. Though only drinking from tiny ceramic mugs that Sister Two also kept in her handbag, the four of us got drunk as apples.

Later that night I woke up in the dark. A cold breeze blew in through the balcony doors, so I pulled the covers closer. I thought I felt something heavy on top of the sheets, but it didn't register through the sleepy, țuica induced haze. The second time I woke up, however, there was no mistaking it. Something heavy was on my legs.

Blearily I looked up. My eyes had trouble adjusting to the dark. Finally I realized that there was a very large, very content cat sleeping on the bed with us. In fact, there were two. Another chubby stray snuggled atop the sheets between Bianca and I.

I slipped out of bed quietly, not wanting to wake Bianca. I gave the first cat a reassuring pet, then picked him up and carried him to the balcony. He did not quietly relinquish his comfort, however, and dug his claws into the sheets. As I pulled him up, he brought the sheets with him!

"Auo!" Bianca cried as the bedding was yanked right off the bed. The other cat slumped onto the floor with an irate meow, then struggled to extricate himself from the tangle of bedspread and blankets.

We finally collared the two vagabonds and dropped them onto the balcony. They glared at us, but then got busy disdainfully bathing the spots where I had deigned to touch them. I closed the balcony door, then helped Bianca remake the bed. We laughed as we snapped the sheets into place and slipped back in.

"You know that's why I insist on a real bed," Bianca chuckled.

"Room for passing strangers?"

"You know how I can't sleep without touching you at least somewhere when we're together," Bianca admitted. "I noticed you were unusually snuggly. I should have known!"

The mood was jovial, but the night called for something more.

"It's time to talk, Bianca," I said.

Her chuckling stopped. The darkness got a bit darker.

"Is it possible," I asked gently, "that we've overcome all these cultural differences only to get caught up in your machismo?"

"What do you mean?" she asked, confused.

"You're macho."

"How can I be macho? I'm a woman!"

"Macho men," I explained, "when things get too close—meaning they can no longer control the situation—will walk away from the whole affair. That's exactly what you're doing. And that's not all. Macho guys will simply ignore something they can't deal with, like you and Piti's cheating."

"What the hell are you talking about?" Bianca asked, rearing back.

"You couldn't control Piti's actions, so you intentionally overlooked his selfishness. You said it's OK because he is a provider. It's OK because he comes back. You are empowering him to continue because you are taking responsibility for his actions. Male-dominated societies require acceptance from *both* sides. Hey, it's not my culture so I won't judge him. I will judge you, though, because you've moved beyond your own culture. You're smart and independent and modern about so many things, yet still stuck in the old days with this one. Then I came along, we fell in love, and suddenly you start acting all macho with me."

"You saying that I'm cheating on you, is that it?" Bianca said, revolted.

"No, I don't think so," I said. "That's not your style. You're a flirt, like me; nothing more. I love that, in fact. But we got too close. You realized you couldn't control the situation any longer. Time to drop it and move on."

"Got it all figured out, eh?" Bianca replied bitterly. "So I am the macho one, yet I am also the weak one empowering my father to cheat. You in there anywhere?"

"Why else would you push that 'don't ask, don't tell' policy so hard? That's just a way to avoid dealing with reality you can't control. I think Piti's cheating hurts you very much, and you're trying to keep potential disappointment with me at arm's length. Is that what happened with Catalin? He cheat, too?"

"Catalin worshipped me," Bianca retorted with a bitter laugh. "You think you're so smart, but you've got it all wrong. You're not even close."

"All right," I said. "So tell me."

"What's the point?" Bianca said, staring ahead. "When you'll never understand."

"It won't matter if I understand or not," I whispered. "When I leave you and ships behind forever. This is it, Bianca."

We looked at each other, just vague shapes in the dark. In the distance, a cat meowed.

"Catalin was not my husband, as you thought my father said," Bianca began slowly. "But he was... somebody's..."

She took a deep breath.

"My... cousin's... husband," Bianca finally said.

Her admission was to the dark, not me.

"You slept with your cousin's husband?" I said, overcome by shock. I was stunned to hear her admit to an affair with a married man. It seemed completely unlike her, based on a thousand intimate little things that I had learned over the years. When it came to intimacy, Bianca was as conventional as they come. No wonder she took such great pains to hide her past.

"He said he loved me," Bianca said simply. "And I knew he did. It was obvious. But in communist days he couldn't divorce his wife. That's why we went to Belgium. We fled. We shamed the whole family. My parents were the laughing stock of the town. When I finally left Catalin, broke and broken and humiliated, they took me back. But they had to forgive me the humiliation I put them through; they're my parents. And

Romania is our home; they can't leave, any more than I can. But you...?"

I said nothing.

"There it is," Bianca said with a sense of finality. "Now that you know, you'll never want me."


## 3


The next morning we rose before dawn for a day trip to Delphi. Quiet seemed appropriate for the ferry across the placid morning sea. The bus roared up a steep, curving road into the mountains just as the pink tinge in the east began to send tendrils of color into the dark sky. Up, up, up we coursed into the dry peaks. The grey rock was covered in green from proliferate scrub, copses of spearing cypress, and thriving juniper. As the bus entered the tumult of the mountains of lower, central Greece, a last look at the sea was past a gargantuan olive grove two millennia old.

On to Mount Parnassus.

The road snaked through a fascinating village slumped atop the brow of a mountain, houses dripping down the steep flanks. The pink tile roofs of Arachova were particularly rosy in the early morning. The main road had been in use for three thousand years, and had obviously not anticipated 30,000 pound tourist buses. Every curve of the corkscrewing street brought us within literal inches of centuries-old—if not millennia-old—houses.

I didn't notice any of it. I was still in shock. I simply could not imagine Bianca having an affair with a married man and intentionally alienating her parents. That was obviously a different woman, a woman of her past she was ashamed of. The Bianca I knew had been forged of that experience and its awful fallout: a woman of fierce determination to remain in control at all costs. She enjoyed play-acting the wild woman and readily hopped from dance to dance, but that didn't translate to hopping from bed to bed. She was too conservative for that. True or false, right or wrong, she had believed that Catalin loved her.

Yet for the first time in our relationship, I was shaken. If Bianca had ever been capable of abandoning—nay, humiliating —her beloved family, then she was capable of playing me for all these years. From outside our relationship, it surely seemed obvious that was what was happening. But only we two knew the truth of each other, and we didn't care what it looked like from outside. Of course, Bianca had surely felt that way with Catalin, too.

Had I really been fighting the good fight, or was it time to run for the hills?

Arriving at the complex of ruins snapped my stupor. Who hadn't heard of the famed Oracle of Delphi? Here kings and conquerors were given a glimpse of the divine will, an ambiguous and powerful portend of the future. At a glance, the ruins appeared to be tumbling down the mountainside, so steep it was, but in fact were tethered by 2,800 year-old foundations. Though trees rose from some temple ruins, many pillars of milky white yet rose to the blue sky. A huge half-moon theater of thirty-five rows still inspired awe. From the top row, the view dropped down the angled tiers of seats, past the stage, past the foundations of ancient temples, to plummet into the fertile valley below. That same angle was unbroken for a thousand feet!

Bianca and I wandered separately through the grounds of the complex. She claimed to be fascinated by the beehive-shaped stone the ancient Greeks believed was the center of the world, whereas I imperiously went further up the mountain to where an athletic stadium had been cut into the living rock. In reality we just didn't know what to say to each other.

No one living knew for certain where the oracle herself had actually performed her duties. She had been positioned in a temple above a fissure, from which hallucinogenic fumes had risen. Thusly intoxicated, the oracle would spout gibberish to be 'translated' by the priests into a prophecy for the paying guest. Alas, over twenty-eight centuries things change, including fault lines.

As I explored, I eventually found myself before the Temple of Apollo, where something happened. I stepped off the Via Sacra—the route that all fortune-seekers were required to walk—to the ruined temple. It was here that fortune seekers gave gifts to the priests and sacrifices to Apollo. Only foundations remained, extending deep along the flank of the mountain. A handful of columns signaled the far end. Stepping onto the entrance stone, I stopped.

There is a disconnect when viewing ruins. What you see is not what once was, and it's up to you to bridge the gap of time. Imagination is required—especially when you know that the people who made all this thought that rock over there was literally the belly button of the earth!

But something here was different.

I dropped down to my knees and traced a finger along the smooth marble. This stone had been the threshold of the main temple since the beginning. Each and every man who sought the famed Oracle of Delphi had been required to step on this very spot. Not just irrelevant kings of the ancient world—the stuff of boring history lessons even in their own far-off lands— but also a man whose name is yet a household word today, all over the world. Alexander the Great, arguably the greatest single conqueror in the history of mankind, had stood right where I was standing now, on this little stone. It was a fact. Time no longer mattered, imagination was no longer required.

And everything became clear to me.

# 4

After a quiet dinner back on Angistri, Bianca and I left the torch-lit terrace and strolled along the beach. Eventually we found a spot quieter than the rest, and rested. The sun had long since set, but the rocks beneath us were still warm. Orange lights from torch-lit cafés behind us cast across the beach to tickle the restless waters.

"I learned something today," I said quietly. "I want to make sure you do, too."

Bianca watched the orange-lit edge of the waves lap over the stones.

"Do you know why people went to Delphi?" I asked. "To get a measure of control over their lives. They figured if they toiled hard enough to get there, they deserved it. They figured if they paid enough of a sacrifice, they deserved it. They believed the gods had ultimate power over their fate, but they would do anything to get a measure of control over their lives.

"You and I both know that was all crap," I added brusquely. "The priests made a killing off selling overpriced sacrificial lambs and expensive trinkets to give to Apollo. The oracle herself was simply high on volcanic fumes and spouting gibberish, and the priests 'translated' it into something you wanted to hear. Usually it was ambiguous enough to always seem right. You left with the illusion of control.

"You, Bianca, are using the ships to pay the heavy price of sacrifice to get that feeling of control. With ship money, you bought a house for your parents. You're atoning for having hurt them in the past. But love isn't about control and you can't buy it. Your parents love you and just want you to be happy, to live your own life. You've done enough for them. If they can communicate that to me, it's amazing they can't get it through to you.

"I haven't given you enough credit. I thought that because you couldn't control Piti's actions, you found other ways of dealing with it, like focusing so hard on 'coming back'. Just like I thought that because you couldn't control my reaction to your past, you hid it and found other ways to deal with it. But you do know that love is acceptance. You and your mother accept that Piti cheats because you both love him.

"I love you, regardless of your past. I may not ever truly understand, but I want you for who you are. I accept who you were. This guilt of yours is from another life. You've reformed, yes, you've atoned, definitely, but you still haven't learned. You're still running scared, scared that you'll lose control and end up selling dubbed tapes in the cold. You've been running a long time. You're running so fast that you're running right through your life."

I toed a rock, flipping it into the water.

"You're running right past me."

Bianca was silent.

"Today I stood in the footsteps of Alexander the Great," I said to the sea. "He inherited all of Greece from his father, the first time it had ever been united. But he dared to demand more from life. He fought for it, and created the largest empire the world had ever known. He looked at the big picture. Until now, I haven't been able to see the big picture. I've refused to see that you are unable to commit."

I took Bianca's hand and said, "We've both made our mistakes, and yet here we are, together again. From here we must move forward together. I want to give you a level of commitment you couldn't get before. No more games. Be with me on the ships, or in America. I want you to marry me."

Bianca continued her silence and stared at the sea. Finally she turned to me and said, "Da."

"Da?" I said, surprised.

"Da," she repeated.

"You mean that's it?" I said, seeking clarification. "I always imagined that she would say 'yes' when I proposed, I guess. Not that I ever really sat around and thought about it."

"As a girl I *did* imagine being asked," Bianca quipped. "And I would always say 'da'."

Bianca and I shared a smile on the dark beach.

"Now to the important stuff," I eventually said. "Let's see if those sisters have any țuica left!"

# 5

That night, Bianca slept so tight to me I could feel her heartbeat. She was stiflingly hot, actually, but that was all right. The blind love I had for Bianca had been exposed to illumination. Across the years and the seas, I had learned much about love, much about Bianca, but most of all about myself.

"There is nothing more enticing, disenchanting, and enslaving than the life at sea," Joseph Conrad had once written.

I reflected on his brilliant, dark novel *Heart of Darkness*. At first I had thought it was a story about adventure. The main character sailed far, after all, to exotic lands. Far from civilization, he witnessed the extreme behavior of men in extreme situations and the cruelty of men unburdened by scrutiny. Conrad was revealing the heart of mankind. But now I could reflect on my own years at sea. I, too, had witnessed the depravity of man. I, too, had tapped the source of the novel's intense loneliness. It was not the absence of companionship or its great physical distance, but the absence of understanding. Rare indeed is the landlubber who fathoms what changes a man of the sea.

What are our responsibilities to each other, and how far must we go to fulfill them? At sea, such things are thrown into particular light. Sometimes it revolves around duty, other times around empathy.

In my journey to be with Bianca, I had gone through a bizarre series of triumphs and setbacks, literal starvation and wanton gluttony, temptation, denial, and other. Through it all, I had learned I could remain true to myself and to my beliefs. Further, I refused to lose my happy-go-lucky self. But I knew if I ever did lose it, I would find it right here with Bianca.

# About Brian David Bruns

Brian David Bruns has adventured in over 60 countries to gather material for his bestselling books and won dozens of literary awards, including the USA REBA Grand Prize. He has been featured on ABC's *20/20* and was anointed Sir Brian by Prince Michael, Regent of the Principality of Sealand (yes, really).

Sir Brian writes of his global experiences with a self-mocking wit and an astute insight into human behavior. His historical fiction seamlessly blends his love of travel and adventure with the fantastical—a sort of Indiana Jones meets Bram Stoker.

After several years living in Dracula's actual hometown (yes, really), he and his Romanian wife now live in Las Vegas with their two old rescue cats, Julius and Caesar.

# Select Books by Sir Brian

*The Gothic Shift*
*In the House of Leviathan*
*The Widow of Half Hill*
*A Cat Herder Goes West*

**Cruise Confidential series:**
*Cruise Confidential*
*Ship for Brains*
*Unsinkable Mister Brown*
*High Seas Drifter*

*Rumble Yell*

**Gone with the Waves trilogy:**
*From Romania with Love*
*Wet Orpheus*
*Gone with the Waves*

For a complete list of titles and audiobooks visit
BrianDavidBruns.com

# Bonus!

The fourth and final book of the series, *High Seas Drifter*, reveals life on one of the most unique cruise ships afloat and what—rather, who—scuttled my career at sea.

*Wind Surf* is the largest sailing ship in the world, yet small enough to visit some of the most ancient ports in existence. Her ideal size, coupled with her expensive itinerary, provides an excellent opportunity to reveal an elite cruising experience beyond the means of most of us.

My time on *Wind Surf* was the pinnacle of my four years at sea. And the end of them. It wasn't the betrayal that bothered me so much, but the lawsuits.

Read the first two chapters here. I hope you enjoy the ride!

—Sir Brian

BOOK 4 of the BESTSELLING
*CRUISE CONFIDENTIAL* SERIES

# HIGH
# SEAS
# DRIFTER

"THIS MAN HAS SEEN IT ALL!"
—ABC 20/20

# BRIAN DAVID BRUNS

# Santorini, Greece

THE HEADLINE WOULD READ "DEATH BY ASS." The newsprint already blazed across my imagination: text bold, black, and all caps. I would have preferred less brevity and more dash. Maybe "Local Man Succumbs to Killer Foreign Ass." Astonishingly, Mom saw this one coming. She always warned me I would die some horrible, unforeseen death if I dared leave my native Iowa. Or the house. I thought she was just being overprotective, yet here I was, thirty years and six thousand miles away, proving her right.

Twenty minutes ago things were going fine. Romantic, even. Not the good kind of romance—another item on Mom's list of Dangerous Don'ts—but the kind of romance that only the sea can invoke, a sea plied by ships of tall sails and peopled with men of courage, curiosity, lust for life. I had once counted myself among their number.

Nine hundred feet below, cool mist lazed atop the gently lapping waters of the Aegean, pulsing to the sea's mysterious, ancient rhythm. Between us and hazy, smoking Fire Island lolled a small yacht, sails furled, barely seen but for a mast piercing the shroud. The mist did not blanket so much as bunch at the cliff's base, perhaps afraid to near that rumbling heap of ash and molten rock rising from the center of the sunken caldera. And fear it should. Such were the still restless remains of a destroyer: the very volcano that in one angry outcry slaughtered the entire Minoan civilization—even as it gave birth to the legend of Atlantis.

Had Poseidon himself been looking from that steaming rock, across his cerulean home and up above the cowering mist, past the satisfying contrast of chestnut brown cliffs, he would have delighted at the shock of whitewashed cottages and sky blue doors. The tiny geometries of man spread liberally atop the brown: thick and wavy like frosting smeared carelessly atop a cupcake, clumps bunching high in some areas, in others threatening to tumble over the steep sides in a sticky white avalanche. Spread, as it were, by the hand of the gods born of this land millennia ago. Long ago the gods destroyed the men living here, even as long ago men destroyed the gods. Man himself was responsible now for the wonder of Santorini.

"And a fine job he has done," my tall companion agreed.

I hadn't meant to speak such wonders of time aloud, being loathe to sound like a poet and stuff. He adjusted his eyeglasses and smiled in his slight, Dutch manner. "The gods were capricious, were they not? But man muddles through and, sometimes, wonders happen."

"Man muddles all right," I agreed, rather petulantly. I had been petulant a lot lately. Ardin lowered his sizable camera to better regard me. Considering what I knew of him, this was a large expression.

"You don't sound very American," he observed.

I dismissed any implied question with a chuckle and said, "I'm just getting a little tired of muddling."

"Aren't we all," Ardin agreed, hefting his camera once more.

He leaned his tall, lanky frame forward, into the wind. After a few crisp clicks, Ardin used the telephoto lens to illustrate the magnitude of the panorama before us: a broken ring of thousand-foot rock rising from a vastness of sea and sky, the point of merging blues indeterminate. "Look at that down there. If you can't appreciate that, you can't appreciate anything."

"I'll appreciate getting down there without dying," I commented drily, clutching tightly to the horn of my saddle. Beneath me, my mount shifted. This nameless beast, who was to be my ride down the nearly vertical cliffs of Santorini, puffed and fussed as much as nearby Fire Island. This was my first mule ride, and I was both surprised and intimidated by the power this humble animal exuded. I felt no safer than had I been straddling the raw power of the volcano. I hoped my beast of burden was not as capricious as the gods.

"If you can drive on American highways," Ardin quipped in his direct, Dutch manner, "surely you can handle a one mulepower vehicle."

My reply was a snort and a smart remark. "Don't you mean one asspower? It's okay. I'm used to flying by the seat of my pants."

"I can't drive!" trilled a voice behind us. "Can we walk?"

I turned in my creaking saddle to view our third companion. A delicate young Asian man clung to his saddle fearfully, skinny knees shifting along the beast's flanks in search of better purchase. With bone-white knuckles gripping the saddle horn, he had difficulty keeping his hair out of his eyes. He shook his head feverishly to keep too-long bangs clear.

"Time to learn," Ardin stated blandly.

That was the umpteenth time Ardin had said such that day, and I noted the rigid Dutchman had not even bothered to turn and look at our fretting companion. Though his posture indicated otherwise, I sensed Ardin sighing and drooping somewhat whenever our charge spoke. Waryo, an Indonesian assigned to replace Ardin as ship's photographer, acted precisely like the large eyed village boy far from home that he was. But his whimpering became simpering sometimes, leaving us to wonder whether he was merely naive or being coy. If the latter, he exhibited it in a most unusual manner.

"If you can't handle your saddle, Yoyo," Ardin continued, still not looking at the Indonesian, "Be reassured by the presence of an actual American cowboy."

Yoyo looked to me longingly for guidance and comfort. I snorted louder than my mule.

When the three of us had departed our ship to enjoy the port of Santorini, we had left the marina via funicular. Ascending to the city so far above was a matter of minutes by mechanical means. But going back we opted for something more... romantic. Despite my recent drop into apathy, I still found the desire to do what the locals had done since antiquity: making the nine-hundred foot traverse on muleback. I would have felt guilty letting the animals labor through the ascent— courtesy of my Catholic upbringing which imbued a sense of guilt over everything—and had therefore suggested we only ride the animals down. Yoyo agreed, if only in order to postpone an action he feared. Ardin, descendent of more practical stock, just shrugged at our foibles.

Dug into the overhanging edge of the cliffs was a corral. It smelled of animals steaming in the late June heat. We had descended an ancient stone ramp and into the striped shade under a roof of unpainted wooden slats. The shadows were not particularly deep, but the outside sunshine was bright enough that our eyes adjusted slowly. We approached several dozen quiet mules, most napping on their feet, a few watching us with large, brown eyes. The flicking of long ears and longer tails was the only movement in this lazy, warm place, barring the occasional snort or shaking head. After a while we found their keeper hidden among them, also mule napping.

The bored Greek came alive when he spied our approach. He rushed over, scraping a sweaty hand through thinning, wind-blown hair, and gleefully took our money. Then he promptly returned to sleeping on his feet.

"No instructions in the seat-back in front of us," I groused. "I have to endure being taught how to use a seatbelt every damn flight of my life, but when first dealing with live transportation, I'm on my own."

We waded into the mass of shifting animals, each man seeking his preferred mount. All were dressed in the same worn saddles atop fraying blankets. Yoyo held his arms in so close as to hug himself, terrified of touching a flank. Selecting our animals at random, we struggled into the saddles. This was a new maneuver for me, but my decent height aided the ascent. Ardin, taller than me at nearly six foot four, had no difficulties whatsoever. Alas, Yoyo was a comical tangle of extremities flashing over the wide barrel of his mount's body.

"In the deserts and ghost towns of Nevada I've seen lots of wild burros," I observed. "And they look just like this. So are these burros or mules? I always pictured donkeys thinner, for some reason. And what the hell is an ass?"

Yoyo exploded into hysterical giggles. Ardin and I both creaked in our saddles to give him dubious looks. Yoyo clammed up. No doubt his nerves were making him giddy. I just hoped he didn't pass out!

To our right rose a wall some twenty feet high, capped by buildings no doubt boasting a whitewashed balcony like every other building on Santorini. Before us dropped the only path, snaking downward at an alarming angle before curving out of sight. It was so steep, in fact, that the road was actually a series of steps. To our left, separated by only a three-foot stone wall, the land sheered away.

"No reins," Ardin noted.

Ardin looked ludicrous atop his mule. In his practical, worn travel clothes and hat he would have cut an impressive figure— almost Indiana Jones-esque—had he been on horseback. Instead, his feet extended far below the useless stirrups and his long, lanky form swayed above the bulk of animal like a lone reed buckled by the wind. Had he a lance, Ardin could have been Don Quixote; a whimpering, Asian Sancho Panza trailing uselessly behind.

"How we start these?" Yoyo asked. His English was not accented so much as broken. He was hesitant to use it and frequently omitted words, but when he did speak his delicate voice rang crystal clear and with excellent pronunciation. Ardin, on the other hand, spoke the superb English of a Dutchman. Next to him, even my native tongue sounded lethargic.

Ardin slapped his mule firmly on the rump and the entire herd began to shift in an organic, pulsing wave. The mass of animal flesh elongated until eventually one third of the nearly three dozen mules broke free of the corral and began descending. Those joining us without riders looked bored, perhaps wanted some exercise, or possibly a change of view. There were only two places in the lives of these animals: top or bottom, with one road between. Two shaggy, happy dogs also joined our procession. The clops of hoof upon stone were softly muffled. It was surprising to see such a large mass moving so quietly.

The quiet did not last long.

What I had assumed would be a leisurely ride was anything but. The nervous anticipation of climbing atop the mules in the corral was not unlike climbing into the car of a roller coaster, the slow start like rising to the first drop. The descent was sheer terror—and without the assurance of a safety harness. After the first bend the ribbon of wriggling road dropped so steeply, so quickly, I seriously thought we were leaping into the blue abyss. My stomach flipped as the herd recklessly plunged with the curves, seemingly out of control but moving ever downward, ever faster. Yet the 'joy ride' was just beginning.

Yoyo's shriek shattered the quiet. The effect was nothing less than the shot starting a race. The dogs began gamely yipping and nipping at the heels of the mules, which began shoving each other with great heaves of bulk. The chaotic mass plunged along the cliffside at a frantic pace. I had never felt so helpless in all my life. I gripped the saddle horn as my mule rammed his way through the crowd directly towards the cliff edge. I felt like I was driving on sheet ice down a steep hill into traffic: no brakes, no steering wheel. The protective wall barely came to my knees while standing, let alone on muleback. The collision felt nothing short of leaping over. I may have succumbed to an unmanly squeal.

My mule remained at the outside of the road for a while, and there I cruised, uncontrolled, just above the wall. I was given a respite as the majority of animals moved inward, to the cliffside, slamming Ardin and Waryo against the wall. The two men were ground against the rough stone, pressed by the sheer tonnage of mule flesh. Ardin prudently kept his elbows in and quietly endured the mauling of his knees, whereas Yoyo squealed bloody murder and flailed everything flailable. Their mules tried unsuccessfully to push away from the cliff, but seemed unable to do so against the might of the others. After several heart—and extremity—rending moments, the beasts flattened their ears, girded their loins, and surged away from the cliff wall. The herd thundered outward, towards the cliff's edge.

Towards me.

My mount took the crush bodily, ears flattened back and head down. His bulk and momentum were forward. Mine were not. I was nearly jettisoned from the saddle when the impact ripped my hands loose. For one horrific moment I looked straight down, down to the tiny waves breaking upon tiny rocks below—waves and rocks I knew damned good and well were not tiny at all. Both feet remained in the stirrups, just barely, which kept me atop the animal.

I had lived a long time with a swelled sense of adventure. I was a happy-go-lucky guy. But this whole thing was shockingly unsafe. Maybe the Greeks felt selecting the muleback ride over the cheaper funicular was self-censoring, or that people were responsible for their own safety. Maybe they just didn't care about safety because they didn't know anybody who had gone over a cliff. But I did.

My friend Will, a teacher famous for offering new students cans of Spam and using Spam haiku to teach math, had gone over a cliffside trail. He free fell the first thirty feet to land on his head upon solid rock. He then rolled down loose scree and rubble to the bottom of a ravine a hundred feet further. Will's head had broken open, and he lay there for hours with his brain exposed. The final protective layer had not been breached, but his right eye had literally been found on the back of his smashed head. Will's unconscious body was so difficult to extract that even the rescuer lowered from a helicopter broke his own leg in the process.

Will's survival had been a miracle by any standard, let alone his full recovery. Luckily his body had been unscathed, but half a dozen experts had to be flown in to literally reassemble his face. They started with his jaw—the only bone in his head unbroken—and reconstructed from there. They lost count of screws after one hundred. Astonishingly, a few weeks later Will was laughing again. In fact, he was even teasing the doctors about how they 'forgot to use a compass' on his tear duct, which had ballooned because it was reoriented incorrectly and tears didn't release outward. One year later he was back in his math room with his beloved pyramid of Spam on the desk. He had a long, thin scar under his hairline, but no other sign of trauma. He joked that his only worry now was receding hairline.

So Will's story had a happy ending. That mountainside had been nearly two hundred feet. I knew it well: I even used to run along its trail! But this was four times higher. I just hoped that Ardin's mount remained on the inside track. Without stirrups I truly feared for his life.

Several hundred vertical feet were traversed in this white-knuckle, gasp-inducing manner. Then suddenly all motion ceased. The herd came to a gentle halt halfway down the cliff. We panted and glanced about, stunned. The excitement was over. The mules, for their part, seemed completely at ease. Heat rose from their bulk. Flies descended. All was calm. Our thumping hearts and sweaty palms were the only evidence of recent chaos.

Ardin gave his mule a decisive spank, but this time it reacted in much the same way as my ex-wife: looking back at him with an expression that plainly said, 'you wish.'

"What now?" I asked, peering tentatively over the edge of the cliff.

"We wait," Ardin replied, gently probing his camera bag for indications of broken equipment within.

"We walk now?" Yoyo whimpered.

"You want to be on the road when the herd decides to resume its descent?" Ardin asked tersely, scrutinizing his lenses.

Yoyo's whining promptly quieted to a low mewl. Until a few moments later, that is, when he suddenly cried out in horror, "I broke a nail!"

"Good," Ardin replied tartly. "Now cut the other one."

I was left to ponder that odd rebuke when Ardin suddenly pointed his telephoto lens downward and began snapping photos. I followed his sight and noted the distinctive masts of our cruise ship, hundreds of feet below: our ship, our home, the *Wind Surf.*

The *Wind Surf* was an unusual cruise ship, to say the least. She was tiny, compared to the mega-liners that plied the world's seas, but also unique. She was an actual sailing vessel. Or, rather, a hybrid. Unlike the windjammer cruises, wherein guests pay for the privilege of handling the sails, the *Surf* was a luxury vessel with hydraulic, computer-driven sails unfurling at the touch of a button. She was designed to reach higher speed under sail than under motor propulsion. And was she ever a sight to behold.

"A ship at sea in God's way," Ardin murmured.

"Getting religious now that our lives are on the line?" I remarked rather insensitively.

Ardin answered with a kind expression. "My grandfather used to say, 'Under sail we went to sea God's way, the way God made the oceans and the winds; we were a part of it. Modern motor vessels fight the sea and the wind.'"

"Your grandfather was a sailor, then?" I asked, impressed. "Old school, with sails and all? My father spent four years in the U.S. Navy but was stationed in the middle of the desert in New Mexico, if you can believe that. He only went to sea one day. Of course, he still got a sailor's tattoo."

"Of course," Ardin repeated with a slight grin. "Both my father and grandfather loved being sailors. They loved being a living part of our heritage as the world's great seafarers. My grandfather started on sailing vessels when he was fourteen years old. Some were still hauling cargo as late as the war, but were phased out because they couldn't outrun U-boats."

"Incredible," I said. "I thought the age of sail was gone way, way back."

"Mostly," Ardin agreed. "My grandfather would tell me stories about it. Usually he was even more pragmatic than my father, rarely finding the beauty in anything. But not when it came to life under sail. He would get poetic about how they lived balanced between air and water, one with the elements. Their schedules were as unpredictable as the weather. In good wind they would sometimes sail around the clock, even up to a week. Everyone worked four hour shifts, one off and one on, for twenty four hours a day. Other times it would lay up in a calm for days on end, with nothing to do but wait. Not very practical in a modern business world. But then, there are always seafaring entrepreneurs in Holland. My father was in shipping, too, and wanted me to follow, but I'm artistically inclined. Serving as photographer on the world's largest sailing vessel seemed like a good medium."

"The *Wind Surf* is the world's largest sailing vessel?" I asked, surprised. Having only met Ardin the day before, I sure was learning a lot from him. A pragmatic artist was someone I wanted to get to know.

"She and her sister *Club Med 2*," Ardin said. "They displace 15,000 tons. Some of the replicas of big ships look a lot bigger with all their sails aloft, but they are in fact far lower and lighter. Most are less than half the weight, which is actually all that counts."

"Still the biggest ship I saw," Yoyo breathed.

"For being 10,000 kilometers from home," Ardin said drily, "You haven't been around much."

"How about you, Yoyo? Any sailors in your family?"

"No," he answered simply. He did not elaborate.

"I will miss the romance of being under sail," Ardin continued. "I was happy on *Wind Surf*, but will be happier at home with my wife in Vietnam."

"Your wife is Vietnamese?" I asked, surprised. Ardin's great height must tower over an Asian body! But I understood the burning, consuming desire for something different. It burns hot. It burns out. But I focused on the positive by saying, "That's my favorite thing about working at sea. It breaks down boundaries completely."

"My future wife is foreign," Yoyo popped up.

"Future wife?" I repeated, somewhat dubiously. "That's the phrase I use regarding Angelina Jolie."

Yoyo glanced up and down the steep road, but all was quiet. No stampede seemed eminent, so he awkwardly fished from his pocket a folded, dogeared photo. He reached out across the shifting mules to show me.

"She's gorgeous!" I complimented upon sight of the young vixen. She was a petite Asian with a round face and dark, beautiful eyes.

"She lives in China," Yoyo said, replacing the photo. "We met online."

Ardin tried unsuccessfully to hide a harrumph. Fortunately Yoyo was too preoccupied with saddle maneuvers to hear him.

"And you, Brian?" Yoyo eventually asked.

"The whole reason I'm at sea was to be with a woman," I replied from habit. While true, there seemed to be a whole lot more to the story now, a whole lot more I didn't want to talk about. I glanced down at the *Wind Surf*, reflecting on how so very, very tiny it looked. It looked equally tiny even close up. "We were here in Greece together just a week ago. I proposed to her here, in a manner of speaking. She even said yes."

"So she'll be joining you soon, then!" Yoyo exclaimed.

"Ships are no place for couples," I said rather sharply. More softly I explained, "She's vacationing with her parents in Romania."

"Romania?" Ardin repeated with evident surprise. It was perhaps the most emotion I had seen since meeting him.

"Yes," I said. "Transylvania. Beautiful country."

He paused before responding, then politely said, "I'm sure."

I chuckled at his obvious effort at restraint. He looked slightly relieved and added, "There's a Romanian woman on *Surf* you'll meet soon. She's... something else."

"A more qualified statement has rarely been uttered," I said.

Ardin's face blanched a bit, no doubt recalling an unpleasant memory, before returning to his usual neutrality. "She hates me, so do yourself a favor and don't mention my name."

"Oh? Why is that?"

"I won't give her what she wants," Ardin said simply. His lips quivered into a hint of a smile and he added, "Ask her if she's found her socks yet."

I was about to inquire further, but was distracted by a visitor from above. A shaggy, brown dog of monstrous proportions came running pell-mell down the road, barking furiously. Even before he met up with our herd, the mules decided this was the catalyst for resuming the descent. Onward and downward we spiraled to the *Wind Surf.*

## 2

The small tender boat muscled through the waves with noisy purpose. I was pressed against the scratched window because both Ardin and Waryo shared the two-seat bench with me. Such was the lot of crew: we were given the tiny bits of space the passengers didn't want. I stared at the crystalline waters, wondering why their soothing blueness did not soothe. The mist had burned off, letting the sun stab as deep as it cared to. My gaze followed the shimmering spears of light down, down into the darkness. It was very conducive to reflection.

I tried to be as enthusiastic about the *Surf* as Ardin. I really did. But where he saw a glorious handful of tall masts I saw a measly handful of passenger decks. That's it. Not thirteen decks, each spanning a whopping 120 feet in width, but just six, measuring a mere 66. Ardin was an artist, so money did not concern him much. I was an art dealer, so money concerned me greatly. In my business, bodies equaled money, and *Surf* didn't carry many. To date I had been modestly successful at my job working on ships. Within a couple months of starting I had been given a ship with 3,000 passengers. Now I got 300.

What was I doing here?

The answer, of course, was that my priority had never been my career and it finally caught up with me. I had come to sea three years ago for one reason: to be with my girlfriend. Ships were her game, so they became mine. She was that magnetic. Bianca was a vivacious and vigorous woman the sun itself set for, seemingly humbled by her excitement at returning to her element of choice, the night. At night she could dance and drink freely, well into the small hours, until exhaustion overcame her. Only then did the sun dare venture back over the world. Bianca's proximity had always been how I gauged my success. Needless to say, my employers had different criteria. I had pushed things too far, too long. Fate finally pushed back, and nobody can out-muscle life.

Suddenly the entrancing light was cut off. I looked up as the shadow of *Wind Surf* overcame all.

I'd already slaved below decks as a lowly waiter and enjoyed the high life as a three stripe officer, honorary as the rank may have been. What new could *Wind Surf* teach? Turns out, quite a bit. Crewing the world's largest sailing vessel was a completely new experience. Because she was so small compared to the mega cruise ships—over a thousand officers and crew on those—interaction here with officers was far more often and far more intimate—as were the difficulties among the crew. For the first time my job and personal goals were trumped by my surroundings.

*Wind Surf* was not merely a floating resort staffed by cheap labor for mass consumption, oh no. She was akin to the fabled sailing life of old. And thusly, perhaps inevitably, she defined my entire outlook as a sailor. I, too, became of the sea.

It didn't start that way, of course. My big ship experiences had to be expunged, a process both painfully fast and thoroughly disheartening. But once freed of stresses regarding my career or my relationship—both obviously now over—once I became of the sea, like the *Surf* herself, I soared on the wind. I learned new things every single day, about the ship, about the world, about myself. Life was as good as I could possibly imagine it, my highest of highs.

Yet *Wind Surf* would be my last ship. Our parting was not a good one. It wasn't just the lawsuit that haunted me after leaving, though that ran into five figures. What made my end at sea so heart wrenching was the humiliation, the indignation. The betrayal. The sea lives up to her notoriety as a harsh mistress. I am ever invigorated by her. I am forever haunted by her.

*Continue reading, I say!*
*High Seas Drifter is available everywhere eBooks are sold.*

# Portoferriao, Elba

DIRECTLY BEHIND *WIND SURF'S* small reception desk in the stern, port side, lay the Photo Gallery. Such galleries on big ships leaned towards large affairs with numerous spotlights, but little *Surf's* was only a glorified corridor accessing the aft pool. The entire back wall and door were glass. The early morning sunlight shot through horizontally like a floodlight, turning displayed photographs into checkered, blinding panels of glossy squares.

"You're late," Ardin admonished, not even bothering to raise his gaze from a glass display counter of photo albums.

"Good morning to you, too," I replied, amused.

Ardin's head snapped up, eyeglasses catching the sun with a flash. I had to look away from the brilliance. The Mediterranean sun was amazingly direct—very different from the ambling, moisture-laden light of the Caribbean I knew so well.

"My apologies," he said. "I thought you were Yoyo. I didn't expect anyone else here this early."

"Haven't seen him," I muttered before launching into complaint. "Is it always this hot in here?"

"*Now* you sound American," Ardin deadpanned. I was in no mood for it, and said as much.

"It was not a rebuke," he defended lightly, "Rather an observation. Americans place a premium on comfort, even at any given moment. By this afternoon it will feel like I'm in Vietnam a week early."

His nod indicated the back wall, where scratches and whorls blazed with snagged light. The door leading to the pool deck was merely an uninsulated panel of glass. Worse, it was warped to prevent fully closing. Humidity wafted in almost visibly. Should the need for battening down the hatches arrive, the photos had much to fear.

Ardin shook his head ruefully and added, "I wonder if I should stay on *Surf*, though. I don't know how my little brother is going to survive."

"I thought your wife was Vietnamese," I said, frowning. "Isn't Yoyo from Java?"

Ardin smiled, apparently enjoying a fleeting thought of his beloved. "She is. I was not implying Yoyo is related to her. God no. But we're all family here."

"Here," I repeated warily. "On the *Surf*, you mean."

"*Wind Surf* is not like other ships," Ardin agreed.

I was beginning to chafe at reminders of how this ship was so different from the norm. Ardin was easily the fourth person I'd heard make such a comment. It made me even more anxious to get back to the big ships, to resume my life. I changed pitch by nudging, "Yo's that bad?"

Ardin grimaced. "He has no concept of selling to his audience. Have you seen his fingernails? Or nail, rather, courtesy of a mule. Most westerners live in a homogenous culture. Yoyo becomes the curiosity. You don't want the guest focusing on the salesman, but rather what he's selling. It is my responsibility to ensure my replacement is up to the task. He is woefully inadequate."

"If he was a good photographer it wouldn't matter, but...," Ardin continued, gesturing to the panel of photographs. "Guess which are his."

A mere glance clearly revealed Ardin's meaning. Ardin's portraits showed guests standing straight, smiling into the camera, the gleam of joy crisp and clear. The latter images were almost entirely out of focus. Yet this was a good thing, for blurry faces maintain anonymity. Far more damning was the guests' lack of forewarning. The result was that Yoyo created an exhaustive—if fuzzy—visual library of embarrassing facial expressions. It was a veritable doctoral thesis on mouths agape, each blur a new and interesting hole in someone's head. One man was even picking his nose.

"You mentioned we would see something worthy this morning?" I asked, presuming it was not that last, hideous photo.

"Ah, yes," Ardin said, stepping from around the counter. A turquoise polo shirt struggled on his tall, spare frame. It was obvious that a ship of *Surf's* size did not have the abundant resources to anticipate a man of Ardin's stature. "We will meet the *Wind Star* this morning."

"And?"

"And that is rare," he explained. "There are only three ships in the fleet."

"And?"

Ardin paused to regard me. With his thick glasses, hands clasped behind his back, and greater height bending down to look over me, he evoked a scolding teacher.

"Because we are not as big as other fleets does not imply we are lesser," Ardin chided gently. "Indeed, I say it promotes value. There are only three small ships plying all seven seas. Meeting up with a sister is cause for celebration."

He then added, most gravely, "Live a little."

Ardin gathered up his camera and bag of lenses, then gestured to the glowing door. He said brusquely, "Yoyo can find us if he wants to learn his job."

I followed him past the pool and up to the top level, the Star Deck. I was still unused to seeing the two sides of the ship so very close together. Three classic Cadillacs, bumper to bumper, were literally the same width. Compare that to *Carnival Ecstasy*, which parked classic cars on the promenade as mere decorations! Until I set foot on a real sailing vessel, with necessarily narrow beam, I hadn't realized just how much modern cruise liners felt like hotels.

"Elba," Ardin said, gesturing to the nearing island of low mountains, abundant flowers, and piles of orange-tiled houses.

"Elba?" I repeated. "As in 'Napoleon's exile' Elba?"

"Yes," he said. "When he escaped here, he went on to ravage the whole of Europe. We will pass directly beneath the smaller of his two palaces here."

The waters narrowed as the island's rugged flanks closed in to form a natural harbor. To our right, past the deep blue, past a slight ribbon of translucent blue-green, then finally past a shifting of sand, rose Elba. Atop a rise and nestled among snarls of vibrant green zig-zagged a centuries-old perimeter of stone. The wall of twenty or more feet hugged the island's edge closely, rising with it to cap a hill at the bay's entrance. From our vantage on deck six, we could just barely see past the wall and into the compound. The garden inside was laid in the forced symmetry the French preferred, enclosed by a cream-colored two-story building and attendant wings. Orange tiles capped all.

"Napoleon's house," Ardin observed. His camera clicked away.

"This is where he was exiled?" I repeated, stunned. "Guess I'm damned with freedom."

Ardin grinned and said, "Royalty live on another plane entirely from us mere mortals. We'll tour his palace later. You'll be fascinated to see his personal furniture and wardrobe. His famous French Marshal's hat is there. You'll see all manner of his things."

"Not his penis, though."

Ardin slowly lowered his camera to look at me. An eyebrow raised.

"It's in New Jersey," I explained helpfully.

Seeing that Ardin was not, in fact, satisfied with my clarification, I continued. "A urologist there has it in his private museum. Saving body parts of great men was in vogue in the 1800's. What, you think I'd make something like that up?"

Ardin's expression was unreadable.

"I mentally file away things like that for moments such as this," I continued into the conversation's sudden vacuum. Then hastily added, "I'm great at parties."

After a further moment of processing, Ardin just shrugged and said, "I can't compete with your connection to Napoleon's penis, but I do have a connection. He gave my family our name."

"What do you mean?"

"When Napoleon occupied the Netherlands, we had no surnames. We all knew who we were—it's a small country—but the invading French couldn't keep track of us. So at his orders they assigned us family names. Before was 'Bob, son of Frank,' and after it became Bob Frankson. That would have been fine, but they also just made things up at random. My family was henceforth known as Prein. Do you know what Prein means? It's the sole of a shoe."

"And people whine about today's politicians," I mused.

"Look," Ardin said, indicating the opposite direction with his camera. "*Wind Star* approaches."

Off the port stern an approaching ship cut cleanly through the water, low and sleek and glistening white. Though she moved towards the harbor mouth under motor power, her magnificence as a sailing ship was undeniable. She had a gentle, curving line that rose in the bow and the stern, that classic deck line of tall ships called the sheer. *Wind Star's* sheer rose up in front with a subtle and compound curve, up and out of the water, to flatten and sharpen into a classic pointed clipper bow. She cut the blue like a swordfish leaping atop the waves, with the unmistakable grace of wind ships of yore.

For *Wind Star*, though built in 1986, was of those romantic tall ships. She was envisioned by a savvy Scandinavian whose family had been tall ship owners since time immemorial in the cold, glacier scarred granite islands of the Baltic, designed from the keel up by the old school shipwrights of the Wärtsila Shipyard in Helsinki, and finally assembled by the craftsmen and polytechniciens of the ACH shipyards in Le Havre on the Normandy coast. She looked nothing like a modern cruise ship, with squared bulk muscling under orders through the water at a criminal twenty-plus feet per gallon of fuel. *Wind Star* danced for the pure joy of it.

Yet *Wind Star* was also a modern ship, the first full-sized sailing vessel built in generations. The French designed computer programs to unfurl her sails and orient her booms so she could react to dangers at sea faster than any crew. And, unimaginable to her predecessors, her computers were designed to operate with a panic threshold of merely eight degrees angle of heel. To yachtsmen, such a heel is utterly insignificant, but modern psychological studies had identified that any angle steeper than eight degrees set off visual alarms in the average passenger's brain that the ship was going over. Thus *Wind Star's* computers never allowed her to go over that heel, even when tacking the wind.

"Did you know that under *Wind Star's* main mast is a U.S. silver dollar from 1889?" Ardin asked. "That's an old shipbuilding tradition. I'm impressed they remembered, considering it was the first tall ship built in two generations."

"How on Earth do you know that?" I asked.

"I'd imagine the same way you knew about Napoleon's penis," Ardin said. Then he mused, "I wonder if *Surf* has one, too."

"No, ships are girls."

Ardin wisely ignored my dick joke.

*Surf* slowed to allow *Star* to pull up along side. Both sisters slipped into the harbor of Portoferriao, side by side and sails full, with nary a dozen feet between. Together they passed the ancient city, dazzling the locals observing from shore. Old men watched silently, sitting heavily on benches, whereas boys squawked like birds atop stone walls clambered upon for a better view. Both ships loosed blasts from their air horns in greeting. The blares bounced off the flanks of Elba in sodden echoes. The unexpected baritones brought even more people out to look. Excitement was in the air.

The closest point of contact between the ships, the wings of both bridges, slid ever closer to each other. Suddenly two lone, white-clad officers stepped out onto the respective wings. Closer, ever closer, then closer still, they came. Had their bridges been on comparable decks the captains could have shaken hands. Alas, *Wind Star's* bridge wing was thirty feet above the waterline and *Wind Surf's* closer to forty. The captain of the *Star* looked up stiffly as his counterpart on *Surf* looked down. As one, they saluted each other. Cameras bristled. Cheers sounded. I yawned.

The captains then disappeared back into their vessels and readied to dock. *Surf*, having arrived first, once again pulled ahead and led the way. As the ships turned, the still-rising sun decided to enter the play. The silhouette of *Surf's* sails projected onto *Star's*, shadow upon white, triangle upon triangle.

Ardin raced off to capture the moment, leaving me to ponder whether or not I was impressed by any of it. No doubt alone of the thousand combined souls on the two ships, I was not. I was mentally and emotionally done with ships—certainly done with this one even before I started.

A renewed flash of officer's whites upon the bridge wing caught my eye. I recognized the strong build of Barney. At least my sense of humor wasn't completely gone: meeting Barney a few days ago still brought a chuckle. It had been the strangest meeting of an officer in my three years at sea.

It had not begun with Barney, however, but rather a bratty youth named Jeff. He was the departing art auctioneer I was sent to replace on über-short notice. It had not been an auspicious beginning. Indeed, it had the distinction of being the shortest handover in my company's history.

I had signed on in Pireaus, the port of Athens. Before both my feet had left the metal gangway at the waterline, Jeff had already cajoled the security guard into handing him my luggage to expedite things. So encumbered, he was not able to accept the handshake I offered. Jeff's sunburned face flushed under the load of my baggage—he was a small man—but he managed to excitedly wheeze, "I'll show you your cabin."

Without a further word he rushed down the corridor, knocking my garment bag upon each and every door along the way. A dozen heads popped into the corridor, looking about in confusion. I felt naughty as a flock of children knocking on neighborhood doors and fleeing. We descended one deck and strode a mere hundred feet before he stopped up short. In one hurried motion he unlocked a door, dropped my bags within, closed the door, and resumed his 'tour' of the ship. Seconds later we were on the main deck beside the ship's small casino. Jeff nodded to a set of metal double doors even as he dropped keys into my palm.

"There," he panted. "Most of the art's in there. Some's in your cabin. Supplies are in a hidden locker by the central stairs. You'll find it. I'm outa here!"

Jeff skipped away. I was so surprised, and he so fast, he crossed half the lounge before I called after him.

"What?" I shouted. "You're leaving? I just got here!"

"Small ship," he called back, only half turning to answer. "Go to the bridge for your paperwork."

He resumed his departure.

"We haven't done the inventory," I reminded him. "We haven't done the handover documents. We haven't done anything!"

"Sundance can stick it up their ass!" he screamed back. An elderly couple relaxing in a nearby booth nearly tumbled out of their seats in surprise.

"Hey!" I reprimanded angrily, striding across the lounge to catch him. "What's the matter with you?"

Jeff retreated with an almost pathological desire for escape. I caught up to him, grabbed his arm, and demanded again, "What's the matter with you?"

"I hate this job and I hate this ship!" he snapped, wiggling free of my grip. "Put whatever you want on the handover report, 'cause I quit!"

I said nothing, knowing well how the stress of the job caused art auctioneers to snap. I had seen better and more seasoned men than this kid crack under the pressure. My very first auctioneer—rookie of the year, no less—had first gone alcoholic, then ulcerated, then impotent, and then bananas. It had taken only two contracts. The second auctioneer and his wife had nearly divorced before quitting. The third went on vacation to Thailand and literally disappeared. An auctioneer trainee friend of mine, so nerve-wracked that she chewed her fingertips to bloody stubs, had nearly endured an emotional breakdown on my last handover. The fact that I hadn't broken yet was clearly a testament to how stupid I was.

"Fine," I finally said. I understood. My first sight of *Wind Surf* had been so disheartening I had nearly gotten back into my taxi with orders to the airport. "Whatever. I'll walk you to the gangway and you'll answer my questions for at least that long, okay?"

Jeff nodded. He calmed upon realization that I wasn't going to force him to stay any longer.

"You didn't even show me the purser," I began, resuming our walk.

"Go to the bridge for all that," Jeff said quietly.

"Where's the handover documentation? You know, your business plans and schedules?"

"I didn't do any. Doesn't matter. Every cruise is totally different: new ports every day, new homeports in new countries every week. No employees. No auctions. No sales. Ever."

I stopped up short. "What?"

"Get used to it. Wait'll you hear about the auctioneer before me," he said derisively. "It'll blow your God damn mind."

"We're here," Jeff said brightly. It had only been one minute. The *Wind Surf* was truly one tiny ship!

"So no advice at all, then," I said bitterly, succumbing to the sickening knot tightening in my stomach.

"Yeah," he said, jumping onto the sunlit gangway. "The tour bitch is psycho."

And he was gone.

To say it was a disheartening introduction was an understatement. My mind reeling, I left to find the bridge. I had never been on a ship's bridge before. Having joined ships after the terrorist attacks of 9/11, bridges had been strictly off limits to unnecessary personnel. Barring the extraordinary revenue we generally secured, art auctioneers were surely the least necessary persons on board.

The search for *Wind Surf's* bridge did not take long. With only three decks of public space, and one clearly labeled Bridge Deck, even Yoyo would have found it proficiently. I approached from an outside deck, nerves growing more taut by the minute. Gathering sign-on paperwork seemed far too trivial a task to be bothering the bridge officers. Small ship or not, these men were responsible for the very lives of hundreds of people. Squinting against the glare, I stepped through the wide, open doorway.

The bridge was a long, wide chamber extending the length of *Wind Surf's* beam, excluding the outside walkway and bridge wings. To the fore was an entire wall of glass stretching above an entire wall of electronics. The panels were only sparsely populated with gauges and buttons, reminding me of the low budget bridge set from the original *Star Trek*. The back of the room was uneven with nooks for reading paper charts, if officers were so inclined, and racks of clipboards and duty rosters and maintenance schedules and such. Overall, the bridge was spacious and bright, clean and airy. Only one man was posted inside. He wore officer's deck whites, which on the *Surf* meant a white dress shirt with epaulets over white shorts.

And he had a guitar.

The officer—second officer, as denoted by his epaulettes— sat upon a stool with his feet propped onto the electronics. He hunched forward and gazed down at his acoustic guitar. Forehead creasing above Oakley sunglasses, he concentrated on placing his fingers properly upon the strings.

I stepped up to introduce myself when he suddenly threw his head back and belted out, "SHOT THROUGH THE HEART!—AND YOU'RE TO BLAME—darlin' you give lo- ove... a bad name!"

His guitar thrummed into the opening riff of the Bon Jovi classic. The sound filled the chamber beautifully. I stood there, immobile and listening, astounded the song continued beyond the opening. After several minutes a slight, handsome man in a stained boiler suit entered from the opposite entrance. He stepped up behind the singer, gave me a smile, and listened along for a moment. Finally he tapped the officer on the shoulder.

The second officer, whose name tag read 'BARNEY', ceased playing immediately. Barney did not rise, however, but merely craned his head back to look upside-down at his visitor.

"We're done painting the rails," he said. "I'll be in the engine room."

"Aye aye," said Barney, even as the other man departed.

With a big grin, Barney looked back at me. "Good morning. What can I do for you?"

"Signing on," I replied. "I'm the new art auctioneer."

"Oh, okay," he said, jumping gamely to his feet. Though we were both over six feet in height, his build was significantly huskier. Offering his hand he said, "Welcome to the family! I'm Barney, Second Officer."

"Brian," I said, shaking his hand. I smiled and teased, "I'm sorry to interrupt your important business."

"Bon Jovi is important," Barney agreed. "We're in port anyway, so there's not much to do. Still, one of us needs to man the bridge. Come on, I'll get you squared away."

That had been several days ago. Since then I had discovered *Wind Surf* was indeed a laid-back ship. No name tags were fine, as were shorts, sandals and no shaving. Hats were fine, too, which I was informed of several times with a rather unusual emphasis: Barney saying cryptically, "Please, man, no more duck hats. I miss hunting and I just wanna grab for my shotgun."

Returning mentally to the present, I saw Ardin speaking with the hotel director, Francois. The Frenchman had distinctly skinny limbs that looked out of place emanating from a middle thickened with age. A bowling ball with sticks. His round head had features rather pinched together and was topped with thinning, oily hair a bit too black to be natural. Dangling from his wrists were several gold chains. His mannerisms were subtly flamboyant, just enough to hint he was probably gay.

"Brian, perfect!" Francois called excitedly with a thick accent. He was so enthusiastic he even clapped his hands together. "You're as big as two Asians. I want to see you in a T-shirt, on the pier, in ten minutes."

"Sure," I said, somewhat hesitantly. I didn't have a chance to ask him why, for he strode away briskly, shaking a fist at the *Wind Star* with a jangling of gold. "This time is ours!"

"What's this all about?" I asked Ardin.

"Sibling rivalry," he answered sardonically. "Welcome to the family."

## 2

The rivalry played out on Portoferriao's pier. *Wind Star* and *Wind Surf* docked nose-to-tail, white masts rising high over the ancient 'port of iron', as the city was called. Very close to the embanked shore rose stacks of tall, Italian-style houses, higher and higher, as the land lifted away from the sea. Between the clusters were moments of stone, shaggy with green. The pier itself, however, was merely a hard strip of soiled functionality. The air was hot and fishy, the concrete just hot.

Francois waited at the gangway with orders to gather all staff members. I joined those indicated, perched atop a line of concrete barriers. Being all young white women in street clothes, I presumed them to be gift shop or spa employees from Canada, perhaps England, based solely and stereotypically on the fact that all had extra meat on their bones. I had learned size to be a surprisingly accurate gauge of first worlders in my three years plying the seas. And, of course, almost no Americans worked on ships but entertainers, who are held to different standards. Near us waited a group of trim brown-skinned men in boiler suits.

With a rattling of gold on wrist, Francois gestured *Star*-side to a gangly man with a particularly prominent nose towering over his own gathering of boiler-suits. "That ugly Frenchman over there is the *Star's* hotel director," Francois explained. "He is a horrible, horrible man. He is also my friend. Last time our ships met, the *Surf* lost. If I have to buy him another bottle of Montrachet after today, I'm firing the lot of you. I'd rather spend my money on celebratory drinks for you."

This announcement perked the ladies right up. I snorted quietly at the edge of the group. Alcohol was the last thing I needed on *Wind Surf*, for a wide variety of reasons.

Francois selected three staff and ordered us to a designated spot between the two ships. I followed a spa girl named Natalie, who was astonishingly long. She stood a whopping six foot two inches tall, even in flip-flops. Long black hair trailed all the way down her back to partially cover her butt in tangles thick with humidity. As if these two rare characteristics were not enough, at the ends of her long arms were two-inch nails painted glossy blue, studded with silver stars. Our third member was a shoppie named Janie, who had obviously been a cheerleader at some point in her life. She pumped her fist into the air enthusiastically, crying, "Let's go *Surf*! Let's show them the stuff we're made of! Whoo whoo!"

We were assigned two yard-long planks fitted with three loops apiece.

Natalie and Janie both bubbled with excitement. I was decidedly less enthusiastic, and remarked sullenly, "Those look like some sort of old school navy tool used to enforce discipline."

"Put your stuff in the loops," Janie explained. "And then the fun stuff happens!"

"Put my stuff in the loops so the fun stuff can happen," I repeated deadpan. "Back in Vegas we have to pay for that."

"Brian first," Francois commanded. "You power through, so the girls are forced to go with it."

"Men always think it works like that," Natalie said sarcastically.

I looked up at Natalie the Oak and observed, "I think I'd like to see a macho guy try that with you."

Seeing that I still didn't understand what was expected of us, Janie explained further. "There are three loops on each plank. That's for six feet. It's a race, silly!"

"My career is languishing and I'm ordered to a footrace?" I complained.

We began sliding our feet into the loops, when short Janie suddenly stopped and craned her neck to exclaim to Natalie, "Your nails are so beautiful! When did you go blue?"

"This morning," she beamed, showing off her nails. "I got tired of red, and last week was black, so I needed something new."

"Focus, women!" Francois snapped.

"Gets kind of lonely down in the spa," Natalie explained sheepishly, leaning closer and nearly tumbling us all.

"They like to do stuff to each other," Janie added brightly.

"We pay a lot for that in Vegas, too," I quipped.

While waiting for the race to begin, we nearly fell over. Our wobbling bodies pressed together so tightly I doubt even a game of Twister offered more intimacy. Natalie was behind me, and gripped my waist with tremendous strength. Her nails dug into my flesh. Painted pretty or not, they scared the bejesus out of me.

Finally the *Star's* team was ready, a trio of small brown seamen standing smoothly in unison beside us. Francois' eyes narrowed.

"No fair!" Janie protested. "They're all boys!"

"Philippe!" Francois called sternly to his counterpart. "Don't you play me."

The opposing Frenchman spread his arms in feigned innocence. The grin beneath his gargantuan nose was evident. "But monsieur!" he protested with a muddy accent, "I give you the advantage, do I not? Even your woman is two meters tall!"

Before Francois could answer, Philippe raised his arm, then brought it down with a shout. "GO!"

We surged forward sloppily. I hauled hard, but hadn't bothered to tell my team which foot to lead with. I led right. They didn't. They didn't go anywhere. I did. I fell forward, nearly crashing to the concrete. Just before I struck, Natalie hauled back on my shirt to save my stuff from a nasty scrape on the ground. Within moments the *Wind Star* team was already halfway to the finish line.

"Get going!" Francois ordered. He shot a glare at Philippe, who was all smiles.

We pushed onward, but Natalie's stride was just too long for me to keep pace with. Poor, short Janie was hopeless in the back. She started going over, and with a wail we all followed. We yelped as soft flesh met hard, hot concrete. Good-natured laughter rose from the audience of both ships, not to mention the locals who had gathered to watch. Despite our second set-back, the race was not yet over, for the *Star* team also tumbled.

"Get up!" cried Francois. "You can do it!"

Untangling our entwined bodies was not an easy procedure. Suddenly Twister seemed easy in comparison: our strapped feet made bodily extraction most... revealing. Natalie's nails nearly ripped my shorts off. Ardin swooped in to document the carnage for posterity.

Surprisingly, we won the race. How is still a mystery, other than perhaps divine intervention. What followed were a handful of races, each with a different combination and order. The all-Asian races were the most exciting. After witnessing the first loss, they regrouped and created a new strategy. They placed their hands on each others' shoulders to stride in better harmony. Asian-on-Asian races moved at an amazingly rapid pace. But the highlight was yet to come. A long rope was laid across the pier alongside the two vessels, the center marked with a prominent ribbon.

"Tug of war!" Janie exclaimed, clapping her hands.

I found myself reluctantly excited, being just macho enough to enjoy a contest of strength. What amazed me, though, was that this contest included officers. My honorary rank of three-stripes was no doubt unrecognized here, but Francois still ordered me to join the men—and one woman, an ensign named Emily—on the *Surf*-side. I was surprised Natalie hadn't been included, but she was apparently too busy showing off her claws to Janie. Francois looked over his team smugly. We appeared obviously much stronger than the competition. Not surprisingly, Philippe threw his knobby arms into the air and cried foul.

"Our ship has half the crew of the *Wind Surf*!" he protested. "We have smaller crew to choose from. I protest that the contest is unfair."

"I think not," Francois retorted. "My biggest man is stationed on the bridge. Is this not enough?"

But Philippe kept protesting. He was specifically pointing at me. The stalemate lengthened. Heat gathered on our still bodies and beaded up. I just wanted to get on with it, or get out of here. Eventually a trim man in a stained boiler suit approached, the handsome fellow on the bridge who had also listened to Barney's singing. He tapped me on the shoulder and said with a delicate Dutch accent, "Thank you. I'll take it from here."

A monstrous wave of cheering crashed over us like a tsunami of enthusiasm.

"What's with the cheering?" I asked Janie, returning to the concrete barriers.

"Ouch!" I suddenly cried, clapping a hand to my shoulder. Giving it a rub, I glared up at Natalie. She had reached down from behind to pluck at my skin with her sharp nails. "What the hell was that?"

"I saw a pimple," she replied sheepishly, adding, "I couldn't resist." For the first time I noticed a blue gem glued to her front tooth, glinting in the harsh sunlight. It matched the blue of her nails.

"That's the XO!" Janie said proudly, answering my pre-pluck question.

"The first officer?" I replied, shocked. "But... that's the guy I saw painting railings!"

As an American, I was used to the idea of 'doers' getting their hands dirty regardless of who they were. Not always, of course, but it appealed to our ideas of equality. As an experienced crew member, however, I knew most officers considered menial chores properly relegated to classes beneath them. This XO either hated being on this ship, with such menial labor, or loved her enough to give her his best. Considering his enthusiastic grip on the rope, I sensed he felt the latter. I liked him already. Obviously Janie did, too, as she was hopping and chanting, "X O X O!"

Yet Philippe's unrelenting protestations delayed the contest interminably. By the time he was satisfied to begin, our team had been whittled down to a mere eight bodies competing against their eleven. I wished I could rejoin our team. Funny how I felt that way only after being booted off. I made the conscious decision to bite back my apathy and view the competition for what it was. Joy buzzed through the crowd, and I passed it along rather than try to douse it. It was not necessarily enthusiasm, but it was a start.

*Wind Star* won. This disgusted Francois so much he refused to reward Philippe after the match, loudly calling him a cheater. Officers rose from hot concrete to dust themselves off with smiles. I just couldn't believe what I was seeing. Officers on the ground in front of their own crew?

No, *Wind Surf* was truly not like other ships.

*Continue reading, I say!*
*High Seas Drifter is available everywhere eBooks are sold.*

Printed in Great Britain
by Amazon